The Opera Singer's Acting Toolkit

The Opera Singer's Acting Toolkit

An Essential Guide to Creating a Role

Martin Constantine

methuen | drama

LONDON • NEW YORK • OXFORD • NEW DELHI • SYDNEY

METHUEN DRAMA
Bloomsbury Publishing Plc
50 Bedford Square, London, WC1B 3DP, UK
1385 Broadway, New York, NY 10018, USA

BLOOMSBURY, METHUEN DRAMA and the Methuen Drama logo are trademarks of
Bloomsbury Publishing Plc

First published in Great Britain 2020

Cover design by Louise Dugdale
Cover image: Opera, *Street Scene*, at the Royal Welsh College, photography by Robert Workman.

A catalogue record for this book is available from the British Library.

Library of Congress Cataloging-in-Publication Data
Names: Constantine, Martin, author.
Title: The opera singer's acting toolkit : an essential guide to creating a role/Martin Constantine.
Description: London ; New York : Methuen Drama, 2019. | Includes bibliographical references and index.
Identifiers: LCCN 2019012585| ISBN 9781350006454 (pbk.) | ISBN 9781350006461 (hpod) |
ISBN 9781350006492 (xml platform)
Subjects: LCSH: Acting in opera.
Classification: LCC MT956 .C68 2019 | DDC 782.1/143—dc23
LC record available at https://lccn.loc.gov/2019012585

ISBN: HB: 978-1-3500-0646-1
       PB: 978-1-3500-0645-4
       ePDF: 978-1-3500-0647-8
       eBook: 978-1-3500-0648-5

Typeset by RefineCatch Limited, Bungay, Suffolk
Printed and bound in Great Britain

To find out more about our authors and books visit www.bloomsbury.com
and sign up for our newsletters.

Contents

Acknowledgements

Huge thanks to Anna Brewer for her support, encouragement and wise words. Thanks also to the rest of the team at Methuen Drama, especially Meredith Benson and Lucy Brown.

Thank you to the more than two hundred young artists who trained with ENO Opera Works, many of whose questions and reflections feature throughout the book, and to the host of extraordinary practitioners who taught on the programme and whose work resonates through these pages: Barbara Houseman, Olga Masleinnikova, Rosemary Brandt, Leah Houseman, Liam Steel, Ian Rickson, Paul Hunter, Cal McCristal, Polly Teale, Lyndsey Turner, Will Holt, Alex MacLaren, Jayke Branson-Thom, Christian Curnyn, Tim Murray, Martin Fitzpatrick and Martin Pacey. With special thanks to my Opera Works co-director Jane Robinson.

Thanks also to the many brilliant young singers, designers, directors and teachers I've had the good fortune to direct and learn alongside at the Royal Welsh College of Music and Drama. Particular thanks to Angela Livingstone.

I'm indebted to those practitioners who have shared their thoughts and experiences in the interviews that feature throughout the book.

Special thanks to Lucy Mellors for her insightful yet always humorous notes, to Dominic Francis for his thoughtful and perceptive comments, to Mark Friend for his terrific images and to Jennifer Fletcher for late night Laban phone calls. Thanks to Toby Farrow, Alan Harris, Simon Armstrong and Liz Hurran for their support. Thanks, also, to all at Gladstone's Library.

Very special thanks to Mike Alfreds and Cis Berry, two guiding lights without whom this book would not have been written.

Above all, thank you to my amazing family for their invaluable support from the North of England and Madrid and to Anna Poole for her consistent encouragement, ideas, belief and understanding.

Permissions

Introduction

Telling the Story

Stories matter. We go to the theatre to witness our world reflected back to us, to explore ideas and feed our imagination. We go to experience the lives of characters transformed by change: to be moved, challenged, provoked, engaged and entertained. A director can achieve a certain amount of this through design: creating pictures and spectacle with set, costumes, light and video. At the heart of every piece of theatre, however, is the performer. The story of the character must live within each of the performers on the stage; it is their story and, ultimately, their responsibility to communicate this to an audience.

Stories in opera *really* matter; to such an extent that the characters are compelled to *sing* them. The drama should be direct and immediate in its expression and yet clear storytelling in opera can be challenging. The singer must negotiate extreme changes of pitch, rhythm and tempo whilst being heard above an orchestra. Yet to truly communicate the story they must do all this whilst being convincingly engaged with the reality of the inner and outer life of their character.

I began thinking about writing this book over ten years ago. I was working with casts of young opera singers and directing them in everything from Mozart to Britten, via Donizetti and Wagner. No matter the repertoire, company, size or location of theatre there was a common theme running through my experiences. Here were teams of terrifically talented young vocal artists, many of whom had trained for seven or more years, making intelligent observations about the operas we were working on and enthusiastically engaged with themes of the story, but there was a problem; the singers lacked the necessary skills to translate their ideas and energy into convincing and truthful dramatic action. Their training had equipped them brilliantly to tackle the demands of virtuosic singing but had failed to provide them with the tools needed to create the characters that needed to sing these words and music. The singers lacked a shared dramatic language and process and, in many cases, a knowledge and understanding of how to collaborate creatively.

It is the aim of this book to give you, the singer and actor, the tools to create truthful characters and, in so doing, enable you to deliver the story of your character, through music and words, with clarity and detail to the audience. The tools are all practical and drawn from a range of theatre, opera and movement practitioners. Some tools will work better for some than others, some will be more useful when creating certain characters or working in particular repertoire or in different rehearsal room environments. As a creative artist, your job is to explore these ideas and exercises, to grow to understand them and to discover which might work best for you. It is for you as an artist to use this book to spur your imagination and create your own, individual and unique, toolkit; a toolkit that you can carry with you throughout your creative journey as a singer and one that will grow far beyond the confines of the pages of this book.

General Challenges for the Singer

It is difficult to think of an artist in another field where mastery of such a wide array of skills is an essential requirement. An opera singer is expected to:

- develop the voice to sing in vastly different houses; from the up-close and intimate to the barn-like international house to the peculiar challenges of the found space
- sing for different media; from live performance to recorded for audio or, increasingly, film
- sing in different contexts; from oratorio, to concert, to the operatic stage
- have a broad knowledge of repertoire and the particular (and fashionable) stylistic demands of these varying schools
- master numerous languages
- speak text on stage
- interpret, create, embody and communicate convincing dramatic characters
- collectively create and bring to life the world of the opera
- dance
- collaborate with a wide range of artists, and respond to their ideas, in order to create the production

Within the opera house itself the competing demands on an opera singer are enormous. The singer at English National Opera, for example, will work with a long list of collaborators including (in no particular order):

- Conductor
- Director
- Other performers; singers, dancers, actors
- Staff Directors
- Choreographer
- Music Staff
- Chorus
- Chorus Master
- Orchestra Manager
- Designer
- Costume Designer
- Costume Maker

- Production Manager
- Stage Manager
- Deputy Stage Manager
- Assistant Stage Managers
- Company Manager
- Casting Director
- Dressers
- Wig Department
- Props Department
- Stage Crew
- Producers
- Press and Marketing team
- Outreach department

Many of those on this list will probably have assistants who will also work directly with the singer. Additionally, most singers will also work with a singing teacher or vocal coach.

However helpful these teams of people aim to be (and from my experience, particularly at ENO, they are usually incredibly helpful), it can all be somewhat overwhelming! When navigating a course through these numerous collaborations, the singing actor ultimately has one responsibility; to truthfully create and communicate the life of a character to the audience through song. Yet even the simplest of acts, that under normal conditions could be achieved without a moment's thought, can seem to become almost impossible to perform convincingly once one sets foot on stage. This is perhaps not surprising when the singer can so easily be constrained by the aspirations of so many other artists. Gathering an understanding of how to steer an individual course through these varying demands is vital, for any singer, to continue to grow and develop creatively.

A Very Brief History of the Singing Actor

The founding principles of opera were somewhat ambitious; indeed, it is no surprise to find the artist at the centre of it subject to so many expectations. Emerging through discussions led by the Camerata, a society of Florentine theorists and academics in the 1580s, about the nature of Greek tragedy, inspiration was initially drawn from Aristotle's *Poetics*:

> Tragedy, then, is an imitation of an action that is serious, complete, and of a certain magnitude; in language embellished with each kind of artistic ornament, the several kinds being found in separate parts of the play ... by 'language embellished,' I mean language into which rhythm, 'harmony,' and song enter. By 'the several kinds in separate parts,' I mean, that some parts are rendered through the medium of verse alone, others again with the aid of song.[1]

---

[1] Aristotle's *Poetics* – VI: Definition of Tragedy.

It was, however, left to the poets and musicians on the edges of such groups as the Camerata to first translate these philosophies into something more practical. Drawing upon these ideals, and previous music theatre forms such as *intermedi* (short performances with music played between the acts of plays at celebrations in fifteenth- or sixteenth-century Italian courts), *recitar cantando* developed as the form to first combine music and words into the first operas; simple accompaniment heightened the emotional impact of the poetic text. The music was intended, not as a decorative element, but to interpret and emphasise action and emotion.[2]

Whilst the ideals at the heart of the birth of this new form seek to be a unifying force, all too often opera has become something of a battleground for opposing sides arguing the predominance of either the words or music.[3] It is the singer who is usually caught in the middle of this.

Acting Styles

Acting styles change with each generation and, whilst it is impossible to assess which age was better or worse, certain factors suggest a shifting emphasis. In the early years of opera, the emphasis on text, the express purpose of the music and the importance of dramatic action as quoted in Aristotle, might suggest a certain style of acting. An early seventeenth-century writer reasons:

> to be a good actor singer one should above all be a good speaking actor – the common run of theatrical audiences takes greater satisfaction in perfect actors with mediocre voice.[4]

By the late seventeenth century, however, the vocal demands of *opera seria*, the scale of orchestrations and the shift in the size of theatres in which operas were presented, all seem to have led to the development of a more conventionalised style of performance. Acting in opera at this time can be characterised as *gestural*. Semi-circles of performers, the most important of whom stood closest to the Royal Box, presented the story through changes in the position of their hands and heads but little else.

The importance of gestures was espoused and set down by a number of significant figures, notably Gilbert Austin and Francois Delsarte. It was Delsarte, in particular, whose codification of gesture had a wide impact; his system of expression was taught internationally and was something of an eighteenth-century guide for performers.[5] Whilst there is acknowledgement in Delsarte's process of the need for the performer to be physically relaxed and in control, there is a disconnect between the psychological factors motivating movement and the resultant behaviour.

There were alternatives to such a conventionalised form of presentation. In the seventeenth century, David Garrick, the great Shakespearean actor known for his naturalistic

---

[2] Pirrotta, N. (1984) *Music and Culture in Italy from the Middle Ages to the Baroque*. Cambridge, MA: Harvard University Press.
[3] Abbate, C. and Parker, R. (2012) *A History of Opera: The Last 400 Years*. London: Penguin Random House. The chapter 'Words and Music' gives a great run down of the various twists and turns.
[4] Savage, R. and Sansone, M. (1989) *Il Corago* and the Staging of Early Opera. *Early Music*, 12/4, p. 501.
[5] Stebbins, G. (1887) Delsarte system of expression.

style of acting, taught the famous castrati Gaetano Guadagni (Gluck's first *Orfeo*).[6] In the nineteenth century, Wagner proposed the *Gesamtkunstwerk*; a 'total work of art' in which music, poetry, dance, design surrender their defining individual elements to find a new freedom in combination with each other. Indeed, the 'Bayreuth Style' became recognised for its tendency toward a naturalistic style of acting.[7] Yet, as late as 1915, George Shea published *Acting in Opera*, a guide to acting gestures in opera, complete with photographs of certain stock poses. His introduction sets out his philosophy:

> in opera the flow of the words is so retarded or hampered by the music, that gestures and attitudes must be inflated and given a duration which would amount to exaggeration even in tragedy.[8]

Critical Response

The results of such acting styles have not always been welcomed. As early as 1755, Francesco Algarotti, a Venetian poet and philosopher, wrote that singers were 'unqualified and grossly defective in the first principles of their arts – gauche in gestures, indistinct in diction and clumsy in movement'.[9] Even today, singers' acting comes under scrutiny with a sideways glance to its historical traditions:

> Keith Warner, who is to direct *Otello* in Covent Garden next month, said the exaggerated stage acting of years gone by can no longer make the cut, particularly once filmed and broadcast in close up on the big screen. Streaming opera in the cinema, he claims, is helping to weed out the 'hammy' over-acting young audiences hate. The development, he suggested, may have encouraged stars and directors to consider a more nuanced performance, which in turn has improved the stage experience for audiences.[10]

Training

With the extraordinary demands placed upon singers, it seems fundamental that training should seek to equip singers with the necessary skills and tools to meet such expectations. This was recognised a couple of hundred years ago by Pietro Metastasio, the librettist upon whose work Mozart's *La Clemenza di Tito* was based, who recognised that singers could only hope to accomplish the demands of opera: 'Through proper training in acting and proper concern for the synthesis of canto (song) and azione (action)'.[11]

More recently it was Stanislavski who focused upon the limitations of opera singer training. Towards the end of his life the great Russian actor, director and teacher, whose ideas have been so wholly embraced in theatre, switched his attentions to opera. He was the director of the Bolshoi (later Stanislavski) Opera Studio in the 1920s, where he taught young

---

[6] Greenwald, H. M. (ed.) (2014) *The Oxford Handbook of Opera*. Oxford: Oxford University Press, p. 402.
[7] Millington, B. (2006) *The New Grove Guide to Wagner and His Operas*. Oxford: Oxford University Press, p. 162.
[8] Shea, G. (1915) *Acting in Opera*. New York: G. Schirmer.
[9] Algarotti, F. (2005) *An Essay on Opera*, ed. Burgess, R. Lewiston, NY: Edwin Mellon Press, p. 34.
[10] Furness, H. (2017) Cinema will save opera for a new generation, Royal Opera House director suggests, *Daily Telegraph*, 27 May.
[11] Savage, R. (1998) Staging and Opera: Letters from the Caesarian Poet. *Early Music*, 26, pp. 584–85.

singers in workshops and directed them in fully staged productions. He noted that, prior to his work, the training at the Bolshoi '. . . was essentially on placement of the voice, the correct producing of notes given without any regard whatsoever for the dramatic form of the work to be brought into being'.[12]

In 2017, the National Opera Studio in the UK published a report into opera singer training and concluded that 'higher levels of skills in acting are now required of opera singers. This is seen as requiring more – and earlier – space being made for drama and movement in the time-table and a greater integration of those disciplines with music'.[13]

ENO Opera Works

The central idea of ENO Opera Works was to introduce singers to the necessary dramatic skills, whilst giving them space to explore them and time to integrate them into their process. The course was developed in response to the company's recognition that young singers often left conservatoire training with a substantial deficit in what was needed for them to progress as an artist within the professional industry.

The course was structured around intensive weekend workshops. Input Weekends introduced the singers to a range of extraordinary practitioners[14] who shared their area of expertise to help develop specific dramatic skills. There was no singing during Input Weekends; the time was spent entirely upon discovering new approaches to creating character. Response Weekends followed each Input Weekend with an opportunity to put into practice newly acquired skills using operatic repertoire. The Input and Response weekends focused on Text, Movement and Text and Music in Action.

Alongside this work on character, the singers worked on their vocal technique with ENO coaching staff and conductors, guided by co-Director, Jane Robinson. In addition, we incorporated a series of professional development classes working specifically with the ENO casting department and performance psychologists and coaches.

The aim of the course was to create a company within a company, in which the singers felt safe to genuinely explore operatic roles through risk-taking and play. The culmination of the course was a rehearsal process for a devised production; the singers collaborated to create an entirely new piece, whilst at the same time applying their newly acquired skills within the rehearsal room. In later years, the singers devised this project in collaboration with emerging designers, directors and stage managers.

When in training it is sometimes difficult to admit what you do not know, to reveal your vulnerabilities, and to risk change. The prospect of exposure, possible failure and judgement is a little too perilous; yet it is the best way to learn. The ENO Opera Works singers were encouraged to bring an open, honest and questioning approach to their work and, as a result, often found that their concerns were shared by others in the group. This helped to bring a keener focus to their process of discovering possible answers.

---

[12] Stanislavski, K. (1998) *Stanislavski on Opera*. Translated by E. R. Hapgood. London: Routledge, p. vii.
[13] Devlin, G. (2017) *Opera Training for Singers in the UK – Executive Summary*, p. 5.
[14] These included Mike Alfreds (Director), Ian Rickson, Lyndsey Turner (Director), Leah Hausman, Liam Steel (Choreographer/Director), Marcello Magni, Rosemary Brandt, Olga Masliennikova, Christian Curnyn (conductor), Jacqueline Branson Thom (Performance Psychologist).

This book aims to share the questions those singers asked over the ten years of ENO Opera Works and to reflect the various journeys we made in seeking to find answers. Sometimes it will reveal the wrong turns we made, the times we floundered and, ultimately, the way in which the developing toolkit helped us to make discoveries.

The Book

This book follows the same structure as ENO Opera Works and seeks to introduce a similarly wide variety of practitioners from various disciplines. There is no prescribed methodology and, although the book draws extensively on the work of Stanislavski, it is rather a series of tools, exercises and approaches that demand your creative engagement. These tools can be used in preparation for rehearsals, in the rehearsal room itself and through performance. Each chapter emphasises a particular approach to the work but, in fact, the chapter on text covers work on movement and the body and vice versa; they simply place the emphasis in a slightly different way. The order that the book lays the tools out in is similarly malleable. If there is one guiding principle in the work, it can best be summed up: explore the process not the result.[15]

The book is, first and foremost, a handbook and a guide. It is not a historiography of different approaches to acting; there are plenty of books that offer this and the best of them are listed at the back of this book for further reading. At times, of course, detail is given as to why a practitioner developed a certain tool; an understanding of this can help to provide an insight into the particular challenges they were facing. It is consoling to know that such challenges are not something you alone might be experiencing. Additionally, the book does not contain exercises for the *singing* voice. I am not a voice coach and, usually, such exercises are best explored directly with a singing teacher.

Aims

The central aim of the book is to answer the many questions singers (you!) have about approaching creating character; to enable you to create your own process that combines the art of building and living a role, with the musical demands and technique of singing. The book aims to do this by:

- engaging you in an active dialogue with your work and process;
- bringing a holistic approach to your work. Stanislavski pioneered a psycho-physical approach to acting through an understanding that the mind affects the body and vice versa. It is my experience that these acting tools also help support the singing voice;
- introducing tools that can be useful in any rehearsal room and that will accompany you throughout your journey as an artist;
- heightening your awareness of how music relates to drama and vice versa;

---

[15] Theatre and opera director Mike Alfreds was an ENO Opera Works contributor from the outset of the course; this is very much his mantra.

- developing a dramatic language that can inform your dialogues with fellow performers, directors and conductors;
- kicking out the fear of making mistakes. For art to be truly alive it must be constantly on the move; there is no fixed point of right or wrong. A true artist must seek to engage spontaneously in the moment and remain open to possibilities at all times, regardless of risk. The tools provide a foundation to forge into the unknown!

The series of tools to create character will only come to life when you begin to try them. I won't prescribe what you must do, or which order you might try them in, but I do suggest you try out all these tools; and not just once. Some will be particularly difficult to master, but they will get easier and quicker the more time you invest in exploring them. Use these tools wherever and whenever you can, so that they become habitual.

A Few Things to Note

1 I will sometimes refer to you as a *singer*, sometimes, an *actor*. The two words are interchangeable when creating opera; you are a singing actor and an acting singer.

2 Throughout the book I tend to refer to Mozart's *The Marriage of Figaro*, in translation by Jeremy Sams. I did not want the book to become a test of repertoire; this piece is both regularly performed and offers a number of terrific roles for young singers. Occasionally, I refer to Mozart's *The Magic Flute*, again in translation by Jeremy Sams, to slightly widen the scope of reference. The book is not meant as an analysis of these operas, they simply provide reference points to illustrate the exercises. There are excellent recordings of both these operas in Jeremy Sams's translations, produced by Chandos; libretti of these translations are available online.[16]

3 In conversations with singers, conductors and directors I refer to a wider range of repertoire and explore how the tools might be used with other operas.

4 All operas referred to in the book are in English translation. The book is the result of my work with predominantly young English-speaking singers at ENO and the Royal Welsh College of Music and Drama. In the first instance, it is much easier to learn new tools when working in your own language. The work places a great deal of emphasis on a deep understanding of the text and, as David Pountney, former Artistic Director of ENO and current Artistic Director of Welsh National Opera, explains, 'The instinctive engagement of all the singers' modes of perception are set in motion so much faster and more directly in their own language and the fact that the audience returns the communication rapidly, as in a tennis rally, serves to heighten the intensity of the relationship between singer and audience.'[17] Of course, some of the sound, rhythm and setting of the original language is lost but what seems to me more vital is that the meaning is directly communicated.

---

[16] Chandos booklets: *The Marriage of Figaro*: https://www.chandos.net/chanimages/Booklets/CH3113.pdf and *The Magic Flute*: https://www.chandos.net/chanimages/Booklets/CH3121.pdf.
[17] Fuchs, P. P. (1991) *The Music Theatre of Walter Felsenstein*. London: Quartet Books.

If you are working through these exercises in a language that is not your first language, it is crucial that you seek to understand the meaning of *every* word you are singing. This should include seeking to bring clarity to the sentence structure.[18]

5   I truly believe you can begin this book at any point. For ease of communication I have separated the psychological exploration of your character from the physical but, in fact, these two factors are completely intertwined. From one production to the next, the order in which you begin your process of creating character will change, depending upon the particular demands of the rehearsal room and role. So, whilst out of necessity a book needs to lay down thoughts in a particular order, I urge you, the reader, to delve in wherever your attention is drawn.

6   The exercises are divided into SOLO and GROUP work. It is part of a singer's life to spend a good deal of time alone learning a role musically. Wherever possible, I encourage you to find like-minded performers and to try these exercises, even the solo ones, together.

7   The book is divided into three main parts:

Part 1: THE TOOLS – this explores the work of many and varied practitioners from theatre, dance and music backgrounds, exploring exercises and tools to create character and how these might be applied to scenes from *The Marriage of Figaro.* This section includes the questions, responses and observations of the young singers training at ENO.

Part 2: IN PRACTICE – this looks at how to apply these tools on your creative journey, from preparing a role, via rehearsal in the studio and onstage, to first performance.

Part 3: INTERVIEWS – a series of discussions with conductors, directors and singers to explore different repertoire, approaches to rehearsal and journeys through a process.

A Manifesto

It is not difficult to find pronouncements of the death of opera. Wagner thought that 'with Rossini died the opera'. Brecht declared its death and denounced attempts to make it relevant through modernist musical techniques or production paraphernalia.

Opera only lives through the singer. If singers deliver the same tired old clichés, fuelled by preconceived notions from other productions, then the best place for opera is in a museum. But when a singer breathes life into a character, moment to moment, and when the character's needs become vital and their desires urgent, when the singing to communicate this is direct and honest, then opera continues to live.

Every artist has a responsibility to ask, why *now*? Why am I exploring this world and the people that populate it *now*? What resonates? What connects to *my* experience and to the experiences of the community we seek to share this story with? What do I bring to this

---

[18] Nico Castell's translations are a tremendous resource but you must *know* what the words mean, not simply have written them under the original libretto in your score to refer to only occasionally.

story? How do we tackle themes of race and gender that reflect a different world from the one in which we now live? How do we tell this story for now?

This begins with a direct and personal dialogue and analysis of the words and music. You, the singer, by doing this must challenge and spur your imagination. You have creative responsibility, not just for producing sound, but embodying within you the layers of story of your character. It is your responsibility to bring *yourself* to the art.

It is not enough to be satisfied with superficial visual and vocal effects. You must seek to make impressions on the emotions; those which will transform you, the singing actor, into truthful, living beings and in turn leave a deep and lasting mark on the audience.

You have responsibility as a singer to interpret the connection between the music and text. Through the decisions you make for your character, you will, in turn, affect the interpretation of those artists you work with. Lose any notions of hierarchy or status; every member of the team is an equally essential part of the task of creating the world. You are a vital and connected part of a collaborative effort to express and communicate the story.

This will be forged through your preparation for, and your active participation in, rehearsals; too often a process is undermined by the distraction of other engagements. A thorough commitment to a complete process of rehearsal is utterly vital; not simply those rehearsals that seem to concern you for an hour or two on a rehearsal schedule but all rehearsals focused upon the task of creating a world.

This book is not a cookbook. You can't simply turn to a page, find the recipe, add the ingredients and adjust the seasoning. You must use it to begin to build your personal artistic toolkit; something that works for you, that you understand and that you can add to throughout your journey as a creative artist.

THINGS TO DO

Before we begin, here are few things to do (in no particular order):

- Devise a fitness programme. Opera is an incredibly physical art form; the act of singing demands breath control and directors and choreographers are increasingly asking for more physical engagement. The fitter you are, the more in control you'll feel.
- Establish a healthy eating plan (see above).
- Break the spine of this book and grab a pencil. Or a highlighter. Make notes.
- Get a notebook. Or a journal. Or a tablet. This is your journey and it's essential to make notes of the various different directions you travel as you take it. I still refer back to my notebooks from theatre school and previous productions to recall useful things I have read or been taught. Distilling your thoughts in your own words provides a record of your creative journey and aids a clearer understanding of your process.
- Ask yourself this question – *what challenges do I face when creating operatic characters?*
- Dream. Imagine. Picture (more of this later).
- Approach the work with a readiness to collaborate and try things out. Play. Take risks.
- Let go of fear! Of course, it is easy to say and more difficult in practice. Make it your aim; exploring a process to create character will help you.

Part One The Tools

1 Foundations: Where to Start

On my first day at drama school a photo of a baby laughing was pinned to the noticeboard. It was signed at the bottom 'love Rudi. See you soon'. Rudi Shelley was a renowned teacher at the Bristol Old Vic Theatre School and the subject of much excitement, having been ubiquitously quoted by the most famous alumni in their various autobiographies. Rudi was in serious ill health and, although he would battle back to the school to teach the new year-group, he was entering the last year of his life. This was his first and most important lesson to us prospective actors (most of whom were in a state of some confusion and proposing various profundities to explain the photo). The lesson was simple: to act, you must play. Like a child you must know how to play and how to find pleasure in the game.

The job of the singing actor is to transform into somebody else; somebody who sings in order to communicate their thoughts, needs and feelings. The central question is *how* do you begin to transform yourself, when all the thoughts, needs, feelings you have will be your own and not those of somebody else? That's the question we're going to explore in this first section of the book.

As we grow older we lose the freedom to play as a child. Society teaches us the way to behave and our experiences mould us. We perhaps develop certain tensions or *blocks* which constrict our imagination and our potential to transform. So, where to start? Well, with *you*.

At ENO Opera Works the exercises that follow were very much the starting point for our journey and work. We continued to return to them throughout the year, integrating them though all our work. They are the foundations for the process of building character; they will free you in body and mind to play and, in so doing, transform.

The Body: Releasing Tension

Every physical action we do is achieved through the constant exchange of tension and release.[1] However, we all carry around unnecessary tension; tension that can make the easiest

---

[1] See Chapter 5, The Body and Movement.

things more difficult to do. As a singer, you will be aware of how such unnecessary tension can affect how you breathe or how your sound resonates. This *awareness* of the particular and individual tension that you habitually carry with you must be brought to the entire body.

This habitual tension affects how you move, sing and, in turn, how you think. You tire more quickly and can risk strains and injuries. Additionally, it is visible and reveals part of your own story, rather than the character's. In order to begin a process of transformation you must become aware of, and learn how to release, tension. Otherwise, not only will doing things become unnecessarily difficult, it will prevent you from embodying new tensions to create somebody else's story.

The process of transformation, in itself, should also be approached with a sense of ease and play. Tension can creep into our work at any moment, especially when performing under the gaze of an audience and the physical contractions that arise from straining to create emotion, or to cover anxiety, do harm to the voice and the production of sound. It also interferes with the revelation of the thoughts and emotions to the audience; delicate, transient, changing moments of feeling become strangled and gnarled.

It is important to note our habits. For example, I tend to carry a very heavy bag on my left shoulder which causes me to lift my left shoulder a little so that the bag remains in place. As a result, even when I'm not carrying the bag, my left shoulder is raised. This tension is visible: it affects the way I walk, the way I roll my shoulder, without thinking, to release tension, the way I sit at a table. This tells the observer something about me; if only that I travel a lot with a heavy bag. This might not be the story of the character I'm playing and is therefore superfluous, or perhaps even contradictory and confusing, information for an audience. As much as possible we want to begin with a blank canvas; a state of physical release and freedom, in order to bring greater control to our bodies, voice and mind and the stories we tell.

We need to get into the habit of breaking our habits and releasing the blocks we carry with us. We can't simply do the following exercises the moment we step into the rehearsal room and hope that they will immediately unlock years of behaviour. We need to find ways of incorporating them into our life; setting the alarm fifteen minutes early, engaging with them on our walk into work, integrating them into the way we approach coachings and so on, in order to be *ready* for the moment we step into the rehearsal room in order to allow us the freedom and control to change.

Awareness

Begin to listen to your body and understand the tensions you carry, in order to learn how to release these tensions. Bringing awareness to your physical state creates a dialogue between your interior reflections and your visible exterior.

> **EXERCISE:** *Understanding Outer Tension*
> **Solo/5 mins**
>
> - Lie on the floor. Tense your left arm, as hard as possible, and release.
> - Repeat this, becoming aware of the different sensation of tension and release.
> - Explore this with different body parts.

- Slowly begin to get up but, almost immediately, stop and release back down to the floor.
- Again, begin to get up. Notice which part of your body moves first; which body part initiates the movement?
- Very slowly continue to get up. Which muscles contract next, and which follow.
- Relax and do the sequence again. Be aware of the parts of the body where tension does not exist.
- Walk around the space. As you walk, bring your attention to where the necessary tension is; you might notice the core, the arms, the buttocks.
- Ask yourself if there is any tension which seems to be unnecessary.
- Is this a part of your body where you would normally feel additional tension? Try to let go of this unnecessary tension by gently shaking out this part of the body.
- Change the speed of your walk and explore how different body parts become more engaged.
- Sit down on a chair. Slowly, at first. Stand up and, now, sit on the floor.
- Which parts of the body engage to enable you to sit? Notice the difference between sitting on a chair and sitting on the floor. Become alert to the muscles that engage with an action and the extent to which they do so.

EXERCISE: *Understanding Inner Tension*
Solo/2 mins

- Picture a moment, in your mind's eye, when you felt stressed. Recall the details of the situation; the place, time, temperature, smells.
- What do you notice about your breathing as you do this?
- Are there any tensions that develop in your body?
- Do they correspond with the unnecessary tensions you noticed in the exercise above?
- Note your tendencies.

EXERCISE: *Extreme Tension*
Solo/2 mins

To illustrate the way in which different levels of tension can affect our ability to perform relatively simple tasks, Stanislavski suggests attempting to lift a piano[2] whilst, for example:

- counting down from 100 in intervals of seven;
- translating, word for word, an aria from one language to another;
- singing.

Let go of the piano. Bring your awareness to the different level of tension in your body. Immediately set about the tasks again; count down from 100 in intervals of seven, etc. Note the difference.

---

[2] Stanislavski, K. (1980) *An Actor Prepares*. Translated by E. R. Hapgood. London: Eyre Methuen, p. 97.

EXERCISE: *The Baby*
Solo/5 mins

Casting our mind back to Rudi Shelley's photo of a baby; observe a baby or, alternatively, a cat. Note, in detail, the way in which they make contact with the surface they sit or lie upon. Which parts of their body contact the surface, how freely do they give themselves to that surface?

Try to imitate this. Be detailed. Are you aware of any particular tension in your body when you do this?

EXERCISE: *Observing Tension*
Pairs/10 mins

- Your partner monitors you as you work through the Exercise: Understanding Outer Tension. They should point out wherever they see any unnecessary tension in your actions. Use the check list below.

- Once you have completed the tasks ask, *How does what they see marry with my own observations?*

- Take a few deep breaths and gently shake out your body; shoulders, arms, hands, torso, hips, legs, feet.

- Try the exercise again, only this time singing (unaccompanied is fine).

- What tensions do you and your partner notice this time? Are there differences from the first time you did the exercise?

TENSION CHECK LIST

Check the following when observing tension in either yourself or partner:

- Jaw released.
- Shoulder blades neither pushed close together or apart.
- Shoulders released and not held.
- Head balanced on top of the spine, not appearing to be pushed forward or back.
- Face relaxed.
- Pelvis released and not tipping forward or back (this can place great pressure on the lower back).
- Thighs released. If there is tension in the thighs, maybe the knees are hyper-extended?

Release

A free and flexible body, as we have already noted, is incredibly important for every stage of your work. The release of tension before you begin work, whether in coachings, rehearsal or performance, is vital. It is, however, important to note that the tension, once released, can return pretty swiftly. It is, therefore, worth considering what might be the root cause of the tension; for example, a physical habit or an emotional block. It is important to explore ways of engaging with this root cause, rather than simply trying to ignore it. Much of this work is individual and deeply personal, and is, therefore, not easy to cover in a book. What follows are some exercises on releasing tension and, as you work through them, I would suggest that you continue to develop a dialogue with yourself and trusted colleagues. How do these exercises make you feel? What do you notice? What is the difference, within and without, before and after these exercises?

It's best to do all the following exercises with bare feet.

EXERCISE: *Feet*
Solo/8 mins + tennis ball

One of the most important lessons I learnt at drama school is to examine what shoes your character wears. The way you contact the floor informs your movement and therefore, to an extent, your internal state. In seeking to release tension, in order to begin work with a blank canvas, the feet are a good place to start.

- Standing, place a tennis ball under one foot.
- Press the ball down onto the floor with the arch of the foot. Do not allow the body to sag whilst doing this.
- Press the ball down onto the floor using the edges of the foot.
- Press the ball down using the heel and then the ball of the foot.
- Find the parts of the foot where the process becomes painful and press further into these parts.
- After four minutes working on one foot, walk around the space.
- What do you notice? How does this foot feel different than the other? Try to describe this feeling.
- Repeat with the other foot.

Do this exercise regularly, perhaps whilst focusing on something else.

EXERCISE: *Align*
Solo/5 mins

Tension is created within the body when the body is unaligned and off-centre. Whilst shaking out body parts has the immediate effect of releasing tension, good alignment offers a longer-term benefit.

- With knees slightly bent and soft, shake out the hands, shoulders, torso, hips and pelvis, legs and feet.
- Stand with your feet directly under your hips with your knees soft. Allow the feet to spread and contact the floor (see the exercise above).

- Find a fixed point across the room to focus upon. Breathe deeply.
- Check the ankles, knees, pelvis are released. Do a figure of eight with the hips to check this, clockwise and then reverse.
- Release the buttocks.
- Relax the stomach.
- Lengthen the spine – beginning at the tail and up to the base of the skull. Be careful not to arch your back. Feel your spine lengthen and your back widen as you breathe.
- Imagine your head is floating on still water.
- Pick your shoulders up to your ears and drop – three times. Allow your shoulder blades to be part of this action and let the arms hang heavy from the shoulders.
- Allow the mouth to open and move the head whilst looking up, centre, to the left, centre, to the right, centre, down and back to centre.
- Scrunch the face tight and release.
- Press your tongue hard against your teeth. Begin on the top row of teeth, at the back of the mouth, and press along the surface to the other side. Repeat on the bottom row of teeth.
- Check again that your knees are soft.
- Bring awareness to your contact with the floor.

Do you feel heavier? How do you feel internally?

EXERCISE: *Roll and Align*
Solo/5 mins + a wall

The spine often takes the brunt of our bad habits; slumping, slouching, rolling our shoulders, pushing our head a little forward or back. Rolling and aligning the spine can help increase flexibility in the spine, give greater support, centre us and, like much of the release work, have a corresponding effect within us. Ask yourself how you feel once you have done a couple of these exercises.

1 Using the Wall

- Stand with your back pressed against a wall, your feet a little wider than shoulder width apart and knees a little bent (as though sitting on a tall stool). Ensure the inside of the shoulder blades, and the back of your head, are touching the wall.
- Slowly allow your head to drop forward, almost touching your chest, and vertebra by vertebra roll down the wall until, reaching your hips, your upper body is hanging over your waist and onto your knees.
- Then, slowly reverse this, from the tail-bone roll up, vertebra by vertebra. Keep the shoulders released, so that they only fall into position as you reach the upper part of your spine.
- Stop when the head is once again resting on the chest.

- Repeat this sequence a couple of times; the final time, allow the head to come to rest on top of the spine.

2 Standing Away from the Wall

- Stand with knees slightly bent and soft, feet slightly wider than shoulder width apart.
- Vocalise a long 'SHA': engage the lips with the 'SH' and enjoy the release of the vowel: 'AH'. Expel all your breath on this release of sound.
- As you do this, flop over your bent knees: pushing the tail-bone back and the chin forward.
- Keeping the head heavy, and using your thighs to support you, move gently to the left and then to the right. As you do so, keep the knees soft and breathe deeply, feeling the stretch down the opposite side to which you have moved.
- Come back to the centre, still flopped over your thighs, with your tail pushed out and your head heavy and free.
- Take a deep breath in.
- On short, repeated 'SH's (releasing only a little of your breath each time) start to uncurl your spine; begin by pushing your tail underneath you, vertebra by vertebra, from the base of the spine. You will feel your diaphragm engage with each 'SH', your belly press against the elastic of your trousers, and each time you feel this pressure, another vertebra moves back into position.
- Your shoulders, and then your head, arrive in the standing position.
- Repeat this exercise three times, each time with the 'SH's getting a little faster than the time before. Keep the lips firm but the neck released as you do this.

EXERCISE: *Align: Semi-Supine*
Solo/10 mins

When you lie down you release the pressures of standing upright. The pressure of gravity, when upright, tends to shorten the body; if you measure yourself in the evening you will be fractionally shorter than in the morning. By lying down you enlist the help of gravity to widen and lengthen the spine, taking the pressure off the invertebral discs keeping you upright. It's also a terrific 'reset', when playing a physically demanding character.

- As you lie down, push your knees up to the ceiling, with your feet planted flat on the floor. Place a book or two under your head, so that your head is in line with the spine, rather than tipping back and putting pressure on the neck and the throat.
- Allow your hands to rest by your side.
- Breathe in through your nose and out through an open mouth.
- Free the head by turning gently to each side and then returning to the centre.
- Roll the shoulders and place wide apart from each other.
- Shake your hands out.

- Gently roll your pelvis: pull up pelvic floor and then pull belly button to floor. The pelvis engages and releases.

- Direct your body through your thoughts, for example, 'my head lets go into the books, my neck releases into the floor, my shoulders move away from each other, my spine is long, my back wide'.

- Imagine a warm red circle in the centre of your forehead. Track a red line from this warm red circle, over the top of the head, down the spine, dividing and running through each shoulder, down the arms through the elbow and wrist and out through each finger. As you map these red lines from the forehead, imagine they carry with them all excess tension out through your fingertips. Retrace these lines five times, from the centre of the forehead and out.

- Repeat the above instruction but, this time, draw the red line from the red circle in your forehead, over the top of the head and continuing down through the pelvis, dividing and running through each leg, down the legs through the knees and ankles, and out through each of your toes. As you map these lines, again, imagine them carrying any excess tension out through the toes. Breathe deeply and repeat five times.

EXERCISE: *Massage 1*
Solo/5 mins + tennis ball + wall

- Use the palms of your hands to vigorously scrub yourself all over; the top of the head, your face, the point your jaw meets your skull, your lips, the back of the neck, your torso, arms, hips, legs, feet. Wherever possible focus on warming the joints. Do not forget about those parts of your back you can reach.

- Taking a tennis ball, find the position against a wall detailed in Exercise: Roll and Align (p. 16). This time, place a tennis ball between you and the wall. The ball should be placed on one side of the spine, beginning at the base of the spine. Keeping your spine as upright as possible, use your back to roll the ball up to your neck and back down again.

- Repeat on the other side of your spine. The ball should gently touch the side of each vertebra as it travels.

EXERCISE: *Massage 2*
Pairs/10 mins

- Partner A stands with soft knees, focusing on a point in front of them and breathing deeply.

- Partner B, using the palms of their hands, scrubs their partner – avoiding all areas that would normally be covered with underwear. The task is to create as much friction and heat as possible, starting with the top of the head and moving down the body to the feet. Be careful not to apply excessive pressure to joints; Partner A will guide you in this.

- Partner B then holds the full weight of A's left arm; A must give the weight of their arms entirely to their partner. B can gently bounce A's arms in the palm of their hands to aid this release.
- B then takes A's arm in the palm of their hands and, starting in the armpit, rolls A's arm (in the same manner that you would roll bread dough) down to the hand and pulls down through the fingers. This is done three times.
- If B stands in front of A, what do they notice? Perhaps A's left shoulder is lower than the right?
- Repeat the process with the right arm.
- Partner A opens their legs slightly wider than shoulder width apart. Partner B stands behind A and places their right leg through A's legs, pushing their left leg behind them. B's thigh becomes a seat for Partner A to sit upon; they sit, flop over their waist and release their head.
- B warms up A's back with the palms of their hands.
- Starting at the base of A's spine, B then moves their thumbs in a circular motion, either side of each vertebra. B makes their way up A's spine towards the base of the skull, applying firm pressure either side of each vertebra.
- B then places the palms of their hands either side of base of A's spine. B then walks their palm slowly up A's back. A presses into the hands and, using the pressure of B's palms, comes to a sitting position.
- B puts their arms under A's armpits and lifts A to a standing position.
- B, still standing behind A, holds each of A's shoulders in each hand, and gently rocks the shoulders forward and back.
- B then places each hand under each of A's armpits. They push A's shoulders up and then release. Do this three times.
- Then, swap over.

EXERCISE: *Energise*
Solo/Group/10 mins

- Walk around the space at a medium pace. Imagine yourself with a purpose; you are travelling somewhere. You are focused, you notice what is around you, you have a sense of ease and release.
- Take this walk into a light run.
- Keeping the knees soft, explore leaping, jumping, running side to side, travelling backwards – try running different distances, directions, speeds.
- Shake out your shoulders, arms, hands, torso, hips, legs, feet.
- Rudolf Laban introduced the idea of your Kinesphere; the sphere of space, always travelling with you, that can be reached by extending your limbs in any direction around you, whilst one foot remains in place on the floor as the point of balance and support.

- We will learn more about Rudolf Laban, his work, and how you can apply it when creating singing characters in Chapter 5: The Body and Movement.
- Stretch into your kinesphere[3] (see Figure 1.1); whilst doing so you will find it useful to connect the core. Connecting the core is detailed in the exercise immediately below.
- Finally, wake up your body by tapping every part of your body. Start with your head and work down to your toes. The theory goes that this allows the brain to remap your body. How does it make you feel?

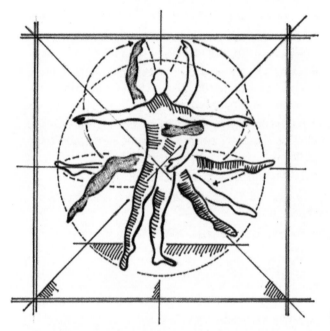

Figure 1.1 Laban kinesphere.[4]

Connection and the Core

We tend to create tension in our body when we place unnecessary pressure on it. Much of our physical strength comes from our centre; what we call the *core*. When we fail to connect the core, there can be an over-reliance on other parts of the body. Strengthening and connecting your physical core helps better support the body during physical activity; particularly the neck, taking the pressure off the spine. Yoga and Pilates place great emphasis on developing core strength.

---

[3] Preston Dunlop, V. (1998) *Looking at Dances: A Choreological Perspective on Choreography*. London: Verve Books, p. 27.
[4] Drawing by theatre and opera designer Mark Friend.

Failing to connect your core during performance can often result in your movement on stage lacking clarity and definition. If want to disappear on stage, work with an unconnected core. To be present on stage – defined in action, with a heightened awareness of others – working with a strong and connected core is incredibly powerful.

Of course, when singing and speaking text your diaphragm needs to be released in order to breathe. It is absolutely possible (and necessary!) to both connect your core and release your diaphragm at the same time; it just might take some practice. Try some of these exercises whilst singing.

EXERCISE: *The Dagger*
Group/5 mins

This is a favourite warm-up exercise that carries an important message.

- The group walks around the space at a medium pace; each player finds different pathways through the space.

- Each player secretly selects one person (1) in the group and keeps as far away from this person as possible.

- Next, after a minute, each secretly selects another person (2). The aim is to keep person (2) between yourself and person (1) at all times. Person (2) is your shield, protecting you from person (1)!

- You will notice the movement in the room changes speed.

- Next, every member of the group is made aware that somebody in the group has an imaginary dagger; no one knows who holds the dagger. For safety, the aim is to be arms-length away from everyone in the space at all times; be aware of those players behind you.

- The group collectively attempt to slow down the tempo of the movement. Try to come to a stop, whilst still keeping as far as possible from person (1), keeping person (2) between you and person (1), and being aware that anyone in the room might be holding the imaginary dagger.

- On a clap, relax for a moment and stop the game.

- On a second clap, restart the game.

- What do you notice? How does your physical state change? How does the physical state of everyone in the group change?

- The game is fun to play and by fully committing to the game you will have entered an important physical state; a state of alertness, with greater awareness of those around you, senses heightened and, crucially, your core connected.

EXERCISE: *Core*
Solo/1 min

This is a quick way of connecting your core. The exercise helps you become aware of the sensation of connecting your core and how this affects your movement as a whole.

- Stand with feet planted on the floor shoulder width apart.
- With knees soft and keeping your spine upright, drop down about ten centimetres by pushing your knees forward.
- To help isolate your pelvis place one hand below your belly button, between your hips, and one hand at the base of your spine.
- Roll your pelvis forward (releasing your knees a little as you do so) and up; think of this roll as following the shape of a 'U'.
- You will feel tension in your thighs, buttocks and tummy area (your core). Walk around the space and release this tension in your thighs and buttocks but remain connected at the core.
- What do you notice?
- Now, release your core and walk around the space. Try to make frequent sharp changes of direction.
- Then, connect your core (as above) and continue making frequent sharp changes of direction.
- How does your movement differ when your core is connected? When is the movement sharper? Or quicker?
- Next, try this while singing. Explore how to breathe freely whilst keeping the core connected.

EXERCISE: *Three Angels*
Pairs/5 mins

This exercise brings your awareness to your body's alignment and to your strength in movement. Work in pairs. A will walk the space as B supports A's body and movement by applying the actions of Three (imaginary) Angels:

First Angel

- B places the thumb and forefinger, four inches apart either side of the tail of the spine, at the top of the glutes.[5] With the motion of a piston, B pushes the thumb and then the forefinger, back and forth, into the top of each glute. This forces one leg forward and then the other and so on.
- Walk around the space with B *powering* and initiating A's walk.
- B lets go of A and A continues to walk with the sensation of their movement being powered by B.
- The fingers act as the trigger for the movement of each leg. They locate the impulse for the forward motion of the leg; this movement begins much higher than we would ordinarily think. By locating this impulse at the top of the glutes, we

---

[5] The gluteal muscle (or backside!) is the main muscle of the hip. Its primary function is in maintaining the trunk in the erect position. The lower part of the muscle acts as the rotator of the legs.

consciously connect the power of the glutes with our walk. Imagine the power in the hind legs of a large cat.

- The First Angel connects us to this powerful muscle; we have strength in our movement.

Second Angel

- B supports the weight of A's head by holding the chin with one hand, and the base of the skull at the rear, with the other hand. B places their thumb and forefinger under the chin; and, their other thumb and forefinger, under the knobbly bits at either side of the final vertebra at the top of the spine.
- B then, very gently, lifts A's skull a little. B must take great care to simply lift up, and not push the skull forward or back. A should allow B to take the weight of their skull.
- It is important that A then leads the walk, slowly, with B simply supporting the weight of the skull.
- B releases A's head and A continues around the space carrying the sensation of this support.
- The Second Angel lengthens and aligns the spine and helps you to feel the sensation of this whilst walking.

Third Angel

- B stands behind A and drops their weight by bending their knees, whilst keeping their spine upright; B will now be lower than A. From this dropped-weight position B takes hold of each side of A's chest and lifts up.
- B ensures not to push or pull the chest forward or back.
- A begins to walk with B continuing to lift A's chest.
- A should take care to release the shoulders.
- B provides all the support for the trunk.
- B releases A to walk alone. A, again, carries the sensation of this movement.
- The Third Angel aligns and lengthens your spine. It engages you with the idea of length in your spine.
- As a final exercise B swiftly triggers the Three Angels, one at a time, and then releases A to walk with the sensation of all Three Angels at work simultaneously. B powers the movement at the top of A's glutes, then gently lifts A's skull and then picks up A's chest from below and behind. Finally, B releases A to walk alone.
- Notice how the Three Angels affect A's walk; does this affect how you feel?
- Try taking the Three Angels into a coaching or rehearsal room. Better still, imaginatively engage them as you walk down the street.

EXERCISE: *Backward Circle*
Solo/5 mins

This exercise helps to centre you physically and emotionally. It is inspired by Tai Chi and I was introduced to the idea by Barbara Houseman during her Opera Works sessions. Barbara suggests doing this movement whilst working on an aria or scene but, to begin with, just focus on the movement itself.

- Stand with feet shoulder width apart and the toes spread.
- Next, create a large circle with your hands. Start with your arms at hip level and push them out away from your body: as though you are holding an imaginary inflatable beach ball, with your palms facing towards your body. Next, bring your arms up to shoulder level (still out in front of you) and then towards you; as though tracing the surface of the imaginary ball. Then push your hands down the front of your body to your starting position. Continue this circle.
- Tai chi is often characterised by slow, purposeful gestures; take your time and create a steady rhythm, with a sense of pushing the air down, without extraneous tension.
- Barbara would always suggest trying the circle in the other direction and observing the difference.
- The backward circle helps you to breathe deeper and slower; it brings with it a sense of calm. It is, therefore, particularly useful in moments of stress; try it before auditions or performances.
- Try the Backward Circle whilst singing; what do you notice?

EXERCISE: *Net Throw*
Solo/5 mins

Engage the core before trying this exercise. Be aware of how the whole body and the breath engages with the action.

- Imagine you are standing in shallow water and just under the water is a small net; maybe twelve inches in diameter.
- Pick the imaginary net up, out of the water, ensuring it does not fold over on itself. Be aware of the weight of water it carries.
- Focus on a spot, about three metres away, to throw the net to.
- Swing the net back, a couple of times, in preparation to throw; continue to support the size and weight of the net.
- Focus on the spot, twist back, support the net, twist forward and release the net on an out breath. Watch where it lands.
- Try this a few times. Focus on breathing out as you release the net. Try this breath out on a comfortable note, that lasts the duration of the imaginary net in flight.
- Repeat the exercise but with a bigger net. Continue to explore how your body and breath connect with the net. Remember to connect your core.

Physical Control and Clarity

An awareness of the tension in your body, together with an understanding of how you connect with your core strength, is essential in beginning to bring control to your body. In turn, you will begin to bring clarity to your physical movements; Stanislavski argues these should be clear-cut 'like notes on an instrument'.[6] This is particularly important when defined and clear notes, played by the instruments in the orchestra, underscore and emphasise your movements.

Greater clarity of movement allows you to develop a wider range of physical expression, leading to the potential for more layered and detailed physical characterisation. As a performer you will be aware, however, of how any tension appears magnified on stage and how, unfortunately, the glare of the footlights only increases this tension. Let's now turn our attention to how we can free the mind to focus upon our imaginative reality and so, in turn, release our physical restrictions.

The Mind: Awareness and Focus

Just as physical relaxation is required for expression through the body, mental relaxation is required for the concentration of thought. Of course, releasing unnecessary tension within the body will help you to focus and concentrate your mind. In turn, greater focus and attention on your character's thoughts will lead to greater physical release and relaxation.

Stanislavski placed great emphasis on what he called the inner creative state;[7] a state in which the performer is ready to receive and build upon the imaginative possibilities the words and music present and highly attuned to the minute meanings of expression in another performer.

Stanislavski asserts that the inner creative state rarely arrives spontaneously and the challenges facing the singer, in the rehearsal room and onstage, are far greater to achieving this state than for the actor. The division of focus between the imaginative reality of the world of the piece and the musical demands of the conductor, in addition to the distracting pull of the audience and, perhaps, the nagging voice of the 'inner critic' present a range of obstacles for the singer. The question for the singer is, how to balance these various demands?

To begin with we will look at how to deal with the audience and the 'inner critic'; quietening these potential distractions will help you to bring your full attention to the other necessary considerations. The 'inner critic' is the internal monitor that many performers carry with them through rehearsals, performances and auditions; an inner monologue providing a running commentary of the work they do. The 'inner critic' is invariably overly harsh, a symptom of doubts and insecurities, feeding these same anxieties.

The ability to be present, moment by moment, in performance whilst at the same time having some small part of your attention on the technicalities of your performance (your 'performer's eye and ear') is crucial. This is what makes you an artist; the duality of focus enabling you to make changes and craft a performance, to connect and adapt with your fellow performers and conductor, whilst simultaneously being alive within each moment.

---

[6] Stanislavski, K. (1980) *An Actor Prepares*. Translated by E. R. Hapgood. London: Eyre Methuen, p. 107.
[7] Ibid., p. 263.

However, the volume of the 'inner critic' can become overwhelming and debilitating. This is a common experience amongst performers; if you are prone to constant self-questioning and self-analysis of every note you sing and gesture you make, then you are certainly not alone.

The Camera is an adaptation of an exercise Barbara Houseman began with when leading her Opera Works sessions. Barbara is a renowned voice coach for actors and has an acute understanding of how self-consciousness can create unnecessary mental and physical tensions. She uses the Camera as a metaphor to represent your attention. When the Camera is pointed in on yourself, you tend to feel self-conscious and judgemental. However, when the Camera points out, into the world, it frees and releases you from self-doubt and self-criticism.

EXERCISE: *The Camera*
Solo/Group/2 mins

This exercise helps to identify those moments when the 'inner critic' is most voluble and illustrates the principles of restraining this internal monologue.

Camera In

- Stand in front of a group of colleagues (if you're not working with a group, use a photo or group of objects). Do nothing, just stand there.
- Now, ask yourself, 'What do these people really think of me?' Imagine yourself through their eyes.
- Notice what happens to your breath.
- Now, begin singing an aria, perhaps one you use for auditions, and continue asking this question, as you sing.
- What physical responses do you notice? How do you feel?

Whenever we did this at Opera Works the response of the volunteer being watched would be incredibly uncomfortable; singers would squirm and shift, desperate to return to the comfort of the group.

Camera Out

- Shake out.
- Stand, once again, in front of the group.
- This time place the Camera's focus on the group. Ask yourself a series of questions about the group. What are each of them wearing? How many are wearing grey items of clothing? How many have brown eyes? How many are wearing trainers? How many wear earrings? And so on.
- What do you notice when your attention and focus is turned out onto others?
- Now, try singing the same aria but throughout, including during the play-in, continue asking similar questions.
- What is the difference between pointing the Camera in and Camera out? How does it affect the voice?

Opera Works singers always felt much calmer, more present and centred, employing Camera Out. The exercise goes straight to the heart of how we can begin to play and, so, create. By heightening our awareness of what lies outside us, we begin to quieten our self-conscious thoughts and discover a connection with our environment and those we are collaborating with.

The more we observe and notice, the greater our curiosity becomes, and the less opportunity our 'Inner Critic' has to turn up the volume on negative thoughts. Bringing our attention *out* begins to attune our senses to the world around us; it enables us to fuel our imagination and react, in detail, to the circumstances that surround us.

Much of the time singing is a solitary pursuit, relying on a great deal of time spent developing the voice and learning music. This can lead to a kind of 'tunnel vision'; a closing down onto a narrow point of focus, in this case, the words and music of the score. This narrowing of focus can translate into the rehearsal room and lead to the risk of not actively hearing the orchestra, or the words another character sings.

We need to activate our senses, in order to effectively employ our Camera Out, to truly engage with the ever-changing world and people that help define us.

EXERCISE: *Active Senses*
Solo/Ongoing

Active Listening

- Lie down and close your eyes.
- Breathe deeply; think of the breath travelling as a wave, in through the nose and slowly out through the mouth.
- Place a hand on your chest and 'listen' to your heartbeat. As your breathing slows and deepens, does your pulse slow?
- What other sounds does your body make?
- Listen to those sounds that immediately surround you in the room: the whirr of a computer, the creak of floorboards, the hum of air-conditioning. Bring your focus to each of these sounds in turn.
- Extend this to the sounds from outside the room. Again, listen to each of these sounds individually.
- Do not strain to hear. Rather, map these sounds in your mind's eye. Where is each sound located? What quality, rhythm, texture does each sound have? What images do they create in your mind's eye?
- Make a mental note of this.
- Now, return to the room and visit each sound again.
- Now, return to yourself. Listen to yourself.

Active Vision

Tunnel vision often occurs when we are anxious about something. Think, now, of something that causes concern and you might experience a sensation of the world narrowing around you. We want to develop vision that is flexible, active, open and 'panoramic'; to include height, width and depth. This means that whilst focusing on something, try bringing your attention to the bigger picture; don't *push* to focus only on one thing. When we focus on something on stage we still need to be connected, in some way, to our fellow performers, the conductor, the audience. This state of panoramic vision – a state where we are open, receptive to information and engaging our peripheral vision – tends to occur when we are at our most relaxed and happy. A few tips to help develop this:

Free Eyes

When beginning to learn a role with the score, allow your eyes to roam freely around the rest of the page. Do not focus only on your role. Begin to notice the information unravelling in the piano score simultaneously: the other characters that are singing, how the orchestra emphasises a particular harmony, etc.

Circles of Attention

- *Small Circle:* step into a room and bring your attention to, for example, the items on top of a table. Look at them for a short moment, try not to fix only on one item but to take in all objects.
- Close your eyes and describe what you saw.
- You can try this with an even smaller *Circle of Attention*; for example, a copy of the score you are learning. Scan over the score, taking everything in, close your eyes and ask yourself what you recall.
- *Medium Circle:* step into a room, allow yourself a moment to notice as much as possible, and then close your eyes and describe what you saw. Bring your attention to those objects that lie at the edge of your field of vision.
- *Large Circle:* this time, look out of the window. Repeat the process in as much detail as possible.

Room Map

- Imagining the tip of your nose has a long pencil attached, draw an imaginary line around all the objects on or against a wall. The tip of the nose must always be parallel with the object it is drawing a line around. If, for example, the wall has a radiator attached, drop down to trace around the radiator. If a picture is hung high on the wall, you need to be on tip toes to trace it.
- As you move along the wall tracing around an object, keep in your peripheral vision the imaginary line you have already drawn. So, you move forward, whilst staying connected with the entire line.

Active Senses

- Bring your attention to each of those senses not yet explored; touch, smell and taste.
- Set five minutes aside to explore each; for example, be led around the room by the different smells you find, try blind-tasting different teas and describing the difference, map the room through touch, with your eyes closed.

This might seem trivial but watch a baby or toddler explore the world and they are always in the moment; testing, discovering, connecting and heightening their senses to a world of possibilities.

Engage

As we develop our toolkit, we will begin to understand that many of the tools within it help us to connect and communicate with those we are creating the story alongside. The way in which we engage with them determines the way our story is told. It is important to develop a full awareness of yourself and your fellow performers; the better you understand yourself and your colleagues, the easier it becomes to connect with them and, by extension, the actions, expressions and emotions of the characters in the opera. As Stanislavski accurately points out, 'Spectators in theatre can understand and indirectly participate in what goes on onstage only while this intercourse continues among the actors.'[8]

Receiving what your fellow singer is communicating is about more than simply listening to the words and music they are singing. You must aim to 'listen' to their entire selves: their breath (its rhythm, tempo, pauses, depth), their tensions and their smallest gestures. Bringing a level of alertness to the unspoken means that you *consciously* note information about your partner your subconscious has probably already collected.

EXERCISE: *Receive*
Pair/3 mins

- Stand facing each other; no more than 30 centimetres apart.
- Do not make eye contact with your partner but focus all your attention on them.
- Listen, look and smell. Notice the tiniest details about them. Study them. Take some time over this. What do you note about them?
- Once the three minutes is up, move away from your partner. Close your eyes and try to recollect everything about them.

This requires a certain amount of trust. Both you and your partner are being very open by allowing each other into your individual personal space; respect this. Thank the other person to bring the exercise to a close.

EXERCISE: *Follow*
Pairs/2 mins each

This exercise is about heightening your senses to your partner's movements and attuning your response to them. It should also help develop your peripheral vision.

- A stands about 50 centimetres behind B. Both A and B keep their knees soft.
- A holds a forefinger, still, at a point behind or to the side of B.
- As soon as B senses movement, they must turn quickly to spot A's finger. Once B has looked directly at A's finger, they then return to face the front (away from A).

---

[8] Stanislavski, K. (1980) *An Actor Prepares*. Translated by E. R. Hapgood. London: Eyre Methuen, p. 195.

- Only once B returns to the front does A move their finger to a new position. B then turns in response.
- The game continues. The aim is for B's reactions in connecting to A's finger to become quicker through the game.
- Swap over at the end of the game.

Communication between performers is more than simply listening to the sung words; thoughts are communicated through an exchange of energy, body language, movement, silences and breath. These factors are the very essence of our communication in life and reveal the story to an audience in a powerful way. Stanislavski was aware that without this continuous communion between singers, stories onstage would fail to reflect the richness and depth of our everyday communication. However, as with so many things, the simplest things in life can suddenly fade away onstage. In response, the singer must constantly sharpen and heighten their senses to better prepare for the demands of the stage.

These next two exercises were instrumental in developing the Opera Works singers' awareness of each other. They demand continuous focus and attention, they necessitate a clarity of connection, they develop the peripheral vision and they help create the state of readiness required for play.

EXERCISE: *The Circle*
Group/Ongoing

- The company stand in a circle facing each other.
- One person begins (A); they make eye contact with someone in the circle (B); A, by raising an eyebrow or smiling at B, seeks consent to cross the circle and move into B's place in the circle; B gives consent for A to move into their place with a clear nod of the head (consent must be given when a player requests to move into your space); *only once B has nodded their consent can A begin their journey across the circle.*
- B then has the time it takes A to reach them, to make eye contact with someone else in the circle (C); seek C's consent to move into C's place in the circle; and, having received consent, begin to move into C's place, vacating their original place in the circle in time for A to take it.
- And so on . . . C makes eye contact with someone else, D, etc.

It is a relatively simple set of rules; one person moves and it creates a chain reaction of people changing places in the circle. However, it rarely plays out so simply. Requests to move are often muddled, nods are unclear, a panicked journey begins without consent having first been sought and so on.

The exercise really gets to the heart of how a company should develop communication with each other. Ideally, the company should develop such a keen understanding that all nods and gestures are imperceptible to an outsider.

Ultimately, a company should be able to play this game whilst singing recit or an ensemble.

- The company stand in a circle facing each other.

- A holds Ball 1. Everyone (except A) raises a hand. A throws Ball 1 to somebody else in the circle and once they've received the ball they lower their hand and throw the ball to somebody with their hand still raised. Once the ball has been passed around the circle, the final person to receive the ball throws it back to A.

- The group has now marked the journey for Ball 1 – it is important to remember who you received the ball from and who you threw it to.

- The group then do the same for Ball 2; except this time the journey of the ball is different. Ball 2 finally returns back to A.

- The game is now ready to begin!

- A begins Ball 1's previously marked journey. Shortly afterwards, A begins Ball 2's previously marked journey. Both journeys are now taking place simultaneously. Once A receives either ball back they immediately re-start the journey.

- To extend the exercise, as both balls travel across the circle, a bottle begins to be passed from person to person around the perimeter of the circle. You now have three objects to keep track of.

- If a ball drops, you pick it up and keep going.

- If the sequence breaks down, you return both balls and the bottle to A and the game begins again.

- The aim is for each ball to make as many uninterrupted journeys as possible.

These exercises help develop our focus and concentration and alert us to our clarity of intention. Additionally, they help foster and grow a shared understanding within a company – a complicité – an awareness that we each need to play our part alongside, and in complete connection to, each other.

SUMMARY

- The body holds tensions that can prevent you fully embodying character.

- By developing an awareness of your own body, and where certain tensions are carried, you can begin to understand how to release tension.

- Connecting the core helps to bring physical control and clarity to work onstage.

- The mind and body are connected and inter-dependent.

- Focusing attention on details of the world outside you helps quieten the 'inner critic'.

- Developing an understanding of, and connection with, your fellow singers brings focus to the clarity of the storytelling.

TO DO

- Integrate work that helps you unlock blocks and tensions: yoga, Pilates, Tai Chi and Alexander technique are terrific for helping you to get to know your body, develop core strength and expand physical flexibility.

- Incorporate the simple release and core work into your everyday routine; let it become habitual.

- Engage your awareness of the world around you; 'listen' to the world for five minutes every day.

- Encourage the team you are working with to integrate the work on developing communication through your process of rehearsal.

Imagination

Heightening our senses to observe the world in greater detail provides the fuel that fires our most important asset: the imagination. The ability to create and believe in fictions, and share these with others, is what separates us from every other animal. The historian Yuval Noah Harari argues that stories are the glue that connect us: 'We cooperate effectively with strangers because we believe in things like gods, nations, money and human rights. Yet none of these things exists outside the stories that people invent and tell one another. There are no gods in the universe, no nations, no money and no human rights – except in the common imagination of human beings.'[9]

Stories have the power to motivate, unite and move us. All art is a product of the imagination and without imagination there can be no creativity. The aim of the singer is to begin to use their imagination to turn the words and music of the opera into a theatrical reality.[10]

The stories we work with in opera challenge us to draw upon and stretch all our imaginative resources; gods appear as lightning bolts, murdered fathers rise from the depths of hell and giants build castles. And yet in each one of these stories very real human lives and emotions unfold.

And in opera we take one further imaginative leap for we must engage our imagination to believe in a truthful world in which everybody *sings* and, in so doing, appeal to the collective imagination of the audience.

The Magic *If*

Stanislavski developed a tool he called The Magic *If* and it underpins all his work. The *If* is a direct and specific appeal to your imagination. So, for example, taking the characters and situations from *The Marriage of Figaro*:

---

[9] http://www.ynharari.com/topic/power-and-imagination/.
[10] Stanislavski, K. (1980) *An Actor Prepares*. Translated by E. R. Hapgood. London: Eyre Methuen, p. 54.

- What *if* I have the money and power of an eighteenth-century Spanish Count?
- What *if* today is my wedding day and I have just discovered my fiancé has a prior arrangement with somebody old enough to be his mother?
- What *if* I have just been ordered to join the army and must say goodbye to the woman I have fallen in love with?

The *If* is also a challenge to action; it engages the active imagination:

- What would I **do** *if* I discovered my husband was cheating on me?
- What would I **do** *if* I learned my employees were attempting to undermine me?
- What would I **do** *if* I'd seen someone jump out of a window, destroying one of the plant pots in the garden I was tending?

Stanislavski described *If* as 'a lever' to lift us out of the real and actual and into the imagined.[11] *If* invites you to work in the first person. Immediately *I* am propelled into the character's world; I empathise with them. This has the effect of engaging and drawing upon our inner life, stimulating the creative subconscious and triggering certain connections between the body, mind and emotions.

In opera the music travels with the story at every moment – the Magic *If* can therefore be extended to include the music as a prompt for our imagination. Again, with reference to characters from *The Marriage of Figaro*:

- What *if* I were a Countess who sings this music?
- What *if* I were decorating a hat for my wedding and in this moment an orchestra was underscoring my life with this music?
- What *if* this was the music of the song I had written to try to express and define my feelings of love?

Of course, sometimes the character you are playing might not be aware of the music that underscores their life but the music can still be used to trigger pictures in your imagination that take you closer to the character's life. By actively listening to the music, and connecting it with the situation *I* (your character) am in, it acts as yet another lever into an imaginary world. You must become your own director – using the Magic *If* to create the pictures, films and soundtracks in your mind's eye.

Stanislavski places the Magic *If* at the very centre of his work, asserting that without it 'There can be no creativeness, no matter how well you execute simple physical actions on the stage. On the stage we must have life but not only that, it must be the life of your imagination which you make real for us.'[12]

Training the Imagination

In order to draw readily on the full power of our imagination we need to train it. Children have ready recourse to imaginative worlds through constant play and they often have a

---

[11] Stanislavski, K. (1980) *An Actor Prepares*. Translated by E. R. Hapgood. London: Eyre Methuen, p. 46.
[12] Stanislavski, K. (1998) *Stanislavski on Opera*. Translated by E. R. Hapgood. London: Routledge, p. 9.

troupe of willing participants to join them; the line between the actual and the imagined is much less defined for children than adults.

Where to Start: In General

- Be keen to observe; look at Exercise: *Circles of Attention* (pp. 27–8).
- Activate your memory; in detail, rediscover moments of your own life by drawing on your five senses. What did you smell, taste, see, hear, feel?
- Heighten your senses; look at Exercise: *Active Senses* (pp. 27–8).
- Travel. Read. Wander around galleries.

Where to Start: In Character

- Engage with the music; allow it to underscore the images or film in your mind's eye.
- Ask Stanislavski's six fundamental questions (we will look at these in more detail later):[13]
  - **Who** is my character?
  - **When** is my character living?
  - **Where** is my character?
  - **Why** is my character here?
  - **For what reason?**
  - **How** will my character get what they want?[14]
- Find a subject in your character's life that interests, intrigues and piques your curiosity. Don't force the imagination, gently coax it.[15]
- Work in detail; focus on the little facts and pieces of information that define your world.
- Use your inner senses; use your inner eye and ear to create the pictures and sounds you see and hear in your imagination.
- Be active; avoid passive observations when using your imagination but, instead, be a central participant in it.
- Whenever you are doing a vocal or physical warm-up exercise, give it an imaginary impetus. (See all Exercises below.)

Your imagination frees you, refreshes you and places you in control.

---

[13] See Chapter 6: Words and Music in Action.
[14] Stanislavski, K. (1980) *An Actor Prepares*. Translated by E. R. Hapgood. London: Eyre Methuen, p. 67.
[15] Ibid., p. 58.

EXERCISE: *Imaginary Impetus*
Solo/Ongoing

Give yourself an imaginative purpose (an inner justification) for every vocal or physical warm-up exercise you do. Ask 'for what reason am I doing this?' and find an imaginative response to it.

For example:

- Whilst practising singing scales, engage your imagination. For example, imagine you are on a desert island and aim each of the notes you sing at an imaginary passing boat; what do you see, smell, hear, feel?
- Look again at Exercise: *Energise* (p. 19) and rather than simply doing the physical actions – leaping, jumping, running side to side and backwards – imagine that you have a reason for doing them. Imagine, for example, that you are the main character in a 1980s arcade game: traverse different environments, collect gold tokens and escape marauding beasts.

Never let your imagination rest; the more active it is, the more accessible it will be when called upon.

EXERCISE: *Visualisation*
Solo/Pair/Ongoing

Use your *inner eye* to see and engage with the images your imagination creates and your *inner ear* to hear distinct voices and melodies.
You:

- Stand in a room. Keep your focus free and wide.
- Look ahead and imagine you can see through the wall in front of you. Travel beyond the boundaries of your knowledge. What do you see?
- Try adding an imaginary soundtrack; the noises might be environmental or alternatively orchestral.
- Now, focus behind you and do the same.
- Now, to each side of you.
- Place yourself at the centre of a real and imaginary landscape.

Your Character: *The Countess* (from *The Marriage of Figaro*):

- Imagine the room in which you spend most of your day; your dressing room or bedroom.
- See the window. Look out into the garden. What do you see in detail? Describe it.
- It is useful if a partner questions and challenges you to continue to develop the images.
- What do you see at different times of the day when you look out of this window? Or, at different times of the year?

- What sounds accompany these pictures? If Mozart were to write music for the view you see, how might it sound? How might that change through the seasons?

Do not be drawn by substitution. For example, do not substitute your own bedroom window into these pictures; rather create something unique to this world. It may, of course, be inspired by a number of actual places.

EXERCISE: *Diary*
Solo/Ongoing

You:

- Do this as a daily exercise. Choose a piece of music; anything is fine but instrumental works best.
- Close your eyes and listen to the music. Begin to picture an imaginary scene, informed by the music, and ask the Six Fundamental Questions: who does this music relate to? Who do I see? When is it? Where is it? Why does this music accompany this moment? For what reason? How does the scene play out?
- Imagine that *you* are the person at the centre of this scene. As you listen to the music again, write a short diary entry for this person, capturing this moment.

Your character: *Figaro* (from *The Marriage of Figaro*):

- Listen to the overture.
- Imagine it is, perhaps, the beginning of the day. When *exactly* is this? Where do you (Figaro) imagine yourself? What action does the music accompany? What are you doing and for what reason? How do you go about it?
- Whilst replaying the overture, write your diary entry for the beginning of the day.
- Try this with other music elsewhere in the opera. Does certain music accompany you at points in the story of the opera that the audience are not privy to? Maybe certain fragments of music are the spur for you to cast your mind back through other moments in your character's life?
- Again, create a diary entry for what you see.
- Write all these entries in pencil; you might want to adapt or manipulate the memories and pictures you create, as you get to know your character better.

These exercises will sharpen and ready your imagination for the moment you meet the world a librettist and composer have already begun to imagine. This world will offer you so many possibilities; you must be prepared to imaginatively connect with it. Your imagination will help you to build belief in the reality of everything a character sings and does. Allow yourself to be imaginatively absorbed in whatever interests and excites your character.

Play and Spontaneity

Your job is to create truthful life onstage communicated through your singing voice, physical actions and engagement with other people and the world in which you live. The challenge is all too clear; life is improvised and spontaneous, whilst opera draws on stories with predetermined plot. The job of the singer is to make predetermined events appear to be unfolding in the present moment for the first time; to be remembering and forgetting simultaneously.[16] Within these set parameters, this process is aided by play; the possibility of being surprised and to surprise.

Play becomes easier when we are physically released, our awareness broadened and our imagination free to roam. Indeed, we are helped by the very nature of live performance itself; we are working with people, for the most part, all of whom are challengeable, suggestible, variable and open to the influence of a multitude of factors. The conductor will make slight adjustments of tempo from one performance to the next, orchestral instruments will alter depending upon the temperature in the pit and an audience's response will vary, depending upon what night of the week it is, the weather outside and the levels of expectation inspired by reviews of a previous performance.

Opera is a careful balancing act of diverse elements drawn together to reveal the most intimate of moments; a flash of doubt in a lover's eyes, the slow growing shame of a betrayal unmasked. The very act of balancing so many elements might seem to promote the appearance of a world alive onstage; the risk of disaster, of veering off balance, keeping all performers present and in the moment. Yet, as a consequence of such terrific risk, the temptation persists to do everything to minimise this danger; too often we hold tight, rely on proven tricks of behaviour and resist adaptation, rather than embrace the potential of the very thing that will keep the performance alive. I am not proposing wild lurches of interpretation from one performance to the next; the form requires discipline. However, it also demands spontaneity, play and glimpses of the unknown.

The musician Stephen Nachmanovitch writes:

> Mozart was perhaps the greatest improviser with pen and paper. He often wrote the fair copies of his scores and parts straight out, inventing the music as fast as the pen would go and hardly ever blotting a line ... The heart of improvisation is the free play of consciousness as it draws, paints, and plays the raw material emerging from the unconscious. Such play entails a certain degree of risk.[17]

Nachmanovitch's observation of Mozart is important. We see scores in black and white, etched with markings, and they appear set, fixed and complete. The idea that Mozart was improvising, his work representing the interplay between the unconscious and conscious mind in the moment, is incredibly freeing for the singer. We are his collaborators. We need to meet him, understand his propositions in depth, in all their many layers, and find a way of rediscovering this initial moment of improvisation to bring to life his music and stories for an audience today. We need to nudge, prompt and inspire our subconscious thoughts to make them present in the moment, and allow them to merge with Mozart's, to create his characters afresh. We must not simply enable the interplay between our own subconscious and conscious thoughts but, this being a collaborative art, also those of our fellow collaborators.

---

[16] Bennett, M. (2017) *Analytic Philosophy and the World of the Play*. London: Routledge, p. 85.
[17] Nachmanovitch, S. (1990) *Free Play: Improvisation in Life and Art*. New York: Tarcher Penguin, pp. 8–9. Nachmanovitch, a musician, explores how improvisation and play relate to an artist's work.

The journey, from the rehearsal room to the stage, is one of discovery; we learn about the world of the opera, the character we are creating and those our character responds to. The most fearless discoverers, and therefore the best learners, are children. Indeed, there is a direct correlation between learning and play.[18] The *way* in which children play is important to note; they generally don't worry too much about failure. If they fall over, they get back up and have another go. This spirit of play and discovery should be brought to your exploration of character and music; within yourself and between you and your collaborators. You need to take risks and venture into the unknown, in order to discover what you do not already know. You must play and risk falling.

Throughout Opera Works we worked with a terrific teacher and improviser, Alex Maclaren, from The Spontaneity Shop. Alex's opening invitation to the singers was to declare an oath; 'We suck and we love to fail!'. This is a big challenge for a singer. Conservatoires and opera companies might not always seem like the easiest places to play but it's important to remember that this is exactly what rehearsals are for. The most exciting singers and actors I have worked with use rehearsals to try, test and explore possible directions. Their sense of play is infectious and usually draws others in.

How do you nurture a sense of play within yourself and the team you are working with? In the first instance, there are a number of *rules* to bear in mind:

The Rules of Play

1 Bring a 'yes and . . .' attitude to all creative collaboration, by listening and building upon others' ideas. See the exercise below.

2 Be ready to offer ideas . . . and just as ready to chuck them away.

3 Seek to build trust between you and collaborators; be responsive to others' body language and aware of the dynamics in the rehearsal room.

4 Find the game. In whatever you do: small playful associations, developments of ideas, entertainments for your partner. See the exercise below.

5 Invite other people to play. Committing to play is difficult by yourself; you need others to join in.

EXERCISE: *Yes and . . .*
Pairs/5 mins

This exercise is a classic improvisation workshop opener and explores different interaction styles, all of which, I am sure, you will be familiar with in one context or another.

No . . .
First, plan a night out with your partner. A is going to make all the suggestions, B is going to consistently reject them.

---

[18] Throughout his book, *Free Play: Improvisation in Life and Art*, Stephen Nachmanovitch argues that the best education systems tap into the close relationship between play and exploration.

For example:

- A – *Let's nip to the pub before we head into town.*
- B – *No, I hate pubs, they're too loud and aggressive.*
- A – *Well, we could jump in a cab and head straight into town.*
- B – *No, I don't have money for a cab and, in any case, I haven't taken a cab since I split up with my ex last June.*
- *And so on . . .*

1. The exercise might be fun, initially; B can certainly begin to relish teasing A and finding ever more ridiculous reasons to block proposals. It is, however, deeply unproductive and reminds us of arguments between defensive colleagues.

Yes but . . .

Next, plan a weekend away together. A, again, makes the suggestions and B appears to accept them whilst ultimately finding a way to reject them.

For example:

- A – *How about Paris?*
- B – *Yes that'd be nice but I've been there before and it rained.*
- A – *What if we go prepared with umbrellas?*
- B – *Yes, good idea, but they're never very effective from the waist down.*
- *And so on . . .*

Yes but. . . is generally not much fun as it quickly tends to sap A's inspiration. This is the template for much workplace dialogue; colleagues wanting to seem to be willing to collaborate but guarding their own position.

Yes and. . .

Finally, plan a fun night in together. A makes the suggestions, B accepts them and builds upon them. A responds in kind.

For example:

- A – *How about we get some nachos?*
- B – *Yes and we could get some salsa to go with it?*
- A – *Yes and some sliced jalapenos to go on top?*
- B – *Yes and we can pick up some beers to wash them down?*
- *And so on . . .*

This is the usually the most fun conversation to be part of. A virtuous circle of developing agreement is created. It will be familiar to you from the kinds of conversations that you have with best friends and with close creative teams.

Yes and . . . is a good basis for improvisation and an incredibly productive attitude to adopt in all creative environments.

Paul Hunter, co-founder of theatre company Told by an Idiot, was an important contributor to Opera Works. Paul's emphasis is on developing interaction and scenes through play. These next exercises are about finding a game to play with your collaborators within a variety of contexts.

EXERCISE: *Find the Game*
Group/Ongoing

Finding a game, whether in workshops, rehearsals or performance, follows a simple structure:

- Find a simple game (something small, perhaps barely perceptible).
- Entertain each other with it.
- Recognise when that game is over.
- Find another game.

Copying

- In a circle, with the group facing each other, someone begins a simple gesture; a scratch of a nose, a flick of an eyebrow, a pout of the lips, etc. Someone copies it. Then the group develops it, playing with it and attempting to amuse each other with it. Once this gesture feels as though it's run its course, someone in the group introduces another gesture.

Twitch

- In pairs, begin by talking about your plans for the weekend.
- A introduces a twitch, which they must appear to be unaware of.
- B notices it and tries to find opportunities to copy it.
- Explore what happens when you twitch at the same time, if the scale of the twitch grows, or if the rhythm alters.
- Try this in front of your fellow singers. Be sensitive to your audience. How do you explore the potential for comedy? Playing with an audience's expectations is important in making them laugh; do you give them what they want or hold off and make them wait?

These exercises work best when you keep the game or the gestures small. A smaller scale restricts you and forces you to be more inventive in playing the game; the game usually becomes more detailed. Don't worry about having to be inventive or novel. The most important thing is to listen to and connect with your partner. Remember, if you're playing a scene from an opera, it's not an invitation to undermine or parody the scene. The game might simply be used to reconnect with your partner, or to refresh the scene and then put the game to one side.

SUMMARY

- Our imagination allows us to fully enter the world of the opera and character.
- The Magic *If* is the key to making us active participants in our imaginative reality.
- Heightening our senses fuels our imagination.
- By engaging in play we can explore the spirit of spontaneity in performance.

TO DO

- Engage your empathetic imagination by utilising The Magic *If*.
- Bring an imaginative impetus to every exercise you do.
- Keep a character diary.
- Employ a 'Yes and . . .' attitude.
- Seek the moment to play a game in your work.

2 A Note about Emotion

Those moments on stage, or in rehearsal, when we *feel* truthfully connected to our emotions, everything seems to fall into place. We are engaged with our inner and outer selves and, as a result, seem to respond spontaneously to our fellow performers and the world of the opera. Understandably, therefore, we *seek* to feel. This impulse for the singing actor is, perhaps, heightened by the music, which seems to suggest particular feelings or emotions. Words and music together take us closer to the result of what might be expressed in a performance than mere words alone; we are provided with additional information from the librettist and composer and, therefore, the score suggests something more complete than a play might.

However, as we'll examine, emotions cannot be simply commanded at will and seeking to *feel* or to play *emotion* risks a forced, demonstrative and generalised style of acting; *showing* the emotion you believe you should be feeling, based upon how you, or others, label a response to the music's emotional content. The words and music written in the score are not the end result. They provide detailed information that you, the performer, must seek to understand, interpret and absorb in order to fire the imagination and communicate, ultimately, to the audience.

The tendency to seek to play emotions – particularly, and understandably, in opera – is so great, it's worth looking at why it is a misguided approach, before beginning to look at those tools which might, instead, lead to a more rewarding process.

Emotion and Psychology

In the 1970s, psychologist Paul Ekman listed six basic emotions that he discerned to be universally recognisable: anger, disgust, fear, happiness, sadness and surprise. He argued that each of these emotions is displayed on the face through a particular and specific pattern of movements. Ekman based his research upon photographs of the faces of American actors enacting certain emotions; he showed these photographs to subjects across the globe and they, for the most part, successfully labelled the emotion the actor was illustrating. The clinching argument for Ekman was that even the Fore people, a remote society in Papua New Guinea isolated from Western influence, recognised the big six emotions.[1] Ekman

---

[1] Ekman, P. and W. V. Friesen (1971) 'Constants across cultures in the face and emotion', *Journal of Personality and Social Psychology*, 17: 124–29.

argued that it proved Darwin's thesis[2] that facial expressions were universally recognisable, in contrast to gestures, which remained specific to a particular place and time. The extension of this argument is that we are pre-programmed to display and recognise emotions from the precise arrangement of facial muscles into facial expressions.

More recent studies into how emotions are made and recognised challenge this view. They suggest a lack of evidence for such facial fingerprints. Certain experiments, whereby electrodes attached to the face measure facial movements, have collected significant data to suggest that there is no verifiable universal link between specific facial movements and certain emotions. Further studies into the supposed standard physiological responses to emotional experiences – such as measuring blood pressure – reveal similar variety, resisting such categorisation.[3] Indeed, looking at the posed photos of actors in the Ekman trial, they appear to be stereotypical, clichéd expressions rather than convincing displays of any *real* emotional experience.

Psychologist Lisa Feldman Barrett suggests, instead, a theory of constructed emotion.[4] She argues against the idea of facial fingerprints, pre-programmed at birth and revealing a set of easily definable emotions, in favour of a view that emotions 'emerge as a combination of the physical properties of your body, a flexible brain that wires itself to whatever environment it develops in, and your culture and upbringing which provide that environment'.[5] Feldman Barrett's argument rests upon the variety of ways in which people define their emotional experience. Her research revealed that respondents used the same words to describe emotions – 'happy', 'sad', 'angry' – but that these words often represented very different emotional experiences. She argues that 'faces are constantly moving and your brain relies on many different factors at once – body posture, voice, the overall situation, your lifetime experience – to figure out which movements are meaningful and what they mean'.[6]

Emotion and the Performer

This recent thesis by Feldman Barrett seems particularly important when considering an approach to character and emotion. Look at the Countess's first aria from *The Marriage of Figaro*, No. 10 'Hear My Prayer'/'Porgi Amor'. When working with Opera Works singers, a first response to this aria would often be that it is a 'sad' aria; the Countess sings about being abandoned by her husband and the music sounds mournful. This general sense of the Countess's emotional state might, indeed, have been supported by coaches, conductors, directors and previous productions; the Countess might indeed be 'sad'. However, this analysis, almost inevitably, leads to the singer *playing* 'sad' throughout the aria.

As a quick exercise, attempt to show 'sad'. Hold this for ten seconds. It doesn't matter if you perform your idea of 'sad' to anyone else but, if you do, ask them for feedback afterwards. Now, show, or replicate, 'angry'. Again, hold this for ten seconds. Finally, show 'happy'.

---

[2] Darwin, C. (1872) *The Expression of the Emotions in Man and Animals*.
[3] Feldman Barrett, L. (2017) *How Emotions are Made: The Secret Life of the Brain*. London: Macmillan, p. 7.
[4] Ibid.
[5] Ibid, p. xii.
[6] Ibid, p. 9.

When Opera Works singers did this exercise, their responses were rarely credible; their expressions were fixed, straining and full of tension! The problem lies with the instruction, not the efforts of the performer. The exercise illustrates what happens when the Countess's Act Two aria is approached with the intention of playing 'sad'. Likewise, a similar effect is often rendered when Figaro's Act Four aria No. 26 'You foolish slaves of cupid . . . you won't believe your eyes'/'Aprite un po' quegli occhi' is approached as 'angry'; the risk of applying such an undefined idea to an entire aria is that it negates the complexities of the moment and limits the possibilities for change presented within the music and libretto. It also increases the likelihood of unwarranted tensions creeping into the body and, importantly, the voice.

The words used to label emotions represent different things to different people; a director might understand one thing by 'sad', the performer, something else entirely. Such labels and words seek to define complex emotional states; states that are always in flux. A single word is rarely adequate to define the journey of a feeling; too often failing to differentiate between the range of colours, depths and textures of an experience and, instead, tending toward generalisation.

Feldman Barrett's research suggests emotions are not the result of commands; physical or psychological. She states that emotions emerge as the result of the interplay between a number of factors. Each time we experience emotion it is unique, distinct and pertaining to a specific and particular moment. The process of exploring and defining these factors can lead the opera singer to an emotional engagement with the part, rather than an attempt to play the resultant emotion. These factors – the character's personal histories, environment, physiology – are the very fuel for your imaginative connection to your character. You must *know* them intimately, the inner eye and ear seeing and hearing, in order to bring these factors closer to you. By imaginatively making these factors *your own*, truthful, changing and varied emotions are more likely to emerge.

The Process

In Chapter 4, under the heading Organising Information: Given Circumstances, we are going to start by exploring how we might dissect a libretto and score to identify the factors that Feldman Barrett refers to. This is the starting point of any process of creating character; underpinned by the over-arching principle emphasising process over result. As Viola Spolin, the famous American acting coach, wrote, 'The emotion we need for theatre can only come out of *fresh experience*; for, in such experience, rests the stirring of our total selves';[7] we must, therefore, go through a process to create the experiences that lead to emotion.

Mike Alfreds, the influential British theatre director, always led the opening Opera Works workshop. He summarises Stanislavski's extensive process in three simple words: *want, do, feel*.[8] As a performer you must *want* something; a motivating force that emerges out of your character's personal history and environment. *Do* something, in order to get your want. And, *as a result of this pursuit of your want*, you will, inevitably, *feel* something.

---

[7] Spolin, V. (1999) *Improvisation for the Theater*. Evanston: Northwestern University Press, p. 219.
[8] We worked with Mike over the ten years of ENO Opera Works. Mike's book *Different Every Night* (London: Nick Hern Books, 2007) is a terrific resource.

Pursuing a process rather than a result can be incredibly freeing. You do not need to arrive, precisely, at a preconceived idea of a particular emotion. You do not need to force a specific emotion out of yourself. Indeed, if you seek to do this, you will likely present an over-simplified caricature that undermines the ever-changing complexities within the score.

3   Creating Character

WHAT ARE THE CHALLENGES WHEN CREATING OPERATIC CHARACTER?

On their first day of ENO Opera Works, we asked singers about the challenges they face when beginning to create dramatic operatic characters:

- *Knowing where to begin from a dramatic point of view.*
- *Understanding how to marry the music and drama, especially before working with directors and conductors. I also find it hard to create all the necessary changes of emotions throughout a role.*
- *Trusting myself to go to the emotional place where I can communicate, without getting too upset. Getting to that place where I can be alive in the moment.*
- *Finding ways to express characterisation and coming up with dramatic ideas.*
- *Knowing how much character prep to do before rehearsals begin.*
- *Knowing what to do with character, without copying how someone else did it.*
- *Understanding how to make interaction with other characters natural.*
- *Making the music seem less two-dimensional; I often learn parrot fashion, if I need to learn something quickly but then it takes me months to imbue it with anything other than surface musicality or 'acting tricks'.*
- *Listening to recordings is great but I sometimes feel I'm trying to be someone else, not myself.*
- *Allowing decisions to continue to develop as I learn more rather than becoming entrenched.*
- *How do I relate to the role? Especially when it feels so different from who I am?*
- *How much of the character can I glean from the music?*

4   Text and Music

Introduction

You pick up a score and examine the words and music. You see the shifting dynamics and the changing rhythms, you note the accented words and the change from one key to the next. You breathe and begin to sing . . . but first:

- Who is this person?
- What life have they led?
- What beliefs guide them?
- How might their past experiences inform their behaviour?
- How might the world in which they live determine how they act?
- What do they think?
- What do they do?
- How might they use the words and music you are beginning to sing to get what they want?
- How might we organise our initial responses to the story, and understand the information we are given in the libretto and score, to explore how this person might behave?
- How do we begin to get to know, understand and ultimately embody the behaviour of this character?

Before singing a note, you must seek to understand *how* and *why* your character sings. Many of the answers to these questions can be found through an analysis of the text. The text in opera really refers to the *whole text*; the words and music combined. Without one or other element, we can only discern a part of the meaning. The words and music must ultimately be indivisible, but in order to begin the process of exploration, it is important to break down the opera into its different parts; to understand each more clearly and their relationship to the other.

The words are the usual starting point for the composer; and so, by exploring the words, we begin to understand the choices the composer had when setting them to music. They provide the context for the sounds, and yet it is easy in opera for the clarity of the words to be overwhelmed by the pitch of the setting, the orchestration or the scale of the house. In Mozart's time the houses and the orchestras were smaller and the orchestration a semitone lower. The original Susanna in Mozart's *The Marriage of Figaro* was only seventeen and yet must have communicated the words clearly, receiving no complaints from the librettist, Da Ponte. The words were the inspiration for Mozart, he spent months searching for the right story to draw upon for his composition and, without them, we understand nothing of the political, cultural or personal themes of the story. Words matter and lead us to understand why the song is vital.

As we approach the task of creating character, it is worth keeping the following in mind:

1 Never judge your character. We all think that what we do, think and feel is normative. We must seek to understand, from the inside what motivates a character's behaviour.

2 Lose fixed notions of your character. For example, the idea of a 'loyal character', or 'an optimistic character'. This tends to fix your character and does not allow room for change. Use instead '*I tend towards* certain characteristics'. A character is continually in motion and all great drama is about interruptions of ritual and habit.

3 Seek to discover a character's habitual behaviour and what, in the plot, places strain on this ritual.

KONSTANTIN STANISLAVSKI

Konstantin Stanislavski (1863–1938) was an actor, director and teacher who devised a systematic approach to creating character. He defined a psycho-physical method of acting that explores the relationship between our psychological functions and our bodies and formed the basis for realism in twentieth-century theatre, opera, television and film. He worked in Russia and was the co-founder of the Moscow Art Theatre and, for the last twenty years of his life, the Stanislavski Opera Theatre Studio (formerly the Bolshoi Opera Studio) between 1918 and 1938. He wrote his findings in three seminal books, *An Actor Prepares, Building a Character* and *Creating a Role.* A collection of his experiences of working with opera singers is published in *Stanislavski on Opera.*

Many of the tools to investigate text that we will explore in the following chapters are drawn directly from Stanislavski's work with actors and singers.

Organising Information: Given Circumstances

The Given Circumstances (or Facts) are the pieces of information within the libretto that relate to anything that is a given before the action of the opera or the scene begins; in so doing, they provide the context for everything that unfolds in the story. The Given Circumstances are not the plot of the opera. Rather, they form the building blocks, or foundations, of the world in which your character exists; once identified, they help inform how your character might behave throughout the story. Collecting all the Given Circumstances, and organising them into groups and lists, is a way of breaking down and managing all the information within the libretto. It is a good place to begin an investigation of character, rather than the first part of a structured exploration.

Given Circumstances tend to fall into a number of categories:

- ENVIRONMENTAL (place, time, weather, etc.)
- CULTURAL (social structure, politics, entertainment)
- PERSONAL and HISTORICAL (your character's biography, family, relationships).

We will examine the important musical information provided by the score in the next chapter.

The process of identifying Given Circumstances provides you with unarguable Facts about your character's world. Categorising these Facts allows you to explore the world of the opera from different perspectives. It also forms the foundation of an understanding of the world of the opera for you and your fellow singers to unite around, helping to dispel some possibly misleading notions of characters received from other productions.

How we understand our reality defines our behaviour. For example, at this very moment, whilst reading this book, you no doubt know where you are. If you happen to be in a rehearsal room, you have a sense of the room's dimensions, the location of the doors and windows, the number of tables and chairs in the space; you are aware of the artificial lighting, of the temperature of the room and how this makes you feel; you know the number of people there with you and what they are wearing. This information enables you to read the book in a manner that, no doubt, represents convincing human behaviour! However, if we were to remove some of the information you have about the room – if, for example, you had no idea of the scale of the room or whether there were any windows, exits, tables or chairs – it would, no doubt, begin to have an effect on how you behave. Your behaviour might become increasingly erratic, as your awareness grows of how little you know about your current circumstance.

It is the same with creating and performing a character. If you are missing information about your character's world, taking the leap to believe the imaginary world to be real becomes much more difficult. How can you hope to behave in a way that seems coherent and detailed to an audience?

There are no short cuts with this process; it requires a methodical reading of the libretto to extract all the information you will need. However, once this process is underway, you become a detective scouring the libretto and score for information to help you create a whole picture of your world.

The libretto will not contain all the information you need. Indeed, many libretti are rather thin affairs; Handel's operas, for example, contain very little information. Therefore, we need to ask Questions about our world, as we collect the Facts from the libretto. How you answer these questions, turning them into Facts, determines your world; detailing your character's reality and, in turn, enabling you to build a sense of your character's history, relationships and environment. This is where Stanislavski's Magic *If* becomes particularly important and where your freedom as a creative artist lies. There is space and room for *you*, within the score. The information given by the librettist is not enough to create a complete world. Collecting the Facts, and Questions, enables you to clearly recognise where your freedom to interpret the opera lies. As Stanislavski states, 'When you create an imaginative life for a part, when you know all the facts concerned with it and you enjoy this – then it becomes a reality.'[1]

---

[1] Stanislavski, K. (1998) *Stanislavski on Opera*. Translated by E. R. Hapgood. London: Routledge, p. 10.

Facts

Collect the FACTS and QUESTIONS, in separate columns, alongside each other on the page. Many Questions will spring from one Fact; note them all down as they come to mind. Draw a line across the page at the end of each scene or act, so that it is clear which information belongs to which scene.

EXAMPLE: *The Marriage of Figaro*

Let us begin with *The Marriage of Figaro*. Some simple Facts are derived from the Dramatis Personae:

- *Susanna is chambermaid to Countess Almaviva.*
- *Susanna and Figaro are engaged.*
- *Figaro is valet to the Count.*
- *Cherubino is the Count's page.*
- *Basilio is the music master.*
- *Don Curzio is a judge.*
- *Bartolo is a doctor from Seville.*
- *Antonio is the Count's gardener.*
- *Antonio is Susanna's uncle.*
- *Barbarina is the daughter of Antonio.*

Here is a list of the Facts from the first scene that we can establish from reading the libretto:

- *There is a room that is incompletely furnished.*
- *There is an armchair.*
- *Figaro has something with which to measure a room.*
- *Susanna has a hat.*
- *The room measures, at least, 43 units.*
- *There is a mirror.*
- *There is to be a wedding; Susanna is the bride, Figaro the bridegroom.*
- *The Count has promised to give Figaro and Susanna a bed.*
- *This room has been 'given' to Figaro by the Count.*
- *Count Almaviva is Figaro's employer.*
- *At the beginning of the opera Susanna is unaware of the Count's gift.*
- *There is a palace.*
- *There is a Count and Countess Almaviva.*
- *The Count has previously made Susanna aware of his desire for her.*
- *This room is located near to the Count and Countess's room.*
- *Don Basilio teaches Susanna singing.*

- *Don Basilio has previously conveyed the Count's virtues to Susanna.*
- *Susanna has received a dowry from the Count.*
- *The Count has previously abolished certain 'feudal rights'.*
- *The Count has looked to reinstate his feudal rights.*
- *The Count has plans to go to London as a minister.*
- *Figaro will be employed as his messenger.*

As you work your way through the libretto, you might notice some information in the form of stage directions. These might simply reflect what happened in a previous production and might not, therefore, be useful or relevant.

Many of the Facts in this opera are derived from the recitative. The arias, duets and ensembles tend to use heightened poetic language and are, more often, an opportunity for the characters to explore their hopes, motivations and feelings.

Questions

Whilst a significant amount of information can be gleaned from the libretto, there is not enough information for us to construct a complete view of the world. The libretto poses many Questions. At this stage, we are not looking to ask questions about the character's motivations or wants; we will certainly come to these, but, to begin with, we want to ask questions that will lead to further Facts.

EXAMPLE: *The Marriage of Figaro*

The libretto of *The Marriage of Figaro* contains more Facts than most operas, perhaps because it is directly adapted from Beaumarchais's play, but even so, the Facts alone offer an incomplete picture.

Here are some of the Questions we might ask from our exploration of the first scene:

- *What year is it?*
- *Where is the Count and Countess's palace?*
- *How large is the palace?*
- *Exactly where is this room in the palace?*
- *Where are the Count and Countess's rooms in the palace?*
- *What day and month is it?*
- *What time of day is it?*
- *What time did Figaro and Susanna wake up?*
- *What might the jobs of valet and chambermaid entail at this time?*
- *Where do Figaro and Susanna currently sleep?*
- *In addition to an armchair, what else is in the room?*
- *What units of measurement is Figaro using?*

- *What is the history of Susanna's hat; did she make it herself and to what extent is it finished?*
- *How long have Figaro and Susanna been engaged?*
- *What is the history of their relationship?*
- *When exactly is the wedding?*
- *What exactly are the 'feudal rights'?*

All these Questions must, at some point, be answered to help create a fuller picture of the world in which you (your character) is living. Where should answers be found?

- *The Libretto and Score*

  This is the touchstone; the words and music are the first place to look for answers to these early Questions. For example, later in the opera we learn more about the nature of the 'feudal rights' and that the wedding is planned for that very day. Whichever production you are in, these Facts are inarguable and become the foundation of an understanding of the world upon which everything else is built.

- *The Model Box*

  Many of these questions will be answered for you on the first day of rehearsals through the model box presentation. You might, for example, learn what period this production is set in, the location of the palace, the size of the room, the location of doors and windows.

  The design might adapt certain established Facts. Some singers have spoken to me about how unsettling a model box presentation can be on the first day of rehearsals, if the designs confound expectations. However, if you have already prepared Facts and Questions prior to rehearsals,[2] you will have an insight into the kinds of questions the director and designer might have asked when designing the opera. The process can arm you with an understanding of the possibilities presented by the libretto; this helps you to see the design presentation as another way of detailing your imaginative world. The design will give you certain Facts and also prompt further Questions; for example, about the specific history of the period in which the designer is setting the production or what your character might see on the fourth wall.[3]

- *Research*

  As you are working through the libretto and writing your list of questions, it is useful to note the Questions that might be answered through research; put an 'R' in the margin whilst compiling the list to alert you to the research you need to come back to later.

---

[2] See Chapter 7: Preparing for Rehearsals.
[3] *The fourth wall* refers to the space between you and the audience and conductor. It is a space which, remaining undefined by scenery, must be detailed by the imagination.

For *Figaro* we might want to research large palaces and gardens in Spain. If you are playing Susanna, you will want to research the lives of chambermaids in a given period. If you are playing Cherubino, you might want to research details of life in the armed forces at this time.

The production you are in might shift the original period the opera is set in; however, researching the history of the original period is always incredibly useful. You will be alerted to the particular tensions of the original period and prompted to search for parallels in the period in which your production is set. Similarly, researching the period and life of the librettist and composer will, perhaps, enlighten you as to where their focus lay in writing the opera. This might bring you closer to an understanding of the themes of the story and suggest your character's function within it; vital information for any storyteller when crafting *how* to tell the story.[4]

The internet is a useful tool for preliminary research but, more often, books and images provide a deeper and fuller insight into the world. Excite yourself by the prospect of digging for possible answers; read literature from the time of the opera, visit galleries with paintings from the period, make a site visit to the location of the opera itself!

The original Beaumarchais play might offer some possible answers for you, that are not present in the libretto of the opera. Many opera libretti draw their inspiration from a previous work and these can provide a further way to detail your world. However, be aware that certain facts from the play might not be useful; the composer and librettist might have intentionally diverted from the original at certain points and you are ultimately working from the opera.

Select the research that is useful to enrich your imaginative engagement and that is pertinent to the particular production you are working on. Discard everything else.

- *Negotiation and Imagination*

There will be Questions that can only be answered through discussions with your fellow creators; the other singers, your director and conductor. For example, if you are playing Figaro there is no information in the opera about how long you have known, or been engaged to, Susanna. If you draw upon the first play (or opera) in the trilogy, *The Barber of Seville*, you might decide that Figaro followed the Count from Seville, once the Count and Rosina (who, once married, becomes the Countess) got together, and only met Susanna after this time. Your research might lead you to the fact that the first and second plays were written by Beaumarchais eleven years apart.

Research provides possibilities but, ultimately, it's up to the collaborators to decide how to answer the questions the libretto and score proposes; this is where your collective imagination and the 'Magic If' become important. What *if* you decide that

---

[4] When discerning your character's function within the story, it is interesting to imagine the character removed from the plot of the opera; what does not happen as a consequence provides you with an indication of the character's function.

this is a whirlwind romance; that Figaro and Susanna have only recently started dating and become engaged? Or, what *if* this is a relationship built upon years of getting to know each other? Either are possibilities but the choice you make will help define your characters' relationship, their behaviour towards each other and ultimately, in part, the production itself.

It is important to interrogate different possible answers. Your answers are ultimately your response to the piece itself; what sort of opera do you want to make? What is the nature of the story you want to tell? For example, if you are playing the Count, the way in which you behave towards Figaro and the other servants might define whether the production is simply a psychodrama of sexual jealousies, or an examination of the growing tensions between different classes; the difference between a personal and political story.

Lists

Having determined the Facts and Questions, the next stage is to divide the information up into even more manageable lists. This can be done at the same time as first working through the libretto; whichever you find easiest to manage. Collate all Facts and Questions under one of the following four headings:

YOUR CHARACTER
This list contains all Facts and Questions personal and specific to your character; helping you build a picture of who *you* are. What is your full name and exact age? Do you have any specific religious or political beliefs? What do you do? What are your physical characteristics? What is your class or status? Where do you come from?

Within this list are all Facts and Questions about your relationships. Who are your family? Where are they? How old are they? Are you married? Single? Have you ever been in love? What is your sexual history?

Also collect all information about the relationships you have with inanimate objects. What personal possessions do you own? What clothes do you wear? What condition are they in? How fashionable are they compared to the fashions of the time?

THE WORLD
This list contains all Facts and Questions concerned with your environment. *Where* are you? *What* surrounds you? *When* is it? What cultural or political events are there? What dances or entertainment? What are the customs or fashions?

As with all Facts and Questions avoid vague, floating answers; 'There are *some* chairs and tables' or 'The garden is *kind of* over there'. Detail precisely; the more certain things are for you, the more secure you will feel in this world.

Gathering this information, in detail, is particularly important when creating a world that is very remote from you; for example, Figaro's eighteenth-century Spain. And this is a fictional eighteenth-century Spain, so it's important to understand how your world might work along different lines. For example, there is little evidence that the 'feudal rights' (the 'droit du seigneur') that form the basis of the drama in the opera actually existed in law in the eighteenth century (although there were no doubt terrible abuses of power) but it is a central Fact in Figaro's world that such rights were enforced.

It becomes even more important that we understand the rules of our fictional world when the world follows wildly different logic from our own. I recently directed Handel's *Semele*, in which Jupiter rescues Semele as an eagle and ultimately kills her in his godlike form of thunderbolts. Our world was defined along the lines of these Facts; there is a god, Jupiter, and he can transform himself into different forms. It is vital that you are aware of the different, and precise, rules and conditions of your world. If the world is translated to another time or place, ask if there are parallel tensions that you can draw upon.

IMMEDIATE CIRCUMSTANCES

List all Facts and Questions pertaining to the events that have occurred in the twenty-four hours leading up to each scene; whether that is before the opera begins or in the time that elapses between scenes or acts. Work in greater detail as the time your scene begins approaches. For example, what happened yesterday for Figaro and Susanna? How did Figaro receive the news from the Count of the gift of the bed? Was there an opportunity to tell Susanna; did he choose not to tell her, or simply forget? Have they already performed certain duties, associated with their jobs, before this first scene of Act One? What room did they enter from? What were they doing in this room?

All this information helps build a foundation of reality upon which the present circumstances rest and helps determine the behaviour of the characters in the scene.

Create the details of the scenes that have taken place offstage before each new scene begins. In *Figaro* the plot is incredibly complex and knowing exactly what your character knows about certain situations, and what they have been doing before they enter a room, is crucial.

FUTURE PROSPECTS

This might be a little more difficult to discern because it concerns information about the plans your character has for events that have not yet taken place.

In *Figaro* the big plan for Susanna and Figaro, at the beginning of the opera, is their wedding later that day. If you were playing Susanna it would be useful to have clear ideas and pictures in your mind's eye of your expectations for your wedding. Where is it to take place, at what hour, who do you expect to be there, how is the room decorated, is there food and dancing afterwards, etc? Beyond this, what are Susanna's plans for the first stage of her marriage? Where does she imagine she and Figaro will sleep? This will help determine Susanna's response to Figaro's news about the Count's gift of the bedroom neighbouring his own.

Stanislavski noted that 'all these facts taken together, give the present tense of the play. There can be no present without the past – all flows naturally out of the past. Neither is there a present without a prospect of the future'.[5] The more detail you have of your character's past and future prospects, the stronger your sense of the character's present conditions will be. Investing in these details will give you more to focus on in the world of your character when in performance and, in so doing, free you from concerns about the audience or your singing technique.

---

[5] Stanislavski, K. (1981) *Creating a Role*. Translated by E. R. Hapgood. London: Eyre Methuen, p. 16.

Imagination

The Facts that form your world will, ultimately, help to stimulate your feelings and emotions but first, you must imbue them with life and meaning. It is easy for the process of collecting Facts, asking Questions and creating Lists to seem rather academic; for the Facts to remain dry and sterile. It is not the Facts in themselves that are of *real* interest but your character's association with, and attitude to, them.

This is where the Magic *If* becomes particularly important; what *if* these were your conditions and circumstances, what *if* you had previously experienced these certain events, what *if* you had clear ideas of a proposed future. The Given Circumstances provide the foundations for this *if*. They are the fuel for your imagination and, as such, you should allow yourself to be drawn to those Facts that excite your imagination. How you explore these Facts, focusing on what seems to be of central importance in a scene, will take you beyond the text and the music to the inner life of your character.

For these circumstances to permeate every moment of your characters' conscious actions, it is important for you to create pictures in your mind's eye; you must make the Facts live for you, in order to bring to life your character's inner life. These pictures can be of your character's past events, or detail your present conditions; what you see when you imagine the 'fourth wall'.

In opera, music scores your character's life and it should also score your character's memories. The composer writes music that transports your character to different places; listen to this music whilst creating such places in your mind's eye. This will help make these musical ideas or motifs real and meaningful for your character. Connecting your imagination to the music of your character's world will help bring forth these imagined pictures in performance, rather than simply prompting a generalised emotional response. We will look at this in more detail in Musical Clues (p. 92).

Fuel your imagination by taking every opportunity to fuse internal images with the music; use every spare moment – walking to and from rehearsals, sitting on public transport – to explore your character's Facts and transform them into living events. The greater the detail, the richer your memories will be. By engaging your imagination, you will cease to judge your character from the outside and instead you will be an active participant in your character's life, looking out through your own eyes at your character's life.

The following exercises can help to further organise your response to the score and, by looking at the opera from different angles, deepen your understanding of your character's world. The information you gather, through these exercises, provides further fuel for your imaginative journey.

EXERCISE: *Character Lists*
Solo

The popular operatic repertoire is relatively small and, as a consequence, it is easy to develop a set of received notions from other productions about a certain piece. Facts and Questions help set us straight as to what is *actually* given by the libretto and what is up for grabs in our interpretation of the piece.

Creating character lists is a way of examining our relationships with other characters by focusing on what we sing to, and about, others and what they sing about us. It is a useful way of examining our character's shifting relationships to others and, perhaps, resetting some of our preconceptions.

Organise these lists by working chronologically through the opera, writing each list on separate sheets of paper. Divide the lists, scene by scene, by drawing a line at the end of each scene. List everything:

- your character sings about themselves, including those things that seem important about how the composer has suggested you sing these lines;
- your character sings about the world;
- your character sings about other characters. Create a separate list, on separate sheets of paper, for each character;
- other characters sing about you. Again, create a separate list, on separate sheets of paper, for each character;

Next, note:

- the imagery your character uses. This can help define the pictures your character sees in their mind's eye;
- *how* you, or the other character singing about you, are instructed to sing a particular line by the composer. How is the line set, with what dynamics, in which key, with any recurring motifs in the orchestration?

When you have finished each list, use three different adjectives to summarise how your character sees themselves or the other character. Ask what the lists tell you about your character's focus throughout the opera. Is there a development in a relationship? Does the music change and guide you towards a particular conclusion?

EXAMPLE: *The Marriage of Figaro*

Let us look at the list the singer playing Figaro would write about Susanna in the first scene:

- *to crown all the joy we are sharing, my Susanna will be wearing a beautiful hat* (music: Susanna and Figaro sing the same melody);
- *Susanna, you're so clever* (music: set as a call and repeat);
- *why so unreasonable?*
- *how can you look this gift horse in the mouth?*
- *Susanetta;*
- *my nagging suspicions are too much to bear;*
- *my dearest darling;*
- *and my Susanna to succour and support you (the Count).*

It is a little early to summarise Figaro's thoughts towards Susanna but if we were to do so, we might select the adjectives: beautiful, clever, untrustworthy.

It is worth noting that in the opening duet between Susanna and Figaro, each character separately sings their own theme, yet by the end of the duet Figaro is singing Susanna's theme with her. This might suggest where the balance of power lies in the relationship, or it might simply reflect the shifting dynamics of their relationship at this moment in the opera. It is worth noting at this point, to see how the this develops throughout the opera.

EXERCISE: *Map Visualisations*
Solo/Group

Do this exercise once you have seen the model box design of your world and, where possible, collaborate with fellow singers to make decisions.

- Draw each space your character inhabits on stage in 360-degree detail. In discussions with fellow singers decide what you collectively imagine to be on the fourth wall.

- In Figaro and Susanna's new room, if there are windows, where exactly are they? What precisely can you see outside? Does Susanna look into a mirror mounted on the fourth wall to view her new hat? By drawing your world, you make it concrete.

- Extend this drawing to a map of your extended off-stage spaces, so that you know the spaces you enter from and exit to.

- In *Figaro* you should draw the house: how one room connects to the other, the doors and windows, the garden. If, for example, you are playing the Countess or Susanna, you should both know, exactly, where the pinewoods you sing about are located on this map.

- Visualise the rooms that are important to you in this house. Create the rooms in your mind's eye in detail. Get to know the house so that it becomes as familiar to you as any other house you have lived in.

- Extend this by detailing the people who live in the house and the different ways the space is used by those of different status. Explore how certain rooms are used at different times of the day or whether particular melodies from the opera connect to certain rooms. Engage your imagination in the same way Christopher Nolan's film *Inception* grows worlds; allow additional spaces to spring up in your mind's eye to bring a fuller picture to your understanding of the world.

- Next, make your visualisation active by putting yourself in the house. Which rooms might you be in at these different times of day or year, what clothes might you wear in different spaces, what conversations might you have and with whom, what memories do you associate with particular spaces.

- Eventually (after your work on Objectives in the following chapter), you might start to detail the wants and desires you have had in these different rooms.

EXERCISE: *Circles of Concentration*
Solo

Circles of Concentration is a tool developed by Stanislavski to help keep you focused and connected to your character's world in performance. It must be prepared prior to performance and is an extension of the Map Visualisation exercise.

- Select an object that is on your character's person; for example, something your character keeps in their pocket or an engagement ring. Study this object and note its physical qualities.

- Create a memory that centres around this particular object; maybe you create the moment Figaro proposed with this engagement ring (if he could afford a ring)? Detail the location, the time of day, the weather, the smells and sounds associated with this memory.

- Then, widen your Circle of Concentration and select an object, or objects, in the *room*. Create a memory associated with this object.

- Widen your Circle of Concentration further still; this time outside the room. Each time you widen your circle, to include a new object or space, follow the same exercise as above.

If there's a particular point in the opera that you find it difficult to remain focused within, try connecting a memory to the music that you hear at this point. In preparation, as you replay the memory in your mind's eye, play the piece of music you want to connect with.

Investing in the detail of the world that surrounds you throughout your preparation, will enable you, at any given moment in performance, to connect with an object or space and immediately re-engage you with your character's reality.

EXERCISE: *Timeline and Diary*
Solo/Group

A simple exercise. Gather all the relevant facts into a character timeline, from the character's earliest memory up to the present moment.

When the timeline comes into contact with other character's timelines, it can be exciting to discuss exactly what might have happened.

Select particular points along the timeline to write a diary entry for the day. Write each of these entries in your character's voice. It is useful to select days on the timeline that resonate within the story of the opera; for example, the day Figaro signed Marcellina's contract, the day the Countess and Count married, the day Basilio espoused the Count's virtues to Susanna.

EXERCISE: *Improvising Pre-Opera or Pre-Scene Events*
Group

This is an extension of the *Timeline* exercise. Select an important event or incident from your character's Timeline that has taken place before the action of opera has begun. With your fellow singers, discuss the Facts of this scene and answer any Questions. Improvise the scene along the lines set out in Exercise: *Events Improvisation* (on p. 119).

When the Countess, in *Figaro*, sings the aria No. 10 'Hear my prayer'/'Porgi, Amor' (at the beginning of Act 2), she is praying that the love her husband once felt for her be rekindled. If you are playing the Countess you might consider it important that, throughout the more hopeful moments of the aria, the Countess has recourse to happier memories of her marriage: for example, the time the Count and Countess first kissed, the marriage proposal, their wedding day. It is much easier to visualise the wedding day, for example, if you have actually experienced some moment of it. To improvise the entire wedding day would, of course, take too much time but you might focus upon a particularly precious moment for the Countess: walking down the aisle, receiving the ring, the first dance.

Similarly, if you're playing the Count, at the moment in Act Three when Barbarina publicly discloses your secret encounter, it is far easier to respond honestly if some moment of this encounter has been lived through improvisation.

EXERCISE: *What If . . .*
Solo/Group

There are certain Facts that you and your collaborators determine. The way in which these particular Questions are answered defines one production from the next. Aim to make choices and decisions that lead to the most dramatically rich situation.

- Explore *how* different Facts can create different behaviour, by first selecting a simple physical action; for example, if you are playing Susanna, it might be to sweep a particular room in the house.

- Do this action a number of times and each time allow the action to be informed by a different Given Circumstance. Try sweeping at 12 noon and then 3 am, in the height of summer and the depths of winter, after an argument with Figaro or a disconcerting encounter with the Count.

- Note the differences that each decision brings and consider how it might affect the outcome of a scene and, ultimately, your character's journey throughout the piece. Changing your character's Given Circumstances will help you to explore the possibilities of dramatic action.

EXERCISE: *Hotseat*
Pairs/5 mins

- Sit opposite your partner; one person is *in character,* the other is a neutral questioner (without opinions).
- The questioner asks questions about the character's life. The singer *in character* answers, in the first person, in detail.
- If the questioner would like more information about a certain subject they say 'expand'; at which point the singer in character talks, in greater detail, exclusively about this subject.
- The questioner says 'continue' to move on.
- As you become more familiar with your character, you will begin to sit as they sit, focus where they focus and answer in a certain rhythm.
- It is useful to do this exercise in short bursts, throughout the rehearsal process. This doesn't need to take place in the rehearsal room and you will often have periods between rehearsals when you can Hotseat with fellow cast members.

SUMMARY

- Collecting the Given Circumstances presented in the libretto and score is a good place to start your process.
- Begin with the external Facts of the world of the opera and use these to detail the imaginative interior life of your character.
- Given Circumstances bring you closer to your character's life as it is lived. They provide a sense of fullness to your character's existence.
- Given Circumstances help you when your character is *not* singing. They help keep you alive and in the moment; connected to your thoughts, the world and others.
- Given Circumstances help create pictures in your mind's eye. This is particularly useful when working in intimate settings and on film.
- You do not need to *play* the information or *show* it. The Given Circumstances will inform *how* you play the scene and *how* your character attempts to achieve their wants.
- Beginning this process before rehearsals gives you a great understanding of the possibilities of your world and character.
- Be ready to discuss, negotiate and change the Facts with your collaborators.
- Every time you play a role, re-engage with the Facts to re-enliven your character's world, rather than simply repeating them.

TO DO

- Work through the score and collect and list all the Facts.
- List and ask Questions that will lead to further Facts.

- Seek to answer these Questions with reference to the score, in dialogue with collaborators, and through research. *How* you answer the Questions and turn them into Facts will determine your characterisation and the overall story of your production.
- Create Character Lists to further organise the information in the score to help you better understand the relationships within the world.
- Use the information to build, layer by layer, an imaginative reality for your character.

Organising Information: Other Approaches

When first picking up a score, your initial task is to ask, who is this character? How do they behave and for what reason? We have looked at how the Stanislavskian approach helps us to organise our first responses to the libretto. Alongside this, there are number of other ways to explore how the information within the score and libretto might inform your early decisions about your character.

The Stanislavski Effect

Stanislavski's approach to acting in opera, theatre and television inspired others to continue his work. In the world of opera, the impact of Stanislavski's work can be seen most clearly in the work and writing of East German director Walter Felsenstein. We will look at how Felsenstein explored the musical information given by the composer in Musical Clues (p. 92).

Elsewhere, and especially in America, practitioners distilled Stanislavski's process into further lists and exercises. I have included these here as they provide a slightly different perspective on the Facts and Questions approach but they reference terms we will explore in detail later in the book.

UTA HAGEN

The American actress and practitioner, Uta Hagen, developed nine essential questions that you can ask yourself as you prepare:[6]

1 Who am I? (To include all biographical details about your character: name, age, where they live, career, hobbies, political or religious beliefs.)

2 What time is it? (What century, season, year, month, day, hour, minute?)

3 Where am I? (Which country, city, area, building or outdoor space?)

4 What surrounds me? (The weather, all inanimate and animate elements within the immediate environment.)

5 What are my given circumstances? (By this Hagen means what has happened in the past, the immediate past, is happening right now in the present and is expected to happen in the future.)

---

[6] Hagen, U. (1973) *Respect for Acting*. New York: Wiley – we will explore in more detail in later chapters.

6 What is my relationship? (Your character's relationship to events, other characters and other factors in your character's life.)

7 What do I want? (What need does your character want to satisfy; what is your character's Objective?)

8 What is in my way? (What obstacles – internal and external – does your character face in achieving their wants?)

9 What do I do to get what I want? (What action does your character take to achieve their Objectives and overcome their obstacles?)

STELLA ADLER

Stella Adler developed her own teaching based upon Stanislavki's process. Although Adler is seen as part of the American method school of acting, her emphasis throughout her teaching was on the importance of the imagination. Adler suggests an actor should begin their process by focusing their imagination on the important details of their character's history. She reduces Stanislavski's six fundamental questions, and Hagen's nine, to 'The Five Ws' that create the background for your character:[7]

1 Who (am I)?

2 What (am I doing)?

3 When (am I)?

4 Where (am I)?

5 Why (am I doing what I'm doing)?

Core Beliefs

At ENO Opera Works we worked with director Lyndsey Turner, who introduced to us the idea of exploring a character's core beliefs as an early approach to analysing character.

This approach is based upon the idea that our behaviours are the external manifestations of the core thoughts that we hold about ourselves, others and the world around us. These central, deep-seated beliefs are often, but not exclusively, formed early in our life and refer to cognitive constructs; for example, *I am* inferior, *other people are* superior. They can inform an automatic behaviour in response to a situation.

In order to develop an understanding of *why* your character acts in certain ways throughout the opera, it's worth considering what core beliefs might underpin their behaviour. This process is particularly useful when considering how characters respond at moments of crisis and, indeed, characters whose behaviour might be extreme. They can help us to understand and accept why, for example, characters fall in love so quickly (Tamino with Pamina in *The Magic Flute*) or extremes of expression can be revealed instantaneously through the music (the Queen of the Night in her Act Two aria). To work with core beliefs is to ask 'What are the particular goggles through which my character sees the world?'

---

[7] Adler, S. (2000) *The Art of Acting*. New York: Applause, p. 169.

Complete the following statements firstly for *yourself* and then for *your character*. It is interesting to begin with yourself in order to bring your attention to those beliefs you and your character share and those which are different. This enables you to target your research in those areas where you need to develop a greater understanding of your character. Try to complete the sentences in as few words as possible:

- I am . . .
- Other people are . . .
- Success is . . .
- Money is . . .
- Fame is . . .
- Women are . . .
- Men are . . .
- Mothers are . . .
- Fathers are . . .
- Art is . . .
- Work is . . .
- Rules are . . .
- The media is . . .
- Sex is . . .
- The people in charge are . . .
- Love is . . .

Those areas – art, love, work, etc. – about which a character might have formed core beliefs will change from opera to opera; feel free to adapt this list. Check in with your character's list before, and after, each act and ask yourself if any of their beliefs appear to have changed; by establishing a set of core beliefs, we can see how the plot challenges them. Extraordinary moments, or situations of great crisis, can change core beliefs and it is an interesting way of exploring your character's journey through the story; you could create a timeline of the formation of your character's core beliefs.

Things to consider about core beliefs:

- They are often distortions; they are not objectively true but subjective ideas held to be true by your character.[8]
- Your character might not be aware of what their core beliefs are.

---

[8] Nettle, D. (2006) *Happiness – The Science behind Your Smile.* Oxford: Oxford University Press, pp. 148–166, provides a clear explanation of how core beliefs can affect behaviour.

- Your character might hold contradictory core beliefs about certain things; these can often create interesting conflict within a character.

- There might be a hierarchy of beliefs; certain beliefs your character holds will be more important than others.

- The adjectives that you used to summarise Exercise: Character Lists (p. 56), might help to provide ideas of your character's core beliefs.

- Consider what has shaped your character's beliefs: trauma, education (school, parents, teachers, their peers), religion, specific experiences or the world around them.

- Ask where particular thoughts lie in the body; for example, your character might associate a certain belief with a feeling in the gut rather than in the head.

A character will often explore a core belief during an aria: they will 'unpack' beliefs, destroy previously held 'truths' or form new core beliefs. For example, the Countess, in her aria No.10 'Hear my prayer'/'Porgi, Amor', seems to arrive at the belief that '*life is* . . . not worth living without love'; Figaro seems to harden a core belief about the infidelity of women in his aria No.26 'You foolish slaves of Cupid'/'Aprite un po' quegl'ochchi'.

EXAMPLE: *The Marriage of Figaro*

The Count's behaviour is, perhaps, particularly difficult to access and understand; his treatment of the Countess, Figaro and Susanna provides the central conflict of the opera. The following are some possible core beliefs that might be informing his behaviour:

- *I am* superior.
- *Other people* are leeches.
- *Success is* fulfilling my desires.
- *Women are* deceitful/undermining.
- *Men are* vulnerable.
- *Mothers are* distant.
- *Fathers are* the basis of my ancestral power.
- *Work is* for others.
- *Rules are* established by me, to be followed by others.
- *Sex is* my right.
- *The people in charge are* divinely ordained.
- *Love is* a fading memory.

These suggestions are starting points and not absolutes; provocations, or food for thought, when playing a scene. Ask *what if* my character holds a certain core belief and explore, in rehearsals, how this might inform your character's behaviour in the scene.

Anthropology

A character's behaviours are informed by the world in which they live. This is why collecting the Facts that relate to the world of the opera is so important; it will directly relate to *how* you act under certain conditions. For example, the varying social classes in *The Marriage of Figaro* will dictate the way in which the characters move and relate to each other, the significance of the *droit du seigneur,* the gender and legal boundaries within which characters' behaviours are restricted.

Simon McBurney, the innovative theatre and opera director, puts it like this:

> What is always interesting to me is to ask – as someone who is in the theatrical profession where you're observing human nature – whether we (in everyday life) are freely participating in our choices or whether in fact it is a product of something else that has nothing to do with you. You have the illusion that you're making these choices, but you're not, it's a consequence of a culture that is a fiction and doesn't exist outside our common imaginations.[9]

Taking an anthropological approach provides a way of grouping together external factors that might impact upon your character's behaviour. This approach is particularly useful when playing smaller or chorus roles. It can bring definition to worlds that contain big, but sometimes nebulous themes, such as nobility or honour. It delineates one world from another; perhaps the servant world from that of the master's world, or a world that is undergoing change. It allows us to understand, in specific detail, the frame of the world within which our characters live; if, for example, you interpret Susanna as a particularly subversive character, the anthropological approach highlights the edges of her world she can kick against.

EXERCISE: *Anthropology*
Group

This exercise must be done in collaboration with your team. Examine, explore and, where possible, define the world of the opera in the following areas:

- power hierarchy or political system
- gender principles
- economic system
- size, scale, borders
- relationships
- work
- rewards, sanctions or punishments
- behaviours that are encouraged or discouraged
- symbolic objects
- religion and gods.

---

[9] McBurney, S. (1996) *The Stage*, 19 February.

Lyndsey Turner suggests defining each part of the world of the opera beginning with, 'This is a world in which it seems ...'; thereby enabling you to develop and change your understanding of the world the more you get to know the opera and the production you are performing in.

These questions often go to the very heart of what the opera is about and it is important to know not only the lines along which the world is defined, but also what your character's response to each of these areas is. For example, how does your character respond to the gender principles in *The Marriage of Figaro* where the state sanctions the rape of a woman by a man of a certain class? In *The Magic Flute,* what is your character's attitude to the teaching of the gods, Isis and Osiris, followed by Sarastro's brotherhood? These factors must be *alive* within the world: understood, debated over, imaginatively engaged with. Just as similar factors absorb us in our own world, so they must engage the characters affected by them in the world of the opera.

Character Traits

Daniel Nettle is a behavioural scientist who examines different personality types and the character traits that define them. Nettle states, 'There are (at least) five broad personality dimensions along which we all differ, and which cause us to behave in certain ways rather than other ways. A great deal of what happens in our interests, careers, relationships, romantic lives, and health follows from where we fall along these continua'.[10] These five broad personality groups are:

- Extraversion
- Neuroticism
- Conscientiousness
- Agreeableness
- Openness.

Nettle devised the NPA test for measuring where somebody lies in relation to these groups. The test can be found easily online and provides a fascinating method for dissecting and categorising your character's behaviour; I have found it useful when exploring characters very different from the singers playing them.

SUMMARY

The way a character views themselves is complex; a multiplicity of views about ourselves can exist, dependent upon the situation we are in and the people we are with.[11] It therefore seems useful that we have a number of different approaches to beginning the process of creating dramatic character that we can use, dependent upon the particular character, opera or production:

---

[10] Nettle, D. (2009) *Personality: What Makes You The Way You Are.* Oxford: Oxford University Press, p. 234.
[11] Carter, R. (2008) *Multiplicity: The New Science of Personality.* London: Little, Brown.

- *Biographical approach*: the Stanislavskian approach of collecting Facts and Questions suggests that we are the sum of all the things that have happened to us. This provides a wealth of information about our character's past and is a helpful approach when we need to create pictures in our mind's eye.

- *Core Beliefs approach*: suggests we are our behaviour and that core beliefs, formed early in life, define the way we behave. This is a useful approach to understanding extreme behaviour.

- *Anthropological approach*: suggests we are the world we live in and all thoughts are societally driven. This is useful when playing characters who, individually, are ill defined by the opera.

- *Personality Trait approach*: suggests that we are predisposed, perhaps due to our genes or physiologically, to act in certain ways. This can help bring definition to our character's behaviour.

TO DO

- Explore possible core beliefs that might trigger your character's behaviour. Create a hierarchy and timeline in response to those places in the opera where new beliefs are formed or old beliefs abandoned.

- Explore ways of defining your world along anthropological lines; research the impact of living within such worlds. Ask what your character's attitude is to each of these parameters.

- Complete the NPA test for your character.

- Collect information to fuel your creative journey and *make it personal to your character.*

- Collect possible 'What *If's*' throughout this early part of your process, to explore in the rehearsal room.

Organising Information: The Music

Walter Felsenstein, director of the Komische Oper in the former East Berlin between 1947 and 1975, was Stanislavksi's most influential follower in the world of opera. He asserted that 'Every instrumental and vocal sequence is dramatic action, and all instructions pertaining to dynamics, meter, and tempo are primarily not technical but expressive indications. In short *everything visual is as much music as everything audible is action*';[12] by exploring every detail of the original score, he believed, singers can 'reveal the entire life of the character, *beyond* the stage action and the text'.[13]

What motivates the music? What does the music represent? The music establishes the mood, the atmosphere, the tempo of the scene, the timing of action: it suggests the subtext, the thoughts and psychology of the characters, the shifting tensions and dramatic events of the scene. However, in line with Felsenstein's assertion, the score must be analysed together with the words and action; music is the principal form in opera but it is only alongside the words and action of the plot that it acquires meaning. Theatre and opera director Peter Hall

---

[12] Fuchs, P. P. (1991) *The Music Theatre of Walter Felsenstein.* London: Quartet Books, p. 20.
[13] Ibid., p. 29.

describes music as a 'mask for drama and like a good mask it can mean anything. A phrase of music begins as something completely neutral ... opera has to be a perfect circle; the drama making the music and the music making the drama.'[14] The action of the plot informs the musical decisions the composer makes; the music, in turn, informs the action of the plot. Felsenstein extends this further by asserting that

> This unity is achieved when the dramatic action *alone* determines all vocal statements, and even the instrumental passages. Only then can the singer recreate a dramatically valid musical score exactly according to the intentions of the composer; only then will they appear sufficiently free and relaxed to turn everything in them and around them into music; and only then will he make singing actually his most expressive device.[15]

In *The Marriage of Figaro*, Mozart imprints dramatic action at every moment through his musical decisions; Susanna and Figaro share the same melody as their understanding of the other grows; Bartolo's pomposity is highlighted by trumpets and percussion; horns underscore Figaro's jealous anxieties; key changes emphasise dramatic events such as Susanna's feigned fainting. We must learn to actively *listen*, to consciously take note of the musical information that the audience will perhaps only receive unconsciously. We must heighten our awareness of the decisions the composer has made and allow them to guide our response to the opera. This is not about attempting to *act* the music – to walk in tempo or illustrate an emotion the music suggests – but to allow the music to inform our analysis of the text and action and vice versa.

Music often suggests the result or outcome of internal or external action. Our understanding of what the composer is suggesting about the world or our character should underpin our decisions about our character's thoughts, motivations and actions; *how* we act, in order to create this music. We must work collaboratively with the composer and librettist, to understand the information they provide and, together with the team in the rehearsal room, use it to instruct our collective creation of the whole story.

EXERCISE: *Musical Response*
Solo/Group

- Listen to a scene and ask, how does the music make me feel? Write down your response to the emotional qualities of the music as a list of adjectives.
- Next to this list, create two columns; in one, ask *how* has the composer has created this effect, in the second, ask *why*.
- This active analysis of the music begins to initiate a direct dialogue with the composer. Seeking to understand their intentions, we begin to work with them, rather than simply experiencing the emotional effect of the music; the emotional impact is for the audience to receive. This dialogue helps inform the decisions we make; *how* we use the music and libretto to tell the story in line with the composer and librettist's intentions.

---

[14] Hall, P. (2000) *Exposed by the Mask: Form and Language in Drama.* London: Oberon Books, p. 77.
[15] Fuchs, P. P. (1991) *The Music Theatre of Walter Felsenstein.* London: Quartet Books, p. 24.

Drama through Music: Theatrical Function of Music

The interplay between words and music – and the inherent tension between the forms – is at the very heart of opera. Music can underpin the meaning of the words or, alternately, work as a counterpoint to them. Music heightens action; we are not in a realistic world but an intensified expression of a character's experience. Music distorts time and, in so doing, impacts upon how we understand the psychology of the character. Plot is often condensed, singing text takes longer than speaking it and yet, conversely, time and space is often given to explore a single thought or feeling that would pass in a flash in a text-based drama.

Music functions to shape the drama in a number of possible ways by:

- revealing the character's subtext; a character might say one thing, whilst the music reveals the truth beneath;
- defining the character's emotional life; the way in which a character feels, thinks and responds to the world;
- defining the speed with which you or other characters think or act; the inner and external tempo-rhythms of your character's life;
- bringing emphasis to a dramatic event;
- defining the atmosphere of the place;
- defining the period or the culture;
- revealing, as an omniscient presence, secrets to the audience unknown to characters (Wagner's leitmotifs being the most obvious example).

EXERCISE: *Words in Music*
Solo

The words are usually the starting point for the composer. They have their own expressive power that will have impacted upon the composer: the varied sound of the vowels and consonants, the rhyme, the rhythm of the verse, the imagery, metaphors, similes, the rhetorical structures.

- Select a scene; write the words out as prose.
- Speak them out loud; what do you notice? How do the words affect you?
- Circle the primary idea in each sentence. Try *speaking* all the words around this idea and only *singing* the composer's setting of the important word that you feel has emphasis. There is no right or wrong answer regarding the word you circle.

The exercise brings our attention to *how* the composer chooses to express the idea through music. We begin to see the relationship between the words and music and the form the composer is working with.

Extension: you might note that each sentence has a grammatical structure that helps take us to the heart of the meaning of each sentence. For example, take Cherubino's line 'What is this yearning burning in me?' We can identify the subject ('me'), the predicate or verb ('burning') and the object ('yearning').

- Try singing these lines and speaking the rest of the words, to explore further the decisions Mozart made when setting the text.

This exercise is useful as it highlights what the character is driving at in each sentence. Cherubino is exploring this idea of 'yearning'. The risk for the singer is that they 'emote' a sense of yearning. The verb suggests what is actually going on within Cherubino; in seeking to define his 'yearning', he locates and labels the sensation 'burning'.

Exploring sentence structure in this way stops us from simply taking the words for granted; instead we explore their meaning, and *how* the character uses them, allied to the music.

The Musical Information

As we explore the character and world of the opera we need to be constantly aware of the information the composer is providing. It is our job to construct the character and world using this material from the score; material that guides us towards the tone, atmosphere, dramatic tempo, characterisation and form of the opera. Alongside the columns of Facts and Questions you collect through your analysis, draw up two further columns: Musical Facts and Musical Questions. The Musical Facts will list the significant musical factors you notice within the scene. The Musical Questions column will propose possible reasons for these Musical Facts. Once you have considered the Musical Questions, alongside the other Given Circumstances, you can highlight what it is your character is *doing* with the music; this will be bound in with your work on Objectives and Actions that we look at later.

This is what to consider when analysing the score:

MELODY
- What is the melodic shape of the scene or aria? What does this reveal about the character's emotional state or the character's journey through the scene?
- Are there significant shifts in the melody and for what dramatic reason?
- How extreme are the modulations or the changes of key in a scene? A shift in key is usually a clear signal of a new message; consider the shift in emotional quality between major and minor.
- Are there certain melodic patterns? Consider the Count and Susanna's duet; by the end of the duet both share the same melody regardless of the gulf in social status between the two.
- How are these factors represented in the orchestra?

HARMONY
- Where do harmonies meld; where do they clash?
- What is the significance of this harmony or discord?
- How might the orchestra provide harmonic support or counterpoint?

RHYTHM
- The rhythm to which the words are set will bring emphasis to certain words or ideas. Consider how this is represented in translation.

- Explore the sound of those words that have been stretched or given additional value.
- Are there words, or points in the orchestration, that are accented? What might they be seeking to emphasise within the drama?
- Are there particular rhythmic patterns that provide information about character? Does the rhythm represent the rhythm of the character's thoughts, or their external action (which may be different), or rather another character or external event?
- How does the rhythmic structure affect you? What might this say about the character?

PAUSES OR RESTS
- How do pauses or rests help to structure the character's thoughts?
- Are they caused by the character's thoughts or feelings or by another character?
- What is communicated during a pause? Maybe it represents a physical action; a thought communicated through a look or a movement.

PHRASING
- How does the rhythm inform when to breathe?
- What motivates the breath? What thought prompts it? When does the idea arrive?
- Is there any information before or after the breath, or any clue in the orchestration, which can help answer this question?

TEMPO
- Consider the composer's tempo markings. Do they suggest anything about the movement of the character's external actions or internal thoughts?
- How does the speed of the scene inform the character's thoughts or actions?
- Where are the changes in tempo and what might these changes represent?

DYNAMICS
- Why is there a shift in dynamics? What is the reason behind this?
- What is the journey of the dynamics? Is there a crescendo or diminuendo and what does this represent?

TONE AND TEXTURE
- What is the tone or colour of the music?
- How does the orchestra establish the tone; how many instruments are playing, which instruments, what melodies, how does this contrast with the vocal line?
- Have certain instruments been chosen to highlight certain characters or themes? For example, Susanna often seems to be accompanied by sensual, warm clarinets.
- Each voice has a particular timbre; what might a choice of voice type represent? Might it reveal something of the function of the character or their social class?

- Are there moments when the voice becomes part of the polyphony, rather than simply sitting on top of the orchestra? What might this suggest about the character's thoughts at these moments?

FORM

- All these factors are organised through the particular form of the opera. The form the opera takes will depend upon the historical context of the opera; it is important to bring an understanding of the history and development of operatic form. For example, the Rossinian code tells us something different from Wagner's leitmotifs and Handel's da capo aria; expression is born through these forms.
- The form provides the restrictions that expression can push against; formality, when challenged, brings our attention to moments of dramatic expression.

SUMMARY

- Every thought and action your character has and does must be informed and infused with the music.
- You must actively listen to the music by bringing your attention to the musical qualities proposed by the composer.
- Within the music we can discover the way in which a character thinks, feels and acts; the rhythm, tone, texture, tempo of these thoughts, feelings and actions.
- The action of the plot informs the musical decisions the composer makes; the music, in turn, informs the action of the plot.

TO DO

- Ask 'What motivates the music? What does the music represent?'
- Mark the Events in the musical score: the significant changes in the music.
- Work through the opera and create a list of all the Musical Facts and Musical Questions by breaking down the score into its various parts, in order to bring clarity to your understanding of the composer's intentions.

Objectives

I want to . . .

Put very simply, an Objective is a want. It is also a need, a desire, an intention, a longing, an aim, a goal, a target. At every moment of our lives we are in a state of want; we have Objectives to achieve, obtain, accomplish, in order to satisfy our desires.

I want to . . . be an opera singer. I want to understand how to create dramatic character, engage with Stanislavski's theory, put into practice some of these ideas, learn from other professionals, broaden my knowledge, relax, sleep and so on.

Objectives determine how we behave. They provide the reason, the *why*, we do things. They are the motor that drives us through our lives. We want something. We do something in order to get it; we take action.

I ... practise singing exercises and engage with my teacher's instructions. I read this book, explore other sources of information, audition, study other singers in operas, explore art galleries, drink herbal tea, lie down. . . . These doing words, verbs, are called Actions; you can read more about Actions in the next chapter.

Every character, at every moment in every opera, is pursuing an Objective. The score contains a series of actions; the words and music the characters sing, the plot, the stage directions. Every action, if it is to be believable, must have a purpose and so must arise from an Objective. An Objective gives every action a character does an inner foundation; they identify, and connect you to, a *need* within the character.

Every note a character sings is in order to achieve their Objective. Without a clearly defined Objective, the character (and therefore you, the singer) has no reason to sing. Your task as a singer is to work backwards to determine the psychological motivation behind everything your character does; you must justify every little piece of action that takes place. An analysis of the character's behaviour through the plot, together with an exploration of the music they sing, will give you clues as to what their possible Objectives might be.

This process of identifying intentions, as described by opera and theatre director Katie Mitchell, is 'like taking an X-ray in which you see the bone structure under the skin';[16] characters' Objectives create the structure of the plot of the opera. Conflicting Objectives, experienced internally within a single character and externally between different characters, provide dramatic tension. By examining and determining the possible Objectives, the foundations of the structure of the story itself become clear.

The difference between life and opera is that in opera you, the singer, must select which Objectives are dramatically exciting and explore how they truthfully prompt you to action. Throughout an opera a character will have many Objectives, varying in importance, scale, duration and intensity. Some Objectives will be carried and sustained through the character's entire life, some the duration of the opera, others just the length of a scene. Certain Objectives will change much more rapidly, throughout a scene, in direct response to events. We'll look at this hierarchy of different Objectives shortly but first we will explore how to work with Objectives.

Exploring Objectives

How do we seek to be in a state of *want*, knowing that we cannot simply command our creative emotions?

First, we must study the plot; what the character sings, and how the music expresses it, will help to determine possible Objectives. The music is tremendously important in guiding us towards the subtext. Literally sitting beneath the text, it provides clues, intimations and inspires our emotions. The music suggests meaning but its exact significance can be ambiguous. It often characterises the *result* of something and so we must seek to understand what it suggests and translate it into clear thoughts for our character.

We must then seek to truly understand and embody these thoughts. Merely knowing what a possible Objective might be, on an academic level, will leave you unable to adapt in the moment of performance. An Objective begins with an impulse towards something or someone, born out of a deep engagement with the circumstances of the character. The

---

[16] Mitchell, K. (2009) *The Director's Craft: A Handbook for the Theatre.* London: Routledge, p. 62.

previous work on the Facts of your character's world brings you closer to your character's situation, the pictures they carry in their mind's eye and the attitudes they carry towards their current experience. This impulse, in turn, will prompt you to seek appropriate words, music and physical actions to get what you want. The act of *doing* something, in order to achieve your want, substantiates your want.

This action is where creativity lies. To simply wallow, passively, in the emotive sound of the words and music, without using them to try to achieve something, does nothing to create an inner life for the character. The thoughts and ideas will simply remain inside you, uncommunicated to an audience, rendering the music an empty vessel. The music must be used to communicate the need to achieve something. The spark of this *need* is fired by an active, imaginative engagement with your character's reality.

EXAMPLE: *The Marriage of Figaro*

Let's look again at the first scene between Figaro and Susanna and, specifically, at the second recitative between the pair. Susanna has just attempted to convey to Figaro the Count's intentions without arousing Figaro's, unfounded, suspicions about her own intentions.

Let's imagine you are playing Susanna and explore the circumstances of her situation at this point in the opera:

- It is the morning of your wedding.
- You are in love with Figaro.
- You have been preparing for the big day, including adding the finishing touches to your hat.
- You have just learned that the Count has promised you and Figaro this room, directly next door to his own bedroom.
- The Count has provided you with a 'handsome dowry'.
- The Count is your employer.
- You live and work here. It is a remote estate.
- Your uncle and cousin also work here.
- There is little opportunity for social advancement and jobs in this society are difficult to change.
- You have not yet told Figaro but you know:
  - The Count has previously attempted to seduce you via your music tutor, Don Basilio.
  - Until recently it was the Count's privilege to sleep with newly wed brides. You have discovered he regrets abolishing these rights.
- Figaro harbours suspicions about your fidelity.
- You have been aware of these suspicions before today.
- You have never been unfaithful.
- You're aware Figaro has sometimes witnessed you flirting with other men.

These are some of the basic Facts for you at this moment;[17] if you were playing Susanna, you would have created a series of pictures, detailing specific incidents and experiences, in response to these simple Facts.

The recitative is preceded by the duet in which you sing over Figaro's line, continually insisting that his 'repeated suspicions are grossly unfair'. Your fiancé, initially, does not understand why you have a problem with the proximity of this room to the Count's. He then moves on to repeatedly insinuate your infidelity, singing that his 'nagging suspicions are too much to bear'. This duet is very much written as an argument: Figaro allowing his doubts, fears and accusations to grow, ahead of Susanna's appeals, reassurances and demands.

Allow all these observations to settle. As Susanna, ask: What do I need? What might I want from Figaro, today, on our wedding morning? Where, in which part of my body, does this need originate? How might the shift from expressive duet to more restrained recitative help to frame my Objective?

Susanna's Objective in this moment might be: '*I want* to set Figaro straight', '*I want* to challenge this nonsense', '*I want* you to wake up and see the situation we are in' or '*I want* you to trust me'.

The inner call to action, at first internal, and then external, must be aroused by the inner imaginative reality of your character's circumstances. You must seek to make these circumstances *your own*; connect to them and have attitudes towards them. By so doing, you will begin to harbour the desires, as yet unsated, that will spark the impulse toward a certain Objective and, beyond, to action.

Notes About Objectives

- *Objectives are holistic*: whilst they might exist in your character's conscious reasoning mind, they often arise from a physical need or desire somewhere deep within your body. It is useful to note that sometimes the character you are creating might harbour unconscious desires that arise instinctively. For example, when working with a singer playing Susanna in this scene, she reported the *need* to dispel Figaro's suspicions, at first, forming in her chest.

- *Objectives seek to balance an off-balanced character*: your character must want something they do not yet have. For example, Susanna does not yet have Figaro's entire trust and so she is driven forward to engage, set straight, challenge, wake up Figaro, in order to achieve her want.

  Many 'love duets' are dramatically problematic because the characters appear to have arrived at the point of achieving their want before they start singing: the other person! However, in order to continue to justify singing, and continue to drive the story forward, the characters must each be seeking *something*, even in a small way. They might be seeking something from their partner, another character or themselves; their Objective could simply be to celebrate their love together, or to confirm their own, and their partner's, feelings.

---

[17] Some of these Facts are not explicitly derived from the score. They were decided upon through the process of Facts and Questions for a production of *The Marriage of Figaro* at the Royal Welsh College of Music and Drama. Some of the Facts listed here, therefore, represent the way in which the singers and I answered the Questions proposed through our collective analysis of the score.

- *The result is not predetermined:* at the moment of seeking something, you (your character) cannot know whether you will get what you want. Susanna is often played as shrewd and *knowing*. However, were she to *know* the outcome of her Objective prior to pursuing it, it would make the scene dramatically meaningless. She cannot be certain that she will dispel Figaro's doubts and he is, therefore, a major obstacle to her achieving her Objective. Obstacles define Objectives; we will explore them later, in Obstacles. As soon as a character has achieved an Objective, or recognises they have ultimately failed to achieve an Objective, a new Objective will emerge.
- *Objectives conflict:* Susanna wants to explain the whole situation; Figaro, fearing the worst, does not want to hear it. The plot unfolds from here. In other scenes it might be that a single character harbours two conflicting Objectives (we will cover this in the section Counter-Objective). It is important to recognise the choices that you have as an artist and work with other singers to select Objectives that bring you into conflict; this is where drama lies. If you both have the same Objective, the scene will quickly become predictable.
- *Objectives and the perception goal:* ask, 'For what reason does your character want to achieve their Objective? What is their perceived goal beyond this Objective? What does the character imagine the result would be if they succeeded in their aim? What would be at stake if they failed? What feelings do these thoughts trigger?' Susanna wants to set Figaro straight in order to fully celebrate their union together; her failure to do so might result in the cancellation of the wedding.
- *Objectives and the relationship goal:* ask, 'What does your character want from their relationships with each other character?'
- *Objectives can seek internal or external satisfaction:* an Objective can provoke either psychological or physical action (or both, one leading to the next). However, to go beyond merely giving an account of your role, you should seek to achieve your character's Objective through outward action.

Hierarchy of Objectives

Stanislavski created a hierarchy of Objectives representing the relative importance of different Objectives and the length of time a character pursues these Objectives. Some Objectives might be sought for a brief moment in response to the immediate circumstances of a character, whilst others are pursued by the character throughout their entire lives, preceding and extending beyond the period of time covered in the opera. The longer a period of time a character holds an Objective, the deeper they tend to lie and the greater they resonate.

Stanislavski named this collection of minor and major Objectives, 'the *score* of the role;'[18] made up of physical and psychological Objectives, and drawing the singer closer to the real life of the character, this provides the foundation and justification for the musical score.

---

[18] Stanislavski, K. (1981) *Creating a Role*. Translated by E. R. Hapgood. London: Eyre Methuen, p. 62.

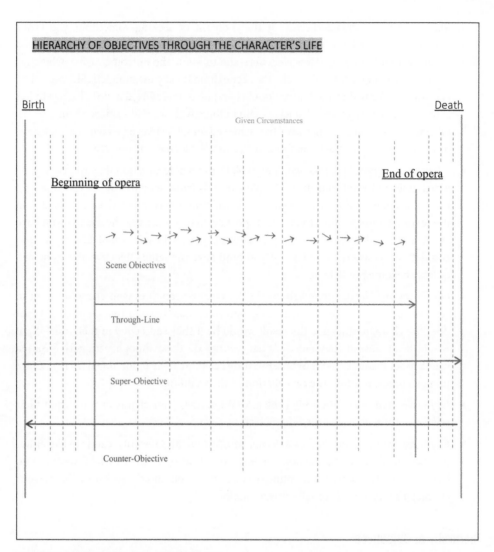

Birth   Death

Given Circumstances

End of opera

Beginning of opera

Scene Objectives

Through-Line

Super-Objective

Counter-Objective

Figure 4.1 Table of Hierarchy of Objectives.

These Objectives, in order of size, with the smallest first, are:

- Scene Objectives
- Through-Lines of Action
- Super-Objectives
- Counter-Objectives.

SCENE OBJECTIVES

Scene Objectives are those Objectives that change most frequently, usually in direct response to Events within the opera. The Objectives are always potentially achievable for a character in that moment and, usually, relate to another character.

A scene can be broken down into smaller sections of action;[19] Stanislavski called these separate sections *bits* or *Units*.[20] Each of these *Units* will be underpinned by a specific Objective the character is pursuing; a new Unit begins when a new Objective forms. Exactly how long each Objective is pursued is for the singer and production to interpret. In Events (p. 114) we look at the factors that might prompt a change of Objective.

Each of these smaller Objectives can be broadly gathered together into one over-arching Scene Objective; something the character is pursuing throughout the entire scene. If there is a major Event in the scene it is possible for a character's wants to change direction and for a new Scene Objective to form.

When playing an Objective by pursuing your character's want, understanding other characters' wants is essential; by listening to other characters, Objectives become transactional. Your character will often be trying to get something from a character who wants entirely the opposite from you; by remaining connected and open to them, whether singing or not, you will, by necessity, begin to adapt and change your Objective in response to their counter pursuit. You will only know if your Objective is succeeding by remaining attuned to the other character's response. If your character is failing to achieve an Objective, it is likely you will need to eventually change their Objective.

The music is an extraordinary guide to understanding what your character wants and when. Listen out for when a change in the music might suggest:

- the beginning of a new thought or new Objective;
- a character closing the book on pursuing a particular Objective;
- two or more characters' Objectives directly conflicting.

Many scores mark such moments precisely and can, in contrast to plays, suggest how two or more characters pursue Objectives simultaneously. The information the music provides must be interpreted and allied to the character's thoughts; the music the character sings and their Objective must be entwined. The singer must make these thoughts their own so that, ultimately, the music becomes driven by the thoughts, rather than the other way around.

The Objectives you decide upon – the choices you make – create the work itself. The words and music lie dormant until you forge your thoughts and creative will through them; they have no purpose until you determine *why* you need them. Alongside this, keep in mind that the decisions you make about Given Circumstances help to raise the stakes and make your Objective even more important or pressing for the character.

EXAMPLE: *The Marriage of Figaro*

Here are some possible Objectives for the recitative after Susanna and Figaro's second duet. The 'What *if*' principle is important. Ask 'What *if*' Figaro and Susanna were to want these Objectives and then explore them, on your feet, in rehearsals. Objectives are best

---

[19] I am not referring to Actions here (we explore these in the next section), but simply the action of the plot, a section of the scene where the plot plays out.
[20] Merlin, B. (2007) *The Complete Stanislavsky Toolkit*. London: Nick Hern Books. Merlin explains that 'bit' and 'unit' mean the same thing but the two terms arise due to different translations.

expressed through verbs as it helps to make them more playable; express each Objective beginning with '*I want to* . . .'. Initially, resist the temptation to over-complicate the character's Objectives. Keep them simple, at first, and they will be easier to grasp (see Figure 4.2):

1   Susanna: *I want to* stop your repetitive thoughts.
2   Figaro: *I want to* prepare myself for the worst.
3   Susanna: *I want to* lay it all out so that you can draw your own conclusions.
4   Figaro: *I want to* get you to move it on.
5   Susanna: *I want to* shock you into action.

How do these Objectives develop – from one to the next – to create a journey of wants for the characters? Susanna must seek to achieve her initial Objective through external Actions. Once the result of this attempt is known, or if a new incident occurs, she must ask 'And *now* what must I do?' The answer provides the next potential Objective. Continue this, asking 'And *now* . . .', to create a thread of Objectives; the continuation of a journey, in one general direction, through the scene.

Looking at these smaller Objectives we might suggest that the overall Scene Objectives for the characters are:

Susanna: *I want* you to fully understand the threat the Count poses.
Figaro: *I want to* demonstrate that I'm in control of every situation.

Recitative's function is to drive the plot forward; there will tend to be more changes of Objective within scenes of recitative. Arias will tend to be motivated by fewer Objectives and are often an opportunity for a character to explore two conflicting Objectives. For example, in Figaro's No. 3 Cavatina 'So, little master, you're dressed to go dancing'/'Se vuol ballare', the shift in dynamics and the repetition of certain phrases might suggest the following conflicting Objectives:

I want to rouse myself to plot revenge on the Count.
I want to calm myself in order not to give the game away too early.

The Handel da capo aria is perhaps the most dramatically challenging of all arias. It usually has three Objectives; one for the first A section, a new Objective for the B section and another Objective for the repeated A section (that is in some way informed by what has happened in the B).

EXERCISE: *The Pen*
Group/5 mins

This is a classic Stanislavski exercise;[21] I adapted it to begin the first Opera Works weekend. The premise is simple and you can try it on others and witness the result.

---

[21] Stanislavski, K. (1980) *An Actor Prepares*. Translated by E. R. Hapgood. London: Eyre Methuen, pp. 33–7.

Recitative

Susanna and Figaro

Figure 4.2 Recitative: Figaro/Susanna.

Announce to the group that you have hidden a gold pen somewhere in the room; a prize will be given to the first person to find it. Give them a five-minute time limit in which to find it.

It does not matter whether a gold pen has actually been hidden. The point is that the participants have a clear Objective and an understanding of why they are pursuing the Objective: '*I want to* find the pen *in order to win the prize*'. The time pressure, and the other participants, raise the stakes and so make the task more interesting to watch.

Every exercise or game in this book (or any other) will have a simple Objective at its core. This tends to focus the player and release them from self-monitoring thoughts and self-conscious feelings. Exercise: The Camera (p. 26) is a terrific example of this.

EXERCISE: *Motivation Challenge*
Solo/Pair/5 mins

In rehearsals, especially when time is short, or when working on a large ensemble number, you might be given 'blocking' (prescribed movements) or choreography. It may be that you are given no reason for doing these moves or actions; the blocking might be set to bring clarity to the visual storytelling or for stylised effect. Just as the score gives you notes to sing without explicitly giving you your motivation for singing them, so this choreography might also be similarly given without justification. It is your job to motivate it; not just generally but in detail. What is your reason for doing this? For whom? To what end or purpose?

This exercise helps you explore how to deal with this challenge. Give yourself a simple action to mime; for example, washing the dishes, measuring a room, fixing flowers to a hat. Then write down five different Objectives, for example:

- *I want to* please my partner.
- *I want to* prove my worth to my employer.
- *I want to* guilt-trip my flat mate.
- *I want to* impress my new colleague.
- *I want to* satisfy myself of my ability.

Note that each of these *wants* establishes a goal and a target; in this case the person who will witness the result of your endeavour. Set a timer on your phone to ring once a minute over five minutes, begin your action, and change Objective every minute.

What do you notice about *how* you do the action? What changes from one Objective to the next? What thoughts occur as you play each Objective? If someone is available to watch you do this exercise, ask them to feedback on your various shifts of movement and focus that they noticed.

THROUGH-LINE OF ACTION

The Through-Line of Action is the character's main Objective that runs throughout the entire opera. You could call it the 'over-arching opera Objective'. It creates the plot and, in turn, is shaped by the plot. It is derived from the subtext rather than the text itself. It links and galvanises all the smaller scene Objectives to create a sense of a character's journey through the story.

The Through-Line of Action, spun from the beginning of the story to its culmination, is subject to creative interpretation. We can bring it to the foreground, or allow it to become a background presence; we can strengthen it or diminish it, speed up or slow down the pace at which we pursue it. The Through-Line is like a piece of music; it responds to the character's music, justifies it, and, at times, acts as a counterpoint to it.

With certain characters, the Through-Line might not kick in until after the opera's first significant event.[22] Most stories begin by laying out the foundation of the world itself – the way the world in the opera has always been. Early on, there will usually be an event that changes this world and so sets the Through-Line Objective for the character for the rest of opera.

EXAMPLE: *The Marriage of Figaro*

We might propose that Figaro's Through-Line of action is:

I want to enjoy/celebrate my wedding day

However, this is a rather general Through-Line and could lead to much passive action. Examining Figaro's Scene Objectives we can see that he spends much of his time in the opera attempting to thwart the Count's sexual advances towards Susanna. The first significant event in the opera seems to be the revelation, by Susanna, that the Count has been making unwanted sexual advances towards her. From this moment, Figaro's Through-Line becomes apparent:

I want to protect/defend my fiancée's honour

A character's Through-Line of Action might end before the opera ends, whether through successful attainment or ultimate failure of their over-arching Objective. Figaro

---

[22] The first significant event is explained in Events (p. 114).

supposes his Through-Line has failed in Act Four, feeling certain of Susanna's betrayal following the news of Susanna's supposed night-time meeting with the Count. It is difficult to discern any clear over-arching Objective taking shape for Figaro after this point other than to expose Susanna (and indeed, *all* women) for her infidelity. For the drama to function, there must be an opposite counteraction; an opposing Through-Line enacted by another character. For example, the Count's Through-Line might be:

> *I want to assert my authority by sleeping with Susanna on her wedding day before Figaro*

The Through-Line is very much the character's Super-Objective, *in action*, shaped by the circumstances of the story. Stanislavski argued that 'The creative force of the Through-Line of Action is in direct proportion to the power of attraction of the Super-Objective'.[23]

SUPER-OBJECTIVE

The Super-Objective is the all-embracing Objective which drives the character through their entire life; it is their ultimate goal, their central core Objective. It is the sum of the smaller Scene Objectives and the Through-Line of Action; it helps bring a sense of logic and connection to all the character's Objectives and actions.

It is difficult to *play* the Super-Objective directly or in detail; it is too general, too big to grasp. Indeed, very often the character will be unaware of what their Super-Objective is. The Through-Line of Action is the active attempt to gain the Super-Objective, framed, as it is, by the particular circumstances of the opera.

Understanding what the character's Super-Objective is helps guide your decisions about the smaller Objectives; all of which will flow in the same direction. It can often be difficult to discern a character's Super-Objective, and the question arises: which do you determine first, the Super-Objective or the Scene Objectives? It is usually only after analysis of entire libretto and score that the Super-Objective emerges but an understanding of the character's central drive can help to define and sharpen Scene Objectives.

EXAMPLE: *The Marriage of Figaro*

All Objectives are subjective and will define the story you choose to communicate to an audience. Here are some thoughts about characters' possible Super-Objectives:

- Figaro: *I want to* . . . have an answer for everything life throws at me/arm myself with answers in order to embrace a joy-filled life/be everyone's friend/be the equal of any man or woman.
- Susanna: *I want to* . . . embrace the joys of life/control my fate/be the equal of any man or woman.

---

[23] Stanislavski, K. (1980) *An Actor Prepares*. Translated by E. R. Hapgood. London: Eyre Methuen, p. 300.

- The Count: *I want to* . . . be in absolute control of people's perception of me/control/be respected as a leader.
- The Countess: *I want to* . . . love completely/embrace all life's experiences/be free to love.

MICHAEL CHEKHOV

Michael Chekhov (1891–1955) was a Russian actor, director and practitioner who studied under Stanislavski at the Moscow Arts Theatre. He continued to develop Stanislavski's work after his death. He was the nephew of the writer Anton Chekhov. He was particularly interested in developing an actor's psycho-physical awareness: work that helps connect the mind and body through the imagination, to heighten physical awareness of the inner psychological impulses and make these impulses present to an audience. He worked in the UK at Dartington College, alongside movement practitioner Rudolf Laban (see Chapter 5, p. 130), and, later, in New York and Los Angeles. He wrote about his work in *On the Technique of Acting* (abridged as *To the Actor*).[24]

EXERCISE: *Psychological Gesture*
Solo/15 mins

Michael Chekhov developed this exercise as a way of helping the actor to physically connect with their character's Super-Objective.

1 • Open and then close your fist; explore this sensation of opening and expanding.
- Then find a way to embody, through gesture and using the whole body, an archetypal gesture to *Open/Expand*; find the point the movement starts from and the end point. Michael Chekhov suggests a Psychological Gesture should begin from your *Ideal Centre* (approximately two inches inside your chest, near your heart).
- Return to neutral: feet shoulder width apart, arms free and released by your side.
- Once you have found the gesture for *Open/Expand*, begin to embody it from neutral, starting at the *Ideal Centre*. As you do this say either, 'opening/expanding/waking up'.
- Repeat but this time extend the movement imaginatively beyond the limits of the body; imagine the movement continues to expand through the fingers, the toes, the top of the head, etc.

---

[24] Chekhov, M. (1985) *To the Actor*. New York: Harper and Row.

- Repeat but this time do the movement quickly.
- Next, speak 'Yes' as you *Open/Expand*; speak when the sensation of *Opening* suggests you should.
- Move around the space and repeat this part of the exercise in different places in the space.
- Leave an imprint in the space.
- Next, as you repeat the gesture, speak a line of any text from an aria.
- Then, as you repeat the gesture, sing this line.

2 • Having determined your Super-Objective, speak it out loud, '*I want to . . .*'.
- Then, find a way to embody, through gesture and using the whole body, an archetypal gesture that represents this statement.
- Again, find the point the movement begins (the *Ideal Centre*) and the end point.
- Return to neutral.
- Once you have found this gesture or frame, from a neutral start, create it again whilst saying your Super-Objective.
- Repeat but this time extend the movement imaginatively beyond the limits of the body; imagine the movement continues without stopping.
- Repeat but this time quickly.
- Move around the space; repeat this process in different places in the space. Leave an imprint in space. Do this at least ten times.
- Then, when you have a clear sense of the gesture, take it inside the body and experience the sensation of imaginatively allowing the gesture to form internally. It will be barely perceptible to a spectator.
- Try speaking 'Yes' or 'No' whilst allowing the inner gesture to form.
- Try shaking hands with someone to reactivate the sensation of the gesture.
- Try speaking a line of text your character sings to activate the inner gesture.
- Finally, sing a line your character sings whilst activating the inner gesture.

Chekhov instructs you to respect the frame you create, or else risk it becoming a cliché. By this he means that each time you activate the gesture, either externally or internally, allow it to connect with your imaginative life: the pictures, wants, feelings you have as your character.

By creating a Psychological Gesture the body begins to release certain sensations. We receive certain information from the body that can, in turn, inform our thoughts and how we seek our Objectives.

Create your character's Psychological Gesture in rehearsals; it is then particularly useful as a pre-show warm up. It awakens the body and mind to the deep-rooted physical sensations that arise from our core Objectives.

COUNTER-OBJECTIVE

The Counter-Objective works in direct opposition to a character's Super-Objective; running throughout their lives, it creates inner conflict and in drama, especially tragedy, will often be partly the reason for a character's unfulfilled ambitions.

As with the Super-Objective, it is often difficult to discern and requires in-depth analysis of the character's behaviour through the plot of the opera. It is useful to consider determining both the character's Super-Objective and Counter-Objective at the same time; each will inform the other.

EXAMPLE: *The Marriage of Figaro*

If Susanna's Super-Objective is to be the equal of any man or woman, her Counter-Objective might be:

- *I want to* please my employers

  or

- *I want to* survive the harsh conditions of a servant's life

Figure 4.3 Recitative and aria: Figaro.

This might account for the confusion she encounters in the Act Two duet with the Count, when she seems genuinely flustered by his advances.

If Figaro's Super-Objective is to embrace a joy-filled life, his Counter-Objective might be:

- *I want to* exact revenge on anyone who gets in my way

  or

- *I want to* ensure I am never cheated on

This creates a conflict within Figaro: his need to seek out Susanna's supposed infidelities works in direct opposition to his drive to embrace the joys of life. This conflict is expressed musically in the accompanied recitative before Figaro's final aria (see Figure 4.3):

1 Figaro's vocal line is suspended in anticipation of Susanna's arrival. The mood could be described as hopeful; he is instinctively lifted by the expectation of her appearance.

2 The confirmation that no-one is there – namely Susanna – unleashes Figaro's darker thoughts. His Counter-Objective takes hold in the aria that follows as he mocks himself for his earlier naïve hopes.

SUMMARY

- Your character is always in a state of *want*, inspired by the Given Circumstances. The Objectives are the trigger for physical action.

- There is a hierarchy of Objectives; living your part consists of creating a score of Objectives driving your character forward. This foundational sub-textual score must be informed by the operatic score. This hierarchy of Objectives creates dramatic logic, a coherent journey through your character's *wants*.

- Scene Objectives change more frequently than other Objectives, in response to other characters' opposing Objectives and the Scene Events.

- The Through-Line of Action is the character's over-arching Objective running through the opera and is the active attempt to attain the character's Super-Objective.

- The Super-Objective drives the character through their life.

- The Counter-Objective is an opposing Objective, pursued by the character, that leads to inner conflict.

TO DO

- Engage with the Given Circumstances and determine your character's main Scene Objective.

- Explore how and when the music suggests changes in Objectives.

- Keep your choices about Objectives simple to begin with.

- By asking 'What *If* . . .' to explore different possible Objectives, you give yourself a range of options to explore and offer in the rehearsal room.
- Determine the first significant event in the opera to define and determine when your character's Through-Line begins and ends.
- Explore the character's Super-Objective; allow it to guide your choice of Scene Objectives. Engage with it through the Psychological Gesture exercise.

Actions

I . . . (transitive verb) you.

An Action is what you *do* in order to get your *want*. It is your want made active; the physical expression of your Objective.

If Objectives pose the question, *what* do you want?, Actions ask, *how* are you going to get it? Actions are your character's tactics for achieving their aims; constantly changing in the face of opposing Objectives and Obstacles. The greater the Obstacle the more tactically diverse a character will need to be to achieve their Objective; the greater the number of Actions a character will do to get what they want. Actions make present the ever-changing inner life of a character. Strung together they create a detailed score of this inner life, mirroring, infusing and bringing definition to the musical score.

The act of doing creates feeling. I *want* something, I *do* something in order to get it, and as a result I *feel* something. If my actions are successful I might feel gratified, happy, relieved; if I fail in striving to get the result I want, I will perhaps experience feelings of disappointment, sadness, guilt. Actions make the imaginative real, they engage us in the *actual* and, as a consequence, we cannot help but experience something; we *feel*.

When working with Objectives our artistic freedom lies in choosing *what* we want, with Actions our choices lie with *how* we get our want and from whom. This will be informed by the music that scores your actions, the Given Circumstances you choose to highlight and the character traits you emphasise.

We express an Action in the following way: as '*I . . . . . (transitive verb) you*'. A *verb* is a doing word; *transitive* means it travels to someone or somewhere.

For example:

OBJECTIVE: *I want to . . . get you to make me dinner.*
ACTIONS: *I* implore *you*/I beg *you*/I urge *you*/I flatter *you*/I guilt-trip *you*/I bribe *you.*

How I implore you, or *how* I urge you, can change, with degrees of variation, each time the Action is executed. Your Action will change depending upon who the '*you*' is you are targeting and how they receive and respond to your Action. Your Actions will always be informed by how your partner in the scene is responding to you.

Actions are ever present; you are *always* in action, *doing* something in order to get something. Indeed, the term *drama* comes from a Greek word meaning *action*, derived from *I do*. So, action in music is the very stuff of music drama and, through the course of the plot,

Actions reveal character. The cognitive behavioural approach to creating character[25] asserts that we are the sum of all our behaviours; we are what we *do*. And what we do is informed by what we think. And vice versa.

The Internal/External Interplay

Action begins with an internal impulse emerging from a desire to achieve an Objective. As we have already explored, this Objective arises from a deep understanding of, and connectedness with, the character's situation. Without this internal drive any external action is empty. This includes the very action of singing; an unmotivated sung word or note *sounds* different from one sung in order to attain something.

Any external Action must be first be *heated* by inner meaning, its purpose reinforced by the *need* to take action. This external Action, through its physical realisation, in turn bolsters and intensifies your inner thoughts. You *experience* through physical action and this experience informs, shapes and moulds your thoughts and feelings.

These inner thoughts and external actions are interlaced, one informing the other, formed by the Facts of the opera itself. The relationship between our outer and inner state can be experienced through Exercise: Psychological Gesture (p. 85).

Notes about Actions

- *Actions bring focus to the sung word:* you *use* the words and music to *do* something; they become tools for your character to get what they want, and, imbued with purpose, they become utterly intrinsic to the drama. Actions help the words live within the music, they prevent moments of inaction, of emptiness, of false expression of feeling. They give every moment of singing purpose beyond simply the aesthetic; singing becomes *actively* connected to thought and intent. When considering Actions, the extraordinary detail in the music – the notes, the pauses, the dynamics, the accented words, the cadenzas – take on meaning; they become *useful* to your character.

- *Actions stop you playing emotion:* Stanislavski devised his system of physical actions in a moment of creative crisis. As an actor and director he felt performances too easily became routine and mere automatically repeated external signals of emotion.[26] When singing opera alongside the huge forces of the orchestra, which is perhaps musically representing an enormous emotional moment for the character, it is difficult to resist the urge to strain to match this volume of emotion with our own *signs* of emotion. Playing the emotion, playing the *result* of an Action, leads to physical and emotional exaggeration and contortion. Who can honestly match the full force of the orchestra? The very point of the orchestration is to heighten and amplify the emotional experience of the characters for an audience; the orchestra does this, so that you don't have to! Playing Actions means engaging in the process which *leads* to feeling; it allows you to focus on something more manageable.

---

[25] See Given Circumstances (p. 48).
[26] Stanislavski, K. (1980). *My Life in Art*. Translated by J. Benedetti. London: Routledge and New York: Theatre Arts Books, R. M. MacGregor, p. 460.

- *Actions offer you both structure and freedom*: The tactics you use to get your Objectives can be determined in rehearsal; this will enable you to construct a detailed direction of travel for your character through the opera. Your freedom lies in exactly how you choose to execute your Actions from one night to the next, in response to your fellow singers, the conductor and your communication with the audience.

- *Actions make the imaginary real*: the process of actually *doing* things helps bring to life the previously imagined inner world of the character. The wants, impulses and Actions must belong to the singer – it is you who will experience and live the part – and, in so doing, communicate the truth of the story to the audience.

- *Actions reveal the story to the audience*: this is best summed up by Stanislavski: 'The point of physical Actions lies not in themselves as such but in what they evoke; conditions, proposed circumstances, feelings. The fact that the hero of a play kills himself is not so important as the inner reason for his suicide'.[27]

Process

Actioning is the process of rehearsing possible *Actions*. When Actioning it is best to explore the process with your fellow singers; your Actions will be defined by what they are doing to you and, in response, theirs by what you do to them.

Even when the process Actioning, as laid out in the exercises below, is not possible due to the particular nature of the rehearsal room you are working in, it is still important to consider what Actions you might play in preparation for a role. Considering different Actions cracks the spine of the character and begins to alert you to tactical possibilities.

This work, eventually, becomes habitual; you should not be able to pick up a score without thinking, *so what am I aiming to do to you when I sing this top C*. To begin with, however, grab a pencil and write down under each line you sing, 'I . . . you'.

Whilst Actioning consider the following points:

MUSIC DEFINES ACTIONS

To begin with, extract from the libretto basic external Actions and write these in pencil beneath each line.[28] For example, Susanna's initial Actions might be:

- *I arrange flowers in my hat.*
- *I invite you (to look at the hat).*
- *I reveal (that I'll wear the hat at my wedding).*

If these Actions move in the general direction of the Through-Line, and seem to be in sympathy with the music, it is possible to begin to discern the character's Objectives. Moment by moment, ask, 'What does the music suggest about *how* I do these actions?' The musical score helps you to interpret the *Actions score* you are creating. As you become more familiar with the character and music, you can adapt and detail your initial Actions. For

---

[27] Stanislavski, K. (1981) *Creating a Role*. Translated by E. R. Hapgood. London: Eyre Methuen, p. 208.
[28] Writing in pencil allows you to continue to change the Action in rehearsal.

example, Susanna's broad Action, *I arrange flowers in my hat*, might be detailed in the following way through her first three lines:

- *I glorify you (the hat).*
- *I delight me.*
- *I confirm the appropriateness of the hat to me.*

The Actions motivate the words you sing. You sing 'Oh, this hat is simply lovely' in order to *glorify* the hat; 'everything a hat should be' in order to *delight* yourself; the repeat of 'everything a hat should be' to confirm the appropriateness of the hat to yourself.

For every one of these Actions, ask, why do I *do* that? The Actions begin to suggest a motivation; the external action informs your choice as to the internal motivating impulse.

For example, Susanna's Objective might be:

- *I want to* enjoy the excitement of the wedding day.

Your character's Objectives, running in parallel alongside the music and action, detail the internal thoughts and motivations of your character. Your complete character score should include your words, music, Actions and Objectives, each supporting, informing, detailing and justifying the other.

MUSICAL CLUES

The mind, the voice and the body are connected. It is important to explore how music might guide your choices about Actions and help strengthen these connections.

The process of thought leading to action tends to follow in the following order:

- you *receive* information (an action from another character).
- you make the *decision* to respond. And breathe.
- you *(re)act* in response.

The composer, and in performance the conductor, will guide *how* this process plays out, determining how quickly you move through this process of thought. The composer also suggests how long an action might be sustained; the end of a phrase might bring to an end the Action, a new musical phrase initiating the next Action.

Look out for the following musical clues when selecting and playing Actions:

- The composer might have written a musical interlude or introduction to an aria; this is an invitation to explore Actions without words. What does the music suggest you are doing? Why are you not yet using words as a way of getting what you want?
- A shift in pitch, or dynamics, or the introduction of certain instruments in the orchestration might suggest a new Action.
- How you play an Action, the texture of an Action, might be informed by the music; soft or harsh, questioning or demanding, or the intensification of a previous Action.
- Certain words might be sung with accented notes; this might suggest the moment a certain Action is emphasised.

- Take note of the rests in the vocal line and the inner psychological workings it might suggest. It perhaps signals the moment the thought process slows to allow time to receive an idea or to form a new thought. It might suggest a moment to recognise whether a particular action has succeeded or failed, or a moment to see a picture in the mind's eye. It might simply be a moment to allow for rudimentary physical action; for example, Figaro's measuring of the room.

- Ask what the music suggests when you are not singing. Maybe there's something in the orchestration that might guide your Actions when somebody else is singing.

- The music often links the journey of your thoughts. Seek to connect the music and thoughts by imagining that the composer is scoring the thoughts in your head and so allow the music to guide these thoughts.

These possibilities are not meant to imply that you should *play* the music by, for example, walking *in time* or measuring every gesture to the music; this would risk becoming mannered and mechanical. However, you must examine the score for every shifting point and ask *why?* Truly *listen* to the music and allow the music to infuse the Actions you do. If you meet the music, your Actions will begin to make sense to the audience of the musical decisions the composer made, in turn, justifying the music.

The score and libretto present the central provocation for you; how am I going to use these words and music to get what I, the character, want? They are invitations from the composer and librettist to join them in creating the whole story.

TARGETS

It is important that your Actions always travel to an external target. Without an external target your Actions risk remaining nothing more than internal thoughts; indistinct to the audience. The target needs to be specific or else the Action will be diffuse and generalised; you must know who the *you* is in the sentence, 'I (transitive verb) *you*'.

Who might your character target? Whoever they want to get something from, whoever they want to change. This could be any of the following:

- *Another character.*

- *Another character not in the space*: they might be next door, in another country, in another world, but you'll need to have a sense of where that space is geographically in order to direct the action in that certain direction.

- *A god or gods*: many operas deal with classical myths or gods; if your character refers to a god or gods, they need a direct sense of communication with them.

- *An object*: the object might be a letter you are investing with hope or a plant pot you have rescued from destruction. It might symbolically represent something greater than the object itself, such as a wedding ring.

- *A place.*

- *A picture in your mind's eye*: this picture might be of someone or something, past or future. It might be real or imagined. In order to target it, you need to detail the picture to make it as vivid as possible.

- *An idea:* this is more difficult to target as it is a non-physical entity, for example, class, honour, power. It might be that you concretise this idea in the form of an object (see Chapter 6: Words and Music in Action) or select someone who represents or embodies this idea. For example, in Figaro's Act Four aria he rails against the infidelity of women. He might choose to target Susanna (last seen in the house) or, depending upon the style of the production, the women in the audience.

- *The Audience:* it will depend upon the style of the production you are creating as to whether your character is *entitled* to access the audience. It might be that the fourth wall is well and truly in place and the character is unaware of an audience. It might be that the piece itself absolutely demands direct address to audience; I recently directed Rossini's *La Cenerentola* and without the audience it would be difficult to discern who Dandini is addressing much of the time. The important thing is this: if you're targeting the audience you need to know what you want to do to them and how you want to change them. To understand this, you need to determine the nature of your relationship with the audience. Dandini seems to see the audience as his best mates, many of his Actions being: I impress you, I nudge you, I excite you, I tickle you.

- *Yourself:* this is a potentially dangerous target! Too often singers will choose to target themselves when singing an aria with the result that the thoughts never become Action; they remain internalised, locked inside the character's head, without ever being sparked by the impulse to external Action. This renders the story unclear, the singer inactive and, as a result, the aria generalised and sentimental. You can, however, direct the Action outside of yourself; for example, if the Action is – I *spur* me – you might imagine spurring yourself as a jockey would a racehorse, or – I *admonish* me – might result in you physically hitting yourself.

There must be some distance between you and your target; otherwise you have no journey to make. A duet between lovers too often ceases to be dramatically interesting after the moment the two singers have touched each other. How you make this journey, indeed how you move, depends upon your target. The theatre director, Declan Donnellan, asserts that all movement is motivated by first 'seeing' the target; and that performers 'see with their entire body'.[29] *How* you move will be informed by the fact that the target is always, in some way, transforming and actively doing something to you. Donnellan suggests, as an exercise, using only the words '*There's you, there's me and there's the space*' to play a scene,[30] in order to explore the fundamental difference between the three utterly distinct ideas. This exercise can be incredibly frustrating as your vocabulary is so reduced but you can adapt the tone, the rhythm, the pitch of these three phrases to bring expression. I often do this exercise with the répétiteur playing the scene and the singers singing '*There's you, there's me and there's the space*' using fragments of their own music.

---

[29] Donnellan, D. (2005) *The Actor and the Target*, London: Nick Hern Books, p. 139.
[30] Ibid.

THE THREE CIRCLES

Targets can be grouped into three different circles[31] that define where your focus is:

- *1st Circle:* are those targets closest to you, including yourself and the pictures that you carry in your mind's eye. Being in 1st Circle for too long can lead to introspection, with the risk that the story is not made clear to the audience.

- *2nd Circle:* are those Targets immediately outside of you. The most common example is another character or an object in the same room. 2nd Circle is a good place to be to heighten your responsiveness to others and the world around you.

- *3rd Circle:* are those Targets some distance from you. For example, they might be a large crowd, someone standing across the road or an idea on the horizon line. In some cases, your character might communicate with the audience in the 3rd Circle. To develop a sense of intimate communication with the audience it is, however, easier to do so by thinking of them as beginning in 2nd Circle; addressing them as though they were in the room with you. 3rd Circle targets can be a fantasy or dream projected by the mind's eye beyond the limits of the space, towards an imagined horizon. The risk of the 3rd Circle is that it can lead to *pushing*; projecting beyond the reasonable limits of the reality of the space for no good reason. For example, your character might be singing directly to another character but the performer is communicating in 3rd Circle, perhaps by demonstrating to the audience. The benefit of 3rd Circle is that, when connected to a clear idea, it can transport the character and audience beyond the naturalistic definitions of the world into other imaginative realities.

It is possible that your character's focus will switch between various targets in all three Circles in the one aria. As an exercise take Susanna's opening line from her duet with Figaro, No. 2 'Supposing one evening the Countess should need you'/'Se a caso madama la note ti chiama':

> *Supposing one morning the Count were to call you.*

Try this line in each of the three Circles. In 1st Circle target yourself; it is an internal thought, you are *picturing* the scene of Figaro being called to work by the Count. In 2nd Circle target Figaro; you are *instructing* him to imagine this scene. In 3rd Circle project the possible scene on the horizon; you are, somewhat dramatically, *creating* the scene for Figaro. It is the same line but the shifting target brings with it different Actions; *picturing, instructing, creating.*

REACTION

All Actions are done in response to a previous Action – enacted by yourself or, more often, another character. This cycle of interaction relies on listening and watching your fellow performers and being open to the possibility of change. The risk of Actioning is that it becomes simply an enacted list of things you do to others, without allowing the Actions of others to affect you and, in turn, your response.

---

[31] We will also look at The Three Circles in Chapter 9: Rehearsals in Depth.

STATE OF *WANT*

It is important that the process of writing down possible Actions doesn't become a test of vocabulary. There is a useful Actions thesaurus[32] which can help prompt thoughts but the word you use has to mean something to you. You might express an Action – 'I urghhh you'; this is absolutely fine, so long as it resonates for you.

This is a physical process and the impulse to act must arise from a felt need or desire in your body, driven by an inner engagement with the Given Circumstances. Your response to this need, perhaps in reaction to somebody else, needs to reach the point where you *must* sing; you *have* to take action.

Actioning

When Actioning in the rehearsal room, bear the following in mind:

- Actioning is physical; be ready to test out Actions on your feet and change them where necessary.

- Do not confuse activity with Actions; Actions are tactics to attain your wants, not generalised bustle.

- Try to avoid using 'I (verb) *to* you' as the Action is more directly driven towards the other character without the *to*. However, sometimes it might release a thought to phrase it in this way.

- Do not play the result. For example, *I seduce you* suggests that you have already achieved your goal. If your character's Objective is, 'I want to seduce you', ask *how* they might do this: for example, 'I tease you', 'I flatter you', 'I encourage you', 'I draw you', 'I touch you'.

- Do not show or demonstrate Actions to the audience; *do* them to your target.

- Be ruthlessly detailed, bold and specific! Do not let a moment pass or an opportunity go when your character could be in *Action*. Even in silence you need to be active.

- Remember that the words and music you have been given are for your own purpose to achieve what your character wants.

- Try to change your partner; get inside their mind, dig away, pursue your goal!

EXAMPLE: *The Marriage of Figaro*

Let's look again at the recitative between Susanna and Figaro at the beginning of Act One. We previously explored Susanna and Figaro's Objectives, now let's look at possible Actions for this scene:

---

[32] Caldarone, M. (2004) *Actions: The Actors' Thesaurus*, London: Nick Hern Books.

Figure 4.4 Recitative: Figaro and Susanna.

Notice:

- The punctuation often suggests the need for a new Action.
- The targets shift from Figaro, to Susanna, to the Count (who is not present in the room).
- When Susanna is being sarcastic, her Actions must be 'sincere' for this to be clear: for example, *I praise you (the Count), I pity you (the Count).*

EXAMPLE: *The Marriage of Figaro*

Let us now turn our attention to a very different scene; the Count's aria in Act Three (see Figure 4.5).[33]

The Count has just overheard Susanna revealing to Figaro that 'He (Figaro) has won the case already'. At this point, the Count is unclear of the meaning of this statement but he is certain that Figaro and Susanna are deceiving him. He wonders whether Figaro will actually marry Susanna and considers the obstacles in Figaro's way: Figaro is still indebted to Marcellina and contracted to marry her; Antonio, Susanna's uncle, is unhappy about Figaro's low status.

Immediately prior to the beginning of the aria, the Count sings recitative:

THE COUNT: Antonio won't allow his beloved niece Susanna to marry such a nobody as Figaro. I will work on Antonio and swell his bloated pride. It will work in my favour. I'll make them suffer.

The Count does not sing for the next four bars, during the play-in of the aria. Look at the play-in of the aria and notice that:

- The orchestra strikes up immediately after the final line of recitative under the instruction *allegro maestoso* (a fast and lively tempo played in a majestic fashion). What does the music in the opening bar of the Count's aria suggest? Does it illustrate the Count's resolve to take action and seize the initiative?
- Intriguingly, the opening bar of the play-in is followed by much softer music in the next three bars. Could this be associated with Susanna? Prior to this scene, during Susanna and the Count's duet, Susanna has agreed to meet the Count later, with a clear insinuation of what will happen. Maybe at this point in the play-in the Count's Action is 'I *picture* you (Susanna)'. Maybe in the Count's mind's eye, he pictures Susanna looking particularly beautiful at the moment she promised herself to him? These opening four bars of play-in must be active; the music has purpose and seems to be suggesting something that the Count is *doing*.

What if the Count's Objective for the aria is:

OBJECTIVE: *I want to* . . . summon my resolve for revenge in spite of my feelings for Susanna.

This Objective suggests an internal struggle, so we could express it differently:

---

[33] Count, No. 17 Recit and Aria 'You've won the case already!'/'Hai gia vinta la causa!'

SCENE OBJECTIVE: *I want to . . .* summon my resolve for revenge.
COUNTER-OBJECTIVE: *I want to . . .* be wanted by Susanna.

Let's now explore what the Count will *do* in order to get his want. Sometimes his Actions will be in pursuit of his Counter-Objective:

Figure 4.5 Recitative: Count.

ACTIONS: –   I *determine* me

           –   I *picture* you (Susanna)

           –   I *adore* you/I *beg* you (Susanna)

           –   I *challenge* me

           –   I *submit* to you (Susanna)

           –   I *replay* my memory of the previous scene/I *accuse* you (Figaro)

           –   I *confront* you (Figaro)

It is worth writing down a couple of options for possible Actions (*adore/beg*) and using rehearsals to test them out.

In Rehearsal

I will often Action a scene with a cast when rehearsing an opera. I break the process down into a number of stages to allow the singers to fully explore the words, music and physical action and the way in which they unite in seeking to obtain an Objective.

By this stage in the rehearsal process the possible Actions will have been discussed with the cast. These discussions will have been informed by the Given Circumstances, the character's Objectives, the opposing Objectives of other characters, other Obstacles and, crucially, the guiding hand of the music. At any stage of rehearsal we might change and adapt our choice of Actions; it's only by getting Actions 'on their feet' that you discover which are the most dramatically interesting to play.

1. SPEAKING

- Be on your feet at all times, initially with your score in hand. Speak the text, do not sing. Firstly, state your Action in a neutral tone out loud, 'I (transitive verb) you'. Immediately following this, physicalise the Action whilst *speaking* the particular line from the libretto.

   For example, using the Figaro scene, above:

SUSANNA *(speaking)*	I <u>stop</u> you *(standing in neutral)*	:	Alright, *(physically stopping Figaro)*
SUSANNA *(speaking)*	I <u>suppress</u> you *(standing in neutral)*	:	shut up and listen *(physically suppressing Figaro)*
FIGARO *(speaking)*	I <u>match</u> you *(standing in neutral)*	:	I'm listening, *(physically matching Susanna)*
FIGARO *(speaking)*	I <u>brace</u> me *(standing in neutral)*	:	tell me the worst *(physically brace yourself)*

- Repeat the scene in this way; each time you repeat, explore different ways of playing the same Action.

Note: For Susanna to be *stopping* Figaro, it suggests that Figaro is *readying* himself to sing. Your character can never assume that they are going to sing the next line. Of course, we know what is coming next, it is written in the score, but the characters do not and we must therefore seek to suspend ourselves in the moment. How? By listening to our partner and responding honestly. The real joy of Actions is that they lay down a sub-textual structure that supports the text and music whilst allowing you to vary *how* you play them from one rehearsal, or performance, to the next. If you are playing Figaro, you can also help define your partner's Action by providing her with an obstacle; for example, by taking a breath to begin to say something, compelling Susanna to have to stop you.

2. SINGING

- Next, speak your Action in a neutral tone out loud, as before. This time, immediately following this, physicalise the Action whilst *speaking* the particular line from the score. The répétiteur will need to play the phrase and then stop, to allow you time to speak the next Action you are about to do. The répétiteur will then continue to play the next phrase, whilst you sing and Action. Remember that at all times you are using the words and music to *do* something; they are as integral a part of an Action as the physical action you make.

- Next, the répétiteur plays the entire scene without stopping; speak each Action (*I (transitive verb) you*) whilst physicalising the Action, in the part of the music where you would normally sing the line. This connects the particular Actions to the musical score.

- Next, ask a colleague who is not in the scene to be your Action's Coach. Hand over your score with your Actions written under each line or phrase; they will feed you your Actions just before you sing and physicalise your Action.

- Finally, play the scene.

Note: As an 'Actions Coach' you need to time the delivery of the Action you are feeding. Where an Action begins and ends with the music is crucial.

This process might seem lengthy but you are always *doing*; constantly informing your internal thoughts through external action. Through repetition, you will be exploring possibilities within each Action and, simultaneously, reinforcing your emotional response to them.

As an extension of this process, Stanislavski suggests doing the whole opera without speaking or singing words . . . just doing your physical Actions.[34] Even if you just do a scene in this way, you will notice how you crave having the words and music to use as your tools to attain your wants.

The director you are working with will determine how the time is used in rehearsals, so these following exercises can be used as part of the process in the rehearsal room, in workshops with fellow singers, or as preparation for a role. When doing any exercises with

---

[34] Stanislavski, K. (1981) *Creating a Role*. Translated by E. R. Hapgood. London: Eyre Methuen, p. 231.

Actions, the key is to aim to remain flexible and responsive. Your Actions will change in response to the director, conductor, other characters' Objectives and the more you get to know your own character. Actions will always give you a range of options, a list of possibilities, to *play*.

EXERCISE: *The Shoe*
Pairs/Group/2 mins

- Each participant in the group selects an individual Action that they want to *do* to the group. They do not share these with anyone else in the group.

- Then, one by one, everyone in the group removes a shoe with the Action they have decided upon.

- At the end of the exercise, report back what you *saw* each person *doing* to the group with the way they removed their shoe.

- This exercise is a great place to begin; it encourages you to use your body and make the Actions physical.

EXERCISE: *Actions Gym*
Pairs/15 mins

- Stand opposite your partner. A goes first, speaking an Action at the same time as *doing* it to their partner: for example, saying 'I dismiss you', 'I comfort you', 'I welcome you', 'I hurry you', whilst at the same time physically *dismissing, comforting, welcoming, hurrying* their partner. B remains receptive and open to what A does to them.

A few things to consider as you do this:

- Start in a physically neutral position.

- Give yourself a context; ask, 'Why might I want to *dismiss* my partner?'

- Find the natural start and end of the Action.

- Avoid apologising to your partner when doing a 'harsh' Action by editing the end of the Action.

- Explore how you can use the words you have, 'I dismiss you', to actually dismiss your partner.

- Use your body and the space to *do* the Action. How do you move towards your partner? How do you orientate yourself to them? What speed do you move? Get the action into your toes and play it boldly.

- If B feels that A was convincing in executing their Action, then swap over. If not, A goes again, exploring other ways of doing the same Action.

- Then, repeat the exercise, only this time without speaking the Action; using only your body and the space. Your partner feeds back what they saw you *do*.

- Then, choose a line from the libretto, for example, 'Here's an end to your life as a rover!'[35] Repeat the exercise; this time, only speak this line of text and use your body and the space to *do* your Action.
- How many different ways can you *do* this Action whilst speaking this text?

EXERCISE: *The Play-in*
Solo/10 mins

Construct a bridge into the moment you begin to sing.

- Select an aria, for example, Cherubino's Act Two aria 'Tell Me What Love Is'.
- Listen to the play-in to the aria; in this example, there are eight bars before Cherubino sings.
- What might Cherubino be thinking? Write a monologue of Cherubino's thoughts for these eight bars. Imagine Mozart is underscoring this monologue; the text needs to fit the music.
- Next, Action the text of your monologue. For every line of text, determine an Action.
- Try speaking the text of the monologue aloud during the play-in.
- Then, try speaking and doing the Actions.
- Then, try speaking the text whilst doing the Actions.
- Finally, just do the Actions without speaking.

The aim is to form a connection between the character's thoughts, external action and the music.

EXERCISE: *The Interior Film*
Solo/Ongoing

If you are singing an aria where nobody else is onstage you could create a film in your mind's eye to respond to; this film could be a past event, a fantasy or a projection of a possible future depending upon the subject of the aria.

Looking again at the Count's Act 3 aria; if you were playing the Count, you might picture the scene between yourself and Susanna. This interior film playing out in your mind's eye can be constructed in whatever style best suits your character's situation and the music you are singing or responding to. You are the director and editor of this film; you choose exactly where in the music to cut from one image to the next, to zoom into close-up, or to pan across the imagined scene and at what speed. The filters, colours and form of your film – whether it be montage, wildly expressionistic or naturalistic – will all be informed by the nature of the music and your character's specific and changing thoughts.

---

[35] *The Marriage of Figaro*, Figaro, No. 9 Aria 'Here's an end to your life as a rover '/'Non più andrai'.

An Action aims to, in some way, change your target; it's vital, therefore, that you connect to your target in order to do so. Only by connecting to your target will you be able to assess the success, or otherwise, of your Action in helping to achieving your *want*.

I was assistant director to the opera and theatre director Richard Jones at ENO and the Royal Shakespeare Company. Richard always emphasised how important it was for singers and actors to point their feet in the direction of their target; the direction led to an actor's direct engagement with their target. However, when singing in a large theatre with an orchestra, it might not always be possible to do this. How do you remain in contact with your target, whilst not looking directly at your target? For example, when you reject someone, you might find yourself turning your back to them; the Action, 'I reject you', is still directed to them. This next exercise engages your imagination to help you remain connected with targets when not directly orientated to them.

EXERCISE: *Connecting Targets*
Solo/3 mins

- Touch a point on a wall on one side of a room; point A.
- Walk directly to another point on the opposite side of the room; point B. As you do so, imagine a line is being drawn from the centre of your back to the point you are walking away from; point A.
- Touch point B. Your back is still connected to point A by the imaginary line.
- Turn to focus on another spot in the room; point C. As you walk to point C, continue to imagine the line between point A and point B and now also draw a line from the centre of your back to point B.
- Repeat this exercise but now, as you walk away from a particular point (drawing the imaginary line between your back and this point) sing a long continuous note, sending it behind you so that it marks the journey of the imaginary line.

Repeat Exercise: Actions Gym (p. 102), but this time try Actions whilst orientated away from your target. Explore how you stay connected. Does the part of your body closest to your target appear more alert? Is this part of the body more receptive to the possibilities of change?

EXERCISE: *Comparing Actions*
Solo/Ongoing

We have looked at the importance of bringing yourself to the role; the idea of 'I am'. This exercise compares your own perceived response to a situation with your character's. It helps you to identify the similarities and differences between you and your character and is useful to do towards the beginning of a rehearsal process.

- Write down a list of physical actions you would undertake if you found yourself in the situation of your role. For example, what if you were getting married today and discovered your very powerful employer, in a world where few jobs exist, had been trying to seduce your fiancée?

- Now, do the same work with the operatic role: list all of the simple Actions your character undertakes in the plot. For example, we can list the simple Actions Figaro does: he avoids listening to Susanna, he suspects Susanna, he listens to Susanna, he questions Susanna, he questions the Count.

- Compare the similarities and differences between your imagined Actions and those of your character. Highlight the points where your Actions differ and ask yourself what different circumstances or character traits might account for this.

Understanding the cycle of interaction – the interplay of receiving Actions, making the decision to respond and then executing an Action – is important in opera when the speed of this process of interaction is dictated by the composer. Even when words are repeated in an aria (Handel's arias being the foremost example), the composer is often unlocking the processes of the mind and giving each stage of the process a moment of expression through a line of music. This simple exercise helps make the thought process physical and therefore more tangible.

EXERCISE: *Clap and Response*
Group/5 mins

- The group move freely around the space.

- One person begins by targeting somebody else in the space and then sending a clap towards them. A clap must have a clear path to its target but the way in which a clap travels to another person can vary; the journey of a clap could be short, sharp and direct or long and arching.

- The person receiving the clap must, together with the person who sent the clap, follow its journey through space. The receiver must clap as the clap completes its journey to them.

- They then target somebody else in the space and send the clap on a different kind of journey to the new target.

- You can, in addition, send a word, at the same time as you send the clap; the word might be spoken sharply or elongated depending upon the nature of the journey. The receiver should clap and repeat the word in exactly the same way as it was sent. They should then send a new word and clap to a new target. The process of clapping/ thoughts breaks down like this:

  - 1st Clap – you *receive* information (an action from another character).

  - Look to find a Target – you make the *decision* to respond. And breathe.

  - 2nd Clap – you *(re)act* in response to the first clap.

SUMMARY

- An Action is something you *do,* usually to another character, to change them, in order to get your *want*.
- It emerges through a connection with your character's Given Circumstances as an impulse to act upon your desires.
- The music and words you sing are your tools to attain your Objective.
- An Action will always have a target.
- Actions provide structure and, within this, freedom.
- Actions stop you aiming to emote.

TO DO

- Study the music to determine what Actions you might be doing.
- Write down, under each line you sing, 'I (transitive verb) you'.
- Use pencil so you can change and adapt your Action as you respond to others.
- Work with a colleague as an Actions Coach to prompt your Actions, just before you take a breath to sing.

Obstacles

An Obstacle is something stopping you achieving your Objective. Obstacles exist internally, within a character, and externally, in the world around them. They define *how* you achieve your want by determining and shaping your Actions. If you want something, whatever you need to *do* to get it will be dependent upon the very thing preventing you from getting it.

Obstacles heighten your Objectives by raising the stakes for your character. If a character wants something and faces no Obstacles, then the stakes are incredibly low; the character's want is immediately satisfied. If a character faces a number of Obstacles, the chances of them achieving their want become lower, the risk of failure greater and, in turn, the stakes increase. Well-chosen Obstacles help create the story itself; all dramatic tension arises from the interplay between a character's Objectives, the Obstacles they face and the Actions they take to overcome them.

Obstacles can be found in three different places:

- *External Circumstances*

  These are environmental obstacles; obstacles found outside of the character and their relationships with others. They can often appear, seemingly, out of nowhere. For example, earthquakes, bad weather, delayed transport, faulty objects, acts of god/s. They are the very essence of the plot-heavy Hollywood disaster movie (a towering inferno, an extraordinary tidal wave, an imminent meteor) or the slapstick comedy (garden rakes, a trail of marbles, a collapsing car).

Act Four of *The Marriage of Figaro* takes place outside at night. This provides External Obstacles for certain characters attempting to make secret assignations but unclear of who exactly they are making them with. Of course, night-time might well be considered a metaphor at the climax of the opera, and in many stories external obstacles – storms, tempests, lightning bolts – have metaphorical significance.

- *Other Characters*

  Very simply: one character wants something from another, and the other does not want to (or cannot give) it to them. This is the essential conceit of most drama, the tactical interplay between characters, and often one character's Objective is another character's Obstacle.

  These Obstacles can play out in the smallest of moments. For example, in *The Marriage of Figaro*, Susanna wants Marcellina to go through the door first and Marcellina wants the opposite. Alternatively, they can drive the action of the entire story. The Count wants to sleep with Susanna; Susanna, Figaro and the Countess do not want him to.

- *Internal Obstacles*

  These are the internal conflicts most characters carry within them. They work in direct opposition to the character's Objectives by hindering, or preventing, them from achieving their overall goal. A character might be unaware of certain Internal Obstacles; their core beliefs will often contain contradictory or opposing ideas. Counter-Objectives fit firmly within this category; they directly conflict with the character's Super-Objective and often result in an uneven, swerving path to the fulfilment of an ambition.

  Internal Obstacles often come into sharp focus in arias. For example:

  - In the Countess's Act Two aria she wants to find the way to get the Count to love her but she wants to protect herself from rejection (so much so, that she is singing about the possibility of death).

  - During the Count's Act Three aria, he wants to explore how to revenge Susanna (and Figaro) but he also wants to get Susanna to want him.

In any scene, these three sets of Obstacles – External, Other Characters, Internal – might present themselves simultaneously. Alternatively, the focus might be entirely on one all-consuming Obstacle. It is up to you (and your collaborators) to choose which Obstacle you highlight at any given moment; the selection should seek to provoke the greatest dramatic tension.

Most Obstacles take a series of Actions to overcome. Once the protagonist in an opera has conquered the major Obstacles, or alternatively been vanquished by these same Obstacles, the opera will come to an end (in Mozart's case usually with a closing chorus!).

Notes about Obstacles

- *Obstacles and Objectives:* When directly faced with an Obstacle, new Objectives begin to take shape. Obstacles help deepen and layer a character's desire and provide the stimulus for change within the character.

- *Obstacles and Actions:* Obstacles bring clarity and definition to Actions. They sharpen the tools you use to get what you want. Actions need the definition and specificity that a real engagement with an Obstacle demands. If Actions are generalised and unfocused they lack vitality and life. Any lack of focus is only heightened by their running in parallel with a musical score of extraordinary detail, clarity, directness and certainty.

  My experience of working with singers is that when the Obstacles are strong and present, the tools to overcome them are similarly defined. Thoughts are clearer, movements more detailed and words more important; the tools combine to carve out an Objective, in opposition to an Obstacle.

  Chapter 6: Words and Music in Action looks at how we make Obstacles solid, visceral elements to engage with and fight against and, in turn, how this engagement brings definition to words, diction, music, movement and emotional experience.

- *Obstacles and Adaptation:* Obstacles challenge the imagination to engage in new approaches to overcome the hurdles they present. They ensure the character is constantly *present* by demanding continual adjustments and adaptations to the variety of Obstacles that challenge the character. Certain Obstacles, for example, might create the need for a character to hide a particular desire which will, in turn, heat or intensify it by restricting the possibility of a direct outlet. Further adaptation will be necessary to attain a hidden desire; the Obstacle will force ever more imaginative Actions under pressure.

- *Obstacles and music:* The music, as always, guides us. Look again at the Count's aria in Act Three;[36] the shift in the music between the first and second bar is extraordinary. The *forte* strings and woodwind give way to *piano* strings and flute. The opposition present within the music directs you to the Internal Obstacles within the character.

  One of Figaro's Internal Obstacles is his inability to trust women. The terror of being cuckolded is marked in the music by the repeated motif of the three horns in the orchestra representing cuckoldry.

- *Obstacles sustain arias and duets:* In certain arias you might repeat the same single line many, many times; why? This is the question you must ask for every line and every phrase; the answer is that the character must *need* to sing because they have not yet achieved their Objective because something is *stopping* them.

  For example, an External Obstacle might help sustain a long love duet; the presence of other people, or a series of physical challenges with a prop, keeping the lovers from uniting. An Internal Obstacle might arise from their desire not to break the moment or the nagging doubt about their lover's true desires.

  Sometimes, it is necessary to work as a dramaturg and construct Obstacles within an aria to give the character a reason to continue to sing. We will look at Handel arias in detail later[37] but it is often necessary to introduce External Obstacles, or the physical manifestation of an Internal Obstacle, to make clear the need to continue to sing.

---

[36] See Actions (p. 99).
[37] Chapter 9: Rehearsals in Depth.

- *Obstacles help your partner:* If you are onstage during another character's aria, it might be useful to consider the aria a duet (or an ensemble if more characters are present). Ask: How can I help my partner continue to *need* to sing? How might I present an Obstacle to their wants? How might this develop and change throughout the scene? This work, of course, will help define your character's Objective.

- *Obstacles and layers:* Internal Obstacles create complex layers of characterisation. Seek out the seeming contradictions within your character; the benevolence of the Count, the frivolity of the Countess.

- *Obstacles and drama*: Obstacles are the very stuff of life; we find catharsis in seeing the struggles we face in life, reflected back in the character's life on stage. *How* the characters change in order to overcome the Obstacles they face is what truly engages an audience.

EXAMPLE: *Marriage of Figaro*

Figaro and Susanna, No. 2 Duet 'Supposing one evening the Countess should need you'/'Se a caso madama la notte ti chiama'.

Susanna's Objective might be to awaken Figaro to the cravings of the Count, however she faces a number of possible Obstacles. Firstly, Figaro's lack of understanding. Secondly, her Through-Line Objective to enjoy her wedding day; she might want to scream at Figaro but this Internal Obstacle tempers her Actions. Thirdly, she might be aware of the External Obstacle of other people in the house; she might want to be more forceful in alerting Figaro but, at the same time, she is cautious of arousing the suspicions of other characters. The dynamics in the duet, shifting from *piano* 'Ding, ding!' to *forte* 'Dong, dong!', as well as being a rhetorical device to wake Figaro, might arise from these Obstacles; the External Obstacle of other people prompting Susanna to keep quiet, overpowered by her Objective to wake Figaro up.

EXERCISE: *Your Obstacles*
Solo/5 mins

Explore the range of Obstacles you face in your own life in trying to achieve a certain ambition.

- Write down an Objective you are pursuing in your life.
- Reflect upon the Obstacles that might prevent you from getting your *want*; classify them as External, Other People or Internal.
- Then consider the various Actions you do to work around the Obstacles.

If you are currently creating a character, find an Objective which might be similar to an Objective they hold. Then compare Obstacles and Actions on both lists. This helps bring you closer to your character and identifies those areas you need to further research.

SUMMARY

- Obstacles work in direct conflict with your Objectives to prevent you from attaining your Objective.
- Obstacles fall into three types: External, Other Characters and Internal.
- The composer often alerts you to these three different types of Obstacles.
- Obstacles help to form and shape your Objectives and Actions.
- Your Objectives are often your partner's Obstacles and vice versa.

TO DO

- For every proposed Objective (Scene/Through-Line/Super-Objective) ask, 'What is in my way?'
- When doing this ask, 'What heightens my struggle?'
- Write down each proposed Obstacle under your Objectives in your score.
- Consider what you need to do (Actions) specifically in relation to these particular Obstacles.
- Research! Seek to better understand the psychology of human behaviour in order to provide more detailed possibilities for the part you are playing.
- Look at Chapter 6: Words and Music in Action for further exercises exploring Obstacles.

Points of Concentration

A Point of Concentration (POC) is a way of actively engaging with the Given Circumstances of the world of the opera. It is a process of bringing your attention to one particular theme or Fact in the opera and allowing your thoughts about this to permeate your experience of playing the scene. By *applying* Given Circumstances and exploring many different Points of Concentration in rehearsal, you begin a process of layering your experience of the world; enriching your imaginative engagement with the world of the opera *on your feet* and with your fellow cast members.

A Point of Concentration will, consciously or subconsciously, warm up your Objectives by digging deeper into the world and giving your wants further stimuli. This, in turn, will affect the way you play your Actions; you might feel you are playing your Actions in a different key. Points of Concentration may also reveal additional psychological layers that are suggested in the orchestration.

Exploring Points of Concentration is a way of allowing your thoughts time to turn over a Given Circumstance and to then experience these thoughts *within* the scene. You cannot plan your response to a Point of Concentration; it will arouse new and unexpected impulses within you and between you and your partners. It is a tremendous way of liberating and freeing your response to the text.

You can bring your attention to:

- Individual Points of Concentration; Given Circumstances that only you choose to focus upon in the scene.

- Shared Points of Concentration; that all characters within the scene will bring their awareness to.

Points of Concentration can include bringing attention to particular:

- Themes and Ideas
- Environmental Facts
- Past Events (immediate or distant)
- Proposed future Events (immediate or distant)
- Other characters and relationships.

It worth noting that director Declan Donnellan prefers to call them *Points of Awareness*,[38] believing that to *concentrate* on one thing excludes all others; Points of Concentration are not an invitation to, furrowed brow, squeeze all conscious thought onto one point. They are instead an invitation to allow your imagination to roam over all the territory connected to a particular Given Circumstance.

Again, Stanislavski most eloquently summed it up when addressing opera singers training at his Studio in Moscow: 'Now go to work, dig down deeper into the song, enhance the highlights and the shadows the way painters do. Stick close to the focal point of your concentrated attention on which your vision is riveted and leave all the rest to be worked out by your subconscious.'[39]

Notes about Points of Concentration

Points of Concentration help to:

- Keep scenes fresh. The challenge for the singer, through rehearsals and performance, is to 'see' and 'hear' things on stage anew, in order to bring spontaneity to a performance. By choosing to see the world through the new lens or filter of a particular Given Circumstance, you will no doubt alight upon new thoughts and ideas in the world of the opera as a consequence.
- Sustain a long performance run. In such circumstances, I will often give a cast a new Shared Point of Concentration for each performance.
- Revitalise a revival of a production and re-energise an audition aria;[40] an over-familiarity with material can deaden it and Points of Concentration help breathe fresh life into it.
- Keep you present within a scene. Too often a Point of Concentration for a performer is the audience and how a performance might be affecting them (or not!).[41] Points of Concentration help to re-orientate you in the world of the opera, giving you less time to consider the audience.

---

[38] Donnellan, D. (2005) *The Actor and the Target*. London: Nick Hern Books.
[39] Stanislavski, K. (1998) *Stanislavski on Opera*. Translated by E. R. Hapgood. London: Routledge, p. 17.
[40] See Chapter 11: Auditions.
[41] See Chapter 11: Auditions.

EXAMPLE: *The Marriage of Figaro*

Here are some possible Points of Concentration to explore in scenes from *Figaro*:

Act One Scene One: Figaro and Susanna prepare for their wedding day.
Shared POC:

- The wedding (the arrangements that still have to be put in place, the people who will be there).
- The time of day; maybe it's 6 am and they both went to bed at 1 am busy preparing for the big day.
- The work they have to do in the house.
- Sex.

Individual POC:

- Susanna: The Count and Basilio/Her first date with Figaro/Her family.
- Figaro: The contract with Marcellina/Money (or lack thereof) and status/His family.

Act Three Scene Two: The Countess and Susanna compose a letter to the Count to arrange a meeting between him and Susanna later that evening.
Shared POC:

- The pinewoods.
- The Count.
- Work relationship.
- The wedding.
- Sex.
- Those who live and work in the house.

Individual POC:

- Susanna: Figaro/Status.
- Countess: Status/Marriage.

EXERCISE: *Point Of Concentration Improvisation*
Rehearsal/Performance

- Before running a scene determine what Point of Concentration to focus upon; is this individual or shared?
- Spend three or four minutes thinking about the Point of Concentration: make present any pictures or thoughts about it. Allow your imagination to roam.
- Walk with these thoughts; allow them to inform how you move.
- Begin to play the scene, focusing on your Objectives but carrying these thoughts with you.

- At the end of the scene: What do you notice? What new thoughts arose through the playing of the scene? How did this Point of Concentration connect to the music; did it connect you or pull you away from the musical tone of the scene?
- Repeat this exercise with a new Point of Concentration; don't immediately return to the same one, as you might start to force thoughts in an attempt to recapture what you have previously discovered.

EXERCISE: *Concentration of Attention*
Solo/Group/Ongoing

In Chapter 1: The Foundations we looked at the importance of heightening your awareness to the world around you. Exercise: Circles of Attention (p. 28) is one way of exploring this.

A similarly useful exercise is to imbue objects within the world of the opera with an imaginary life that in some way resonates for the character. For example, your character might wear a wedding ring that connects to memories of their wedding day or there might be a guitar reminding them of the first time they kissed their fiancé. Throughout rehearsals you can endow these objects with meaning by creating these pictures and memories that link them to the character's experiences.

In performance, you will then be surrounded by numerous Points of Concentration; objects that help draw you back into the life of the character. The more you detail these images in your mind's eye, the richer the experience of connecting with the objects.

SUMMARY

- A Point of Concentration is a way of making the Given Circumstances of the opera active.
- They change the filter through which you see your character's world and thus affect the way you seek your Objectives.
- They will connect your Actions to the tone of the music in different ways.
- They are to be *layered* throughout rehearsals to enrich and enliven your imaginative reality.

TO DO

- As you work through the scenes of the opera select Given Circumstances that can become Points of Concentration.
- Throughout rehearsals explore different Points exploring the varying textures they bring to the playing of the scene.
- Play your Objectives; don't allow the Points of Concentration to overwhelm them.

Events

An Event is a significant moment of change in the action of the opera; a moment that incites a new Objective to form for all characters present in the scene.

You want to achieve an Objective, something unexpected occurs, you change your Objective in response to this; the Event is the moment something happens to change your Objective. Events are like 'sign posts along a road';[42] identifying them serves to signal the formation of a new Objective for the character.

These turning points in the scene are often signalled in opera by a shift in the music. These shifts often suggest the length of time an Event takes. Events have different lengths; from the time it takes somebody to appear unexpectedly from a cupboard, to the dawning realisation of a deception. Correspondingly, an Event might be marked in the music by one striking chord or change of key, whilst others might emerge more slowly through shifting dynamics or gradual change of tempi; *rallentando* or *accelerando*.[43] These shifts in the music marking Events often mirror the thought processes of the characters.

Some Events will only be discerned from the libretto. For example, Events occurring during simple recitative will not usually be marked by a change in the music. Contrastingly, a significant musical shift might take place, whilst the libretto suggests no apparent change; the music brings our attention to a change within the scene that perhaps the characters are not commenting upon at that moment.

By identifying Events we begin to divide the opera into tangible parts, each separated from the next by a significant moment of change. By forming an agreement with your fellow cast members as to where exactly each Event begins and ends, Events collectively begin to form the spine of the story.

By giving a name to each of these Events, labelling them to denote their significance in the story of the opera, we begin to create a tangible sub-textual score that sits in parallel to the musical score.

Not every change in situation is an Event; the change must generate new Objectives for those characters present. For example, when a character enters a room it can sometimes cause you to stop what you are doing and sometimes create no significant change.

Notes about Events

- As you work through the score mark an Ⓔ in pencil whenever you see an Event in your score.
- Ideally, do this in rehearsals with the rest of the cast as it means you are all working together to identify where all your characters need to change Objectives. As a result, you can work together to represent these changes as clearly as possible. If nothing changes in a story or, just as importantly, if this change is muddied, the engagement of the audience risks being broken.

---

[42] Stanislavski, K. (1981) *Creating a Role*. Translated by E. R. Hapgood. London: Eyre Methuen, p. 148.
[43] *Rallentando*, a gradual slowing down. *Accelerando*, a gradual speeding up.

- It is still worth doing this process by yourself as it helps you identify the big shifts in the story. It creates a channel, with markers and signals, through which you can navigate the Through-Line of the opera.

- There will be other smaller shifts that prompt individual characters to change their individual Objective; we looked at these *Units* of Objectives in the Objectives section (p. 79). Make a note of these.

- Once you have marked all the Events in the opera, and given each of these a name, make these Events part of *your* story. The story is driven and defined by those moments that change Objectives.

EXAMPLE: *The Marriage of Figaro*

Let us take a look at an Event that is clearly marked in both the music and the libretto; the point in the Act Two finale of *Figaro* when Susanna steps out of the cupboard, at the same moment when the Count and Countess are expecting to discover Cherubino.

- The Count's Objective, having retrieved the key to open the cupboard, might be: *I want to* reveal Cherubino to shame my wife or, more simply, *I want to* kill Cherubino.

- The Countess's Objective might be: *I want to* calm the Count or *I want to* protect Cherubino.

- Susanna's Objective: *I want to* hold my nerve.

Figure 4.6
Events
illustration.

The music before the Event gives us a clear sense of *how* the Count and Countess might be pursuing their Objectives. The beginning of the Event is marked with a two-and-a-half beats rest. This is the very moment the Count must open the door to reveal Susanna.

The Event continues; we hear a *piano* phrase in the orchestra marking the moment the Count *registers* the Event, 'Susanna'. The Countess takes longer to register the Event; the same phrase is repeated to score the process of the Countess registering her maid, 'Susanna'.

The Event completes. We might label this EVENT: Susanna's Reveal.

What new Objectives are formed after the Event? The music seems to suggests Susanna's Action; it is controlled, considered. The instruction, *Andante con moto (Slowly, but with motion),* also supports this. The music has a quality of suspension, especially in contrast to the fury of the strings before the Event; could this suggest that the Count and Countess's Actions are more internal, that they are *doing* less externally?

- Maybe the Count and Countess share their new Objective: *I want to* work out what's going on.

- Susanna's new Objective might be: *I want to* act as though nothing has happened.

THE MAJOR PRE-OPERA EVENT

Every opera will have a major Event that occurs before the action of the opera begins. It will inform the world of the opera and the way in which the story unfolds. It is important to consider how your character was affected by this pre-opera Event.

In *The Marriage of Figaro* the major pre-opera Event might be the engagement of Figaro and Susanna. More immediately, it might be the news that Susanna has received, that the Count is regretting relinquishing the *Droit du Seigneur,*[44] or it could be the moment the Count gifts Figaro and Susanna the bedroom next to his own.

THE FIRST SIGNIFICANT EVENT

This will always fall in the first act of an opera and is the moment the foundations of the established world begin to shift.

In *Figaro* it is the moment Figaro finally realises that the Count is pursuing Susanna. Where this Event begins and ends is clear from listening to the music. The Event takes quite a long time, the whole length of Susanna's verse in reply to Figaro during their second Duet in Act One.

EXAMPLE: *The Marriage of Figaro*

- EVENT: Figaro's Realisation

Susanna:
Supposing one morning the Count were to call you,

---

[44] The *Droit du Seigneur* is a supposed legal right in medieval Europe allowing feudal lords to have sexual relations with women of a lower class. It is not clear that this ever actually existed but it is a terrifying literary device which defines much of the action in *Figaro* and serves as a metaphor for the ongoing class and gender relations.

our sweet little Count were to call you.
Ding ding! Ding ding!
And to send you a long way away.
Ding ding! Dong **dong!**
If he wants me he knows where to find me; he'll
be there behind me.

- Listen to the music; the Event begins with the shift of music as Susanna's melody mirrors Figaro's, albeit in a minor key variation of the same melody.[45] Maybe at this point Figaro senses something is happening. The Event lasts until the horns underscore Susanna's 'Dong dong!':[46] the moment the Event finally culminates, with Figaro's realisation landing rather heavily alongside the horns (introducing the idea of cuckoldry).

    If we were only to analyse Da Ponte's words, without the music, it would be less clear where the Event was; indeed, we might even suppose that the Event landed on the following two lines, 'If he wants me he knows where to find me; he'll be there behind me'.

- The possible Objectives before, and after, the Event might be:

Figaro: I want to promote the benefits of this room.	**EVENT: Figaro's Realisation**	*Figaro:* I want to avoid anything that arouses my sexual jealousies.
Susanna: I want to lead you to an understanding of what's been happening.		*Susanna:* I want you to share the horror of this situation.

THE MAJOR ACT EVENT

Every Act will have one major Event, the significant turning point of the Act.

Each production will decide which Event it wishes to emphasise. In Act Two of *Figaro*, for example, it might be the Count's discovery of the Countess's locked door.

THE OPERA'S MAJOR EVENT

Every opera will have a major Event; it might take time to discern but working this out will give you a sense of where the Through-Line is driving towards. It will also lead you to ask if the Major Event causes a break in your character's Through-Line.

Every production will be defined by the Events it chooses to bring particular attention to. It is important you understand how the emphasis you and your collaborators bring to the story affects your character.

---

[45] This occurs on *The Marriage of Figaro* (Chandos) CD 1, track 4, 0.39 s.
[46] *The Marriage of Figaro* (Chandos) CD 1, track 4, 1 m 03 s.

The MGM Rule

Every Event suggests a change of Objective; the greater the change, from one Objective to the next, the greater the drama. The importance of identifying Events was highlighted by a story that director Nicholas Hytner told whilst I was assisting him on his production of Philip Pullman's *His Dark Materials* at the National Theatre. He recalled his first day on set of the very first film he directed in Hollywood and a producer's reassurance, 'Don't worry – it'll all be fine, so long as you remember the MGM rule'. Nick didn't know the MGM rule. Apparently, it goes like this:

If you are directing a scene in an office and a secretary is about to receive some bad news, make sure, as the secretary taps away on the computer's keyboard, that outside the sun is shining, the office junior has just brought them a coffee, the boss has just complimented them on their work. The phone rings. The secretary picks up the phone. They receive the news their father has died.

Conversely, if you are directing a scene and the secretary is about to receive some good news, ensure that outside it is raining, that the coffee has just spilt over them and that the boss has just landed an extra pile of work on their desk. The phone rings. The secretary picks up the phone. They have won the lottery.

As a creator of stories, you need to be aware of the possible decisions you can make to heighten the drama. Of course, you are not designing the *mise en scène* – it's not your call if it is raining outside or not – but you can help determine certain Given Circumstances and explore how they raise the stakes for the Objectives you play. Find Objectives to play that go on a big journey from one Event to the next; Objectives that are clearly changed by an Event.

Shared Units

Each part of the libretto or score through which one particular Objective is sought is referred to as a Unit. As Events are moments of shared change (the Objectives of all characters present are affected), we can call the section between each Event a Shared Unit.

Labelling

Events create the spine of the narrative; a sequence of turning points, triggering new Objectives. By labelling each of these Events, giving each Event a specific title, we begin to define *our* story.

It is also incredibly useful to collaborate with your team to label each act of the opera in the same way. 'Act One' denotes nothing in particular but, for example, *The Discovery of the Count's Mission* begins to make the story, *your* story.

EXERCISE: *Montage*
Rehearsal/5 mins

- Having decided upon the pre-opera Event and the major Act Events, create still 'snapshots' of each of these moments.

- If you can work with the répétiteur to do this, ask them to play the lead-up to the Event. As the Event approaches all cast members walk into the scene playing the Objective they are seeking at this moment. As the Event lands (and as all the singers arrive in the space), find an attitude to the Event in character and freeze. Hold the 'snapshot' for five seconds and leave the scene carrying your new Objective.
- Do not plan the 'snapshot' you are about to create. Respond in the moment and in silence.
- By the end of the exercise you will have a collective series of snapshots of the major turning points in the opera. Of course, these will change as you work through the piece but they may give you some initial thoughts about the shifting relationships between characters and the way in which the plot develops.

Improvisation frees the performer to respond spontaneously to dramatic events. For the singer, this means that time is no longer governed by the score; you are liberated to respond instinctively in the moment. The process can therefore be useful as a way of exploring reflex physical reactions to Events; in scripted or scored performances there can be a tendency to restrict the range and scale of our physical responses in an attempt to appear 'natural' or, conversely, to embellish them in an attempt match the scale of the music.

Events help to structure an improvisation. They provide a pathway for a scene to develop, marked out by clearly defined turning points each signalling a change of Objective. At the same time, the exact moment of an Event in an improvisation is unplanned, thus affording the freedom for impulsive responses.

The following exercise provides the framework to explore the ideas in the opera by establishing an improvisation, structured through Events, based on a real-life incident linking thematically to the opera. This provides the opportunity to explore *how* we might instinctively respond to such ideas; our reflex physical impulses unrestrained by the relative confines of a score. The responses to these associated themes, experienced in the improvisation, can then inform the possible behaviours of those characters in the opera experiencing a similar situation.

The exercise is also a useful way to become familiar with working with Events.

EXERCISE: *Events Improvisation*
Group/15 mins

- Choose a theme from *Figaro*. Let us imagine you are playing Cherubino and want to explore the theme of unrequited love.
- Cast your mind back to a time in your own life when you experienced or witnessed unrequited love. It is useful if the memory you select occurred in one geographical location. Also, avoid particularly traumatic territory.
- Replay this memory for yourself and identify the Events in the memory. Begin and end your memory wherever you like but limit the number of Events to no more than five.

- Determine how many actors you need to relive this memory and cast from your team.
- Tell your team the Given Circumstances of the memory: the size of the space, the objects in the space, the exact location of any doors or windows, the time of day, the weather.
- Give them brief details about relationship histories.
- Tell them about the Immediate Circumstances; what has just happened before the first Event.
- Tell them the Events; label the Events.
- Suggest the Objectives for each person in the scene before, and after, each Event.
- Mention any particular Obstacles that characters might face.
- Give your team a minute to ask any Questions.

Without any rehearsal, your team will play the scene. Note that you have not given them any dialogue to say (unless one of your Events features an exact line of text). Your team will use the words they need to get their Objective.

The rest of the room should observe. Ask, were the Facts of the world clear? Can you distinguish the scene Events? What were the physical responses to Events?

EXERCISE: *Scene Improvisation* Rehearsal

Translate the work from the previous exercise into the opera, if possible, at an early stage of rehearsal.

- Read through your scene and determine, with the rest of cast, the Events of the opera.
- Label these Events.
- Pitch possible Objectives before and after each Event.
- You should already know the Given Circumstances of the world at this point so remind yourself of these; cover relationship histories and the immediate pre-scene circumstances.
- Ask which Obstacles might be present for your character in this scene.

Now play the scene without reference to the score. You will, no doubt, have already learned the words and music. However, in this improvisation you will only be speaking. I have noticed how often words slip from the memory when not allied to music. However, do not worry about this during this exercise; simply focus on playing your Objectives, and changing your Objectives in response to each Event.

What do you notice when you do this? How important do the words seem? Are the Events provoking a real change in your Objective? Are there any Facts of the world which appear unclear? Question with rigour and answer honestly.

I understand that these exercises might sometimes be difficult for you to suggest in certain rehearsal rooms. However, in training young singers to develop as collaborative creative artists I have found it tremendously useful for them to have an understanding of possible processes. This exercise is tremendously useful to allow you the time to focus on the parallel score you are creating; the score of Events, Objectives, Actions and Obstacles.

SUMMARY

- An Event is a turning point; a moment in a scene that affects all characters present in that scene by changing what they *want*.
- An Event can be found in the music, the libretto or both.
- Events vary in duration.
- A Shared Unit is the part of the score between Events distinguished by certain Objectives.

TO DO

- Engage your colleagues; work through the entire score, marking Events with Ⓔ.
- Give each Event a distinct name.
- Label each Act.
- Prioritise Events; pre-opera, first significant Event, the major Act Event, the major opera Event.

Further Text Tools

Emotion Memory

Emotion (or Affective) Memory is not a tool I would use in my process with singers. I refer to it as it was a substantial part of Stanislavski's earlier acting toolkit, prior to his later emphasis on physical Actions. It was, however, adopted by many twentieth-century practitioners and is therefore something you might have heard about; I think it might therefore be worth covering briefly. I am also aware that certain performers have found it useful in helping to connect to the emotional life of the character. Amongst the most influential advocates of Emotion Memory were those proponents of what became known as *Method Acting*: Lee Strasberg and Uta Hagen.

Emotion Memory has its roots in the work of French psychologist Théodule-Armand Ribot. Working at the same time as Stanislavski, Ribot identified that emotions could be triggered by the process of memory; the reliving of a past event, with particular emphasis on the recall of the five senses (referred to as Sense Memory). At its core is the idea that you are both internally and externally affected by memory. Stanislavski, early on in the development of his continually evolving system, suggested that 'feelings drawn from our actual experience (could be) transferred to our part – giving life to the play'.[47]

---

[47] Stanislavski, K. (1980) *An Actor Prepares*. Translated by E. R. Hapgood. London: Eyre Methuen, p. 164.

The risk, however, is that it leads the actor to aim to play the result; the emotion. The emphasis is placed upon examining how you behave when you *feel* a particular emotion. Yet, as we explored in Chapter 2, it's very difficult to define a particular emotion; feeling is rooted in the very specific circumstances of any given situation.

Stanislavski's later emphasis on physical Actions and the body – the interplay between the physical aspect of thought and the mental aspect of action – superseded his earlier ideas. He recognised that the emotions an actor feels need to arrive from a fresh experience.

Seeking parallels between our own experience and that of a character can be useful; it can bring us closer to an understanding of their situation.[48] However, it is also well worth noting the differences between ourselves and the characters we are playing, in order to highlight those parts of the character that require particular focus. Analysis of the text and detailed research can help bring us closer to such an understanding. Seeking affinities can be risky as they potentially lead to a sense of 'Well, *I* wouldn't do this' when, of course, it is not *your* story. You will bring yourself and your points of reference to the part but they must be informed by your analysis of the opera and further relevant research; particularly important when dealing with operatic characters in the midst of extreme circumstances.

Meisner Repetition

Sanford Meisner (1905–97) worked initially alongside Lee Strasberg. Both were heavily influenced by Stanislavski but developed divergent paths. The central tenet of Meisner's work is the importance of an actor's focus being on other people; for the actor to listen to others, rather than to themselves.

In the Actions section we acknowledged that it can be easy to get stuck asking, what am *I* doing? One of your challenges when working in opera is that your focus is constantly driven back onto yourself and your voice. Meisner's work frees you up to connect with the other people in the scene and places at the heart of the work the question: what am I doing in *response* to *you*? It encourages you to actively listen to others, to allow yourself to be affected by them, to follow your impulse in response to them and vice versa. It is about engaging you with your character's target; every action received prompts a decision and then a (re)action.

Developing the ability to be *in the moment* when acting in opera is particularly challenging because there is already a predetermined rhythm, tempo and pitch; a non-singing actor can vary these factors moment to moment. It can therefore feel as though there is less room for manoeuvre; that is exactly the reason why it is so important to seek out your freedom to play within the form to avoid simply repeating predictable patterns.

Meisner's exercises seem very simple but their purpose is to get you to do something deceptively difficult in rehearsal and performance; to forget yourself and to explore responses that have not been predetermined.

---

[48] Look back at Events (p. 114).

1. Simple Observation

This is a really simple observation exercise. You need to listen to what your partner says and repeat it. Be detailed and truthful.

- Face your partner either sitting down, or standing in neutral.
- Close your eyes.
- Open your eyes. Take in your partner, from head to toe.
- One person will begin (let's say A) by making a very simple, truthful observation about their partner; the first thing they see. It should be something objective and unarguable. For example, 'You have brown eyes' or 'You have a scar on your upper lip'.
- Partner B will receive what A has just said and repeat it; simply changing the '*you*' to '*I*'. For example, 'I have brown eyes' or 'I have a scar on my upper lip'.
- This exchange continues with the words remaining the same but the way the words are spoken – their underlying meaning – changing:

  Partner A: You have brown eyes.

  Partner B: I have brown eyes.

  Partner A: You have brown eyes.

  Partner B: I have brown eyes.

  And so on . . .

- *How* you say this line of text will change – intonation, volume and pitch – but allow this to happen naturally and in response to what your partner has just said, rather than forcing it, imposing something, or trying to 'entertain'.
- In moments the exchange might become a little automatic or even feel slightly absurd; that is often just part of the process, keep going!
- Listen to your partner and very real moments of connection will occur.

2. Extension: Continued Observation

Try the exercise again. This time, when a new observation about your partner occurs to you – say it. For example:

Partner A: You have brown eyes.

Partner B: I have brown eyes.

Partner A: You have brown eyes.

Partner B: You raised your eyebrow.

Partner A: I raised my eyebrow.

Partner B: You raised your eyebrow and smiled.

Partner A: I raised my eyebrow and smiled.

Partner B: You raised your eyebrow and smiled.

And so on.

- The more detailed you become about how your partner is changing, the better.
- Keep the observations about external factors rather than making emotional judgements, for example, 'You're happy'.

3. Extension: Subjective Observation

As you develop trust and confidence with your partner, you can extend the repetition exercise so that you begin to make subjective observations; those observations that you *believe* to be true:

Partner A: You have brown eyes.

Partner B: I have brown eyes.

Partner A: You have brown eyes.

Partner B: You look nervous.

Partner A: I look nervous.

And so on.

This exercise can be deeply affecting, so it is always really good to have an observer to steer you or reflect back what they notice between the two of you.

4. Extension: Sung Repetition

I've tried this with Opera Works singers and, although challenging at first, it seems to open you much more directly to your partner.

Go through exercises 1–3 above, but allow yourself to *sing* your observation. Keep the singing very simple at first, with gentle support, and allow it to develop naturally.

5. Extension: Text Repetition

This exercise can be extended to your work on the libretto. Speak your character's words with your partner; you and your partner repeat each other's line, until the line has been fully understood and received. When the need arises, move onto the next line.

When exploring Meisner's work keep the following in mind:

- It is about your partner.
- It is about allowing yourself to be open and affected by what your partner says and how they say it. Respond to this rather than simply repeating words.
- It is about allowing yourself to be changed.
- It is, ultimately, less about words and more about behaviour.
- Take time to reflect upon what you noticed with your partner.

This exercise involves repeating the last few words of your partner's line, before moving onto yours. Its purpose is to alert and connect you to what you are reacting to. It is particularly useful when exploring recitative. Try this exercise speaking at first, and then singing. If you need to adjust the octave you are singing in when repeating your partner's line, so that it is comfortable for you to sing, do so.

As an example, let us look at the recitative just before the Countess and Susanna's duet in Act Three:

Countess	That's amazing! But how did the Count react?
Susanna	*But how did the Count react?* His face was a picture and the varnish was cracked!
Countess	*His face was a picture and the varnish was cracked!* Careful! If we enrage him, we may not defeat him. Now what have you arranged? Where are you going to meet him?
Susanna	*Where are you going to meet him?* In the garden.
Countess	*In the garden.* Let's fix a place. Write to him.
Susanna	*Write to him.* My lady, I wouldn't dare.
Countess	*My lady, I wouldn't dare.* I'll take the blame. Yes, we'll disguise it as a poem. Let's say, a song to the breezes.

Text and Music: Conclusion

Through this work you have two lines of perspective running in parallel alongside each other.

The first line is that of the character you are creating and playing. You must see the world of the opera from their perspective, through their eyes. Each time you play, you must engage in the detail of their life, their relationships, their attitudes.

The second line is that of the artist; the actor-singer. In the first instance you need to be curating the perspective of the character and, alongside your team, the world your character lives in. You will be making decisions that excite the imagination, that raise the stakes, that nourish the need for action. And then, when in action, this line of perspective will bring awareness of the road ahead for the character, the Through-Line, and the way in which you are navigating your way through the story.

The singer playing Figaro knows there is a line that must be drawn through the opera; beginning at the moment of Figaro's realisation of what might be lost in his duet with Susanna ('Dong!'), through to the moment he rails against all women in Act Four. *How* this line is traversed, how the journey is travelled, creates the story.

SINGERS' RESPONSES TO TEXT TOOLS

- *Actioning translated recitative into something real; I didn't need to follow the rhythmic notation.*

- *The structure of Events and Objectives serves to give you freedom – it takes away self-consciousness and holds you in the present.*

- *I no longer felt the pressure to create the perfect Susanna/Countess Duet – it just felt like a conversation.*

- *I think these exercises allow us to take control of music as a resource – as a singer – music is always owned by someone else, the conductor/orchestra/coach/teacher – so bringing the storytelling element back into it actually makes singing a primal exercise.*

- *Different tools work for different scenarios; not one size fits all. You can't do everything at once, it's a layering process; adding layer upon layer, then you make discoveries. It's a way of making the music make more sense.*

- *Doing Actions helps the THINK, BREATHE, SING idea.*

- *Actioning doesn't allow any time to obsess over mistakes, as you have to move onto the next tactic straight away.*

- *Prior preparation, having all the foundations in place, meant that I was able to connect to my body more, which in turn made it easier to sing!*

5 The Body and Movement

WHAT CHALLENGES DO YOU FACE WHEN CREATING A PHYSICAL OPERATIC CHARACTER?

- *I carry a lot of tension in my body and push my head forward.*
- *I run out of ideas quickly.*
- *Me too! But I'm also wary of doing too much.*
- *I feel I show my character with my top half of my body but stop about half way down. I demonstrate, rather than inhabit.*
- *I try to release my jaw but end up developing tensions elsewhere; I seem to put my hand into a claw.*
- *I act a bit and then stop and sing – the physical character doesn't seem to happen when I sing.*
- *My range of movement is very limited. I tend to stick to things that seem to work and find them quite boring.*
- *I've never felt like I'm not me. I've never felt – movement wise – that I'm not responding exactly as I would.*
- *When performing in a concert, my hands shake.*
- *I'm quite tall, so I find that when I'm performing with someone shorter I over-compensate and lose all sense of good posture.*
- *How to move naturally without tension in a recital or audition. How to feel free whilst remaining still. I tend to feel self-conscious.*
- *How to keep movement real when the opera is over the top and exaggerated.*
- *When I'm creating 'trouser roles' – how do I feel like a man?*
- *I don't know what to do with my hands.*

Introduction

Many of these challenges are specific to the individual performer. Some, however, might well be very familiar. Many actors and singers feel that they have unresolved issues with their physicality and are only too aware of how this impacts their characterisation on stage.[1]

---

[1] If you're the one performer I've yet to meet who is exempt from this category, please jump to Chapter 6: Words and Music in Action!

Such concerns are often not helped by the physical demands of singing. The tensions required to produce a particular note at a particular volume often translate into constrictions in the whole body. This is why the work on release in Chapter 1: Foundations is so important to do whilst singing. These challenges are incredibly common, so don't worry, it's normal! To begin with, grab your notebook and write down *your own* response to the question, what challenges do you face when creating a physical singing character?

Our body is our home. We might feel we know it incredibly well and yet we are often unaware of the stories we tell through our body and movement. And so, we remain unaware of how to begin to tell new stories through our body.

The Given Circumstances set our course, define our story: revealing who these characters are, where they are, when they are, how they got here and why they are here. These pieces of information are the fuel for our story. We must adapt ourselves to them and transform into the likeness of the person in these Circumstances.

In order to be ready to embrace the possibilities of the text and score we need to be in a state of readiness. This means being not only vocally but also physically and psychologically prepared. Use those exercises in Chapter 1: Foundations to develop a sense of release, alongside a heightened awareness, a flexible imagination and a spirit of play.

Your body is your instrument to deliver your story to the audience. And what we say *without* words is often just as powerful as the words we use. This non-verbal communication is expressive and we have recourse to it already. We are doing it *all* the time. A nod. A gaze. The way in which you close this book and place it on the table. All will express something to the observer; everything we do communicates. Indeed, you cannot *not* communicate. We have all already learned to do this. We are all socialised, we all participate in a shared, patterned way in order to survive!

The key is to become aware of what you do and then do it again, deliberately and with awareness of intensity, speed, tension, weight, direction and more; all of which can be varied to different effect. Movement is not something you need to go out and acquire; it's something you already have. It is just about becoming more aware of what it communicates. And if you're clear in your intention of what you want, the expression, or story, will follow.

The theatre is a psycho-physical domain; for every thought, internal action, leap of emotion, there is a corresponding breath that leads to the external.[2] This external action, driven by a clear intention, is what the audience hears *and* sees and, ultimately, what it believes and feels.

The artist, instrument and medium are all one. In order to express our finely tuned intentions, we need to expand our palette of movements to discover a fuller range of physical expression through which to build character. We need to do this within the physical limitations that singing brings but we also need to explore the edges of these limitations. This chapter will seek to introduce how to achieve this by focusing, primarily, on the work of Rudolf Laban and Jacques Lecoq. We drew on the work of these two practitioners throughout Opera Works; the singers connected to at least one or other of the differing approaches. Laban is more analytical; Lecoq more playful. Their work creates similar results but offers different ways of thinking about physicality.

---

[2] Artaud, A. (2017) *The Theatre and Its Double*. Richmond: Alma Classics, p. 260.

It will not be possible to address every specific question that each of us has about our physical expression but I hope that through an emphasis on detailed observation, a heightened awareness and a range of approaches, these tools help you address your concerns in a way that makes them easier for you to resolve.

Music

Music moves us, internally and externally. We drink, eat, dance, shop, romance and support sports teams, moved by the kinetic power of music. The score moves. The conductor does nothing but move to conjure the sound of the orchestra. And this relationship between the two forms is so intrinsic that we often use the same words to describe movement and music. Many of the words you refer to in the score are shared with choreographers; you are obviously familiar with the use of tempo, rhythms, structure and patterns.

The following exercise is a good place to start our exploration of movement and story.

EXERCISE: *Follow the Leader*
Pairs/15 mins

- A begins to walk around the room at a medium pace.
- B follows A, step by step.
- B studies the movement of A's feet:
  - How do the feet strike the floor? Does the heel hit first, or the ball of the foot? Do they land hard or soft, how do they roll once they have landed? Are both feet the same in their movement?
  - B replicates in detail the movement of A's feet.
- B studies the movement of A's knees:
  - Do they bounce? Are the knees aligned over the feet or do they point out or inwards?
  - B copies A's knees.
- B focuses on the movement of A's hips and pelvis:
  - How much swing is there? Is the movement more prominent to the left or right side? Is the pelvis rolled forward or back and to what extent?
  - B mirrors A's hips.
- B continues to study the movement of the individual parts of A's body:
  - The torso and chest: pushed forward, inclined inwards, moving freely or held?
  - The shoulders: what degree of tension is there, is one raised higher than the other?
  - The arms: how much do they move, does one arm seem to power the movement, how released are they?
  - The head: how does it rest on top of the spine, does the chin protrude or do they instead lead with the forehead?
  - The focus: where does A seem to look mostly, what draws their attention?

- B scans up and down A's body, putting the movement of each of A's body parts into their own body; replicating in detail.
- Once B is moving as A, A drops out and watches.
- What do you see? For all B's observations this is not an exact replication of A's movement; it is a heightened expression, as seen through the eyes of another. But what story is reflected back to you? Do you recognise yourself and your movement? Are you surprised by anything?
- B can next extend this movement, identifying what they perceive to be the defining features of A's walk and exaggerating it. Try this on a count from 1 to 10, with 1 being the most reduced state and 10 being the most exaggerated.
- B will likely create a caricature of A's movement but, when watching, bring awareness to what B chooses to focus upon.
- Before sharing your reflections, swap over and repeat the exercise; A follows B.

Laban

RUDOLF LABAN

Rudolf Laban (1879–1958) was a choreographer, teacher and theorist of movement and dance. He was born in Hungary and initially studied architecture at the École des Beaux-Arts in Paris. His study of buildings in space led to his observations of the moving body in space. He worked throughout theatres in Europe and the States and his ongoing investigations led to a detailed analysis of the components of human movement.

Laban's approach to movement was informed through his early study of buildings in space. Look at the room you are currently sitting in. What would the architect have needed to consider when designing this building?

The dimensions, the shape, the light, the texture of the materials needed to build, the flow of traffic through the space, the colour, how it interacts with the neighbouring buildings, the foundations, the location and size of the windows and doors and so on.

What do I need? How much of it do I need? How do I order it? These three questions connect the architect and the performer onstage.

Laban asked these questions to break down the structure of physical movement in much the same way that you, as a singer, will analyse a piece of music. You are given information by the composer to understand their intentions regarding rhythm, tempi, flow and weight, without which you would not know how to approach playing or singing their compositions. Laban breaks down physical movement in a similar way. His approach helps you to see the constituent parts of movement and label them and, by so doing, gives you the tools to construct movement in the way you intend. Laban's work in this area led him to create his own notation of movement not dissimilar to a musical score.

To understand Laban is to have all the ingredients of movement to select from. Stanislavski wrote that when creating a character, we have to be 'an engineer or mechanic to comprehend and fully appreciate the action of our motor apparatus.'[3] Laban gives us the motor mechanics handbook.

You have a *home* body; a body that, through movement, reveals *your* individual story. Your body is also an *instrument* through which to reveal the story of the *character*. This duality can often prove problematic; after all, the audience are here to see the character's story, not yours. Laban's work presents creative choices to help break habitual patterns of behaviour, in order to move away from our *home* body and develop a more responsive *instrument*; to become aware of different notes, in order to create different sounds.

We create expression through movement. By adjusting one component, the whole psychology of a character can seem to be transformed. The big question is, what do you intend to convey; what you want the audience to see? The expression of character, of behaviour, is carried through the movement of the body and this expression changes if you change your intention. Laban's work brings our attention to the structure of movement and how modifications in the various components of movement can change expression. Movement in everyday life is spontaneous and functional but in order to create physical character we must be deliberate and expressive. Laban's work gives us a wider range of options to choose from in order to change our movement and alter our creative expression. Laban's process could be summed up with three simple words: 'observe, select and create'.

The Structural Model of Movement[4]

The structural model is a way of breaking down and naming what we *see* in every movement. It is as though we have different pairs of spectacles that each allow us to see movement through a different lens, each lens highlighting a particular aspect of movement.

The model is made up of five intrinsic components, all of which are present in all movement. These structural components of movement are the essentials without which movement could not exist.

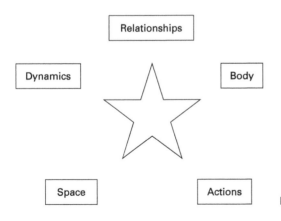

Figure 5.1 Structural Model of Movement.

---

[3] Stanislavski, K. (1999) *Building a Character*. Translated by E. R. Hapgood. London: Eyre Methuen, p. 52.
[4] The work originates from Laban and Valerie Preston-Dunlop. I was introduced to it by two brilliant teachers, Rosemary Brandt and Olga Masleinnikova, both of whom are practitioners at Trinity Laban, London. Preston Dunlop, V. (1998) *Looking at Dances: A Choreological Perspective on Choreography*. London: Verve Books, pp. 77–155 is particularly useful.

The model provides a vocabulary for movement, helping us to define what we are doing with our bodies; movement becomes something we can more readily comprehend, grasp hold of and adjust in line with our intentions.

The model presents five different ways to analyse movement. By bringing your focus to one of these five components and changing it, the other four will shift at the same time. The components relate to:

THE BODY

- The structure or posture of the body; the face, joints, arms, legs and how they co-ordinate.
- How we isolate certain parts to bring focus.
- The surfaces of the body and how parts of your body contact other surfaces of an object: the floor, a table, a chair, or somebody else.
- How you touch. The many aspects to touch; duration, weight, force, energy, intensity, reception. Is the touch received by another person and, if so, how? Does another person touch you?

ACTIONS

- Rather than the 'Actions' we have previously looked at as part of our analysis of the libretto, this relates to simply what we do physically; either with a part of the body or the whole self.
- There are only eleven basic actions but an infinite way of doing them. They are:
  - turn (the whole body rotates)
  - jump (a hop, or leap, one- or two-footed)
  - travel (from one point to the next)
  - transfer of weight (a roll, a pivot)
  - stillness (which requires tension)
  - twist (part of the body rotates)
  - fall (release to gravity)
  - open (to reveal the body)
  - close (to remove the body from show)
  - lability (that edge of a cliff moment, teetering on the brink of balance)
  - gesture (a part of the body moves – in an everyday or abstracted way).
- Every action has a three-part rhythm: preparation/action/recovery.

DYNAMICS

- Relates to *how* the actions are performed or 'the dynamic qualities of rhythm'. The dynamics are the adjectives of movement; reflecting upon how the body is moving in relation to time, weight, space, and the flow of energy.
- It is important not to confuse movement dynamics with the dynamics referred to in a musical score, relating simply to volume of sound.

- It includes the dynamics of the *breath* in the preparation and recovery part of an action.
- Dynamics are expressed in opposition to each other, for example, *free* and *bound*.
- Dynamics add texture, colour and variety to movement.
- Every movement has a visible rhythm which can be characterised in one of five ways. We will explore each of these ways in the section on movement dynamics below.

SPACE
- Where you are and how you relate to it; your level of engagement with it.
- This includes the floor space or the different levels in the space (high, middle or low), your personal space (kinesphere) and the entire space.
- It relates to how you move through this space, usually characterised through curves or direct lines.
- What shapes does your movement make in space? What directions do you travel in?

RELATIONSHIPS
- This relates to the people, objects, music with whom the actions take place.
- It also concerns relationship with space, time and flow.
- Relationships might be expressed through unison, canon and pause, gaze, orientation, distance, levels, touch and weight transfer.

These components are all interconnected. You focus and change one and another will shift in response; this will become clearer through doing the exercises below.

GIVEN CIRCUMSTANCES
We can use the structural model to break down and analyse your own behavioural patterns. The way we might naturally move has been formalised into certain patterns through our social interaction; we learn *how* to behave socially in order to survive! Our movement means different things in different situations and characters operate in relation to, and in the context of, certain social parameters. The patterns of behaviour these parameters inform concern bodily contact, physical proximity, gesture, posture, facial expressions, eye focus.

Ask, what are the Given Circumstances in the opera that define these factors? Consider how your movement would change if you:

- wore certain clothes;
- lived with particular social or political conditions;
- were subject to certain social codes based upon class or gender;
- had your character's health conditions;
- ate particular food.

How does your character respond to these factors? Do they follow patterns or break them? Are there restrictions placed upon their behaviour and movement?

This is a warm-up exercise that helps you explore the five components of the structural model. Each task in the exercise places particular emphasis on a certain component; these are marked in parenthesis. Be aware that a change in one component can create a shift in another.

- Travel around the space. Do not make eye contact with anybody else. (Action/Space/Relationships)
- Make sharp 90 degree turns as you walk. (Action)
- Travel in direct lines. Travel in curved lines. (Space)
- Change the position of your feet as you walk. (Body)
- Present your chest, knees, hips, hands, elbows as you walk. How does it feel? (Body)
- Change the orientation of your elbows. (Body)
- Shift your focus; look up, look down. (Body/Relationships)
- Change the speed you walk: very fast, fast, medium, slow, very slow. (Dynamics)
- Try stopping together as a group (without negotiation). And then starting to walk together. (Relationships)
- Walk around the space whilst making eye contact with a partner. (Relationships)
- Extend this contact with others; nod, smile, wink. (Actions)
- Every time you pass someone, share a brief moment of touch. Use different surfaces of your body. (Relationships, Body, Action)
- Walk around the space, searching for the 'gaps' between bodies in the space. Be the first person to get into those gaps. (Space/Relationships)
- Walk alongside your partner. Shift the rhythm of your walk; one person may lead. Vary your orientation; you may face towards, away from, at an angle to your partner. (Relationships, Dynamics)
- Vary the distance between each of your kinespheres. (Relationships/Body)

As you work through this warm-up, be clear, focused and present in your choices. Bring your awareness to the rest of the group and, in particular, the partner you are working with. If you lose focus, watch your feet. Following your feet is useful if you ever feel self-conscious in performance; bring your focus to one body part, for example, your feet in space.

Dynamics

We are going to focus, in particular detail, on one of these five components of the Structural Model; Dynamics. Later exercises explore the other components.

Dynamics in music concern the relative volume of a piece, whereas movement dynamics relate to the *qualities of rhythm*. Rhythm is something, as a musician, you will be acutely aware of; your journey through an opera is broken into metric rhythms, structuring your character's time into notational units.

Different rhythms exist within us; our heartbeat, our thought patterns, our breath. They are visible through our gestures, walk and actions. All rhythm in movement is visible as a result of the interaction between tension and release in our bodies. Our bodies are subject to gravity and through our movement we use energy to counter its effect. When energy yields to gravity, there is release; when energy counters gravity, there is tension. The visible qualities of rhythm are the result of the ebb and flow of this tension and release.

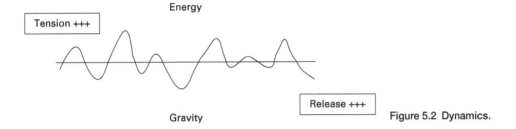

Figure 5.2 Dynamics.

Rhythmic Constructs

All rhythm in movement is made up of the fluctuation in the output of energy; this can vary, resulting in different expressions. Sometimes this output of energy increases through a movement, sometimes it decreases. The way in which energy travels through a movement Laban defines as the Rhythmic Construct. Every movement can be described as being made up of one of only five Rhythmic Constructs.

IMPULSE

- We see an impulse when the movement begins fast and decelerates towards the end. There is decreasing output of energy through the movement.

- For example, try standing up; you need more energy at the beginning of the action, and this is where we see the fastest part of the movement takes place.

- An impulse tends to be an outward movement, with deceleration into the unknown.

- Laban writes an impulse in this way, with the accent at the beginning of the movement, marking the point of greatest acceleration:

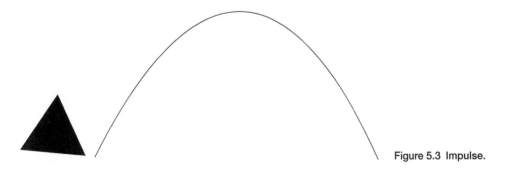

Figure 5.3 Impulse.

IMPACT

- The movement begins more slowly, with acceleration occurring towards the end.
- There is increasing output of energy through the movement.
- For example, punching a cushion; the action is fastest at the end.
- An impact tends to be a direct movement, with acceleration into the known.
- Laban notates this with the accent at the end:

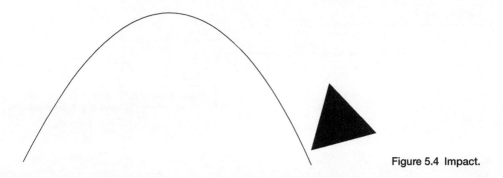

Figure 5.4 Impact.

SWING

- Acceleration is to the mid-point of the movement, followed by deceleration away from the mid-point.
- Gravity or release causes the movement to accelerate to, and decelerate from, the mid-point; there is no force involved. For example, walk and bring attention to the movement of your arms as you do so.
- The movement tends to be indirect.
- Laban notes the movement with the accent at the mid-point but leaves the accent open to suggest the absence of force:

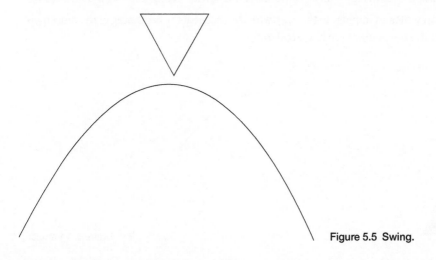

Figure 5.5 Swing.

REBOUND

- Acceleration is again to the mid-point, followed by deceleration away from this point.

- The pattern is similar to a Swing but the acceleration is the result of force or tension, not release. For example, imagine dabbing a hot kettle or stepping out into a road only to immediately step back to avoid an approaching bus.

- The movement tends to be direct.

- Laban illustrates this force with a shaded accent:

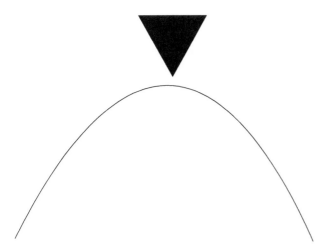

Figure 5.6 Rebound.

CONTINUOUS

- There is no acceleration or deceleration; the movement is constant throughout.

- This requires complete control of energy, with no release and no increase of tension.

- The movement therefore has no accents. Imagine carrying a tray of tea cups, each filled to the brim with hot tea, whilst taking care not to spill any liquid.

- Laban notates this with a straight line:

_____   Figure 5.7 Continuous.

Organic and Inorganic Movement

Breathe in. Breathe out. We naturally tend to do this on an *Impulse*. Laban would describe this as an *Organic* movement.

The examples given above to illustrate each Rhythmic Construct are *Organic* movements; the way in which particular movements naturally tend to be ordered. For example, you tend to stand up on an Impulse and sit on an Impact.

If you were to change the Organic Rhythmic Construct with which you did a particular action (for example, standing up on an Impact and sitting down on an Impulse), Laban would call this *Inorganic*; it is the less efficient way to structure a movement.

Here are some examples of actions alongside their Organic and possible Inorganic Rhythmic Structures:

Action	Organic	Inorganic
Throwing a punch	impact	impulse
Reaching for a full glass of water	impulse	rebound
Leafing through the pages of a very old book	continuous	swing
Holding hands with your loved one	swing	continuous
Pushing a button to call a lift	rebound	impact

By looking at the particular structure of Organic movements and deciding what it is you want to highlight, you can bring emphasis to a movement by making it Inorganic. Understanding movement means understanding how you can create expression.

Consider how, by exploring different Rhythms, you might highlight a particular moment in the opera and bring the audience's attention to this; for example, a shift in Rhythm might suddenly reveal the effects of age, expose a hidden intention, or uncover a moment in the history of a character as carried through the body.

Understanding the Rhythmic Constructs of movement enables you to bring precision and detail to your physical expression of character; in so doing, it frees you from the generalised movements which can often result in unnecessary tensions.

EXERCISE: *Rhythmic Constructs*
Solo/Ongoing

- As a brief exercise, look around at the small actions or gestures people are doing around you and categorise them as Impulses, Impacts, Swings, Rebounds or Continuous Rhythms. Write down the actions and their corresponding Rhythms. Sometimes it might be difficult to discern a particular Rhythm; this is perhaps because a sequence of little movements is strung together. If so, break them down into single actions.

- Alongside each of these movements and Rhythms, note whether they are done Organically or Inorganically.

- Alongside those movements you have categorised as Organic, write down an Inorganic way of doing this same movement.

- Finally, try repeating these movements, firstly with their Organic construct and then with an Inorganic construct. What do you notice? What effect does it create?

Rhythmic constructs are a way of helping us to identify *how* movement is structured. Having done this we can then, if we so wish, change that structure. Movements can be used Organically or Inorganically to manipulate the feeling you want to create.

For example, your walk might normally be characterised as a series of Swings. If you change this and walk instead with a Continuous construct, you would create a significantly different story. An observer might imagine you were, perhaps, suffering a traumatic experience. Your internal thoughts might shift as a consequence.

You might notice that someone tends to gesture using Impulses; this might create the impression of them as energetic, keen, ready. Another person's tendency might be to gesture using Impacts; they might appear aggressive, forthright, dogmatic. Another might suddenly adopt gestures that Swing when a lover enters or, if the person is the secret object of their affections, it might be that just one of their arms Swings.

If you are playing Cherubino, for example, you might want to study the Rhythmic Constructs of the gestures and movements of somebody you know fitting the character's description. This enables your study to be a specific analysis of somebody of a different age and gender to yourself, rather than relying on a generalised idea of a teenage boy.

Rhythm carries expression. By changing the rhythm, we can change the expression. In performance, to *do* something is not the result, it merely serves the result. *How* you do something is where the story truly lies. As storytellers, the *how* is our chief means of communication with an audience. You might change the rhythm of an action or a gesture to highlight a particular moment in a story, a major Event that you want an audience to notice and to reflect upon, or you might wish to emphasise a particular character trait or relationship. People, and therefore characters, quite naturally inhabit different places on the tension–release spectrum. As a performer, it is really useful to be able to access the whole spectrum to create, and bring definition to, the expression that you want to convey.

EXERCISE: *Exploring Rhythmic Constructs*
Solo/10 mins[5]

Carry out a series of actions, firstly with Organic Rhythms, then with Inorganic Rhythms. What do you notice changes from one sequence to the next?

Action	Organic rhythms (first exercise)	Inorganic rhythms (second exercise)
Travel forward	Swing	Rebound
Travel backward	Swing	
Turn to the right	Impulse	Continuous
Turn to the centre	Impulse	Swing
Transfer weight to a body part other than the feet	Impact	Impulse
Stand up	Impulse	Impact
Gesture	Impact	Swing
Gesture	Impulse	Rebound
Gesture	Impact	Swing

---

[5] This is a terrific exercise to explore Organic and Inorganic Rhythmic Constructs from Rosemary Brandt. I would do this exercise to music; if you are working on a particular opera, try it to some music within the piece. Otherwise, Scriabin or Chopin piano preludes are good to work with!

Efforts

Laban asks: what is the visible result of effort? For example, the difference between punching someone in the face and reaching for a glass of water is slight in terms of how we organise the body; both rely on the extension of the arm. The attention is therefore brought to the *strength* of the movement, the *control* of the movement and the *timing* of the movement as each of these are very different. Motion Factors define the quality of visible effort in a movement. They offer a system for understanding the subtle characteristics of movement with respect to inner intention.

Laban suggests there are four key Motion Factors common to all movement; Time, Space, Weight and Flow. Each Factor is defined through its two opposing extremes. The movement between these extremes is where the potential Rhythm exists.[6]

Motion Factors

Each of these factors travels between two opposing elements:

- WEIGHT

  Light _____ Strong

- TIME

  Sustained _____ Sudden

- SPACE

  Flexible _____ Direct

- FLOW

  Free _____ Bound

It is useful to consider these Factors quantitatively; weight measures force, time measures durational length, space measures the degrees of angles walked in space, flow measures the degree of continuity.

Laban provides a vocabulary for movement and how he describes each of these four Factors is helpful when creating physical character; the actor, he says, 'derives a certain inspiration from descriptions of movement that awaken their imagination'.[7] Explore the descriptions of the each of these Motion Factors on your feet.

WEIGHT

- Weight travels between *light* and *strong* movement.

- Rather than thinking of weight as measured in grams and kilograms, consider the amount of force in a movement. The lighter the movement, the less force or energy is used and the more release to gravity. The stronger the movement, the more force or energy is used and the more tension is created.

---

[6] Preston Dunlop, V. (1998) *Looking at Dances: A Choreological Perspective on Choreography*. London: Verve Books.
[7] Laban, R. (1988) *Mastery of Movement*. Binsted, Hants.: Dance Books Publication, p. 21.

- Weight can best be clarified by working with a partner. Give your weight to them in two ways:
- Firstly, place your arm gently upon your partner's shoulder, giving them very little weight and imagining your arm as light as a feather. The weight you are giving your partner is defined as *light*.
- Next, your partner begins to walk away from you. Take their hand, pulling down and away from the direction in which they are walking. The weight you are giving your partner is defined as *strong*.
- Laban would sometimes interchange the terms *weight* and *force*.
- Compare the sensation of an imaginary cord, connected to the top of your head, lifting you upwards, to the sensation of wading through deep, boggy marshland.

TIME

- Time travels between *sustained* and *sudden* (or broken).
- This relates to the duration of a movement and how your movement, your journey through the space, is characterised in relation to time. Sustained journeys are long, continuous, unaccented; sudden journeys are broken, split up, shorter.
- Compare the sensation of walking into the wind on top of a high cliff, to blowing a dandelion and trying to catch as many of the seeds before they fly away.

SPACE

- You travel through space in *direct* or *indirect* (flexible) movements.
- You travel from A to B by taking the clearest, straightest, unswerving line, or you take a veering, unfocused, winding route to your destination.
- When moving through space, think of carving lines into the space; moving directly you will carve straight lines, moving indirectly you will carve curved lines.
- Compare the sensation of walking headlong down a long narrow corridor, to trying to weave your way back to your seat in an overcrowded bar.

FLOW

- The flow of energy through your body moves between a *bound* and *free* quality.
- This might be more difficult to imagine but relates to restriction or release in your movement.
- Compare the sensation of an imaginary cord pulling tight every muscle in your body, to running down a huge, grassy hill with your arms outstretched.

Explore the sensations of each of these Motion Factors. Note that all the words on the left-hand side of the page have an affinity: light, sustained, flexible, free. For example, if you lift your arm in a light way, you might notice that your movement could also be described as moving in accordance with these other Motion Factors.

Similarly, the words on the right-hand side, their opposites, often have an affinity; strong, sudden, direct, bound. For example, if you plant your hand on the desk in a strong way, it will often also be direct, sudden and bound.

These affinities do not always apply. By intentionally changing one or other of these qualities in combination, we shift the expression.

Efforts of Action Drive

Laban unites three of these Motion Factors – weight, time and space – in different combinations to define how the Effort or energy we use characterises our movement; in so doing, Laban categorises eight archetypal ways in which we behave. Laban called this 'Efforts of Action Drive' because each type of movement is defined by Effort combined with an inner intention or drive; although they are external physical states, they also relate to a character's psychology.

To different degrees, we all embody these basic movement qualities at various times of our day or life, but we will have affinities with particular qualities; those which we feel most at home with. When you work through the Efforts of Action Drive in the exercise below, it is worth noting which combinations feel more recognisable or comfortable for you. Understanding your own movement affinities will help you to break certain patterns in your own behaviour that might not be helpful to your physical characterisation.

Effort	Weight	Time	Space
Floating	Light	Sustained	Indirect
Gliding	Light	Sustained	Direct
Dabbing	Light	Sudden	Direct
Flicking	Light	Sudden	Indirect
Wringing	Strong	Sustained	Indirect
Pressing	Strong	Sustained	Direct
Thrusting	Strong	Sudden	Direct
Slashing	Strong	Sudden	Indirect

Things to remember:

- The Efforts of Action Drive are usually holistic and each has a *centre* in the body where the movement tends to lie.

- Efforts might define our thoughts and state of mind.

- We can therefore have an outer and inner Effort. These Efforts can be different, with one Effort *covering* or *hiding* another.

- Efforts usually involve the whole body; however, we can give different Efforts to different body parts. For example, our hips might be Gliding whilst our eyes might be Flicking.

- Flow, although not one of the constituent parts of the archetypes, still relates to certain Efforts. Flow is unusual in that within the same Effort of Action Drive, different circumstances might suggest either a bound or free flow.

Begin by first embodying each of the Motion Factors in the space, in order to experience their distinct and opposing qualities. Try each of these archetypal movements one by one:

FLOATING: light, sustained, indirect.
Centre: above the head.
Flow: free.
Imagine a sense of weightlessness, of being blown by the breezes, without direction. The movement has the quality of air; lift the arms, imagining currents of air supporting them from below, and allow these currents to change your direction – to gently push and roll you – through the space. The movement is sustained, so will lack any accents or sharp turns. It can help to think of a sense of suspension; an almost dreamlike state, lifted above the world below.
Character Tendencies: tend towards the meditative, spiritual and religious reverence. Floaters might be artists, dreamers and those who rise above, or avoid, the practical considerations of everyday life. They might be under the constant influence of drugs.

GLIDING: light, sustained, direct.
Centre: the centre of the chest.
Flow: mostly bound.
You know where you are going and travel there with composure and effortless ease. You have a sense of alignment within the body. Imagine you are ice-skating; that you move without any friction. Run your hand over a flat smooth surface. It requires a certain amount of tension to control the smooth motion; you might Glide with fluency as you walk a tightrope. Imagine you are the puck on an air hockey table.
Character Tendencies: tends to suggest a character of a higher social class. Someone who assumes themselves above others and can be arrogant or dismissive. Alternatively, Gliders can be elegant, graceful, balanced and assured. They might be counsellors or diplomats.

DABBING: light, sudden, direct.
Centre: level with the chin and shoulders.
Flow: free or bound.
Imagine the action of a nurse gently dabbing cotton wool on a wound whilst being mindful of the potential pain, or a painter (Monet or Seurat) carefully applying the final dots to their masterpiece. Try this with your hands; you will have a target. Notice the *rebound* rhythm in play. Then try dabbing with your head, and next your whole body. Notice the shift in flow; as the cotton wool dabbing nurse, the flow of your hands might be free but when using your whole body to dab, tension is required as you move away from your target.
Character Tendencies: someone who supports, nurtures and achieves practical solutions: sociable, makes thing come together. A Dabber could be a nurse or a busy personal assistant.

FLICKING: light, sudden, indirect.
Centre: on level with eyes and ears.
Flow: free.
Flick crumbs off a table, a fly from food, a stray hair from your face, a football up in the air. How: this action is more commonly done with hands and fingers, specifically the back surface of hands, but it can extend to any part of the body. Imagine walking in the Scottish Highlands and being harassed by a couple of gnats; use your feet, legs,

hips, torso, shoulders, elbows, nose, forehead to lightly flick them away. Your whole body begins to flutter.

Character Tendencies: tending to nervousness, lacking in responsibility, preoccupied and easily distracted. Flickers could be silly or flirtatious: obsessed with their own appearance or the appearance of something or somebody else.

WRINGING: strong, sustained, indirect.

Centre: stomach.

Flow: bound.

Imagine wringing out a massive wet beach towel: twisting the body left and right, the hands in opposition. Try moving this action out, above, or below. Involve the feet in this action, twisting into the ground. Be aware of your action and the almost exact counter-tension in your body coming into direct opposition. Imagine this effort without the resistance provided by an object; imagine the large towel *inside* your gut, heart or head.

Character Tendencies: prone to worry, anxiety, brooding and obsessive behaviours; turning problems in on themselves and tending towards avoidance. Alternatively, Wringers can be deeply sensual, illustrated through an enjoyment of sex or food.

PRESSING: strong, sustained, direct.

Centre: close to ground.

Flow: bound.

Try pressing against a wall, firstly with your hands and then involve other body parts. Imagine a giant mattress stood vertically on end and press your whole body into it. Then, walk whilst imagining pushing against the mattress. Imagine someone behind the mattress is pressing in the opposite direction. Or imagine pressing into very strong winds. As you press in one part of your body, a counter-tension in the rest of your body comes into play; it gives you a sense of strength and connection with the ground.

Character Tendencies: stubborn, insistent, inflexible, unimaginative, solid. Alternatively, Pressers can be loyal, thorough, persistent and methodical. They might be pen-pushers or bureaucrats; in favour of rules and regulations.

THRUSTING: strong, sudden, direct.

Centre: solar plexus/diaphragm.

Flow: bound or free.

This effort is sometimes also referred to as *Punching*. Try this; clench one fist and punch in all directions of your *kinesphere*. Each punch will always have an imaginary target; it is a direct movement. Extend this exercise to other body parts. Now, imagine fencing; lunge and thrust your blade into your opponent. Be aware of the necessary counter tension in all thrusts and punches; the rest of the body resists each action's drive to pull you too far forward. The effort is also sudden or broken, it gives way to obstacles (unlike Pressing which is consistent and sustained), and then moves toward its target.

Character Tendencies: tending towards ambition, motivation, aspiration, achievement but also aggression, driving and bullying. Thrusters are managers, rulers, dictators, entrepreneurs and the goal-orientated.

SLASHING: strong, sudden, indirect.

Centre: lower stomach/pelvis/groin.

Flow: mostly free.

This is a particularly violent and unpredictable Effort. Imagine a drunk man looking for a fight, wheeling his arms about in search of a target. Or slashing into a large canvas of a painting, then repeating with a series of 'Z'-like movements. Try this same action with your torso or, jumping, with your feet.

Character Tendencies: unpredictability, violence, recklessness but also characterised by a freewheeling adventure-seeking spirit. Slashers are lacking in control, unfocused and prone to lashing out. They could be psychopaths or wild risk-takers.

EXERCISE: Efforts Exploration
Group/45 mins

- Walk the space from one point to another embodying a particular Effort. When you reach a point, turn and change one Motion Factor: either weight, time or space. By so doing, embody a new Archetype. Walk to a new point in the space and repeat.

- Once you've journeyed through all eight Efforts, select one to explore in more detail. Try sitting down, doing small tasks, shaking somebody's hand, exploring objects in the room. Explore the difference between holistically embodying this and placing this in only one body part.

- Allow this Effort to infuse your state of mind; your thoughts start to *Float* or *Thrust*. You might be drawn to certain thoughts influenced by your state. In turn, let these thoughts infuse your breath. Your physical actions will strengthen this inner dialogue.

- Next, reduce the expression. Imagine you are currently at level 7 or 8, on a scale of 1 to 10. Begin to slowly bring the physical volume down. By the time you reach 1 it will be within you, hidden from the outside world. Carry it around with you. Shake hands with somebody and allow it to be externally activated to level 3 or 4.[8]

- With this first state inside you, attempt to *cover* it with another state. Your internal thoughts might be *Dabbing*, whilst externally you are displaying the state *Gliding*. This requires some practice.

- Now try an Effort in one particular body part and another Effort in a different body part. Your feet are *Pressing* but above the waist you are *Flicking*. As you become more confident you can add further detail to this.

- It is useful to have some of the group observing, whilst others in the group are exploring the Efforts. Reflect back what you saw and how clear the expression was. The more detailed you are, the clearer your expression will be communicated.

- Finally, write all of the eight Efforts on individual pieces of paper. Repeat this and place all sixteen pieces of paper into a hat.

- Each member of the group takes one piece of paper; they begin to embody the Effort on their paper. Walk, talk, perform short tasks. The aim is to find the person who shares your Effort, simply through observation. Once you believe you have found this person, do not discuss, but continue tasks until the game has finished.

---

[8] Such levels are only approximations and not absolute measurements; they are a guide for yourself, so that you can gradually increase or decrease the external expression, or physical volume, of an action.

Gesture

Laban incorporates all gestures under the Actions branch of the Structural Model. As we examined in the Introduction, the standardisation of gesture and emotion in operatic performance was in large part to blame for much of the criticism of acting in opera. However, gesture is a crucial component of our means of physical expression. *How* and *when* we gesture reveals something of who we are and highlights what we consider is particularly important when speaking or singing.

As a quick exercise, get a group of five or six singers to sit on chairs in a line, facing the rest of the group (at least five metres away). Instruct those on the chairs to sit on their hands throughout the exercise and to tell a memorable story from their childhood. All storytellers must all speak at once. In the cacophony of recited memories, you will probably catch only fragments of sentences and the occasional word. Bring your attention to the storytellers' movements; what do you see? In all likelihood you will see a series of nods, twitches, shrugs. Ask the storytellers to free their hands and continue their stories and, in all probability, these movements will now be transferred to the speaker's hands.

We have to gesture when communicating. We usually gesture with our hands but, otherwise, with other parts of our body. We use gesture to emphasise the words that we feel need particular emphasis or stress, those words we really want the listener to hear; movement and sound bound together by intention!

Each person will also have a repertoire of gestures. Look at the storytellers on the chairs and notice their distinct qualities. What Rhythms do they move in? *Impulses, Swings*? Which Efforts characterise their gestures? Are there particular parts of their story where these shift?

These individual, detailed gestures are character traits that form part of your toolkit to create character. Start observing people and, magpie-like, steal their gestures. Create a palette of possible gestures for your character. If you want to stress a certain word, and obviously the music might guide you with accented notes or pauses – or wish to highlight a particular moment – you can use your character's gestures in an Inorganic Rhythm to heighten them.

Gestures become especially useful in ensembles:[9]

- when everyone is singing at once, gestures help to communicate certain words in order to continue to tell the story.
- to keep *alive* our physical engagement with our character.
- to communicate an important moment or event within an ensemble. The moments are usually marked by a musical shift; it might be useful to change the Rhythm of a gesture or to heighten the gesture with a shift in Effort in order to clearly communicate this change to the audience.

As a singer performing expressive characters in large spaces, the risk is that you make gestures bigger in an attempt to communicate your thoughts. Actually, this tends to lead to a lack of clarity and risks cliché. Gestures are much more readable, whatever the scale of the space, if they are defined, detailed and motivated by clear thoughts. Of course, in larger spaces it is important that you bring an energised quality to your gestures. This can be done by intensifying the character's impulse to action; placing yourself imaginatively within the

---

[9] See Chapter 9: Rehearsals in Depth.

Given Circumstances and identifying where the *need* to achieve an Objective begins in your body. It might be useful to raise the stakes for your character to heighten their Objective. Allow the need to grow from this point and infuse the entire body.

EXERCISE: *Exploring Gestures and Rhythm*
Solo/15 mins

We can bring definition to our gestures by thinking about the rhythmic construct which defines them. This might seem rather mechanical but it brings greater control to our expression. This exercise explores how we can bring particular attention to our character's gestures by using Organic and Inorganic Rhythms. Rhythms can heighten, detail, abstract and draw attention to gestures.

- Select six gestures you might do. Each one of us has a wide repertoire of movements to draw from. For example, push back your hair, scratch your chin, squeeze your nose, push up your glasses, crack your knuckles, nod your head.
- Order these gestures in a sequence from 1 to 6. Run this sequence.
- Now discern the Organic Rhythms that define these gestures.
- Repeat this sequence using the Organic Rhythms to sharpen and clarify your gestures.
- Now do this to music, keeping the gestures in time.
- Now switch the Rhythms with which you do your gestures; make them Inorganic. For example, push your spectacles further up your nose; an Organic Rhythm for this movement might be *Impact*. Now try this action on an *Impulse*. Create an Inorganic sequence for all six gestures.
- Now repeat this entire exercise for your character. This brings awareness to your character's traits and explores how you can expand your choices.
- This exercise creates material, so is particularly useful for devising.[10]

The following exercises refer to all elements of the Structural Model. Some exercises will bring emphasis to one particular branch; for example, an exercise might bring our attention to the use of Space in the movement. Be aware, however, that as we shift and adapt through the exercises, the other branches of the Model will also be touched upon and changed.

EXERCISE: *Spatial Relations*
Pairs/10 mins

This exercise emphasises the importance of *relationships* and *space* in the communication of story.

- Stand opposite your partner and make eye contact.
- A will remain where they are. B moves to a different point in the room; towards, away from or around A.

---

[10] See the Devising section, p. 197. When devising you can add other people, canon and music and vary the orientation and speed to create a complex sequence that might ultimately be useful in an Ensemble.

- B explores how they make the journey to a new point; what speed, what rhythm. B may choose to withdraw or maintain eye contact throughout the journey.

- Keep it simple to begin with. Let thoughts and stories occur to you but do not seek to play out a narrative.

- After five minutes, swap over.

EXERCISE: *Efforts/Rhythmic Constructs Actions Gym*
Pairs/15 mins

This is an extension of the Exercise: Actions Gym (p. 102), exploring Rhythmic Constructs and Efforts.

- In pairs, both select a particular Effort to work with.
- Stand opposite your partner. A begins by speaking an Action whilst *doing* the Action to their partner: I *urge* you, I *admonish* you. B receives the action. Both *do* and *receive* whilst embodying their Effort.
- Remember to use your whole body when Actioning and to explore the Effort holistically.
- Repeat, Actioning without speaking the Action line.
- Repeat, Actioning whilst speaking a line from the libretto.
- Repeat, Actioning whilst singing a line from the libretto.
- Only move onto another Action if your partner has confirmed that the Action was clear.
- Reflect upon how different Efforts changed the quality and the story behind the Action. Did it create new textures? Did certain Efforts seem to fit more clearly with the sung line than others?
- Now, repeat all of this but work with an Internal Effort, in parallel with an External Effort.
- Do not reveal to your partner which Efforts you are working with. Discuss after the exercise to see how clear your physicality was.
- Repeat the whole exercise but using Rhythmic Constructs. Any gestures used in doing an Action will be done in a certain Rhythm: *Impulse, Impact, Swing, Rebound* or *Continuous.* Explore using Organic and Inorganic Rhythms.

EXERCISE: *Isolation*
Pairs/5 mins

This exercise emphasises the Body part of the Structural Model. It explores how to highlight certain body parts through isolation. The exercise is a way of getting us to think about how story might be expressed through emphasis of separate parts of the body.

There are twelve ways in which you can highlight a particular body part:

Isolation

Focus

Presenting

Touch

Leading with

Repetition

Initiating

The end place of a movement (the opposite of initiating)

Stillness

Hiding

Location

Frame.

- Choose three of these ingredients and focus your attention on one body part; for example, feet, knees, hips, left elbow, or surface of torso.
- Improvise[11] a simple scene with your partner or play a scene from *Figaro*. Do not reveal which body part you are bringing emphasis to prior to the scene.
- Ask if it was clear which body parts you were highlighting.
- This might be fun to explore with a scene from *Figaro* in which a character might legitimately want to bring attention to a particular body part; for example, in the scene with Marcellina, Susanna might want to draw attention to her engagement ring finger.
- It is easy to overtly highlight body parts but the exercise becomes much more interesting when you reduce your physical volume; it forces you to be more tactically diverse and more detailed in your attempts to isolate.

EXAMPLE: *The Marriage of Figaro*

Figaro and Susanna, No. 1 Duet 'Fifteen . . . sixteen . . .' / 'Cinque . . . dieci . . .' (see the extract below).

Listen actively to the music. Does it suggest the Rhythm of movement of the character, either internally or externally? Consider how certain Motion Factors might relate to the music.

Of course, it is worth considering that the music might not be your character's music, it might instead reflect another character's thoughts or movement. Consider how certain musical phrases seem to belong to certain characters. Are there oppositions within this music? Do shifts in rhythm suggest a shift in a character's internal or external Rhythmic quality?

Let us again look at the first scene of *Figaro*; the music poses many interesting questions that relate to the character's movement. We get information about the pace of the music – *allegro*. Is this brisk liveliness the internal or external tempo of one or both of the characters?

---

[11] See Exercise: Events Improvisation (p. 119).

1 The music suggests Figaro is measuring the room at the beginning of the play-in, as the same phrase is repeated just before he sings each of his measurements. The crochets in the 2nd bar – regulated, ordered, always on a D – give us perhaps a sense of *how* he is moving. Maybe he is *Gliding*?

2 The order of these initial bars is always followed, in the first two beats of the next bar, by the slurred crochets; perhaps Figaro slips whilst measuring?

3 These little slips become more frequent in the 5th, 6th and 7th bars. Do they, perhaps, suggest a different Inner Rhythm? Something set against the Outward Rhythm? If Figaro is trying to *Glide* through his task, it might be that internally he's *Pressing*; a simple shift in terms of Weight, from Light in *Gliding,* to Strong in *Pressing*.

   Maybe there is an Obstacle? The measurements might not be adding up the way he had hoped and he is beginning to realise that the new bed will not fit?

4 Susanna's theme kicks in at the 9th bar; what does it suggest? *Floating*, perhaps?

5 This phrase is almost interrupted by another phrase in the 11th, 13th and 15th bars. Maybe it suggests Susanna's inner rhythm. It sounds fluttering, excited, nervous; is Susanna's Internal Effort *Flicking*?

From the introduction of the first duet we have some possible Efforts to play:

	Internal Effort	External Effort
Figaro	*Pressing*	*Gliding*
Susanna	*Floating*	*Flicking*

6 If we look a little later in the duet, something exciting happens! Susanna's rhythm changes and she seems to adopt Figaro's rhythm. Maybe she shifts her Effort, also, to match his; *Pressing*? Figaro's *Pressing* runs in parallel until point 7 . . .

7 . . . when Susanna seems to *Press* home her Objective. This might also be the first Event in the duet because at 8 . . .

8 . . . Figaro adopts Susanna's rhythm. Maybe Figaro illustrates that he, like Susanna, is also *Floating*?

Alongside Efforts consider the other components of the Structural Model:

- Space: we know from the Given Circumstances that the room Figaro is measuring is a small one. How do they both use the space? How do they move around it?

- Relationship: what is Figaro and Susanna's physical orientation towards each other? How much do they look at each other? How close are they throughout the scene? And for how long? Do they touch each other? If so, it should be with clear intent, not arbitrary; touch rarely is.[12]

- Actions: what are they doing? And how? Is there a particular Rhythmic Construct that underlies their gestures? Susanna's music suggests that she might seem to travel between *Swings* and *Impulses*; Figaro's, between *Impacts* and *Rebounds*.

- Body: how do they stand or sit? Which body part do they lead with?

---

[12] See Chapter 9: Rehearsals in Depth.

Act I

(Scene: An incompletely furnished room, with an arm-chair in the middle. Figaro has a ruler in his hand; Susanna is seated at a mirror, trying on a small, flowered hat.)

No.1. Cinque... dieci...

Duettino

Figaro and Susanna

Figure 5.8 Act One Scene One.

Figure 5.9 Act One Scene One.

Figure 5.10 Act One Scene One.

How you *write* the story through movement creates and expresses the story. Develop an awareness of the choices you have, framed by the Structural Model, and use rehearsals to actively explore your choices; you begin to see possibilities in space, within relationships, in your body, in the actions you do and through the rhythm of your movement. Developing this awareness will reduce the need for 'blocking' in staging (which, more often than not, restricts the development of character) and place you, the singer, in a position of creative control.

SUMMARY

- Laban gives us the ingredients of movement through the Structural Model: Actions, Body, Space, Relationships and Dynamics. Expression is built out of these ingredients.
- Rhythmic Constructs define the movement rhythm of every action: Impulse, Impact, Swing, Rebound, Continuous.
- Laban defines four key Motion Factors: time, space, weight and flow. These can be internal or external expressions.
- Efforts are the archetypal movements created from different combinations of three Motion Factors: time, space and weight.
- Your body is an instrument through which to reveal the story of the character.
- By adjusting one element of your movement, the whole psychology of your character can seem to be transformed.

TO DO

- Clarify your own movement tendencies.
- Observe movement and label it; collect movement ideas to create character.
- Have a clear intention of what it is you want to express in the story through movement.
- Remove generalisations; be specific!
- Consider the ingredients list presented in the Structural Model; how does it help create 1) character and 2) the movement within the scene?
- Consider your character's movements; are they led by particular Body Parts?
- Explore possible Internal and External Efforts for your character throughout the opera.
- Explore a palette of gestures for your character.

Lecoq

JACQUES LECOQ

Jacques Lecoq (1921–1999) was a teacher and practitioner whose work focused upon the techniques of physical theatre and movement for performance. His philosophies emphasise the importance of collaboration.

Born in Paris, he trained as a physiotherapist, and began to analyse the geometry of movement of the body in space.[13] His early work as an actor took him to Italy for eight years, where he explored *Commedia dell'arte*, the mask and Greek tragedy and chorus.

He founded L'ecole Internationale de Théâtre Jacques Lecoq in 1956. The school continues to train many leading actors, directors and choreographers.

---

[13] Lecoq, J. (2000). *The Moving Body*. London: Methuen Drama, p. 3.

Lecoq's work and practice introduces a range of approaches to bring awareness to the body, alongside tools for creating character through movement. At Opera Works we worked with a number of practitioners who trained under Lecoq; each brought a different emphasis to his teaching and extended his work in a variety of ways.

Lecoq's toolkit explores:

- the translation of physical technique into dramatic situation;
- scales and levels of performance;
- Mask and the State of Neutral;
- animal work.

Lecoq's work is experiential and best understood through *doing* the exercises. These exercises emphasise the importance of play and the imagination and the development of a physically engaged state. They also explore how working within certain constraints can lead to a clearer definition of expression.

As a teacher and practitioner Lecoq saw his role as placing obstacles in the performer's path, in order for each performer to better find a way around them.[14] Many exercises help access the scale of operatic worlds by pushing ideas to the physical and psychological extremes. In turn, they also explore how to reduce that scale so that, whilst expression remains alive within the body, the singer can work without strain being placed upon the voice.

I have divided these exercises into two categories; those that are particularly useful for developing the scene and those that relate specifically to developing physical character. Engagement with all these exercises will develop your physical technique and increase your awareness of the possibilities of movement and your body.

Some of the following exercises originate directly from Lecoq himself whilst others derive from those who trained and worked with him. They all capture the essence of his approach to storytelling. Work, as always, barefoot and in comfortable clothes.

As a brief warm-up exercise, I recommend doing Exercise: Ball Throw (p. 31).

Scene Work

BAMBOO

The following exercises use a bamboo stick[15] to help to create a dynamic spatial relationship between performers, as well as improving movement and coordination skills.

The bamboo helps to connect the internal and external at the same time. It engages the whole body with the work. It brings a fluidity to your work; the bamboo does not bend, so

---

[14] Lecoq, J. (2000). *The Moving Body*. London: Methuen Drama, p. x.
[15] The bamboo stick is an extraordinarily useful training tool; get along to your local garden centre, buy a couple! They need to be about shoulder height. Get some medical gauze, wrap around each end and tape it on; ensure they are padded and comfortable to use.

you must work around it. Perhaps most importantly, when the stick falls to the floor (which it will do again and again), it is a reminder that you have failed! And that failing is not necessarily such a problem; indeed, it is absolutely necessary to continue to learn. The very act of simply picking up the bamboo and replacing it, with perhaps greater determination not to let it fall again, brings a terrific perspective to your work; no one 'ever became great or good except through many and great mistakes!'[16]

EXERCISE: *Balance, Control, Focus*
Solo/20 mins

- Working by yourself, place the bamboo horizontally along the top of your head, from front to back. Walk around the space, attempting to keep the bamboo stick in place.

- When the bamboo inevitably drops, catch it before it hits the floor and hold the position in which you catch the stick for five seconds. Remain completely still, before replacing the bamboo stick on top of your head and continuing.

- This moment of poise as you hold the stick is important. Firstly, the necessity to catch the stick demands that you are always alert to the possibility of it falling; your knees, in particular, remain responsive and ready. Get low to the floor and remain soft footed. Secondly, how the stick falls determines how you catch it and so places your body in space in unusual, unpredictable positions. Be aware of the line and shape of your body and what story this might tell.

- Become more adventurous with how you move about the space. Try running, travelling backwards, sideways, at different levels. Jump. Leap. Do tasks. Keep pushing yourself.

- Try the same exercise again but this time balancing the bamboo on the crook of the arm, or horizontally or vertically on the fingertip.

- A few things to remember:

    At all times remain aware of the obstacles in space around you.

    Connect your core.

    Unlock your knees.

    Do not stamp your feet.

    When balancing the stick vertically, focus on the far end of the stick to help you balance.

- Try this exercise with an aria or, if rehearsals allow, in a scene with others.

- What do you notice? Does the exercise ground you? How does it affect the breath? How does it change or sustain thoughts?

---

[16] William E. Gladstone.

EXAMPLE: *The Marriage of Figaro*

We used this exercise to explore the Countess's cavatina (No. 10, 'Hear my prayer' / 'Porgi Amor') and it really helped the singer sustain their thoughts with energy throughout. There are a number of challenges with this aria. First is connecting the rather long introduction to the first line of sung text. We began this exercise during the play-in. The physical concentration required to balance the bamboo seemed to immediately engage the body and thoughts throughout the play-in and through to the first line. Second, these are big thoughts – the Countess is contemplating a life without love – and they are carried through the aria *larghetto* (fairly slow), so energy is needed to keep them alive, especially in those bars where the Countess is not singing; the bamboo exercise demands a consistent focus that seemed to translate into the singing. Third, the big challenge with this aria is that because the Countess is contemplating death, the temptation can be to play 'sad'. Rather, consider that the Countess, who we know as the ever-resourceful Rosina, is attempting to strike a bargain, perhaps through prayer. The Countess sings 'may his love be reawakened or forsaken let me die' and the singer therefore needs to explore the implied tension in the proposition of a deal throughout the aria; the tension between investing in hope and finding the resolve to die. The exercise requires a great deal of control and focus, which somehow frees the singing; it draws you away from the temptation to play emotions, towards the immediacy of the situation.

PUSH AND PULL

Everything we ever do can be reduced to push or pull:

- We can pull or push others or objects.
- We can be pulled or pushed by others.
- We can pull or push ourselves.

These two essential actions can go in all directions; backwards, forwards, up, down, to one side, diagonally. Certain individual body parts may emphasise the action. The action itself implies a target: an object, a person, a god, a space to be pulled towards or pushed away from. The action and target can be physical or psychological.

EXERCISE: *Push and Pull*
Pairs/Group

This exercise explores all these elements of push and pull and is particularly useful in scene work for making the psychological push and pull, the underlying subtext, visceral and present.

- Working in pairs, hold a bamboo stick between the forefingers of your opposing hands. Exert a little pressure to keep the stick secure between your fingers.
- Move around the space, working together to try not to let the stick drop to the floor.

- Become increasingly daring in your movement together. Explore sitting down, changing speed and rhythm, rolling on the floor, whilst always remaining linked together by the stick.
- As you play, allow stories between you and your partner to unfold. What do certain relationships in space remind you of? What happens if your free hands touch?
- Extend this to working with other pairs to increase the number of people, sticks and connections. Be playful in how you discover the possibilities of moving with the sticks. Attempt to weave between each other, create knots and unravel, move over, under and through each other.

Extend this to working on a scene in pairs:

- First improvise a scene in silence; you will know what the character sings but, rather than singing, explore the underlying push and pull in the relationship between two characters by keeping the connection between you and your partner with the stick.
- Next, sing and play the scene whilst remaining connected by the bamboo. The exercise makes visible the sub-textual connection between characters. You *feel* someone pulling away, you literally *push* into somebody else. Explore the extent of the force of the push and pull so that you play with different levels of force. Acknowledge the moments where the word you or your partner are singing to each other seem to contradict your physical relationship.
- Extend this work in pairs by placing the bamboo between each of your foreheads and playing a scene. Explore when you make eye contact. Move slowly to begin with. This exercise will make the scene more direct but certain associations within the scene, not previously alighted upon, will become apparent.
- After exploring the scene in this way, immediately play the scene without the sticks.
- What do you notice? Is there a *heat* between you and your partner? Are there new connections between the characters? Have certain undercurrents become more present? How do you use the space now?
- What happens if you connect the bamboo to different body parts in certain scenes? For example, your shoulder, sternum, just below the belly button.
- Extend this exercise to ensemble work to explore the connection between three or more characters.

A few things to remember:

- Develop a ping pong dynamic between you and your partner. Rather than both pushing and pulling simultaneously, develop the rhythm of your partner moving, and then you moving, and so on; this will give you more time and space to understand the implications of what is happening.

- Be tactically diverse. When improvising scenes for the first time, you are not bound by staging or 'blocking', all your attention is on the underlying currents revealed through your relationship to each other in space. Ideally, this will then lead directly to staging the scene. If you are in a rehearsal where things are staged early on, try using bamboo sticks to energise the space between you and your partner.

- Always look at each other, unless it seems important not to.

- Explore how you use your free hand (if the bamboo is connected through the hands).

- When moving from using the bamboo to playing without the bamboo, make the transition as swift as possible so that the physical connection that was created by the bamboo is not lost.

I find the bamboo exercises exciting; they help us to mark the space between characters and, by so doing, help us appreciate the difference even a shift of a centimetre can make between two characters in a scene.

The bamboo exercises also help us to define physical characterisations. Are certain characters more likely to push and pull than others, or are they more passive and more likely to be pushed or pulled? From which parts of the body does your character initiate the push or pull? Do you feel a particular affinity with your character when exploring these exercises?

EXAMPLE: *The Marriage of Figaro*

Look at the scene between Susanna and Marcellina in Act One, beginning with the recitative and leading to their duet No. 5, 'I bow to your grace, after you / Via resti servita'. At the beginning of the recitative the two are not singing to each other and, yet, everything they do is in response to the other. The bamboo ensures this unspoken, or unsung, connection is alive. The final lines of the recitative clearly imply the force of the push and pull dynamic:

Susanna	(*I'd better go*)
Marcellina	(*I'd better stop her*)

When exploring the duet with bamboos in rehearsals, we noticed how the connection with the bamboo helped to define the different ways of *pushing*. The women throw repeated insults at each other but physically they jabbed, needled, stabbed, twisted, propelled. We also noticed how, even when Marcellina seems to want to pull away ('*Oh, this is unbearable, I'm bursting, I'm bursting with rage*'), by continuing to be physically connected to Susanna with the bamboo, it helped heighten the internal tension within Marcellina; she wants to leave but, actually *feeling* Susanna's presence, also wants to *push* her once more.

EXERCISE: *Balancing the Space*
Group 20 mins

This exercise demands an acute awareness of our partners' physical movements and invites for our response to them. It increases our awareness of how relationships in space reveal the story to an audience.

- Set a circle of chairs, with a large circle of space in the middle. Imagine this space is a plate balanced upon a pin at its centre.

- The first person enters the space. They walk to the centre of the plate and upon finding the centre, they turn 360 degrees to take in the entire group. They stop, facing one of the group, and walk backwards to invite this person into the space.

- This invitation is to balance the plate on the pin. Wherever the first person travels around the imaginary plate, the second person must imagine that they are a counterweight to their partner and balance the plate accordingly.

- The first person can move around the plate in either direction, or towards or away from the centre, or across the centre point. The second person must always balance the plate.

- If the plate is unbalanced with the second person failing to counter the first person's weight, then whichever member of the group sitting in the circle of chairs nearest to the point where the imaginary plate is most unbalanced, must step into the space to balance the plate.

- At this point, the first and second person join together as one team. The third person is now in control, testing the newly formed team, attempting to make them unbalance the plate or to accidentally split in opposite directions.

- Once the plate is unbalanced again, a fourth person enters the space. Player three then joins the first and second player as a team, and so the exercise continues.

- Notice the stories that unravel. Where does the power lie? How much movement is required? How do shifts in tempo, rhythm, direction and intention confuse and confound the opposite player/s?

Throughout Opera Works we had the great pleasure to work with Marcello Magni. He introduced this exercise with terrific emphasis on the first person's entry into the space, asking: how do you own this space? How do you physically introduce yourself to your audience? How do you say *this is my territory* without turning the audience off? How do you spark interest in the game from the beginning? Player after player would stand up and rarely make it to the centre spot before betraying through their movement a lack of self-belief or revealing a preoccupation with something other than that exact moment; and would be sent back to their chair to try again. Marcello likened this to a gladiatorial ring; the performer must take the moment, the space and the audience with them, in order to tell a story.

EXAMPLE: *The Marriage of Figaro*

We used this exercise when working on the Act Two finale, No. 15 'Out you come, you vile seducer'/'Esci omai, garzon malnato'. First, the Count takes the centre and invites the Countess into the ring. Explore if and when there is a change of leader during this exchange (in an adaptation of the original exercise, we allowed the leader to change over without discussion). Then, as Susanna enters, the Count and Countess join the same team and Susanna seeks to unbalance them.

Adaptations of the conventional rules continued when we played the scene. For example, at the *allegro* when the Countess sings, '*I cannot believe it, Susanna, where is he?*', the Countess joined Susanna's team and left the Count alone. However, it might also be interesting to look at the Count and Countess remaining on the same team, despite the asides the Countess is making to Susanna. When Figaro enters, the game becomes even more interesting. It is important to explore how the relationships unfold in space within the confines of the rules of balancing the plate.

It is also worth noting that the exercise – played, as it is, in the round with audience watching on all sides – demands that the players are not only in contact with each other but also with the edge of the space (where the imaginary plate will tip if unbalanced) and, thus, the audience. It heightens the performers' awareness of the story being told to the audience and how to use the space to reveal the subtext to this audience. No matter how naturalistic or abstracted a production is, you will need an awareness of the audience on some level: you must consider how to open up the story to the audience, where best to place yourself to reveal an Event, how to angle yourself on stage to allow yourself or your partner to be heard.

Physical Characterisation

UNDULATION

Lecoq describes undulation as 'the human body's first movement, underlying all locomotion'.[17] Undulation is the result of the physical effort exerted by the body in response to gravity. The movement tends to be centred in the pelvis as the point of leverage against the ground and from there transmits to other parts of the body. Lecoq explores the entire body going through one full undulation and suggests that different points on this cycle physically represent different stages of a person's life.

---

[17] Lecoq, J. (2000). *The Moving Body*. London: Methuen Drama, p. 75.

To begin with we should look at how to complete an undulation:

- Firstly, stand upright, your legs apart (as though standing over a small hedge) and pushed out, so that you are on the outside edges of your feet.

- Imagine a coin is thrown onto the wall directly opposite; at the moment it is thrown push your head forward as though to follow the coin's flight.

- Then follow the coin's journey with your nose, down the wall and along the floor towards you.

- Imagine that upon reaching your feet the coin travels up your body; continue to follow it with your nose. As the imaginary coin journeys up your body, you press each body part in contact with the coin forward, in order to be able to properly follow its journey; from shins to chest.

- Lean back as the coin rolls up your chest in order to continue to look at it.

- Still leaning back, the coin rolls over your chin, nose and arrives at your forehead.

- At which point you impel it forward once more towards the wall.

- Figure 5.11 illustrates this movement.

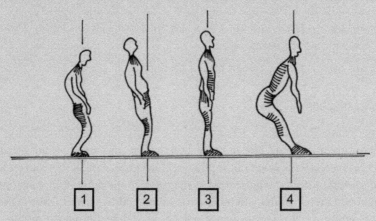

Figure 5.11 Lecoq undulation[18]

- Once you have mastered the Undulation, it is interesting to play with pausing at various points along the cycle.

- You might pause at the points illustrated above; Lecoq likened (1) to someone in old age, slouched and burdened by time, (2) to the mature adult leaning backwards (3) to the upright mid-life adult and (4) to the frame of a child – inquisitive, propelled forward.

- By pausing at random moments along the cycle you will begin to discover different postures that might seem to suggest different characters.

---

[18] Drawing by theatre and opera designer Mark Friend.

- Walk with this posture. As you do so consider the distance between the character's feet, the length of their stride, where in the body they are balanced, whether they roll their hips, if they seem to be being pushed forward or pulled backward, their resistance to gravity.
- Allow this frame to begin to inform your character's thoughts; where does their focus seem to be? How do they relate to other people? How do they enter or leave a space? How do they sit or stand?

EXERCISE: *Reverse Undulation*
Solo

- Try the undulation in reverse. Start by looking up and then imagine the coin drops onto your chest. Track the coin down your chest. Then follow the coin onto the floor and away in front of you. Then imagine it rolling up the wall and onto the ceiling.
- These movements suggest an external initiation, in contrast to the first undulation which suggests an internal drive.
- Follow the same process as above by exploring possible points at which to stop. The reverse undulation might prompt you to explore alternative postures.

EXERCISE: *Body Parts*
Solo/Group

When exploring these undulation exercises also consider which body parts the character might be led by. Imagine that all the character's movement is driven forward by one particular part of their body, as though a barely perceptible thread were attached to this body part and pulled forward by an unknown force.

- Explore the impulse for movement. Begin by being led by the different features of the face (the forehead, the nose, the lips, the chin) and then the chest, the stomach, the hips, the hands and fingers, the knees, the feet.
- Be aware of the amount of tension that each particular body part holds when leading the rest of the body: is it bound or free?
- What direction does each body part seem to travel in: is it direct or flexible?
- Does your focus naturally land at a particular level?
- What do you see when your colleagues do this exercise? Who are these characters?
- How do you feel when certain body parts lead you? Each time you do this exercise, write down adjectives to describe the feelings you notice.

A character might be led by different body parts depending upon who they are within the scene. For example, Susanna might be led by her eyes or nose when with Figaro but by her sternum when serving the Countess. Explore how this might create different layers to your character. We all have a multiplicity of different personas given different circumstances; how might these be revealed physically?

States of Tension

As we have already explored through Laban's work, movement is the visible result of the interplay between tension and release. There is always tension in the body and Lecoq categorises these different levels of tension to create seven identifiable States of Tension. We will each have experienced these States of Tension, informed by certain events. We will have an affinity with a certain state, a disposition to engage with life in a particular way.

Each State is defined through a series of different images and the best way to understand these is to explore them on your feet, State by State, ideally within a group. The common thread through all these States is the need to move forward; through all States you are always in motion:

STATE 1: THE LEAD BLANKET

Lie on the floor, limbs uncrossed and head released. Imagine a lead blanket pressing down on top of you, formed to the specific contours of your body, the weight of the blanket equally distributed over every part of your body, pressing you into the ground. Find the will to move. Push against the blanket in a constant attempt to get up. Make a consistent effort to resist the weight of the blanket.

Now, making an imaginative leap, imagine enough layers of the blanket have been removed to enable you to roll onto one side and lever yourself up to a standing position. The blanket will be repositioned over your shoulders, neck and head, continuing the downward pressure. The sensation is such that you should feel that all your muscles have been stripped away, your body resembling the frame of a tent, almost buckling under the extraordinary weight of almost unbearably heavy material. To lift a foot, to initiate a step, will place too much weight on the remaining standing leg; you will overbalance and fall over. Your skeletal frame, with widened stance dug into the ground, is the only resistance to the overbearing pressure. You can barely shuffle around the space.

STATE 2: SPAGHETTI/CALIFORNIAN COOL

Now imagine that your limbs, your torso, indeed your entire body, is spaghetti. You have no knees, hips, ankles, wrists or vertebrae; all have been replaced with spaghetti. Your body moves almost entirely freely, barely bound by tension, subject to the pull of gravity and the weight of your own body. If your head, the heaviest part of your body, moves one way, the rest of your body will follow; perhaps the hips acting as counter-weight. Your limbs may move in entirely different directions. Your muscles have more tension within them than State 1 but the movements of your muscles are akin to a slinky dog toy; as a result, this can be a rather enjoyable State to inhabit.

Reduce the movement down, connect it to an internal sensation, and the State becomes more like a hippy in 1960s California, lolling casually down the beachfront promenade. Any attempt to high five passers-by will likely miss but you will be *cool* with that; State 2 generally embraces a care-free attitude.

STATE 3: ECONOMIC/EFFICIENT

State 3 uses the exact amount of effort to execute a task. The expenditure of energy is acutely accurate. Every movement is precise; there are no spirals or undulations.

Every task is carried out with a certain simplicity and never overcomplicated by an attempt to do two things at once. State 3 has no attitude to anything other than an appreciation for order. You turn. You see something unaligned. You walk over to it. Your pace is steady; neither fast nor slow. Your arms swing simply enough to propel your walk. Your head, shoulders, hips are all aligned. If an obstacle, or another person, momentarily obstructs your journey, you simply wait until the obstruction has moved on. And then you continue. You arrive at your destination. You carry out your task in a deliberate and ordered way. You turn to face the room. If another task presents itself, you move towards it in the same economic and efficient manner. There is no variation.

STATE 4: CURIOUS/ALERT

There is a further increase in tension. Your awareness of the space and the possibilities within it heightens. In State 4 there are *endless* possibilities. There is barely enough time to explore everything but, nevertheless, you charge at every sound, texture, object, person, surface, smell, colour and taste with eager anticipation. Your movements are constantly forward and back. You have the readiness of a dog about to chase a ball. You are alert to everything and fascinated to discover the possibilities within the space. You are on the balls of your feet, exploring with the great intensity and furious intrigue of a toddler. Once something catches your eye, you drop whatever previously so absorbed you, and immerse yourself in the delights of new discoveries.

STATE 5: DEMONSTRATIVE DIRECTOR/MELODRAMA

State 5 is expansive, open and direct. Intentions are clear and they are signalled demonstrably to others. Ideally, State 5 executes very little, other than directives to others. The body is used as a means to distinctly semaphore these instructions; not unlike an air steward on a plane indicating the exits. Another way to think of State 5 is that you are the leading protagonist in your own 1920s German expressionist film; grand melodramatic gestures, heightened responses to everyday events, suspended emotions worn resolutely on the exterior.

STATE 6: PASSION

Imagine the amount of tension required to push over a tree, or to lift a car off a person trapped beneath; this is the tension required in State 6. It is the passion experienced the moment your team is on the cusp of scoring the winning goal of a cup final, or when somebody prangs your beautifully restored vintage car. It is not about playing anger or fury, although when in this state you might well appear to be angry or furious, and it is not about shouting. It is about finding intense expression in your body and gestures to express a moment of intense feeling. State 6 never achieves and never resolves; it is always on the edge. It is also exhausting to sustain State 6 for any great period of time. You must find the opportunity to release this pent-up tension, to discover the inevitable ebbs and flows within each moment, in order to continue in this State.

STATE 7: TRAGEDY

State 7 is the most extreme state of tension. It is an expression in response to the moment the worst thing that could happen, happens. You make a sustained appeal to the gods or you slam your fists into the ground; you reach, arms outstretched, in fruitless appeal or damn the earth for your plight. The body is in continuous motion;

however, the tempo of this movement is restricted by muscles bound with extraordinary tension. If you make a sound, it is an endless scream, like the noise we might imagine emanating from Edvard Munch's *The Scream*. Every part of the body is engaged, stretched or compressed, in an endless gesture.

Note:

- When exploring these States, it can be useful to improvise speech or singing. Ensure you adequately support the voice; especially in States 6 and 7. These States must not result in shouting. I have noticed that State 5 can quickly result in singers barking orders at each other. Focus on bringing the tension into the *body*; fully physicalising each State, rather than placing tension in the voice.

- Initially, explore these States at a heightened level; it will help you draw the distinction from one to the next. The States become more useful, however, when reduced down to a smaller physical volume; sometimes it might be effective to reduce the States to a level that is barely perceptible. Herein lies the possibility for detailed work rather than generalisation.

INTERNAL STATES OF TENSION

States of Tension can be carried *within* you; an *Internal* State of Tension informing your response to the world but covered by another, *External*, State. The Given Circumstances of the opera will suggest the reason for a disparity between Internal and External States. For example, imagine an interviewee in a job interview who has already unsuccessfully interviewed for fifty jobs. They might be in Internal State 1; a sense of already being defeated, or on the edge of giving up. However, in the job interview the applicant might cover State 1 with State 4, to suggest to the prospective employer that they are curious, alert and engaged with the potential job. It is always dramatically interesting when the External State, perhaps informed by certain cultural standards and codes, gives way to an Internal State; it might only be for an instant but it visibly reveals something of the character. This is something composers play with repeatedly in opera. This flash of an Internal State might only be apparent in the orchestration but, in such cases, it is vital that the singer is seen to have created this music through their physical state.

EXERCISE: *A States of Tension Journey*
Solo/Group 10 mins

It is useful to play with the transition from one State to the next. The more familiar you are with this tool, the more you can use it. These exercises can help to clarify the difference between each State and the very moment of transition from one State to another. This transition might be initiated by an Event and the shift from one State to the another can therefore help define a turning point in a scene.

- Firstly, draw an imaginary line across the space from one corner of the room to the furthest point. Walk this line, beginning in State 1, travelling through each State, and reaching the end of the line in State 7.
- Travel back along the line, this time from State 7 back to State 1.
- Next, get into a group of three with one chair. Person A and B aim to get C to sit in the chair. C is the perfect obstacle and finds many and various ways to refuse. A and B begin in State 1 and move through each of the States; an observer claps every thirty seconds to mark the transition into the next State.
- Play this exercise again, but with person C working from State 1 through to 7.
- Then again, with each person starting in different States and moving through them at the same time.
- Next, the group improvise a simple scenario; travelling to work in the morning, going into battle, rehearsing an opera. Improvise this scene whilst working through the different States collectively.
- Write 1 through to 7 on separate pieces of paper, twice over. Four players take two pieces of paper each, keeping the numbers of their pieces of paper secret. The first number represents their Internal State, the second their External State. Establish a simple scenario; a park bench at lunchtime or a bus stop and a delayed bus. One by one the players take to the space and, at certain points, for specific reasons, reveal their Internal States. Observers watch to discern the Internal and External States of the players.
- It can be exciting to combine the bamboo exercises with States of Tension. It helps develop greater fluidity in the transition between States. The constraints that the bamboo imposes seem to help frame with greater clarity the distinction between one State and the next.

The feedback your trusted collaborators can give you is vital, especially when working on movement tools. We are often unaware of the stories we tell through our bodies and it is only by listening to such observations that we can begin to heighten our awareness to our physicality and adapt in order to fully express our intentions.

EXAMPLE: *The Marriage of Figaro*

Too often, when watching opera, theatre or film, you will see singers and actors remain in one State throughout their entire performance. Many actors in soap operas on television seem to too easily get stuck in State 3; with an occasional shift into a shouty State 6.

The Duet in Act Three between the Count and Susanna, No.16 'How could you be so cruel'/'Crudel! Perchè finora', can be enlightening when using States of Tension. It is worth exploring a different combination of States to see which yields the most dramatic tension.

For example:

	INTERNAL STATE	EXTERNAL STATE
Count		
How could you be so cruel, making me suffer so?	3	3
You were so cruel, making me suffer so.	4	3
Susanna		
A girl needs time to ponder, should it be yes or no?	3	2
Count		
Then you'll be there this evening?	4	3
Susanna		
You speak and I obey.	6	3
Count		
Swear you'll be there to meet me.	6	5
Susanna		
How could I stay away?	1	2

That the Count and Susanna could often share External State 3 might suggest the external pressures of a supposed illicit romance in public; if somebody were to discover them, they would need to present 'normality'. Susanna's shift into State 2 – a freer, more flirtatious State – would be a conscious decision, in order to persuade the Count of her promised intentions. The Count might tend to dictate and State 5 might be a familiar State for the character.

States of Tension are easy to change and give you a clear grasp of exactly *what* it is you are changing and *when*. Using them can be an early way to discover the possibilities of a scene or a way of freshening up a scene that seems to have become stale; when playing a scene in rehearsals and in performance, you might have a tendency over time to err towards one particular State.

I think States of Tension are particularly useful for singers. They allow you to create visible tension in your body without having to create emotional tension which, more often than not, creates tension in the throat and restricts the voice. Of course, as we have seen through the work of Michael Chekhov,[19] your physical frame will inform your interior emotional life but States of Tension provide a way of specifically managing and controlling the amount of tension you play with.

As a director, I find States particularly useful when working with a Chorus. It provides a way of uniting a group's response to an Event, for clarity of storytelling, whilst affording the performers freedom to respond individually within each of the States.

---

[19] Objectives (p. 73).

Animal Work

The study of animals can be a tremendously liberating way of creating physical character. It is something Lecoq encouraged as a way of bringing you closer to the study of the human body; you begin to see how your body moves in contrast to other animals. However, to study and embrace animal movement pushes you to work at your physical extremes of expression, outside the codes of civilised human behaviour. It provides a framework to physically articulate a character's less socially acceptable motivations.

Animals are led by instinct. They are responsive to the moment, always present, with no sense of obligation to the future or past. This quality of being in the moment, unrehearsed, is something that, as a singer, you must develop in order to suggest that the music you are singing is being communicated for the first time, in response to a spontaneous event.

Animal work is part of the journey of characterisation; it is not an end in itself. Even if you are playing a character in, for example, Janacek's *The Cunning Little Vixen*, there is a process of anthropomorphic realisation of a character that will integrate human behaviours and movements. Regardless of which operatic world your character inhabits, this can be a useful *way in*. It requires you to see the character from another physical perspective and, as animals have simpler behavioural codes than humans, helpfully enables you to simplify your approach to character.

Which animal might your character most be like? Does the music suggest certain characteristics that you associate with certain animals? How does the melodic structure, the tempo, the rhythm, the words that the librettist has used, guide you towards a choice? Does your character have a particular function in the opera that allies them to a certain animal?

When initially choosing an animal to study, try to avoid apes and chimps, due to their similarity with humans. Also, avoid choosing fish; they always prove problematic for obvious reasons!

The most important place to start your study is at a zoo. If this is not possible, seek out your animal elsewhere; a family pet, the internet. Observe the animal in detail by making notes, drawings, or taking videos. As you watch, try to capture, embody and replicate the distinct qualities you observe.

ANALYSING ANIMAL MOVEMENT
Break down the animal's movements into the following categories:

Contact with the Ground

- How is the animal's contact with the ground different from your own?
- What kind of surface is their natural territory and how does this affect them?
- How much weight do they give the floor? How is this weight distributed?
- How do they balance? For example, chickens carefully place their feet down as though walking on hot coals, the padding dog has a firm, secure placement, the parade horse prances as though in stilettos.

Movement Through the Spine

- If the animal is a quadruped, how does this affect the movement of their spine? Consider the flexibility of the cat's twisting and arching spine.
- How much does the spine power the animal? Consider short-limbed undulating reptiles.
- Look at the flight of birds and the width of their wing span. Consider how the limbs extend from the spine and where the movement originates.

Breath

- What rhythm and tempo does your animal breathe in? Try to tap the rhythm of the breath out for yourself and then extend this sensation of rhythm to your whole body.
- When singing, you obviously won't be able to replicate the animal's breath using your own breath. Translating the rhythm and tempo of their breath to another part of your body can, however, communicate an essential quality of the animal.

Focus

- How are their eyes positioned and how does this angle cause them to orientate themselves to best see?
- What does your animal look for; what attracts them?

Other Senses

- Which other senses does the animal rely upon? Do they, for example, lead with their ears? How much information do they gather through taste?

Sounds

- What noises do they make?
- Does this connect in any way to what or how your character sings?

Attitude

- How do they spend their day and how many different attitudes can you observe them in? A cat grooms, prowls, brushes up against a leg, curls up in self-protective rest, skittishly chases a ball, prepares to attack, etc.
- How do they transition from one attitude to the next?

Space

- How do they use the space? Do they move directly or indirectly?
- How do they orientate themselves to an object?
- What level do they live at? How do they share this space with others?
- Are they singular creatures or part of a herd?

Your observations of animals will be limited by the time you can spend watching them; this will likely only be in one environment. It is therefore useful to research further into the particular habits of this animal; details about their natural habitat, their eating and sleeping habits, etc. Further details will be filled by your imagination. The approach is therefore similar to playing a human character.

EXERCISE: *Becoming Your Animal*
Solo/Group 20 mins

- Now move from observation and analysis to workshopping your animal. Wear comfortable clothes and ensure you warm up and down, with particular focus on those areas of your body that might be working harder than usual through this work. You will require great flexibility, especially in your spine. If you are creating a quadruped, it is a good idea to use knee pads when working on all fours.

- Begin by focusing your attention on one part of your animal's movement. You will have analysed this part of their movement already; now visualise it in your mind's eye. Very slowly begin to translate this element of their movement into your own body; adopt and replicate their behaviour in detail.

- Start by examining how your animal contacts the ground. Attempt to give the floor the same sense of weight and a similar amount of contact with corresponding surfaces of your body.

- Now, focus on your animal's breath (its rhythm), focus, senses, sounds and attitudes.

- Work by yourself and, for the moment, do not interact with others in the group.

- Throughout this work it is important to bear in mind that your physiology is different from that of your animal; in most cases this will be rather obvious! You will need to consider how to adapt its movements in order to translate it to your movement. You will need to make choices and judge which elements more clearly represent your animal. Additionally, certain elements will be impossible to replicate. For example, if you are creating a squirrel the rapidity of its breath would cause you to hyperventilate. The rhythm of a squirrel's breath is a distinguishing feature of the animal's behaviour, so it might be that you instead place this rhythm elsewhere; your foot might tap the same rhythm.

- Once you have worked through all the elements, arrive at how your animal might use this space. Where might they feel safe? Where might they hunt or forage for food? It might be useful to speak your animal's thoughts out loud; a stream of consciousness helps to make the thoughts more present.

- The room you and the group are working in will now resemble a strange kind of zoo. Begin to notice the other animals in the space. Allow interaction to develop slowly. Are there animals similar to you? Are there predators? Are there those that might intrigue or attract you? As relationships between the animals develop in space, engage imaginatively with your animal's motivations.

The next stage of the process is to look at how you can translate these movement traits to help create character. There are two ways of doing this:

Human Animal 1

When you fully embody your animal, we might define this as playing at Level 10. In order to translate your physicalised animal into a human character, the animal needs to become socialised to the extent that one might not look twice as they walk down the street; aim to reduce your animal to Level 3. To do this, imagine that the movement is drawn within you, leaving only elements of the animal movement visibly present. For example, if you have studied a quadruped, as you reduce from Level 10 to 3 you will now find yourself on two feet, the undulation of the spine will be less extreme, hooves will become hands and claws will become fingers.

These Levels do not follow any sort of consistent measurement; they are simply an imaginative guide. You will make choices; certain traits will remain present, others will no longer be perceptible. You will be left with the essence of your animal: the alertness of the dog, the undulation of the cat, the drive of the bull. These are elements that correspond to a kind of human behaviour and hopefully reveal something about your character.

- Walk around the space embodying your animal at Level 3.
- Do you make eye contact with others? How do you use the space? Where is your attention drawn? Observe how others are moving.
- Now make physical contact with another person; shake their hand and perhaps offer a greeting.
- As you walk around the space, triggered by a clap, leap from Level 3 to Level 7. You will still be on two feet but the more extreme animal movement submerged under your skin will be released; your physical frame will again capture the particular tensions your body previously held.
- Continue walking around the space at Level 3. Now, use the moment of shaking hands as the trigger to leap to Level 7.
- In performance, is there a point when you might choose to reveal this heightened animal physicality in the same way? Is there a trigger within the opera? Perhaps the audience will witness only a flash of revelation; maybe at an emotionally charged moment, when the chains of civilised behaviour are loosened.

Human Animal 2

Another way of making the transition from animal to human is to imagine you have replaced certain parts of your animal body with human parts. For example, you might retain an animal torso but discover you have human limbs.

- Imagine falling asleep as your animal; find a space in the room to do this. When you awake discover that your animal limbs have been replaced with human limbs. Explore how you would begin to move, how your animal motivations respond to this transition.

- Then explore how your behaviour translates into an improvised scene. For example, all the animals are pupils in a school room; there is one teacher. How do these animals with human limbs become socialised? How do you behave in this human context?

- This exercise gives you an opportunity to explore certain gestures, traits and movements that you can select and incorporate into your process of creating physical character.

EXAMPLES: *The Marriage of Figaro/The Magic Flute*

I have found animal work in opera to be incredibly important. Opera is already a heightened world and the clarity of the music, and the ideas contained within it, demand a similar physical clarity in order for the audience to believe that the music has emerged out of the person and their actions. Animal work gives us immediate access to such abstraction. The decision you make about which animal to explore for your character will be entirely individual and based upon how you meet the ideas of the production. In recent productions of *Figaro* and *Flute* that I have directed, the singers layered their exploration of their characters through a process of embodying the following animals' behaviours:

- Figaro – a bear
- Susanna – a meerkat
- The Count – a bull
- The Countess – a badger

- Tamino – a young dog
- Pamina – a lioness
- Papageno – a fox
- Papagena – also a fox
- Queen of Night – a (male) peacock
- Sarastro – a rhino

The Neutral Mask

During Opera Works we worked closely with director and choreographer Leah Hausman[20] who introduced us to the principles of the Neutral Mask. The Neutral Mask is the first mask Lecoq introduced to his students and, whilst not in itself a tool directly leading to physical characterisation, working with the Mask provides an extraordinary wealth of information about how your body and movement reveals story. It is also useful to look at the principles of the Neutral Mask before looking at other masks, for example, those masks featured in *Commedia dell'arte* (crucially important in much operatic repertoire).[21]

Of course, as a singer it will be a rare occurrence to be in a production that requires you to wear a mask. I used large animal masks for characters, Moppet and Poppet, in a production

---

[20] See Chapter 13: Approaches to Rehearsal.
[21] Character Types and *Commedia dell'arte*, p. 178.

of *Paul Bunyan* for Welsh National Opera and it was a challenge to ensure the design allowed for the singer to hear the orchestra and for the voice to project. However, the Neutral Mask is a powerful tool for teaching the performer about themselves, their relationship with the audience and the very nature of theatre itself. This tool could feature at the very beginning of this chapter, or indeed at the very beginning of the book, as it offers a starting point for your work and a number of fundamental lessons. Through my work with singers, however, I have also been aware that Neutral Mask work can initially feel exposing and intimidating; feelings that usually give way to profound reflections. It is important that you explore this work in a safe, positive and supportive environment. As with all these tools, the crucial thing is to experience the mask with observers; gather a group of like-minded singers to fully explore.[22]

The Neutral Mask is about creating a state of *being*. The mask has no character, no sense of past or future, no ambition or desire, no experience of conflict or knowledge of human history. The mask has arrived *here* for the very first time. Once you place the Neutral Mask on, you *are* what happens in this very moment.

Wearing the Neutral Mask initially reveals the story *you* tell; the stories present in your body and movement. As you continue to work with the mask, you must seek to embody the qualities of the mask; to discover a sense of balance and neutrality.

THE MASK IN TRAINING

The neutral mask, in the end, unmasks

Jacques Lecoq[23]

Working with Neutral Mask helps the singer in a number of ways:

- It clarifies and defines your movement. It offers to increase your physical control by helping you experience and observe the composition of movement; bringing your attention to tempo, rhythm, posture and gesture.
- It helps channel expression through the body, rather than through the face.
- It liberates by taking the pressure off the need to *perform* and underlining the importance of simply *being*; the perfect state of awareness for the performer to investigate creative possibilities.

It is not uncommon for singers to feel adrift and uncertain of where to move onstage; unclear of what to do with hands or how to change habitual physical behaviours. Neutral Mask work helps creates balance. It highlights the idea that less is more and that an economy of physical expression is vital in clearly conveying the story. This is important when using the body to create sound; extraneous movement can lead to distortions. The emphasis on channeling expression through the entire body becomes a requirement when working on such a large stage as English National Opera's home, the London Coliseum. Yet Mask work also reveals the true intent behind gestures and guides us away from grand presentation, towards something more truthful.

---

[22] Lecoq used a leather mask created by Amleto Sartori and, where possible, similar masks should be used. There are, however, much less expensive simple white masks that can be purchased more widely. John Rudlin, in the appendix to his book *Commedia dell'Arte – An Actor's Handbook* (Abingdon: Routledge, 1994), brilliantly details how to make a range of masks, if you are so inclined!
[23] Lecoq, J. (2000). *The Moving Body*. London: Methuen Drama, p. 39.

EXERCISE: *Wearing the Neutral Mask*
Group/A Neutral Mask/5 mins

To begin with, shake out the body and assume a neutral stance before placing the mask on:

- Feet shoulder width apart, in parallel;
- Shoulders released, hands by the side, fingers down;
- Hips aligned below shoulders;
- Knees soft and weight slightly forward on the balls of your feet;
- Chin level with horizon, eyes focused towards the horizon.

The group should sit two metres in front of you and observe. The following takes place in silence.

- Face away from the group and place the mask on (this moment should be done in silence; there should be a sense of ritual and anticipation).
- Turn and stand facing the group.
- Breathe deeply and slowly.
- The group proceed to give simple, clear notes and instructions to help you achieve a state of physical neutrality; balanced, aligned, free of tension.
- Once the group has helped you find this state – present and composed – stay for a moment, your eyes resting on the horizon.
- Turn away from the group and remove your mask.

The act of concealing the face brings the audience's attention to the rest of the body. They see your body and the story it tells. Their feedback is crucial to help you find alignment and balance; it must be given and received in the spirit of generosity.

EXERCISE: *Waking Up*
Group/3 mins

Again, in silence, with the group facing you:

- Place the mask on, facing away from the group.
- Close your eyes and drop your head; a moment of rest. Remain with your back to the audience.
- In your own time you awake, *as though for the first time*, and turn, with that same sense of neutrality you experienced previously, to face the observers. Allow the mask to lead your turn; in general, the mask is alive when facing the audience.
- There is a sense of *receiving* the audience as you face them.
- Try some simple gestures; point at an imaginary object on the horizon, open yourself to the sky, turn to focus on a new target. The slower the gestures, the stronger they will be.

- Turn away from the audience, the head trailing, with a sense of departure.
- Take off the mask.

What did the group see? Which gestures resonated? What was unclear? Did they feel you retained neutrality throughout?

How did you feel? Did you experience a sense of freedom? Which gestures felt more connected to that sense of neutrality? How did you connect to the breath?

EXERCISE: *The Sea*
Group/5 mins

This is a reduced version of Lecoq's 'Fundamental Journey' which sees the Neutral Mask wearer traverse an imaginary landscape through forests, over mountains, along rivers; an epic journey through the natural world.[24] Through this exercise resist telling a story; *see*, without attitude.

- Face away from the audience, shake out, breathe deeply, and place your mask on.
- Turn slowly into an imaginary landscape covered with a white mist. Walk a few steps through the mist.
- As the mist clears you see, *for the first time*, the sea.
- Watch it. Allow the picture to become vivid.
- Notice a stone by your foot, bend down and pick up the imaginary stone: look at it, look at the sea and throw the stone into the sea. See the stone land in the water.
- Breathe in the sea. Allow your breath to take on the rhythm and the tempo of the waves. The breath drops into your body.
- The mask and you are one; *become* the sea. Embody the rhythm and tempo of the imaginary sea. Stay with this for a couple of minutes.
- Release the sea and come back to a state of neutrality.
- Turn away from the sea and take off the mask.

You can extend this exercise to explore the other elements; fire, air and earth. Imagine transposing the energy of these elements into your body in the same way. Explore the rootedness of the tree in earth; the sense of roots growing out through the soles of your feet. See the flickering flames of a fire and explore the difference between embodying the intensely vibrating blue centre of the flame and the more gently flickering outer edge of the flames. Always push yourself to your limits when embodying these elements but keep yourself, and others around you, safe. Then, reduce the physical volume of these embodied elements.

Exploring the mask and elements in rehearsals can lead directly to your work developing physical character. Rick Kemp, in his book exploring neuroscience and acting, writes of actors developing muscle memory. He suggests that experiences explored in rehearsals

---

[24] Lecoq, J. (2000). *The Moving Body*. London: Methuen Drama, pp. 42–3.

when creating a role 'remain engraved in the body of the actor ... reactivated in him at the moment of interpretation'[25] This work can capture and instil the essence of a physical quality that can resonate within a character at a given moment in the drama.

EXAMPLES: *The Marriage of Figaro/The Magic Flute*

Figaro, in his Act Four aria, No. 26, 'You foolish slaves of cupid . . . you won't believe your eyes'/'Aprite un po' quegli occhi', is in a state of barely restrained fury. The horns (suggesting cuckoldry) resound in the orchestration, a constant reminder of the infidelity he imagines his new bride to have committed; the strings build in ferocity, finding occasional release as Figaro recognises the cruel irony of the situation; the patter of words grow to a flurry, with little space for breath. This intense fire rages through Figaro's music and needs to be present within the singer. The mask work on elements – in particular, fire – is a good way to access the essence of this moment. The movement can be also be reduced so that it is alive only, for example, in the hands and fingers.

The Magic Flute is filled with symbolism derived from Mozart and librettist Emanuel Schikaneder's fascination with Masonic practice and allegory. The evocation of the four elements is present throughout and it is possible to divide the characters into each of these elements.[26] The Three Boys are clearly associated with air: their voices soar above the rest of the world, the simplicity of the wind accompaniment. When directing the opera, I worked with the singers playing the Boys with masks and the element of air. They pictured a balloon buffeted by the breeze and then worked to embody this quality throughout rehearsals.

SUMMARY

- Lecoq emphasises the importance of your relationship with your partner: the bamboo stick makes this connection visible.
- Balancing the Space and Neutral Mask work brings an awareness of the partnership you form with the audience as a communicator of the story.
- Collaboration is central to creating an environment in which you can explore the extremities of physicality in a safe and supportive environment.
- The work brings an awareness of your body and the possibilities of storytelling through movement, through applied constraints.
- His work emphasises the maxim of *less is more*, through the economy of movement.
- Undulation, States of Tension, Animal work and Mask work provide a series of tools for creating physical character.

---

[25] Kemp, R. (2012). *Embodied Acting: What Neuroscience Tells Us about Acting*. Abingdon: Routledge, p. 86.
[26] Chailley, J. (1972) *The Magic Flute, Masonic Opera*. London: Gollancz, is an enjoyable journey through the opera's use of such imagery.

TO DO

- Begin by finding a state of neutrality with the help of a trusted colleague or group.

- Continued engagement with these tools builds your physical technique and increases your awareness of the possibilities of movement and your body. The more familiar they become, the more useful they will be when creating character.

- Make a note of your inner responses and feelings when working with these particular tools.

- Leah Hausman instructs us to 'reduce the sauce' of the movement; to boil a movement down to its essential rich essence. Stanislavski supports this instruction, claiming: 'an excessive use of gesture dilutes a part as water does good wine'.[27]

Character Types and *Commedia dell'arte*

Archetypal characters are those that are defined by their patterns of behaviour and the function they serve in the story. They are quickly recognisable to the audience and characterised through identifiable qualities. The psychoanalyst Carl Jung identified a range of archetypes common through Western literature:

- Hero

- Lover

- Mentor or Old Sage

- Earth Mother

- Companion

- Innocent or Child

- Trickster

- Shape Shifter or Magician

- Shadow or Villain.

Characters do not always conform exactly to their archetype; they might embody certain qualities or they might change throughout the story. As a singer you will often have to play certain types of character that exist outside of your individual experience; you might play an older or younger character, a king or god, a man or woman. These characters might exist in an entirely imagined reality.

How to approach creating physical characteristics for these characters? Firstly, by research and observation. You cannot simply play a generic old man or a young girl; you need to create an individual and very particular old man or young girl. Of course, their behaviour might be informed by certain uniform qualities – restricted movement or

---

[27] Stanislavski, K. (1999) *Building a Character*. Translated by E. R. Hapgood. London: Eyre Methuen, p. 74.

diminutive stature – but these need to be detailed and specific to each character. Find someone similar to such a character in real life and physically capture their movement in the same way you did in Exercise: Follow the Leader (p. 129). Consider how a particular State of Tension might help you embody a certain quality; add to this the specific details of the character's Given Circumstances. Once you have explored and selected the possible movement traits of this character, you must then *live* with the character; make their physical behaviour habitual by setting aside ten minutes each day to inhabit their everyday movement. Most operas feature characters in times of crisis, but it is useful to explore the movement of your character when not in crisis; ask, how would they cook, walk down the street, read a book?

Of course, if you are playing a character from another period then research into their clothes, formalised gestures they might have employed, dances they engaged in, will be paramount. The important factor to remember is that through these formal patterns of behaviour, *real* people exist. The way they engage in these social rituals will be informed by their character Facts and their Objectives.

EXERCISE: *Moulding*
Pairs/5 mins

This is an exercise to explore with a fellow cast member:

- Refer back to your Character Lists; look at the adjectives you used to summarise everything you sing about your fellow cast member's character.
- Your partner stands in neutral, eyes closed.
- You are going to position your partner into the physical frame that defines how your character sees their character, using the adjectives outlining your character's opinion of them to guide you.
- Mould your partner as a sculptor would mould clay; gently push, pull and place your partner into a position that represents the epitome of your character's view of them.
- Both you and your partner should remain silent during the exercise. Your partner should allow their body to be moved into the positions you place them. You should be as detailed as possible but use only touch to communicate.
- Once you are finished, stand back and ask your partner to open their eyes.
- They become aware of the shape you have created and how this makes them feel.
- They begin, slowly at first, to allow their breath to move them. They begin to move around the space, keenly holding onto those particular tensions that you have created in your body.
- As they move, they should notice how the physicality informs their behaviour and thoughts.
- Once your partner has walked for a minute, swap over. Discuss your observations at the end of the exercise.

> **EXAMPLE:** *The Marriage of Figaro*
>
> When working with young singers on a production of *The Marriage of Figaro* a frequent question arose: *How do I play Marcellina (or Bartolo, Antonio) when I'm in my mid-twenties?*
>
> Here are some pointers:
>
> - Research. Is there someone you know, or someone you might find in your local town centre, who in some way resembles the character you are playing? Maybe only in part? Your eventual characterisation will be formed from a composite of different references. Watch them, in detail: their gestures, their rhythm and tempo. Analyse which body parts seem to lead their movement.
>
> - Slowly Undulate, stopping at various points on the cycle. Explore, in collaboration with colleagues, those points that appear to best represent your character's stage of life. Work in detail; a shift of a centimetre in the position of the shoulders, for example, might make all the difference between a caricature and a character who appears 'real'.
>
> - Most importantly, the way we move is habitual. Moving like somebody else, especially somebody very different from ourselves, requires a good deal of practice.
>
> - Remember to always stretch out after doing this work to release unfamiliar tensions.

Operatic Archetypes

Much operatic repertoire, at least up until the mid-nineteenth century, can be defined by certain plot and character conventions; governed by language and tone. These recognisable forms were delineated through specific recurring ideas and helped make stories more immediately accessible to an audience. In Italy, opera was defined as *seria* or *buffa*, in Germany, *romantische* or *singspiel,* and in France, *grand opéra* and *opéra comique*. Each of these, in turn, were defined by certain character types allied to certain voice types:

- Hero; Lover; Prince (tenor/castrati)
- Heroine; Lover; Princess (soprano)
- Companion; Father; Villain (baritone)
- Companion; Mother (mezzo-soprano)
- High-priest; Patriarch (bass).

Commedia dell'arte ('comedy of the artists') was the major influence on *opera buffa, singspiel* and *opéra comique*. It was a form of improvised street theatre, with mask, music, dance and simple costumes, originating in Italy in the sixteenth century. The performers were troupes of travelling professionals who played a range of masked, stock characters. These were recognisable through their distinctive personalities and behaviours, from one story to the next. The form takes its roots from the market place and the pedlars, quacks and charlatans pitching their potions, pills and inventions. It is, therefore, an oral tradition – stories were not written down – and one which prioritises contact between actor and audience.

Commedia inspired a host of writers and librettists of the day: Molière, Beaumarchais, Marivaux, Goldoni (who first coined the term *Commedia dell'arte* in the eighteenth century to draw a distinction between written and improvised plays).[28] *Opera buffa* usually featured *Commedia* characters in plots set in the present day. This allowed for more direct social commentary than *opera seria*; a form more used to dealing with historical or mythical stories. Today the influence of *Commedia* can be seen directly in the films of Charlie Chaplin and Buster Keaton, the work of Picasso and Hockney, English pantomime and, more widely, the stock characters of such television comedies as *Fawlty Towers, Blackadder* and *The Office*.

Commedia Masks

Unlike the plain, open, Neutral mask, *Commedia* masks are richly characterful; the personality of the stock character is crystallised in each mask. Upon wearing, the actor subsumes their own personality and *becomes* that character. The characters live in the present; there is no sense of past or psychological reality. They are drawn from all levels of class, each defined by the desires that drive them. The masks are accompanied by a set of stock gestures and props associated with each character.

Commedia and Opera

Opera's roots are inextricably linked with *Commedia*; indeed, *Commedia*'s combination of drama and song is similar to that of the *intermedi* of the fifteenth and sixteenth century which were a source of inspiration for early writers of opera. Italian, French and German librettists later drew directly from the cast of *Commedia* stock characters to populate their comic operas. Characters in certain operas by, for example, Mozart, Rossini and Donizetti might have different names, and appear in diverse situations, but will share a similar function and set of personality traits; for example, Mozart's Figaro and Rossini's Dandini (*Cenerentola*) are drawn from *Commedia*'s Arlecchino, whilst Donizetti's Norina (*Don Pasquale*) and Mozart's Susanna originate from *Commedia*'s Columbina.

Commedia and the Singer

Understanding these stock characters can be enlightening when playing the operatic character from which they derive; it can help clarify your character's motivations, physicality and function within the plot. Of course, in opera, each of these stereotypes must be imbued with the truth of their situation, or else they become empty and superficial. Within the frame of the archetype, the reality of the story and subtext suggested by the music must be alive within the performer.

The value of studying *Commedia* also lies in exploring the principles and spirit of the form in performance. Lecoq's early training in Italy embraced *Commedia* or, as he referred

---

[28] There is terrific detail of the background and history in Rudlin, R. (1994) *Commedia dell'Arte: An Actor's Handbook*. Abingdon: Routledge.

to it, *La Commedia Humaine* (*The Human Comedy*); 'It's about misery, a world where life's a luxury ... In commedia you die of everything: desire, hunger, love, jealousy.'[29]

Playing *Commedia* we become aware of the imperative of rhythm in comedy, the possibilities of a direct relationship with the audience, the structure of thoughts, the sense of a physical phrase and, of course, the primacy of play.

Stock Characters

The main masks of *Commedia dell'arte* are:

THE SERVANTS

- *Zanni*

  The lowest of the low; the generic servant working for any of the Masters or Lovers. Zanni can be male or female, is always hungry, sleeps whenever and wherever possible (usually standing up), has strong survival instincts but lacks intelligence. Zanni is driven by sex and hunger. His function is to be the servant of anybody and to create accidental chaos.

- *Arlecchino (Harlequin)*

  The central servant character. Usually servant to Pantalone and in love with Columbina. His name means little devil; he can be crafty (if not the most intelligent) but never nasty. Can shift shape and sometimes has magical powers. His function is to hatch plots or deliver messages, most of which go wrong, although he is rarely the central loser in the story.

- *Brighella*

  He is the little boss servant, often a shopkeeper, with higher status than other Zanni. He is consistently hungry and thirsty. Quick witted but can be malicious, deceitful and volatile, although he is always up front about this. He will do anything for money. Often gives advice to the Lovers and makes sure never to lose his status.

- *Columbina*

  Servant, usually to the *Inamorata (Lovers)*. She is intelligent, literate, resourceful and something of a gossip. She has no monetary ambition and is the lover of *Arlecchino*. The precursor of the *soubrette*. She *knows* everything and comments on it all with a generous spirit. She is usually the messenger for the Lovers. Often pursued by the older men.

THE MASTERS

- *Pantalone*

  Highest status of all the characters; he is the rich old man. He is usually the father of one of the Lovers. He is miserly and terrified of losing his money. Lascivious, driven

---

[29] Hiley, J. (1988) 'Moving Heaven and Earth'. *The Observer*, 20 March, p. 40.

by lust and believes everything can be bought. He often inappropriately pursues much younger women and, as such, is the subject of ridicule.

- *Il Dottore*

  High status; the authority on most, if not all, subjects (or so he would have you believe). Often father to one of the Lovers, he is a friend and competitor of *Pantalone*. Often speaks Latin (the *Commedia* idea of *grammelot* is useful to employ if playing *Dottore*; it is a nonsense language made up of an indistinguishable jumble of words). A heavy drinker. In stories he tends to take up a lot of time and space on stage. If he marries, he is usually immediately cuckolded.

- *Il Capitano*

  A swaggering Captain from another land. In all likelihood not an actual soldier but, as he is an outsider, no other character can prove this. An arrogant, ego driven show-off whose cowardice is usually revealed by the end of the story.

THE LOVERS

- *Inamorata*

  The leading lady, high status and almost always in emotional turmoil. She is vain, self-absorbed, impatient and prone to outbursts of jealousy. The Lovers are usually at the centre of the plot and the authors of, often misplaced, messages transported by Zanni. She is often pursued by one of the old men.

- *Inamorato*

  The leading man, high status and in a similar state of persistent emotional turmoil. He is vain, self-absorbed, impatient and prone to outbursts of jealousy.

EXERCISE: Commedia *and Rhythm*
Pairs/One Person to Lead Clapping Ongoing

The spirit of *Commedia* relies on a performer's ability to connect with their fellow performers in the moment. It requires spontaneity and a sense of the connection with the rhythm of the scene. We will look at this in further detail in the next Chapter: The Clown.

- One person claps: 1, 1-2, 1-2-3, 1-2-3-4 and so on up to 10. In response you create a random action on each clap; any spontaneous physical shape or gesture. Freeze on the final clap of each section.

- Then, repeat this with a partner. Up to the count of 5, both make random physical actions individually; only make eye contact with your partner on the final clap of each section (whilst frozen). From the count of 6 onward (1-2-3-4-5-6 . . .) ensure that whilst continuing to make random physical actions you remain in contact with your partner; create any shapes together and ensure you are physically connected by at least one part of your body. Always make eye contact and freeze on the final clap of each section.

- Repeat this exercise, only this time in the character of one of the *Commedia* characters. Use the exercise to explore how your character's attitude informs your actions and interaction with the character of your partner.

EXERCISE: Commedia *and The Inner Monologue*
Pairs/*Commedia* Mask[30]

When working without words, all actions must be underpinned by a continuous inner monologue, in the voice of the character. All action and gesture will therefore be initiated and supported by your thoughts; carrying intention and meaning.

All *Commedia* characters have stock masks, stock characteristics and stock movements. The Zanni mask has a heavy brow and a long nose (the longer the nose, the more stupid the Zanni).

This exercise employs the stock movements of Zanni. Here is a list of Zanni's physical traits to explore through the exercise:

- head constantly moving independently
- low centre of gravity, with torso arched forward
- one knee always bent, with the other straight
- fast, nervous movements of hands
- sleeps standing up with legs crossed; one foot hooked over the other knee
- to walk: continually shifts weight between bent and straight legs, head pecking
- when happy, skips from side to side
- when running away, legs kick out front and arms move in opposition
- when proud, Zanni struts like a chicken.

To begin with, one person watches and one person places a Zanni mask on:[31]

- enter the space with a clear intention and walk through the space
- remember something important you have previously forgotten; you stop
- turn to the audience to share this moment
- exit in the same direction as you entered.

Note:

- Have a clear inner monologue throughout your scene.
- Remember, less is more.
- Check in with your partner to see what they thought your inner monologue was. Ask if your thought processes were clear.
- If you and your partner are on the same page, swap over. If not, go again.

---

[30] This can be a very rudimentary mask – it could be that you simply adapt a Neutral Mask to give it some of the features of the *Commedia* character.
[31] See Exercise: Wearing the Neutral Mask (p. 175) for how to first place the mask on the face.

Thought Process

The moment that you look to the audience to share a specific event, as in the exercise above, has been evocatively described by mask practitioner Toby Wilsher as 'like opening up the face of a clock and momentarily seeing the cogs turning. The actor has a phrase in their head that can be shown through a slight gesture or intake of breath. This can be directed straight to the audience. Once finished, the clock face closes up and the action continues'.[32] This idea takes us to the heart of why mask work is so crucial for the opera singer:

- Opera often plays with time. The effect of music can be to suspend a character's thought process and, by so doing, bring focus and attention to the thought process of a character. However, the audience will only follow what you are thinking if every step of your thought process is clearly and logically progressed and physically connected. When working with masks we are generally not using words, so the only way to make our thoughts clear is through our movements. In some small way our thoughts always move us, and so long as our thoughts are clear they will be communicated through the body.

- There are certain steps we take before acting: we receive information, we understand it, we decide to act and then we act. This sequence might vary from moment to moment; for example, to truly *understand* something we need to acknowledge it, turn it over, picture it and embed it, before arriving at the decision to act.

- Whilst words may be repeated, the music shifts beneath them giving us indications and clues as to *how* the thoughts might be travelling. If the words and music cannot both be seen to have been initiated by a unifying thought, then repeated words are rendered nonsensical and the music, merely pleasurable sound. Thoughts must be as clear as the words and music they underpin.

- Mask work and the inner monologue viscerally connect us, in character, to our thoughts. The mask reveals to us, through performance before an audience, the extent to which we are honouring a truthful process of thought.

EXAMPLE: *The Magic Flute*

Tamino is the *Inamorato* in *The Magic Flute*. Look at his first aria in Act One (No. 3 'I've never seen a face so fair'/'Dies Bildnis ist bezaubernd schön'). He has just received the portrait of Pamina from the Three Ladies and it has aroused unexpected and unfamiliar feelings within him. In response, we hear his inner monologue. The words, however, are often repeated and it is important to listen to the stresses in the music to understand how each of these repeated lines marks a new step in his thought process.

Without singing, and wearing a Neutral Mask (to save on make-up!), try speaking Tamino's inner monologue to yourself. Ask the répétiteur to play the aria as you work and allow the music to guide your thoughts; expand on the actual words of the libretto to mark the journey of your thoughts with keener distinction.

---

[32] Wilsher, T. (2006) *The Mask Handbook*. London: Routledge. Toby was Artistic Director of Trestle Theatre Company.

For example:

Tamino

What is this fire consuming me?	What is the *strange feeling* in my chest, in my heart?
What is this fire consuming me?	Really <u>what</u> is this thing?
(The music answers)	Ah . . .!
I know . . .	That's *it*
I feel the pain of love	I'm *experiencing* the pain of love.
I know it	I *know* it
I know it	I *hold* it
I know it	I *understand* it.
It is love	I've *alighted* on the word: love.

Direct Address

Clarity of thought becomes even more important when your thought process is shared with the audience; the clock face opening. This is a common conceit in opera: the shared aside to the audience, or the direct address aria. Each thought communicated to the audience must be clear, present and progress logically, for the audience to understand and believe in you.

EXAMPLE: *The Magic Flute*

Papageno embodies many qualities of Arlecchino and seeks to build an immediate connection with the audience from his first entrance; he introduces himself, his work and his dreams, directly to the audience in his first aria, No. 2 'I'm sure that there could never be a more contented man than me'/'Der Vögelfanger bin ich ja'.

In the Act Two finale, Papageno makes a direct appeal to the audience to save his life:

Papageno

Who can save me now,

if only someone here would be my wife

Lovely ladies, save my life.

Say the word and save my life!

The idea for Papageno to appeal begins at 'if only' and grows throughout this line (until 'my wife'). The clock face opens throughout this line before his direct appeal to the audience; we must see the cogs working to generate his idea. Papageno casts the audience in two distinct roles: close confidante and potential lover. When addressing the audience, the singer must have a clear attitude towards them.

Throughout this section Mozart leaves empty bars for Papageno to await the audience response. It is in these silences that we again must see behind the clock face; the singer playing Papageno must have a clear inner monologue, for the audience to continue to follow his story.

The most revealing section of this aria should be the moment Papageno counts to three before proceeding to hang himself. Mozart leaves this section entirely unaccompanied, handing over all responsibility for the rhythm of the scene to the singer. There is terrific freedom for the singer; it is a moment that can be, simultaneously, sublimely comic and heartbreakingly tragic, marking the knife-edge transition between hope and despondency. The rhythm of these transitions is left to the singer but will be determined by the speed with which each individual thought travels.

The Arlecchino mask is a useful tool to help clarify the thought process in this aria; it requires the entire body to be engaged with each nuanced movement of thought.

Less is More

Commedia mask work underlines the idea that every movement we make onstage reveals a thought and tells a story to the audience. When observing others in the mask, you will notice that extraneous movements clutter this communication; it is vital that every movement is borne out of a clear intention. Stillness can be incredibly potent, for it allows space for the intended movement to begin and end.

I have written about 'reducing the sauce' of a movement.[33] If movement is overly expansive, nuance and detail risks being lost; the delicate interplay of thoughts and transitions from one idea to the next can easily be eclipsed by unmotivated movement.

The opera and theatre director Peter Hall wrote: 'it is more intriguing seeing a character trying not to express emotion, than one constantly demanding our attention'.[34] Hall is promoting the idea of physical restraint, over expressive abandon. When the character is *trying not* to express an emotion, they are working with an obstacle. Obstacles are incredibly important when considering how to reduce the scale of a movement; the pressure of an opposing force, acting upon the character's objective, resulting in a heightening of dramatic tension.

The Physical Phrase

Just as a sung phrase will have a natural length, the same applies for a physical movement; a physical phrase. As you work become aware of the beginning and end of this phrase. For clarity of storytelling you and your partner must together acknowledge this physical phrase; you may choose to share it, or to work off each other; however, to ignore it clutters the picture.

---

[33] See Lecoq (p. 154).
[34] Hall, P. (2000) *Exposed by the Mask: Form and Language in Drama*. London: Oberon Books. There is a terrific chapter on Mozart's Ensembles, pp. 71–102.

In opera, the journey of an idea is usually marked by music; the physical phrase must therefore be informed by the music. This does not mean moving in time, or choreographing a scene, but it does mean listening and being sensitive to when the music suggests beginning, ending or landing a movement.

Lazzi are routines, gags and bits of physical comic business that litter *Commedia* performances as dazzling little side shows of no significant consequence (other than all-important laughter). Lazzi never drive the story forward and work as a brief diversion from the main plot; for example, Arlecchino somersaulting whilst holding a full glass of wine and not spilling a drop, a chair accidentally pulled away as one of the old men moves to sit down and so on. The routines are often technically demanding, requiring a good deal of rehearsal to make them appear effortless. The performer must always have a small part of their consciousness on the technical mechanics of the Lazzi, whilst appearing completely immersed in the action of the story.

In opera, and particularly *buffa,* there will often be orchestral phrases allowing room for such physical action. The more aware we become of how the music informs this action, the more it will appear that the thought, music and action are interlinked.

EXERCISE: Commedia *and Lazzi*
Pairs, Threes and More/*Commedia* **Mask**

Improvise a simple scene between *Commedia* characters and introduce moments of Lazzi. Always improvise these scenes with musical accompaniment, so that you can develop the connection between action and music.
   For example:

- A first date between the Lovers. One of the Lovers is constantly diverted by a piece of paper stuck to their shoe, whilst the other becomes increasingly alert to the burgeoning spot on their nose.

- Arlecchino attempts to deliver a love letter to the Inamorata but, having seemingly lost the letter, only presents her with the various, and increasingly odd, contents of his pocket.

- Brighella serves Il Dottore and Inamorata dinner. Brighella is covertly attempting to steal Il Dottore's food. The Inamorata is awaiting a covert meeting with the increasingly late Inamorato. Meanwhile, Il Dottore is trying to impress the Inamorato with his new cane.

Try working on such a Lazzi by yourself, prior to the improvisation, and then aim to find a moment to introduce it into your improvisation, in order to surprise your fellow performers and delight your audience.

One of the first operas I worked on as an assistant director was a production of Offenbach's *Orpheus in the Underworld* at Opera North. Opera singer Eric Roberts played Jupiter and sought out any, and every, opportunity to introduce Lazzi into the production; chairs were flipped, impressive routines danced and costumes unravelled. Eric was often to be found in the rehearsal room, during the lunch break, working up these little routines. By the time of the performance, they were executed with complete precision and balletic panache in absolute sympathy with the music; flippant amusements, over in a flash, that aroused much mirth and, due to their brevity and seeming effortlessness, never distracted from the central story.

EXAMPLE: *The Marriage of Figaro*

Beaumarchais, the writer of the original play of *The Marriage of Figaro*, later adapted by Mozart and Da Ponte, was highly influenced by *Commedia dell'arte*. The stock figures that he draws upon to create the characters in *Figaro* are easy to see:

Figaro – Arlecchino

Susanna – Columbina

The Countess – Inamorata

The Count – Pantalone

Bartolo – Il Dottore (in *The Barber of Seville*, Bartolo is more clearly drawn from Pantalone)

Cherubino – Inamorato (occasionally dressed up as Inamorata and Il Capitano)

Antonio – Brighella

Other characters embody elements and combinations of other masks.

In rehearsals for *The Marriage of Figaro* I found it a useful starting point to explore the stock characters from *Commedia*. We would improvise the story of the opera in the *Commedia* style; firstly, silently in masks and then, retaining the physical style but removing the masks, singing certain scenes. It helped the singers to develop a keener connection with the audience and to experience the part through their whole body. It released them to take time to explore the comic moments of the plot; for example, we discovered moments of Lazzi with Figaro getting caught up with tape measures in the first act and Susanna overwhelmed by a quantity of ribbons in the second act.

SUMMARY

- Operatic characters and plot are often defined by certain storytelling conventions; an understanding of these conventions helps bring an understanding of the language of the piece and a character's function within it.

- *Commedia dell'arte* was a direct influence on *opera buffa*, *singspiel* and *opéra comique*.

- An understanding of the central tenets of *Commedia* can help develop an understanding of the rhythm of comedy, the clear communication of a process of thought, the connection with the audience and the idea of 'the physical phrase'.

TO DO

- Explore the conventions of *Commedia* through improvisation with the stock characters.
- Identify *Commedia* characters alive in contemporary stories and throughout operatic repertoire.
- Identify your character's function in the plot, in relation to other characters.
- Play with the idea of *Lazzi* to music, to develop your understanding of the 'physical phrase'.

The Clown

We are all clowns, we all think we are beautiful, clever and strong, whereas we all have our weaknesses, our ridiculous side, which can make people laugh when we allow it to express itself.[35]

Lecoq

The spirit of *Commedia* and the clown are inextricably linked.[36] In *Commedia*, working within the confines of an established character, the central lesson the mask teaches us is not to *act*, but to *be*. The spirit of clowning is to *be yourself*; to reveal, to strip away and expose your weaknesses, vulnerabilities and naïveties.

The clown is the side of ourselves we spend most of our time attempting to hide; defined through hope and, more often than not, failure. When the clown feels certain that they will succeed, such failure is usually more painful and, as a consequence, funnier. Clowning is not really about learning routines or doing silly walks but about asking what it is about ourselves that makes others want to laugh; it is about locating where the impulse for comedy and laughter lies in any moment. The desire to make the audience laugh, and to keep making them laugh, is the clown's primary motivation; they will break every code and disregard all conventions to achieve it. For the clown, the central relationship is with the audience. It is an immediate, genuinely playful and unpredictable relationship and requires the performer to be in a constant state of reaction, surprise and vulnerability in order to develop it.

Clowning and the spirit of play can seem at odds with much of what is necessary in opera. Opera brings together an extraordinary range of diverse elements and balances an array of conflicting demands; as a singer you must hit the spot to find your light, navigate unfamiliar design worlds, be heard over an orchestra, all whilst precisely following the conductor's beat. The risk is that, in all the necessary structure put in place to bring an opera to the stage, we lose the most important thing: the real human being at the centre of the story and their direct communication with the audience.

We all, no doubt, recognise those astonishing performances when the drama makes us sit on the edge of our seat, when the music is alive and when we feel a connection to the

---

[35] Lecoq, J. (2000). *The Moving Body*. London: Methuen Drama, p. 154.
[36] Lecoq suggested that there are six different levels of play. Each of these levels offers a different way of releasing the actor's imagination and creating an effect on the audience. They are: Tragedy, Psychological Realism, Melodrama, *Commedia dell'arte*, Buffoon, Clown.

honesty and openness with which the performer communicates their story; we experience the sense of possibility that might arise from these moments. We will also recognise the difference between performances of opera that have genuinely made us laugh and those that merely present received ideas of comedy.

The following games and exercises will not equip you for a life in the circus – complete with red nose and massive shoes. They look, instead, to place *you*, the performer, in difficult situations. The exercises seek to engage you with the reality of needing to find ways to overcome genuine obstacles; the result being that the audience witness an *honest* response to such difficulties, rather than *acting*. In so doing, these games aim to help you to explore what it is to be spontaneous, to improvise, to reveal yourself and to embrace the possibility of things going wrong.

Finding the Game

EXERCISE: *The Clapping Game*
Group/10 mins

This exercise is the perfect way to explore the alternately joyful and frustrating direct relationship with the audience.

- One person volunteers to leave the room. Whilst they are gone, the rest of the group devises a simple sequence of action that, upon their return, the volunteer must carry out. Keep this sequence relatively simple to begin with; as your familiarity with the game grows, introduce props or items of clothing into the sequence.

- The volunteer enters to a rapturous round of applause and attempts to discover the pre-determined sequence, simply by doing it.

- The rest of the group, the audience, guide and encourage the volunteer only through applause. The closer the volunteer gets to the next part of the sequence, the louder the applause becomes; contrastingly, the further away from completing the next stage of the sequence, the less applause they receive.

- Other than the sound of applause, the game should be played in silence throughout.

Note:

- As you play the game, be in constant contact with the audience. Do not give up! Keep exploring possibilities to discover what the sequence might be.

- The audience should look out for the volunteers' small moments of despondency or frustration and, by contrast, their moments of hope. These are the moments when it seems the performer reveals themselves most and they are often the funniest moments to watch.

A clown will always attempt to find a game, whatever that game might be. They might initiate the game themselves, or respond to somebody else's invitation to play; the only motivation is to play an action simply for the fun of it.

For example, a character walks seductively towards another in order to kiss them; a man slams a door in a show of vexation; a woman sits down intimidatingly before striking a deal. Now try all these scenarios and find the game in the action; in walking seductively, in slamming the door, in sitting down slowly. You will begin to find the pleasure in an action. John Wright, co-founder of Told by an Idiot, writes:

> If the work is playful it becomes a pleasure and when you're enjoying yourself you get bolder and take more risks. Choices proliferate. Problems become more manageable because our perspectives change once the work becomes a pleasure.[37]

This idea seems particularly important when performing in opera; the relative expense of the form can make play and risk-taking seem less likely.

A simple exercise to discover *finding the game* is for the group to stand in a circle and for one person to trigger an action that others might copy. Allow time for the group to develop and play with the action; a pout, a wink, a little hip swivel.[38] The purpose of the game is to amuse the rest of the group and, once a particular action has run its course, to find a new action.

The sock game is a particularly good game to employ when a scene in rehearsals is becoming a little predictable.

- Everyone in the group removes their socks and places them down the back of their trousers. At least half the sock needs to be visible over the waistline.

- A space in the room is defined; a square, a circle.

- The Objective is to grab as many other people's socks as possible and place them alongside your own. As soon as a player is without any socks, they are out of the game. The winner is the person with all the socks.

- As more players are eliminated, it is a good idea to reduce the size of the playing space.

- From my experience, this game can get quite intense, so it is always worth pointing out that this is a non-contact game!

Extension:

- The game gets really exciting when you play it within a scenario. Create a scene, for example, where everyone is a servant in a large house. Place the socks, again,

---

[37] Wright, J. (2006) *Why is that so Funny: A Practical Exploration of Physical Comedy.* London: Nick Hern Books, p. 27.
[38] See Chapter 1: Foundations.

down the trousers and, without using text, begin to improvise the scene; whilst cleaning takes place, the servants attempt to steal the sock off the Head Butler or, indeed, the other servants, without anyone noticing.

- Next, improvise a scene with only one word. For example, two brothers are reunited at an airport after years apart but you can both only use the word 'No' throughout the scene. Additionally, try to take the socks from each other without undermining the emotion of the moment.

- Next, improvise a similar scene but only sing one word. For example, a factory owner is showing the local mayor around their new factory; both can only sing the word 'Yes' to each other. Play with tempo, rhythm and pitch and, at the same time, attempt to take the socks from each other.

- Try the sock exercise with a scene from an opera. For example, in *The Marriage of Figaro*, play the game in a high-stakes scene such as the beginning of the Act Two finale, or the Count and Susanna duet in Act Three.

- Always find a moment to discuss what you noticed: how was the scene affected by playing the game?

- The real pleasure comes in keeping the game as small as possible, so that an audience *might* almost miss it. Do not comment on the game – just play it.

Finding the game can help bring fresh life to a scene; it raises the stakes and heightens the performer to the possibilities of new impulses in the drama. This is particularly important in opera, where the multitude of technical requirements can restrict spontaneity.

We once had a debate in Opera Works about whether *finding the game* in performance potentially undermined the integrity of the scene. Might performers upstage others in search of laughs? Would the competitive spirit of the game undermine the collaborative effort? Great discretion is required; the merits of introducing a *game* are based upon the repertoire and tone of the production. *Finding a game,* for example, is more likely to be useful in comedy than tragedy. The most successful *games* are those played at such a low physical volume that they are barely perceptible. They re-engage the singer with the need to listen to other singers and, in so doing, can help to reinvigorate a scene.

Restrictions

The more difficult you make life for your character, the more creative your character is forced to be in order to overcome these difficulties; as a performer, your options proliferate. This exercise is about introducing physical Obstacles for your character; Obstacles that might prompt the audience to look again at the possible revelation of your character's hidden Objectives.

EXERCISE: *Restrictions*
Solo/Group/10 mins

- Try walking on the side of your feet. Then, with your toes turned up. Next, only on the balls of your feet.

- Run, hop, jump with these restrictions. Find a partner with the same restriction and try jumping together and landing at exactly the same time.

- Then, attempt to get your partner to jump but without jumping yourself. If you jump, they have to jump; if you do not jump, their feet must remain firmly planted on the ground. *Will you jump, won't you jump?* In polite society, a true Gentleman can only sit once the Lady has been seated. *Will she sit, won't she sit?* This *'yes, no'* dynamic is always exciting to play with. Explore it in *finding the game*.

- Next, walk with your toes scrunched up under your feet. Imagine you are wearing the most exquisite shoes, proudly displaying them to all; the most coveted shoes in town. But they are two sizes too small and unbearably painful. Allow a little of this pain to leak out. Make the audience look twice. First, they see the vain pride and then, on closer inspection, another story reveals itself.

- Now, engage a partner in conversation. Look down on your partner's clearly inferior shoes. And then depart, hobbling, gracefully.

The revelation of subtext is always thrilling for an audience. A character saying one thing, whilst simultaneously undermining their words through an unconscious tick or *tell*, takes the audience beyond words into the subconscious world of a character.

Status

It is impossible to think of an opera, or indeed any story, where a character's Status is not at the centre of the drama. *The Marriage of Figaro* is defined by the time in which it was written; French society's tectonic plates are shifting beneath the characters' feet. The Count is terrified of being outwitted by scheming servants; Susanna is compelled to navigate the twin challenges of the time: gender and class. Of course, much comedy is to be found in the gulf between where a character thinks their Status is, and where it actually lies. Class is not always the defining factor in Status. Barbarina's revelation of an affair with the Count is both funny and painful; both the Countess and the Count suffer a public indignity which lowers their Status.

The Status Bridge

- Establish an imaginary bridge in the rehearsal room. This is a particularly narrow bridge and only one person can pass at a time. If two people cross the bridge at the same time in opposite directions, one would have to return to the side of the bridge where they began their journey in order to allow the other person to cross first.

- One player stands at either end of the bridge. They each take a playing card; the number on the card is their *perceived* Status. In this exercise Status is measurable on a scale of one to ten, with ten being the highest, and dictates who has the right to cross the bridge first. Neither player knows the number on the other's playing card.

- As they approach each other, each must assess the other's Status. Based upon this assessment, they must judge whether they will retreat, to allow the other to pass, or plough onwards and demand the other gives way in their favour. Of course, they might judge themselves to be higher Status and magnanimously allow the lower Status character to pass first.

- The negotiation between players whose cards are numerically close to each other is always interesting.

- Try this exercise, at first, in silence. Then repeat, speaking.

The Party

- A party is thrown. One player hosts and sets the scene.

- All other players take a card before entering the party and, without looking at the number on the card themselves, hold the card to their forehead for everyone else to see. The number represents your *actual* Status; the way others see you.

- The object of the exercise is to determine, before the host calls time on the party, what your Status is, in response to how others treat you.

- Play this improvised scene initially without talking, perhaps simply to some suitable musical accompaniment. This places the emphasis on the physical behaviour of the party-goers.

Alex MacLaren, co-Artistic Director of The Spontaneity Shop,[40] worked with us throughout Opera Works. He breaks down Status behaviour in the following ways:

---

[39] We look at this further in Devising (p. 197).
[40] The Spontaneity Shop are an improvisation and training company who specialise in exploring story and behaviour. We look more closely at some of their tools in Chapter 11: Auditions.

- High Status behaviour is characterised through stillness (especially the head), calmness, strong eye contact, decisive gestures, wide stance and sustaining pauses.
- Low Status behaviour is characterised through small purposeless movements, breaking eye contact, 'ers' and 'ums' in speech and closed-off body language.

Try employing these Status behaviours when you play both exercises.

EXAMPLE: *The Magic Flute/The Marriage of Figaro*

A few years ago, I directed a production of *The Magic Flute* at the Royal Welsh College of Music and Drama set in a circus: Sarastro was the all-controlling ring leader, the Queen of the Night a fading cabaret singer, the chorus a broken troupe of acrobats and Papageno, of course, the clown. The setting gave us an ideal opportunity to explore the spirit of clowning throughout the process and through into performance. Opera singer Emyr Wyn Jones played Papageno and, throughout rehearsals, we encouraged the ensemble to be his audience; the clapping game and the sock game became the spine of our process. All the characters, with the exception of Pamina and Tamino who we considered outsiders, were performing in some way. Simon McBurney's incredibly playful production of *Flute* at ENO saw Papageno and Papagena breaking the fourth wall convention by strolling through the stalls, ad-libbing and engaging the audience in vaudevillian routine.

When directing *The Marriage of Figaro,* I found that the characters in the beginning of the Act Two finale – the Count, Countess and Susanna – were becoming increasingly aggressive towards each other. I was concerned that this tone might create an imbalance in the production and overshadow other important layers in the scene. It is an extraordinary scene; dangerous, dark and yet teetering somewhere between farce and tragedy. I introduced the sock game and it seemed to release the singers; they acknowledged that, at the same time as pursuing the Objectives of their character, such as *I want to shame you, I want to prove you are as low as I think you are, I want to defend my honour*, the characters were also presenting a version of themselves. The exercise introduced the idea of game-playing into the scene; as well as pursuing Objectives, the characters also had to hide certain secrets.

Throughout *Figaro* rehearsals I established an imaginary Status ladder; a line-up of the characters, with their position in the line determined by their Status in the world of the opera. At the beginning and end of each scene, I would ask the singers to form the Status ladder in order to see the movement in Status that might have occurred through the scene. This was always negotiated in silence. The exercise underlined our awareness of the political implications of all transactions throughout the opera.

SUMMARY

- Clowning is about finding spontaneity within the conventional form of opera.
- It is about revealing yourself and embracing the possibility of things going wrong.
- Finding the game, exploring restrictions and Status are central to clowning.

TO DO

- *Find the game* in each scene in order to explore the line between character and performer.
- Explore the possible physical restrictions that might limit, or make life difficult, for your character.
- Consider your character's Status before and after each scene. What is their Status journey through the opera? Is there a difference between their perceived and actual Status?

Devising

Each year of training on ENO Opera Works would culminate in a devised public performance. A selection of scenes was chosen by vocal director, Jane Robinson, from a wide operatic repertoire. The choice of scenes was based upon each individual singer's vocal development. The scenes were, therefore, rarely thematically or narratively linked and the aim through the rehearsal process was to explore how, as a company, we might weave these separate scenes together to create one unified story.

The reason for this was threefold; firstly, by presenting more than a selection of opera scenes we could increase the time spent on stage for each singer and, therefore, their performance experience. Next, my experience of watching scenes performances in conservatoires was that there was often a lull at the end of one scene – the point at which the audience's attention would naturally wane – leading to a battle at the beginning of the next scene to win back the audience's focus. A cohesive production would aim to carry the audience's attention throughout. Finally, I was keen to expand the singer's creative toolkit and deepen their understanding of those tools they had already been introduced to. The final Opera Works Input weekend was led by members of such theatre companies as Frantic Assembly, Complicité and Told by an Idiot, where the singers were introduced to the ideas behind collaborative improvisation and devising stories; the devised end-of-year performance gave the singers a perfect opportunity to test out and develop these tools.

These are important skills to develop. New opera is now frequently developed through the workshop process, following the lead of the development of new writing in theatre. These short, intensive workshops will usually be targeted at the dramaturgical needs of the composer, librettist and creative team. Singers will be expected to collaborate in the creation of a new piece by contributing ideas, improvising scenes and, quickly, creating characters that may not have even existed at the beginning of the workshops.

The development of, and necessary investment in, new opera is vital for the form to continue to move forward. If opera is to succeed in being more than simply an artistic form belonging in a museum, it must seek to reflect the stories of today from a wide variety of cultures and communities. Singers, as the primary communicators of these stories, should be at the heart of this development, supporting the work of the composers and librettists.

Alongside this, more time is also being given by opera companies to develop production ideas prior to rehearsals. Leah Hausman, co-director, with Terry Gilliam, of ENO's productions of *Benvenuto Cellini* and *The Damnation of Faust*, would gather Opera Works singers for a series of workshops to explore, investigate, challenge and develop the ideas of the production, before the pressure of the rehearsal period began. I was assistant director to Phyllida Lloyd on ENO's production of *Rhinegold* and the early part of the process was spent improvising; we improvised scenes that preceded the scenes present in the opera, prior to improvising the actual scenes, with the singers using their own words to explore the central themes and ideas.

These tools therefore can be used to develop new work or, alternatively, new ideas for established repertoire. They can inform an improvisational approach to work. The tools also bring our awareness to the process of creative work in any environment and to the narrative structure of stories; central to the work of any creative storyteller.

The Process

The following are important to bear in mind when beginning a devising process:

- The Rules of Play, detailed in Chapter 1: Foundations (p. 38), are the starting point when establishing any devising process; bringing a '*yes, and . . .*' attitude, a readiness to offer ideas, seeking to build trust and inviting others to play, are crucial for establishing a creative environment. This is the same for any rehearsal period but the demands are even greater when devising a performance without the guiding hand of the score and libretto.

- Restrictions inspire creativity. Creating a structure to work within brings focus by narrowing your options. Set clear bitesize tasks.

- Bring a spirit of spontaneity to the process by learning to follow the impulse that lies in the moment between reaction and action. Too often this impulse is destroyed by overthinking and editing; the aim should be to reduce the time between inner reaction and outer action, so that the audience sees only visible impulses.[41] This is achieved by bringing limitless attention to your partner and accepting their proposals rather than blocking them.

WALT DISNEY'S THREE ROOMS

Walt Disney apparently had three separate rooms that he and his team used when creating a project:

- Room 1: The Ideas Room.

  A room to dream up any ideas for a project, for brainstorming and asking 'What *if . . .?*' Doubters not invited! This is a room to imagine, free from the shackles of practical considerations.

- Room 2: The Making Room.

  A room for the realists. Taking one of the ideas from Room 1, this is the room where you work out *how* to realise the idea. You consider what the ingredients might be, how

---

[41] Grotowski's theory of *via negativa* is a process of eradicating blocks that sit in the way of this impulse. You can read about his work in Grotowski, J. (1975) *Towards a Poor Theatre*. London: Bloomsbury.

these work together and what the end result might look like. This is the room where an idea hits the real world.

- Room 3: The Editing Room.

  Taking the actual result of the idea from Room 2, Room 3 provides the opportunity to cast a critical eye over the work; to place the work under the microscope and, where necessary, edit, cut, shape and refine.

The Three Rooms propose a clear distinction between each stage of the creative process. They can be metaphorical 'rooms' framed by periods of time but it is important for all creators of the work to recognise which room they are in, at any point. If most of the group are in the Ideas Room but one person believes they are in the Making Room, the fragile fragments of ideas risk being crushed under the weight of real-world considerations before having had the time and space to fully form. Similarly, if the group have moved an idea into the Making Room, the ethos of the Ideas Room will disrupt the necessary practical considerations. The Editing Room should only be entered having first visited Rooms 1 and 2; the risk is that the principles of Room 3 seep into the creative process too early, tearing apart any idea or half-formed work.

Every Room needs its own fuel. The Opera Works devising process always began in Room 1 with the singers working alongside designer Will Holt, who would have assembled a series of mood-boards to help ignite the collective imagination; collections of images, links to video clips and clippings of articles.

Devising Warm Ups

These warm ups develop the work on spontaneity that we looked at in Play and Spontaneity (p. 37).

EXERCISE: 123
Pairs/3 mins

- Stand facing your partner. Between you, count to three in a constant loop; get to three and return to one. (A: 'One' B: 'Two' A: 'Three' B: 'One' A: 'Two' and so on.)
- Next, substitute 'One' with an agreed simple action or gesture: a jump, clap, nose grab.
- Next, substitute 'Two' in the same way, and then 'Three'.
- It sounds easy but in playing the game our thoughts often stop us from simply responding to our partner.
- Expand: try counting to five and following the same sequence.

EXERCISE: *Text Improvisation*
Pairs/3 mins

Do not discuss this exercise before doing it; you must listen intently to your partner to understand the story they are proposing and meet them in that story.

- One player will determine where the scene takes place. This will only be communicated through the playing of the scene; the other player must discern, in the moment, where they are.
- Both players walk into the space. The following text is spoken:

  A: 'Hello'.

  B: 'How long have you been waiting?'

  A: 'Ages'.
- Do not determine who will say the first line.
- Play this scene many times over; each time listening carefully to your partner.

Note:

- Consider how to communicate the location of the scene to your partner.
- Be aware that your partner might cast you in a certain role; go with it. How do you respond?
- Play with physicality, rhythm, relationships in space and *how* you speak the text.

EXERCISE: *The Journey*
Pairs/Group/5 mins

This leads on from the 'Yes and . . .' exercise (p. 38), and requires the spirit of that exercise translated into your whole body.

- One person suggests an action and the rest of the group (including the person who suggests it) enacts it. For example:
  - 'We are walking along a cliff-edge . . . (the group mime walking along a cliff-edge)
  - and then we discover a cave . . . (the group go into the imaginary cave)
  - which narrows to a tight tapering tunnel . . .' (the group snake along the floor)
  - And so on . . .
- The idea is to build a collective journey that everyone in the group immediately agrees to take.
- Next, try the exercise with your eyes closed.
- What do you notice about your response to the instructions? What are the challenges of this exercise?

- Be barefoot in the space and imagine the floor is a giant canvas. Use the soles of your feet to translate, or *paint,* the story of your life on the floor.

- Imagine you are able to apply different textures, shapes, lines and patterns. Explore the use of space and rhythm to express your major life events.

- Now, try this for a character you are beginning to create. Certain biographical details may, as yet, be unclear. Think of this as an abstract expressionists canvas; how would Jackson Pollock or Mark Rothko express this character's early or teenage years?

This exercise gives you the freedom to instantly translate something literal into another form: imaginary lines on the floor. It demands spontaneity; if you stop and think about the exercise it becomes absurd. It is a good way to reduce the gap between reaction and action; the journey of the character's life springs impulsively from the soles of your feet onto the canvas.

- Extension: Try this exercise whilst singing an aria and focus, instead, on the journey of the character through the aria. It is useful to begin painting before the aria begins; what has been happening for the character before the play-in begins?

Story Structure

This leads directly onto an analysis of the structure of story. The devising process seeks to create new stories. An understanding of a traditional story arc enables you to adapt and transform the arc to tell your story, in the way you want. It also helps bring definition to a character's journey through an established opera; the mapping of the development of your character's Objectives in the context of the overall story.

The structures of most stories, when laid out, are remarkably similar; as an audience we respond to familiar patterns. The structural map, below, will, no doubt, feel incredibly familiar. However, by bringing our attention to structure, we begin to ask important questions about the stories we are telling, whether those stories are centuries old or newly formed.

A STRUCTURAL JOURNEY

The Beginning	*Once upon a time . . .*	This is the foundation of the world your character inhabits; the way it has *always* been.
The First Significant Event	*Then, one day . . .*	The foundation of the world the protagonist/s inhabit is destroyed.

The Middle	Because of this event. . .Because of this event. . .Because of this event. . .Because of this event. . .Because of this event. . .	The series of consequences that lead on from the first significant event; the central characters struggle against obstacles. The cause and effect.
The Climax	Until, ultimately . . .	The consequences culminate in a final struggle, leading the character towards success or failure.
The Resolution	And ever since then . . .	A new foundation is formed.

This, of course, is an extreme reduction of plot structure: sub-plots weave through this central plot, often in a similar fashion. Christopher Booker's *The Seven Basic Plots* examines, in detail, the manner in which different genres of story structure contrast, asserting that all stories conform to one of seven basic plots; overcoming the monster, rags to riches, the quest, voyage and return, comedy, tragedy and rebirth.

This simple exposition of structure raises interesting questions when placed alongside the opera you are rehearsing:

- What is your character's routine?
- Is their routine changed by the First Significant Event of the opera?
- What is the nature of your character's struggle?
- How can your character's journey be seen as a series of interlinking consequences?
- In what way is the world of the opera different by the end?

These plot points are important to identify. They enable you to bring emphasis to the turning points in a story, in order to construct a coherent and plausible story arc for your character; they act as a check list for clear storytelling.

DEVISING STORY

The simple story arc forms the basis for devising story. Throughout this central spine of plot will run a multitude of Events (see p. 114), each marking a turning point in each of the characters' Objectives. Structuring an improvisation involves establishing the main events in the scene, determining the character's Objectives before and after an event, and shaping the Given Circumstances within which the Events take place. The integrity of any story rests on the validity of the cause and effect, from one Event to the next; each Event is caused by the previous one and has an effect on the future plot. The Given Circumstances help to raise the stakes within the story; they help make the Events matter to each of the characters.

EXERCISE: *A Story String*
Group/5 mins

This exercise explores two important factors of storytelling: cause and effect, and raising the stakes.

Cause and Effect

- The group sit in a circle. The first person starts off the story with a simple story proposition. For example, 'Jack wanted to sell his cow'.

- The next person in the circle picks up the story and adds a new sentence to it. This new sentence always begins with '*because* . . .', in order to take the story forward and explore the consequence of the previous statement. For example, '*because* Jack wanted to sell his cow, he decided he must travel to market', '*because* Jack decided to travel to market, he determined to buy a map', '*because* Jack determined to buy a map, he needed to find some money' and so on.

- Every story must be formed through a string of consequential Events. Without this, the story simply falls apart.

Raising the Stakes

- Again, in a circle, one person starts off a story with an opening sentence.

- The next person in the circle has a choice; they can move the story on in the same way as before using '*because*', or they can raise the stakes by beginning their sentence with '*but the stakes are so high because* . . .'. For example, 'Jack wanted to sell his cow', '*but the stakes are so high because* he needs the money from the cow to get medicine for his sick mother', '*but the stakes are so high because* this is the last cow they own' and so on.

Consider your character's journeys through each aria, scene and act, in the opera you are rehearsing. The central questions for a creator of work must be: *What* do I want to reveal through these journeys? And, *how* do I want to reveal it? These questions remain central when devising a new piece.

Director Declan Donnellan has two rules about raising the stakes in drama;[42] they certainly apply to opera. They are:

1 There is always something to be won and something to be lost.

2 Whatever is to be lost is exactly the same size as whatever is to be won.

For example, if Susanna's Objective is 'I want to have the perfect start to my marriage with Figaro', what is at stake is the possibility of *not* having the perfect start to her marriage. Both possibilities exist for the character; this possibility of loss drives the character forward.

---

[42] Donnellan, D. (2005) *The Actor and the Target.* London: Nick Hern Books, p. 51.

Creating Material

The choices we make when asking *how* to reveal the story to the audience define our work as artists. When devising new work, we need to be aware of the range of tools that we can draw upon; I have listed the tools that we used during our Opera Works devising process below. In addition, we worked with practitioners who introduced us to a range of physical theatre tools that helped us to express the stories we wanted to tell.[43]

EXERCISE: *The Flock*
Group/Music/Various Objects/20 mins

This exercise develops an ensemble's awareness and focus. It is also a valuable tool when creating material. Working with music provides a point of reference for the group to either work with or against.

- The leader stands at the front of the group, the rest of the group arranged randomly behind them.
- The leader begins to move around the space and the group follow: stepping together, dropping to the same level, heads aligned at the exact angle. The group should keep the focus wide and forward, and remain in contact with the leader through their peripheral vision.
- When the leader turns 90 degrees or more and stops, the person who is now at the front of the group takes over as leader.
- This can be extended so that, through the journey, the leader adds a consistently held gesture: pointing in certain directions, waving a hand, pulling an item of clothing.
- Now, add objects to the exercise. For example, the group might each carry a coat, a piece of paper or a tea-cup. Keep your focus at all times on the object; when the leader shifts the angle at which the object is held, the group follow simultaneously.
- Now, explore the difference between focusing on the object and focusing instead on another target: the audience, a certain character, a window.

The choice of a particular object can highlight a certain aspect of the opera. For example, the group might each carry a coat, whilst downstage a character sits alone, shivering (this might relate to Colline's aria in *La Bohème*). The group can act as a chorus, to reveal something of the protagonist's subtext in the scene, or alternatively, the group might capture what is happening in the world of the opera at a given point. For example, in the fandango in the third act of *Figaro*, the chorus might work collectively with bulls' horns, in order to highlight the ever-present threat of cuckoldry. The choice of object, and how the group interacts with it in relationship to the space and other characters, helps create the story.

---

[43] Liam Steel, Georgina Lamb and Imogen Knight created work, over many years, with physical theatre company Frantic Assembly; their contributions to Opera Works were vital in helping the singers explore the expressive possibilities of the body and movement in creating story. This work formed the basis of the stories the singers devised for their end-of-year production.

Élan – French def. Internal movement aroused by a strong feeling that drives one to act in a certain way or to manifest a feeling; impulse.

This exercise brings clarity to physical storytelling through its structuring of movement onstage. It brings the performer's attention to the idea of the physical phrase that we looked at in Character Types and *Commedia dell'arte* (p. 178).

Pairs

- Player A does a simple movement: they circle a chair or walk to a table. Bring your attention to the beginning of the movement (élan) and the end (stillness).

- As soon as Player A stops their movement, Player B begins theirs; Player A's stopping initiates Player B's élan.

- You must respond to each other's energy; the rhythm and tempo that Player A finishes their movement with is the same energy that initiates Player B's movement. Look to change the energy of the movement, through the journey of the movement.

- The exercise continues in this fashion. Be incredibly clear with this handover of energy and ensure that there are no gaps in movement; the trigger from stopping to starting should be immediate.

- Do only one complete movement. Do not walk around a chair, breathe, and then sit down: this is two movements. Be clean and clear in your execution of a movement.

- Keep the movements real; do not be tempted to turn this into a piece of abstract contemporary dance.

Group

- Now work in groups of three or four. Repeat the exercise but if, when one player stops, two players immediately begin to move, they must continue on a journey together (not necessarily in step). They must be complicit in how they change energy and aim to stop together.

- The movements can be gestural or they can consist of just walking, sitting or shifting positions.

- Now try placing the activity around a table, or just using the movement of the hands, or restricted to remaining in contact with a piano, or constrained by an imaginary box on the floor.

Explore this exercise when creating a devised piece or when staging a scene. Richard Jones' production of Handel's *Rodelinda* for ENO embraced the principles of this exercise throughout. The singers were allied to each other and to each musical phrase. It was incredibly subtle, but the effect was to create an intrinsic connection between the characters, the space and the music.

EXERCISE: *Physical Essence*
Solo/Ongoing

The Physical Essence of a character is sub-textual information revealed through seemingly unconscious movement; the ostensibly meaningless, small movement betrays the hidden truth about the character or the journey they are on. Find a metaphor, simile or idiom, relating to the character's state or journey. Translate this into one condensed movement and sustain throughout the journey of an aria or scene. For example:

- if a character has to make a difficult journey, it might be as though they are *walking on glass*;
- if a character feels trapped by a past decision or an historic event, they might be trying to *free themselves from chains*;
- a character might be trying to *keep a lid on the situation*;
- or described as having *a bee in his bonnet*;
- or as being *joined at the hip to another character*.

These ideas are translatable into simple movement and this movement will perhaps reveal to the audience something of the character, in addition to what is being sung. When exploring this exercise, it is important to simply invest in the physical idea of, for example, *walking on glass*, rather than 'acting' a scene.

EXAMPLE: *The Magic Flute*

Explore *The Magic Flute*; how might you define the Physical Essence of certain characters' journeys at specific points in the opera?

- Try singing Pamina's aria (No. 17, 'Now I know that love has vanished'/'Ach ich fühl's, es ist verschwunden') attempting to engage Tamino's attention, whilst imagining you are barefoot and the floor is covered with glass.
- The Queen of the Night is perhaps imprisoned by her feelings of anger towards Sarastro. Explore the Queen of the Night's aria (No. 14, 'The wrath of hell is burning in my bosom'/'Der Hölle Rache kockt in meinem Herzen') whilst discreetly trying to slip one hand through an imaginary handcuff. How does the music guide, or work against, the physical engagement with this idea? Maybe there's a release during the cadenza? Maybe the hand is again restrained in the section that follows?
- Throughout Monostatos's aria (No. 13, 'All the world is always lusting'/'Alles fühlt der Liebe Freuden') he is very much *keeping the lid* on his sexual desire for Pamina, until the very final bars when the playout suggests he is acting upon them. Sing this aria imagining that you have a small container of combustible material in one hand and are trying to suppress the lid of the container with the other.

- Explore Papageno's first aria (No. 2, 'I'm sure that there could never be a more contented man than me'/'Der Vogelfänger bin ich ja') with the idea of him having a bee in his bonnet; the bee literally buzzes around within Papageno's hat and dictates the direction and tempo of the movement.
- Or look at Papageno and Papagena's duet (No. 21, 'Pa-Pa-Pa') whilst they are literally joined at the hip.

Explore how long an idea can be sustained and recognise once it has run its course. The music can guide you here: for example, the bee has most definitely flown away for the third and final verse of Papageno's aria.

Physical expression of such ideas should be small yet intensive. The advantage of this for the singer is that, whilst the Physical Essence might communicate an inner tension to the audience, the actual tension within the singer's body is minimal and placed very specifically in a certain part of the body.

Discerning the Physical Essence is a simple way of defining a character's physical journey through a part of the opera. The Physical Essence prompts you to look at what is travelling beneath the surface of a character – hidden from what they choose to reveal to the world – and encourages you to consider *how* to reveal this to an audience.

Devising a Toolkit

There are entire books dedicated to the process of improvisation and devising; I have listed some of my favourite books at the back of this book. However, it is worth noting the tools from the creating character toolkit that we have already explored, which can prove invaluable when creating and devising new work:

- Status
- Gesture
- Spacial relations
- Rhythmic constructs
- Laban and Lecoq's work with body parts
- Laban's Efforts
- Lecoq's States of Tension
- Unison
- Stillness
- Rhythm
- Pace
- Orientation
- Focus
- Tableaux.

SUMMARY

- The tools for devising can be used when developing new operatic work, exploring production ideas or simply creating character.
- Walt Disney's Three Rooms suggests the separation of the different stages of a process.
- An understanding of the structure of a story helps us to bring particular emphasis to the telling of a story.

TO DO

- Always bring a 'yes and . . .' attitude to any process.
- Explore creating new stories; they are the future of opera!
- Consider your character's journey through an aria, scene, act or opera and ask how you reveal this to audience.

SINGERS' RESPONSES TO MOVEMENT TOOLS

- *Using different choreographic forms, or types of movement, has released unexpected phrasing and interesting new intentions connected with the music. I thought opera was a ridiculously strict form in itself, so that there was no chance you could add anything else to it successfully, but it seems you can.*
- *It will be helpful when working in opera to have clear intentions behind movements, not just behind the text. The tools open up a new level of body awareness and therefore new things to explore; they helped me understand my own physical tendencies and choices.*
- *I came back to the idea of 'reducing the sauce' again and again; it has had a real effect in the way I sing. For example, in an audition I recently had (which I got), I have a point in an aria I used to go down on one knee. That was a bit much, so I reduced it into a simple head nod, which apparently caught the panel's attention simply because of the meaning behind it.*
- *Isolating body parts is really useful so that tension can be created and communicated but without detriment to the voice.*
- *States of Tension help to access states which we do not often find ourselves in; life and death situations. They help to access characters that are very different to us, characters from different periods of time and those of different gender.*
- *The tools enable you to maintain your effort and rhythm qualities, even when they are very different from those of your scene partner – so their energy doesn't bleed into yours.*
- *Bringing awareness to my physicality releases a lot of tension in awkward areas of the body – especially the voice! I noticed that when everyone focused on something different, it transformed everyone's breath. It freed it up and it became more present and therefore more exciting!*
- *If I play clear Actions and intentions, if I think about the Given Circumstances, I find I tend not to worry about how I 'become a man' when playing a 'trouser role'.*

6 Words and Music in Action

CICELY BERRY

Cicely Berry (1926–2018) was the Voice Director of the Royal Shakespeare Company from 1969 to 2014 where she worked alongside directors such as Peter Brook, Trevor Nunn and John Barton. She taught all over the world, including pioneering work with Nós do Morro in Rio de Janeiro, directed an acclaimed production of *King Lear* for the RSC and published five books, including the seminal *Text in Action*.

Her teaching focuses on two main areas: helping actors develop their speaking voice and empowering them to develop their own response to the text. It is this second area of Cicely's work that we will focus on.

The majority of people in Shakespeare's day were illiterate: plays were heard, not read. Cicely Berry's work emphasises the need to hear, and feel, what is happening in the language to fully understand the meaning, and subtext, of the text itself. Shakespearean verse with its predetermined rhythmic structure, use of heightened poetic imagery and dramatic devices such as soliloquies and chorus, shares a number of qualities with many opera libretti. The challenges for the actor in accessing the verse are similar to those faced by the singer accessing the libretti and music, this takes us to the heart of Cicely's work and why it is so important for the opera singer. She aims to help the actor speak the text for *now* – to truly hear the language and respond to it individually – rather than simply honouring a received way of speaking the text.

It was in response to working with Cicely alongside actors at the RSC, and experiencing how profoundly important her tools were for these actors, that I established ENO Opera Works; I was keen to explore how to translate her ideas into tools for opera singers. Cicely led a number of the early Opera Works sessions, followed later by the voice teacher and director, Barbara Houseman, a colleague of Cicely's at the RSC whose thorough and thoughtful response to Cicely's work is also referred to here.[1]

The work invites us to explore the music in the words, and the words in music, through tools that unify text, music and the body; indeed, the exercises encapsulate Stanislavski's psycho-physical approach by emphasising the complete connectedness of thought, breath,

---

[1] Houseman, B. (2008) *Tackling Text and Subtext: A Step-by-Step Guide for Actors*. London: Nick Hern Books is an incredibly valuable resource.

voice and body in action. Cicely's work helps us to understand the 'total text'; the words and music combined. Underpinning the work are two guiding principles relating to pleasure and politics. She invites the performer to find the pleasure and delight in the sound of the word and the messy, chaotic, visceral experience of singing thoughts in action and she reminds us that 'speech (and song) is always political. The story matters'.[2]

Thoughts in Action

The process of writing a play or opera is not about putting down on paper, in words and music, a series of logical ideas. It is about a writer capturing the way each character, in a manner unique to each of them, expresses their thoughts, feelings and responses to the world within and around them. The character we see and hear emerges out of the rhythm of the language, the choice of words, the notes on which these words are sung and their shifting dynamics. The result is formalised in the libretto and the score but it still represents something 'visceral and primal'.[3] The risk is that our initial response to the words and music is similarly formal; we sit down to read through the text and stand still at the piano to sing through the music. To truly understand the character, we must seek to heighten our awareness of the rhythms and sounds of the words they are singing. Through a visceral physical engagement with these elements we get closer to the movement and journeys of the character's thoughts, closer to the underlying subtext.

   Sound moves us; a change of key, an underlying rhythm, a shift in tempo, all create different and profound emotional responses and resonances in the listener. The *sound* of words, less often considered in opera, has a similar power to move the audience; violent words disturb, lively words awaken. Words provide vital context in an opera and language changes the quality of the note, as Anthony Legge, former Head of Music at ENO, observes, 'The sound and timbre of the language all add greatly to the resonance of your voice'.[4] The rhythm and sound of the language tell us something about the way in which the librettist perceived the character. The composer responded to these words by choosing to accentuate certain qualities through the music the words are set to and underscored by. As a singer you need to, firstly, be alert to this and, secondly, seek to understand *why* the words have inspired the composer,[5] to take you closer to their underlying meaning and into the heart of the world of the opera.

The Psycho-Physical Approach

Sound moves the body and the moving body creates sound. The diaphragm is located close to the celiac (solar) plexus, a mass of nerve-endings near the stomach that collects a good deal of information about your emotional state and vibrates as you speak or sing. Conversely, bringing expression to your thoughts through the singing voice requires an enormous physical exertion; the body must be fully engaged to create, support and sustain the sound. It is clear to see the connectedness of Stanislavski's psycho-physical approach to acting.

---

[2] From an interview with Cicely Berry, Stratford, July 2016.
[3] Ibid.
[4] Legge, A. (2017) *The Art of Auditioning*. London: Edition Peters, p. 22.
[5] See the later interview with composer Jonathan Dove in Chapter 12 (p. 328).

Training for singers too often separates the words from the music, and the mind from the body, yet they are all clearly related and must, ultimately, be indivisible. As I have emphasised throughout the previous chapters, when bringing your attention to the processes of *thought* and emotion, the *body* is intricately connected, and vice versa.

The physical act of singing is an evocation of an image in the mind of the singer. The singer must *see* these images in their mind's eye for their words to fully paint such pictures in the audience's imagination, the *words* must capture and express this image. When the sound a singer creates is disconnected from any such image, it is merely a whirr of technical acrobatics designed to show off the athleticism and *beauty* of the voice, with no clear intent to express anything beyond this.

Words are action; they move and travel in parallel with our ranging thoughts. By bringing awareness to the rhythms inherent in the text and how one word or sentence knocks up against the other, by embodying them and moving with them, by exploring how the particular sounds of the words express need or feeling, we get closer to what the character is feeling and wants to express. Cicely Berry's tools raise our awareness of this 'wonderful, but subliminal, connection between the meaning of words, their sound and physical movement involved in making them'.[6]

Cicely's tools directly explore:

- The meaning of the opera through the structure and sound of the words.
- The subtext of the opera through 'displacement strategies'.

We will explore the words of the libretto, in the first instance, and then look at how the tools can be applied to the music. Cicely's tools are primarily about placing the singer and the story at the centre of the work. They bring the singer's attention to:

- the possibilities of the language; the variety of energies, rhythms and movements of thought which can be found in any text
- your individual response to the language; its sound, movement and structure
- how punctuation and grammar in the score reveal the character's thought process
- where the image lies; the size and scale of imagery and how you inhabit these images in mind and body
- the importance of listening in order to keep ideas alive
- how the music informs your understanding of characters
- how we can deepen our connection to singing words in other languages
- our physical relationship to thoughts and ideas.

These tools are quick to access. Cicely, however, always stressed how important it was to find time to explore and note your own responses. The tools require a decent amount of space and preferably, although you can work alone on a number of the exercises, other people; the tools are inherently playful and working with them is a communal exercise. Discover a sense of play throughout your work on these exercises and find the delight in hearing the

---

[6] Berry, C. (2008) *From Word to Play: A Handbook for Directors.* London: Oberon Books, p. 1.

words spoken out loud. Some exercises will open up a multitude of possibilities within a scene or aria, others will not. Do not worry, move onto the next one.

Opera can sometimes suffer from the weight of its illustrious history, causing performers to be overly reverential, a bit careful, a little too polite. This is also this case with Shakespeare; an actor can too easily hold the verse at arm's length and, seduced by the sound of their own voice, forget to engage with *why* they are making these sounds in the first place. These exercises are messy, physical and occasionally chaotic but by engaging with them fully, they provide a set of invaluable tools to access the meaning of the words and the music on a primal level.

What follows are my recollections of working on the exercises that Cicely developed. Over time, as I have worked with singers, and with Cis' generosity and input, I have adapted the exercises where necessary to better suit the opera singer. Throughout this section I have interspersed the responses of singers who worked with the tools at ENO Opera Works and the Royal Welsh College of Music and Drama.

WARM-UP

You are going to speak the words out loud to experience their particular resonances and vibrations; so first, you need to warm up the body and the voice.

EXERCISE: *Spoken Text Vocal Warm-Up*
Solo/10 mins

- Stand with the knees soft, feet shoulder width apart. Roll the head slowly in a circular motion in each direction, with the jaw dropped and released. Rotate the shoulders three times back and then forwards; include the shoulder-blades in the rotation. Isolate and circle the hips.

- Roll the head so that your chin is touching your chest; continue this roll down the spine. Bend the knees so that the upper half of your body is released over your hips. Shake out the torso to either side.

- Squat and breathe into your lower back, five times. Then, hug your arms around your rib cage and breathe deeply, five times. (See Exercise: Roll and Align (p. 16).)

- Breathe down and hum on a comfortable note. Tap or shake your body to feel vibrations in different places. Five times.

- Repeat this but drop the jaw after initiating a hum; quietly speak M-AY for 10 counts. Then, M-EE, M-I, M-OH, M-OO. Repeat this with different consonants.

- On one breath, focusing on a target, speak each vowel three times through – AY, EE, I, OH, OO. Imagine you can see the sound travel forwards towards the object, carried on one's breath.

- Next, chew imaginary toffee to warm up the lips. Paste your teeth with your tongue, clockwise and then anti-clockwise. Check that there is no tension in the neck.

- Feel your spine lengthened and your feet firmly planted on the floor. Point to a spot in the room, say 'ay', add a consonant to the sound, 'ay-b', and throw an imaginary dart at the spot, releasing the dart on the consonant. Move through all vowels – ee-b, i-b, oh-b, oo-b – and then change consonants.

Text and Music: Structure, Sound, Language

The following exercises can be done largely by yourself. I would recommend you build them into your process when beginning to learn a role. Begin each exercise by first speaking the words, when learning new music notice what the words reveal to you. These observations will help form the foundations of your characterisation.

Speaking the text at the very beginning of the process frees you up to make observations about the character and story, rather than immediately note bashing or focusing on counting rhythms. It also helps you to understand the composer's intentions when you begin to sing the words.

Structure

These exercises explore the movement and journey of thought. When walking the space, do so with a sense of purpose. The exercises are useful at any stage of the rehearsal process but particularly as a first stop at the beginning of your process; they are quick and incredibly informative. I have suggested testing them out with an aria to begin with but they can just as easily be done when singing recitative, duets or ensembles.

> **EXERCISE:** *Walking the Punctuation*
> **Solo/Ongoing**
>
> - Read your aria out loud, score in hand. Walk the space briskly, making sharp changes of direction on every new thought or every grammatical punctuation in the text.
> - Do it again, walking faster, but this time also turn on every musical punctuation; every marked breath, rest or interlude.
> - Next sing your aria, turning on all musical and grammatical punctuation.
> - What do you notice about the number of turns you make? How does it make you feel? What does it tell you about the character? What differences do you notice when you sing?
> - The punctuation signals all the little shifts and changes of thought your character has. By *walking* them in the space – by physicalising this journey of thought – you bring your awareness to *how* this journey of thought is made.
> - This is particularly important for highlighting all the repetitions, each of these separate thoughts must be a distinct step on the journey of the character.
> - By doing this exercise we might lose a sense of the overall meaning of an aria but each physical action will bring us closer to the emotional state of the character.
> - Characters are what they *do*, rather than merely what they think. The movement throughout this exercise represents thoughts in *action* and so help construct character.

- Read your aria out loud again and walk the space as you speak, this time turning only at the end of a sentence.

- Repeat this exercise whilst singing the aria.

- What is the difference from turning on every punctuation? Do you get the sense of the whole thought?

- This exercise helps make sense of the words again following the previous exercise. It often brings us closer to *walking* the musical line or phrasing that the composer might have written. It reflects the idea that we carry thoughts of different size within us, at the same time. We need an understanding of the over-arching thought and, alongside this, its composite parts.

EXAMPLE: *The Magic Flute*

Queen of the Night, No. 4 Recitativo and Aria 'Don't be Afraid, my dearest son!'/'O zittre nicht, mein lieber Sohn'

> **Queen of the Night** Don't be afraid, my dearest son! *(two bars of strings)*
> For you are noble, fearless, strong . . . *(two bars of strings)*
> So hear a mother's plea, do not ignore me, a wilderness of sorrow lies before me.
> Alone, abandoned and forsaken, how I recall that dreadful day, the day I saw my daughter taken.
> A wicked man,
> a wicked man stole her away.
> In waking, in sleeping, I still hear her weeping, her trembling, her shaking, her poor heart was breaking.
> I saw her sorrow all too plainly:
> Ah, help, ah, help!
> I heard my daughter say.
> Alas, she pleaded with me vainly, for all my power had drained away.

When exploring this aria with these two exercises we notice:

- In the recitativo, when the Queen is not singing, the music carries the thoughts. We must still walk the music, changing at the musical punctuation.

- When singing this aria, we notice the second '*wicked*' is set over a full bar. When we walk the journey of this thought, we physically connect its length. It prompts us to seek a reason as to why the Queen does this.

- Turning on the punctuation; '*In waking, in sleeping, etc*'. becomes pretty frenzied. You get a clear sense, through the structure of the sentence, of the agitation she is experiencing by recalling this memory. We also note that it is simply one long sentence; we must embody the sense of the thought developing through to its culmination '*I saw her sorrow all too plainly*'.

- The next sentence is a whirlwind of thoughts; it is important to note that the punctuation here suggests each '*Ah!*' is a separate and distinct thought.

SINGERS' RESPONSES TO WALKING THE PUNCTUATION/THE SENTENCE

- *I did not realise that the thoughts were so long but that, also, there were so many smaller thoughts along the way.*
- *It helped me discover different emphasis and brought my awareness to how the character changes.*
- *I had a much clearer sense of intention; it helps to give an overall aim through the aria.*
- *'Walking the sentence' keeps a line through the thoughts rather than cutting up the sentence into musical phrases. It keeps the breath going and preserves the musical line or intention of the text through any rests.*
- *Makes you realise the contrast needed in repetition within a song. The little physical journeys are all distinct, so the sung lines need to be too.*
- *It's useful to think of the punctuation and how it differed from the placement of the musical breaks – trying to figure out why the composer put those breaks there, is like figuring out what it means when Shakespeare broke the pattern of the verse.*
- *The exercises were especially useful on the recit – they helped point out which rests I should take my time on and which were just added to fill the measure.*
- *'Walking the sentence' helped to emphasise the importance of the beginning of each sentence and thought.*

EXERCISE: *Changing Chairs*
Pairs/Ongoing

- Place two chairs next to each other and, as you speak through the aria, change chairs on each musical or grammatical punctuation.
- It is a good idea to speak your words to a target. For example, the Queen of the Night should sing her first aria to Tamino sitting opposite. If it is a duet, have two sets of two chairs facing each other.
- Make sure that you have actually sat down before continuing to speak.
- Notice how one thought provokes the next.
- Now, try this singing. The répétiteur will have to be eagle eyed to continually stop and start.
- What do you notice this time? Is there a sense of *landing* ideas? What is the difference when you sing it? Do you notice that you are landing ideas within the musical structure? Does this give you a sense of ownership of the music; even when not singing?

Papageno, Tamino No. 5 Quintet 'Hm! Hm! Hm!'

> **Papageno** (*pointing to the padlock on his mouth*)
> Hm! hm! hm! hm! hm! hm! hm! hm! hm! hm! hm! hm! hm! hm! hm! hm!
> **Tamino** Poor Papageno, I can see you have been commanded not to speak.
> **Papageno**
> Hm! hm! hm! hm! hm! hm! hm! hm! hm! hm! hm! hm! hm! hm! hm! hm!
> **Tamino** Alas I'm powerless to help you. The spell is strong and I am weak.
> **Papageno** Hm! hm! hm! hm!
> **Tamino** I cannot tell how
> **Papageno** Hm! hm! hm! hm!
> **Tamino** I can help you.
> **Papageno** Hm! hm! hm! hm!
> **Tamino** The spell is strong and I am weak.

This exercise was incredibly useful to do when working on this scene from *The Magic Flute*. Whilst certainly a good thigh workout for the singer playing Papageno, it served to underline two things:

- Papageno's frustration became rooted in the thought, body, word and music.
- It gave the singer time to consider the thoughts behind each of the 'Hm's'; namely, the actual words he was trying to express but could not because of the padlock on his mouth. It gave time to create a clear parallel line of text that Papageno was trying to sing.
- By changing seats both singers experienced a feeling of being in the moment and present with the thought.
- Tamino's 'I's' seemed to be more important. He is moving in order to speak, there is a need implicit in the action, and this seems to emphasise the importance of the beginning of the line.

SINGERS' RESPONSES TO CHANGING CHAIRS

- *The process of moving from one chair to another gives you more time to connect to thoughts behind idea.*
- *It alerts you to the tiny punctuations you might otherwise miss but which signal a shift in thought. You have to put some physical effort in, so it makes these shifts matter.*
- *The thoughts became clearer.*
- *It really helps identify the need for new thoughts in repetitive arias.*

Note:
- Opera libretti often contain much repetition. A repeated line can move the speaker and the listener; it often intensifies the intentions or reveals the heart of the emotion.

The music suggests *how* a repeated line is to be sung and these exercises provide the time and physical engagement to ask *why* the character is repeating a line.

- These exercises alert us to the primary and subordinate ideas with the line. They help us to understand how a character's thoughts are organised, when a character switches target, when they are in dialogue with themselves and what the driving force of their argument is, suggested through the way in which the thought is structured.

- The rhythmic structure of a line represents the emotional state of the character. By embodying the rhythmic structure, we get close to the character's emotional state without 'acting an emotion'.

Sound

The following exercises alert us to the sound of the words in the music and the possible meaning that these sounds carry. The meaning is revealed through a sensory, rather than intellectual, engagement with the sound; it often takes us close to the essence of a thought or feeling.

CONSONANTS

The consonants tend to carry the meaning and sense of the words. The sounds of consonants affect us through their varying percussive sounds.

EXERCISE: *Release of Emotion*
Solo/Group/Ongoing

Kicking

- Take an object – a shoe or plastic bottle – and, whilst first speaking, and then singing, kick the object around the space.

- Notice the words that seem to jump out. Are they always the words that the composer has emphasised in the music? Note how the consonants seem to become particularly present.

Jostle

- The group stand in a circle shoulder to shoulder. Whilst the text is spoken, and then sung, the group jostle, push and gently shove each other.

- As you try to sing, the breath will be misplaced and the rhythm of the aria will be knocked about by the physicality of the exercise but you might become aware of other qualities of sound.

- After the exercise, it is worth immediately standing aside from the group and singing the aria again in the context of the scene. You might still be a little out of breath but the exercise might have released other ideas.

- What do you notice? The exercise usually brings out textures in the words that were previously hidden. The text can feel alive, vital and energised. A muscularity in the text is highlighted; the words seem to carry a punch.

Figaro No. 26 Aria 'You foolish slaves of Cupid'/'Aprite un po' quegli occhi'

> **Figaro** You foolish slaves of Cupid, how can you be so stupid?
> Just look at what these women are, you won't believe your eyes,
> you won't believe your eyes, no, no, you won't believe your eyes.
> Slavishly we adore them, prostrate ourselves before them.
> We're worshipping the devil, the devil in disguise,
> the devil in disguise, the devil in disguise.
> They wheedle and chivvy us until we give in,
> perverse and lascivious, they drive us to sin;
> these tigresses, pawing us and clawing us so sweetly;
> these comets that shine on us and blind us completely;
> these roses that prick us, these vixens that trick us,
> these daughters of Circe who show us no mercy,
> the monkeys that cheat us, the spiders that eat us,
> these witches, the bitches, pretending to love us,
> you know it is true, you know it is true, yes, yes, it true.
> I see that you know what I'm saying, I see that it's happened to you.

Speak through this aria of Figaro's whilst doing these two exercises. What do you notice?

- Both exercises reveal the rough-edged texture of the words; the alliteration of 'devil in disguise' becomes more pronounced.

- Certain words become more urgent when pressing against the physical obstacle of the person next to you; some words more explosive, or percussive, as you kick your shoe.

- The words become more 'present'; particularly important considering the tempo of this aria and the need for clarity of text when singing at this speed.

EXERCISE: *Exploring the Consonants*
Solo/Ongoing

- Go through your aria and speak only the consonants in the text.

- For example, the Figaro aria becomes *Y flsh slvs f Cpd, hw cn y b s stpid?*

- Having worked your way through the text in this way, immediately sing through your aria in the context of the opera.

- What feelings does this release? Does it tell you anything about Figaro that you had not already noticed?

- The exercise highlights the idea that the meaning of the aria lies in the consonants. Images often seem to be clearer having done this exercise. In this example, the exercise seems to emphasise the fertile thoughts alive in Figaro's mind.

VOWELS

Vowels carry the emotional expression. What is the tonal quality of this expression, are the vowels bright or heavy? How does the choice of vowel take us into the character's interior world?

EXERCISE: *Resistance*
Group/Ongoing

- One person speaks their text whilst trying to reach another person, or a particular target. Two or three of the group hold the person back physically.
- Speak first, then sing.
- It is important that the group do not block the view of the target for the speaker.
- If it seems appropriate, the group might release the speaker at a given point and then re-engage the resistance.
- Notice the words coming from a deeper place in the body and how important the breath becomes to express the character's ideas.

EXAMPLE: *The Magic Flute*

Queen of the Night, No. 4 Recitativo and Aria 'Don't be Afraid, my dearest son!'/'O zittre nicht, mein lieber Sohn' (p. 214)

- Look at this aria again. The Queen has a number of potential targets: Tamino, the memory of the day her daughter was taken, Sarastro, Pamina, herself.
- When we explored the aria, we had different people from the group representing these targets the Queen is trying to reach.
- Certain vowels become lengthened, for example:

  alone, abandoned and forsaken

  a wicked man stole her away

- When the aria was sung, the exercise seemed to have provided emotional justification for the elongated vowels; they were filled with a sense of searching. This was felt in the body, not simply understood in a literal way.
- In this way, we seemed to access the underlying meaning of the aria. The Queen of the Night is a strong woman but, at this moment, she is vulnerable. She is clearly manipulating Tamino but underlying this is the need she feels to rescue Pamina and defeat Sarastro.
- Immediately after exploring the exercise we repeated the aria in the context of the scene. The singer was rooted, connected to her body; the Objective to persuade Tamino was underpinned by a physical need.

EXERCISE: *Exploring the Vowel*
Solo/Ongoing

- This is a similar exercise to exploring consonants. Work through your text speaking the vowels only. Add an 'H' to the front of every vowel to avoid making the shorter sounds glottal and give each vowel its true length.

- What is the impact of this? The vowel sounds suggest the emotion of the character.

- For example, look at the beginning of the Queen of the Night's aria, 'alone, abandoned and forsaken': HA HOH HA HA HUH HA HOH HAY HE. The vowels have a groaning quality and a sense of pain.

- Repeat this *speaking* the sung vowels and note the difference.

- Then, sing only the vowels – this will help create the rhythm of phrase – but will also connect the sense of the character you derived when speaking the vowels.

- When doing this do not be tempted to start *playing* the emotion.

SINGERS' RESPONSES TO EXPLORING THE VOWEL

- *Breaking down the text into its constituent vowels helps to put it 'on the body' and 'in the voice', making it easier to sing.*

- *'Ho hi ha' (glottal) helps me connect the breath with the words more by driving the breath through the vowels of each word.*

- *The exercise of phonating only the vowels is one commonly used in singing practice in order to attain the line and phrasing of a sung phrase or to support a more legato line. Applied to text it allows us to comprehend the line of each phrase: the start, the end and emphasised points in between. Vowels control the tone of what one says and sings and, in turn, the emotional expression; this exercise gives added meaning to my singing practice.*

LANGUAGE

The choice of a particular word tells us much about the world of the opera; its tone, its character, its quality. It also brings us close to the images that the character sees and lives with.

EXERCISE: *Three Times Through*
Solo/Ongoing

- This is an exercise originally introduced to Opera Works by Barbara Houseman. Say each word or short phrase three times. Slow the speech and allow the word to drop in and to connect.

- It sounds incredibly simple but it gives us time with each word to make a personal association with it. The words have time and space to resonate. Pictures might develop in our mind's eye as we repeat the word.
- Then, sing the word or short phrase three times through. Allow yourself to vary the rhythm and the tempo but keep the pitch the same.
- Ask a partner to close their eyes and listen to you speaking or singing the aria through again. Ask them what they see.

SINGERS' RESPONSES TO THREE TIMES THROUGH

- *It provided a way to discover further colours in each word.*
- *It's great for connecting with a language that isn't my own. I focused on the sensation of the word itself – the shape, the sound – and it released feelings and thoughts. Each word became more significant.*

EXERCISE: *Physicalising Words*
Solo/Ongoing

- Place your score on a music stand or similar in order to free up your hands. If you are working in a room with others, keep your back to them to save being distracted.
- Work through your text finding a physicalised image for every word; you can create a still or moving image.
- The physical images you create with your body will also correspond to images in your mind's eye; you might create an imagined visual context for your physical image to live within. The very act of physicalising a word might spark pictures.
- Ally this work to the music by singing each word as you physicalise the word.

SINGERS' RESPONSES TO PHYSICALISING WORDS

- *Unlocks different ways of interpreting a word or phrase.*
- *Helped me break away from the stiffness that can come from trying to play a 'regal' or 'noble' character.*[7]
- *Focusing on each word can help to rediscover what inspired the composer to respond to the text in the way they have.*

---

[7] See Character Types and *Commedia dell'arte*, p. 178.

- *I was working on Rosina's aria 'Una voce poco fa'/'A voice a little while ago'[8] and found violence in the words that I hadn't noticed before; 'victory, viper . . .'. I'd always thought of it as a cheeky aria but there is more strength and viciousness in the character than I had been playing.*

Note:

- These exercises help us to translate abstract ideas into something tangible.
- They help us to notice the smaller words. The words, 'now, then, if, but, either, or' are words on which the character's reasoning balances; an argument or reality is formed through the use of these words.

Displacement Strategies

These next tools, or *strategies*, were developed by Cicely in response to specific challenges she found actors facing in the rehearsal room. The tools bring together and unite much of the work on creating character through the mind and body.

The strategies work on a number of different levels:

1 They help uncover the meaning that lies beneath the surface of the words and music by introducing a particular Point of Concentration into the playing of the scene. These Points of Concentration are usually physically engaging; the meaning becomes *felt* through the whole body.

2 They introduce a physical Obstacle which informs an intensified engagement with the body, words and music.

Cicely calls them displacement strategies because they literally take the mind elsewhere. This can be incredibly liberating. When rehearsing a scene, the focus can too often be on the specific act of singing the words and music. The strategies stop you thinking about the singing; your mind is diverted and preoccupied with something else and your technique takes over. My experience of using the strategies is that they usually bring focus, connection and clarity to the singing.

In many ways the strategies build, and develop, a subconscious connection to the language that enriches our understanding of the opera. This connection, on a profound level, helps develop the sense that our *actions* and words belong to us.

The choice of which particular strategy to best use, in any given scene, is crucial. It is, however, usually a case of trial and error, until you get to know the tools. In Opera Works Response Weekends we played with all the strategies, on a range of repertoire; some worked, others fell flat. It is about letting go of seeking a particular result and experiencing the tools for yourself, unpacking what you have discovered at a later point. The strategies are listed, therefore, in no particular order. I have listed examples of scenes, from *The Marriage of Figaro* and *The Magic Flute*, that we explored with a particular exercise when rehearsing these operas with young singers at the Royal Welsh College of Music and Drama.

---

[8] Rosina's Act One aria from *The Barber of Seville*.

EXERCISE: *Task*
Solo/Ongoing

- Carry out a simple but engaging task whilst singing the aria or scene. For example, pick up paperclips, arrange chairs in the space, fold paper into envelopes.
- Consider the music as you do the task; allow the music to inform the movement. In turn, the music should be seen to have been initiated by the task.

EXAMPLE: *The Magic Flute*

The Queen of the Night, No. 14 Aria 'The wrath of hell'/'Der Hölle Rache'

- The singer playing the Queen folded clothes and packed them into a suitcase whilst singing this aria. During the exercise certain words became allied to certain actions; this seemed to reinforce the Queen's need to communicate. The use of the words became more precise and there was a keener location of targets: as a result, clearer thoughts were conveyed.

EXERCISE: *A Circle*
Group/Ongoing

- The singer stands in the centre of a circle of people. Their Objective is to find a way through the circle. Those in the circle aim to block the singer's escape.
- It might be that you introduce a target outside of the circle that the character is striving to reach.
- Explore the impact of this physical Obstacle on the words. How does pushing against a physical barrier help to root the sound? Does it seem appropriate to push against the group on a specific line or piece of music?

EXAMPLES: *The Magic Flute/The Marriage of Figaro*

- Tamino, No. 1 Introduction 'Have mercy'/Zu Hilfe!'
  - Tamino's introduction needs a terrific amount of sustained energy, it is at the beginning of the opera and kicks the story off. In the story he is running away from the snake but metaphorically he is trapped, he has nowhere to run to. The circle physicalised this metaphor and demanded an engagement with the entire body, which helped the singer sustain the energy.
- Figaro, No. 3 Cavatina 'So, little master, you're dressed to go dancing'/'Se vuol ballare'

○ Figaro's cavatina is a response full of ironic spite that conceals violent intent. It is formalised in a dance, a minuet, but Figaro is responding to a desperate situation; he is trapped by his class and by his master's intentions to sleep with Susanna. The circle makes the idea of entrapment tangible. When we used this tool, the singer's words punched against the circle and his actions united with the music with real *purpose*; the exercise revealed, and made present, Figaro's underlying impotent rage.

EXERCISE: *Spaces of the Mind*
Solo/Ongoing

- Travel to a new space in the room and arrive at this new space before singing a new thought.
- Do this whilst singing; work with a keen-eyed, sensitive répétiteur!
- This tool is about the processes of thought. It is useful when exploring any aria as it gives you time, on each journey, to consider why the previous thought leads to the new one.
- It also allows you to mark how long every journey is between thoughts, sometimes you might only want to take a couple of steps, sometimes your journey to the next thought will be much longer.
- When you sing the aria through afterwards, the music will dictate the speed of one thought travelling to the next; you will probably need to compress the thoughts you have discovered through the exercise. Importantly, however, there will be clear thoughts to *actually* compress; often, thinking within the confines of the music for the first time allows no time to construct a thought.
- The sense of arrival, in a new space, makes the thought feel very present.
- Thoughts become three-dimensional within the space; they are represented by a particular part of the room. This means you literally inhabit them. The music will give you a sense of what this space is like; you do not need to be literal about this, it might be that the space has a particular temperature, colour or texture. These sensory details are often much quicker to access afterwards and help you to unite your thoughts and the music.

EXAMPLES: *The Magic Flute/The Marriage of Figaro*

- Papageno, No. 2 Aria 'I'm sure that there could never be. . .'/'Der Vogelfänger bin ich ja'
  - ○ The setting of Papageno's aria can sometimes seem confusing; sometimes the music suggests a new thought, whilst in contrast the words suggest that the thought needs to be sustained over a number of musical phrases. This exercise

clarifies exactly when new ideas arrive. It also clarifies that each time Papageno blows his pipe, it is a new idea, or an extension of the previous thought.

- Sarastro, No. 15 Aria 'Before our holy altar'/'In diesen heil'gen Hallen'
  - The tempo of Sarastro's aria is *larghetto*; we found the challenge for the singer was keeping the thoughts alive and present, especially when there are so many repeats. The exercise gave time, through each journey from space to space, to consider why a new space is different from the previous one; it encouraged the singer to consider each repeat as a new thought.

EXERCISE: *Inner and Outer Landscape*
Solo/Ongoing

- Two or more spaces on the floor mark different areas of thought: for example, the rest of the world and you, the here and there, or the past, present and future.
- Mark lines on the floor to define the separate areas and travel from one space to the next as the aria or scene demands.

EXAMPLE: *The Magic Flute*

Sarastro, Act Two opening dialogue, 'My brothers'

My brothers who serve the great gods Isis and Osiris,/Tamino has approached us in search of the goals to which we all aspire./It is our duty to help him./ Such is his worth that Pamina has been chosen to be by his side. // That is why I took her from her mother, a woman who hopes to use her magic to destroy our temple./ Tamino will help us defend ourselves against her.

The lines mark the possible shift into either the past, the present or the future. This exercise begins to open up the language; we see the possibilities for change within a line. Sarastro leads his followers through what has happened in the past, where they are now and what he hopes will happen in the future; he is taking them on a journey. I have marked // to suggest the moment that Sarastro travels even further into the past.

EXERCISE: *Drawing a Picture*
Solo/Ongoing

- Draw a picture whilst singing your aria. The picture should relate in some way to what you are singing about.
- It is important to focus entirely on this task and not seek to engage with any other character through the exercise.
- Find a way of connecting the task to the music (without simply drawing in tempo).

- Papageno, No. 20 Aria 'If only I could meet her'/'Ein Mädchen oder Weibchen'
  - Papageno drew his ideal woman; his imaginary Papagena. The process made the prospect of what he is longing for real and added specific detail to such phrases as 'no sweetheart could be sweeter'.
- Countess, No. 19 Aria 'I remember his love so tender'/'Dove sono i bei momenti'
  - The Countess drew a picture of the perfect moment between herself and the Count; a memory of the time he proposed to her. The exercise explored the bitter-sweet quality of the music throughout, particularly on the repeat of 'So much love can disappear'/'di quell labbro menzogner!'. There was a tangible tension as she forced herself to draw the treasured memory from the past, whilst singing about how devalued the memory has now become.

SINGERS' RESPONSES TO DRAWING A PICTURE

- *This strategy helped with 'just being'.*
- *I struggle to connect with my emotions when singing – drawing a picture released the emotion. It made me concentrate on the story and I didn't worry too much about technique; the voice was freer and I was completely 'in the zone'.*

EXERCISE: *Concretising Thought*
Solo/Pairs/Group/Ongoing

- Identify a major theme in your aria or scene and represent it with a physical object; ideally a 500ml half-filled plastic water bottle.
- The object becomes a metaphor for such concepts as love, power, injustice, God, the past, etc.
- You might use two or more different objects to represent ideas that are present or conflicting in the scene.
- Consider how you pick up the object, weigh it, explore its texture, its size.
- Use the space around you to develop an active relationship with the object/idea.
- Explore how you use the music, the interludes, the pauses, the melodic shifts and the changes in rhythm, to explore the idea through the object.
- It is worth noting that the object is not a replacement for a living person; your concentration would then be on imagining what their response, moment to moment, might be, rather than playing your Objective. The exercise is a way of making something intangible, tangible.
- The exercise underlines the importance of having a clear target; even when the target itself is an idea or concept.

- As you play your scene remain as focused on your Objective as always. It is especially useful to explore the object/idea through your scene, whilst others observe and write down what you are *doing*; write down the transitive verbs that define your Actions. This feedback gives you a palette of possibilities when you return to your scene.

EXAMPLE: *The Marriage of Figaro*

The Countess, No. 10 Aria 'Hear my prayer'/'Porgi, Amor'

- We used two different bottles to explore this aria; one represented death, the other, the Count's love.
- The exercise brought to life the tension between these two possibilities for the Countess; the aria became much more active as a result.
- The singer's interaction with the two ideas was very much guided by the music. This connected the music to the thought and action, with the result that the music appeared to be being generated from her inner dialogue; this began in the play-in:

Figure 6.1 Countess aria.

1 The Countess sees the two bottles; love and death. She recognises what they represent.

2 She moves towards 'love'.

3 She picks 'love' up slowly.

4 She cradles it to her, experiencing what it is to hold these memories.

5 The Countess sees 'death'.

6 She tries to resist the possibility of death.

7 She holds 'death'.

8 She weighs 'death' and understands its meaning.

9 She again sees 'love' and rekindles hope in it.

10 The Countess acknowledges the presence of 'death'.

11 She clings onto the hope of 'love' in response to this. Investing in this hope moves her to sing her appeal.

This is not staging; it represents what the singer discovered when exploring this exercise. Once the singer had played the exercise through a few times, we lost the bottles, and played the scene again: the Countess, alone, in her dressing room. The singer remained engaged with ideas that had been discovered through the exercise – the conflict between love and death – in her thoughts and through her movements.

SINGERS' RESPONSES TO CONCRETISING THOUGHT

- *Concretising thought makes your thoughts present, easily readable and tangible.*

- *I found out so much about the ideas in the scene; much more than if I'd just sat down and thought about it. It was playful and freeing.*

EXERCISE: *Marking Thoughts*
Solo/Pair/Group/Ongoing

- You need a blank piece of paper and a pen. Throughout your aria, put a tick on the paper at the end of every thought. This can be a part or whole thought.

- If the aria explores two conflicting ideas, you might draw a line down the centre of the paper to represent each side of the argument and land thoughts on one side, or the other.

- You begin to think of the notes you are singing as active thoughts. Add up how many thoughts at the end of the aria.

- In a duet, both characters mark a tick after every thought. The singers should take particular pleasure in marking a tick, or scoring a point, when they land an especially strong thought, so as to develop a sense of one-upmanship!

- This exercise underlines that words, sung in a particular way, can be tools, or even weapons, to help achieve your Objective.

EXAMPLES: *The Magic Flute/The Marriage of Figaro*

- Figaro and Susanna, No. 2 Duet 'Supposing one evening the Countess should need you'/'Se a caso madama la note ti chiama'
  - The Figaro and Susanna duet has a lot of space between the lines the characters sing to each other; they are leaving time for the other one to get up to speed with their argument. The singers filled the time in the music by playing with *how* they marked their tick; sometimes very slowly to show they were giving the other time, sometimes a huge tick marking a particularly strong idea that had been landed.
- Pamina and Papagena, No. 7 Duet 'A man in search of truth'/'Bei Männern, welche Liebe fühlen'
  - In *The Magic Flute* duet we drew a couple of additional lines down the paper; the lines marked the distinction between those thoughts each of the characters were communicating to the other character, and those they were unpacking for themselves.

EXERCISE: *Building Structures*
Solo/Pair/Group/Ongoing

- Using any objects within the rehearsal room – tables, chairs, bags – build a literal structure or monument that represents an idea within the opera, whilst singing your aria or scene.
- Consider *how* you connect the words and music to the action of constructing your monument. What is your attitude to the idea you are building at any given point? This should be represented by your contact with each individual object. Do you connect with it lightly or roughly? Do you respect the act of building this idea? Or do you build it in spite of yourself?
- Explore exactly *when* an object is picked up and placed down: on which particular word or chord. The exercise really helps to connect the beginning and end of thoughts with the music. Your thoughts will not usually begin *on* the first word you sing, but at some point before it; the thought needs to inspire the breath to sing the thought. Very often there is music to mark the beginning of a thought. Similarly, explore exactly when an idea is delivered, or *lands*.

EXAMPLES: *The Magic Flute/The Marriage of Figaro*

- Tamino, No. 3 Aria 'I've never seen a face so fair'/'Dies Bildnis ist bezaubernd schön'
  - The monument represented 'Love' for Tamino. In the first part of the aria Tamino, struck by an unfamiliar feeling, was seeking or searching for a meaning from the

objects. Occasionally he distanced himself from them, as though they were unexplained, mysterious notions. The construction took place at a slow tempo. Once he had discovered that he was building a monument to Love, the building became much more open, encircling, celebratory.

- Susanna and The Countess, No. 20 Duet 'The breezes . . .'/'Sull'aria'
  - The monument represented the 'Future' for the Countess and Susanna. The exercise helped to explore the moments the two were collaborating and those moments where they were finding the thoughts for themselves. The building of the structure helped to reveal the moments of doubt, the moments the weight of responsibility felt more burdensome, and those moments where the task became painful. It also pinpointed those times in the duet where they were resolved and determined to construct the 'Future' they both wanted.

Note: the relationships the characters have with the ideas are often defined in terms of verbs: Action words. The relationships they have with the objects are externalised; making the thoughts vital, extant and clear for the audience.

SINGERS' RESPONSES TO BUILDING STRUCTURES

- *I stayed connected to the subtext – like a giant physical point of concentration. I used the words differently in response to the POC.*
- *I felt my body was engaged with the music. I felt like I was generating the music.*

EXERCISE: *Covert Relations*
Group/Ongoing

- Two volunteers patrol the perimeter of your acting space; they are guards. When either of the guards travels from one side of the space to the other, you must stop singing. You can resume the scene once they are still.
- Do not interact with the guards; they are simply there to stop you singing. You may, of course, imagine them to be certain other characters in your opera.
- Again, it requires a skilled répétiteur to stop and start playing the music in line with the patrol's movements.
- This exercise underlines the value of your communication in any given moment; in this way it intensifies your need to achieve your Objective.
- It also breaks up the rhythm of the scene. Breaking the pattern of a scene can often lead to noticing new things about the scene; it helps you see the situation from a slightly different perspective.

EXAMPLES: *The Magic Flute/The Marriage of Figaro*

- Pamina, Three Boys No. 21 'Are you the one I love the best?'/'Du also bist mein Bräutigam'
  - ○ Pamina is conflicted; she has the knife and intends to kill herself but needs to overcome certain Obstacles to do this. The exercise seemed to heighten these Obstacles, with the result that the words were used more energetically to pursue the Objectives. The Three Boys' music is often becalming but the exercise was useful for engaging them in the peril of the moment.
- Count, Countess, Susanna No.13 Trio 'Come out of there Susanna!'/'Susanna, or via sortite!'
  - ○ The trio in *Figaro* is similarly high stakes and the threat of violence and potential humiliation seemed to be intensified with the repeated suspension of the scene. The volunteer patrol took on the persona of the rest of the household. When the music was suspended before a repeated line, the moment of silence gave time to consider why the line *needed* to be repeated. There are moments throughout the trio when one or more characters is not singing; the tension between the characters must exist even when the singing stops. The exercise helped sustain this tension by consistently frustrating the singers.

SINGERS' RESPONSES TO COVERT RELATIONS

- *The next thought becomes especially important with the implied threat that it may never be spoken.*
- *It brings our attention to how to sustain thoughts through silence: to connect silence with thought, pregnant with need. Listen to John Cage's music and the way he plays with silence; it is heard as clearly and absolutely as a note struck on a piano.*
- *The words really matter!*
- *It brings a greater awareness of the rhythm and dynamics in the music.*

EXERCISE: *Making Contact*
Group/Ongoing

- As you sing, you pursue eye contact either with members of a group, or with just one other person; they all deny you eye contact.
- It helps if the other players know the music; they can reject contact at a specific moment to help suggest that the action inspires a certain response in the music. It underlines the idea that many arias are actually duets (or ensembles) and that the

other singers in a scene need to sensitively work with the music to create the necessary interaction; be it as an Obstacle or otherwise.

- You can use the whole space to attempt to contact someone or, alternatively, restrict the exercise to being sat around a table. Restricting the action means the singer's pursuit, and the group's rejection, must become even more detailed and specific.

EXAMPLES: *The Magic Flute/The Marriage of Figaro*

- Three Ladies, Tamino, Papageno No. 12 Quintet, 'Why, why, why?'/ Wie, wie, wie?'
  - The *Flute* quintet is obviously all about the Three Ladies attempting to make contact with Tamino and Papageno with varying degrees of success. The challenge in this scene is two-fold; there are lots of repeated lines and the tempo is *allegro*. Both these factors risk undermining the veracity of the Ladies' attempts. The exercise brings unerring focus to seeking your target and achieving your Objective. The result in our rehearsals was that the Ladies became brilliantly tactically diverse; it freed up their movement and brought great intent to each word.
- Barbarina No. 23 Cavatina 'I have lost it'/'L'ho perduta, me meschina!'
  - In Barbarina's cavatina the singer faces the challenge of searching for something they know they will not find. Initially, in rehearsals, the search for the pin was quite generalised. We then used this exercise; Barbarina pursued the entire cast for an answer but in seeking their help, found no response. This connected the singer to the character's sense of isolation at this moment and the previous generalised searching was replaced by the search for something real; in this case, eye contact. When we translated this back into the reality of the scene, the singer seemed to have a connection with both the feeling of loneliness and the *need* to resolve the situation.

EXERCISE: *Shifting Alliances*
Group/Ongoing

- This tool is useful for accessing the subtext of political scenes; it keys into the Lecoq theory of push and pull we looked at in Chapter 5 (p. 154).
- Sit at a table with a number of chairs around it (more chairs than players). With every line you sing, make the decision to move towards, away from or around another character (or group of characters).
- This exercise encourages you to consider the effect you would like each line to have on other characters throughout a scene and demands that you engage physically to express this. Even if the scene, once staged, is relatively static, you will have an awareness of how each line represents the potential for shifting allegiances; the lines will continue to carry this idea of movement.

EXAMPLE: *The Marriage of Figaro*

Marcellina, Figaro, Bartolo, Don Curzio, Count, Susanna No.18 Sextet 'Darling boy, let me embrace you'/'Riconosci in questo ampleso'

- There is a lot of information to be unpacked in this scene; Figaro is reunited with his parents. The exercise helped to make clear the shifting dynamics of the scene, establishing the historic allegiances that each character brought into the scene and emphasising the varying degrees of acceptance felt by each character, as the news of Figaro's parentage is revealed.

EXERCISE: *Barriers*
Pairs/Group/Ongoing

- Create a physical barrier using objects in the room. The barrier should either defend you from the outside world, or seek to block another character in.
- This is similar to Exercise: Building Structures (p. 229), but, invariably, engages others who might be assisting you or working against you. Likewise, consider *how* and *when* you place an object down with the music.

EXAMPLES: *The Magic Flute/The Marriage of Figaro*

- The Queen of the Night, No. 14 Aria 'The wrath of hell'/'Der Hölle Rache'
  - The Queen builds a barrier between herself and Pamina; threatening to kill the love she has for Pamina, if she refuses to kill Sarastro. By making the metaphor literal it absolutely connected the Queen's thoughts to the music and words through her actions. During the exercise, Pamina began to dismantle the wall, just before the Queen's first cadenza. Pamina's action seemed to inspire the cadenza which, for the Queen, became full of jubilant resistance to her daughter's efforts.
- Cherubino, No. 11 'Tell me what love is'/'Voi, che sapete'
  - The Cherubino aria seemed to work best when we addressed it as a trio between Cherubino, Susanna and the Countess. In the action of the scene, Susanna is supposed to be accompanying Cherubino on guitar but the exercise freed Susanna to play without a guitar. Cherubino started to tentatively build a wall around himself and the Countess. Susanna at times encouraged and, later, began to dismantle the wall. The Countess questioned Cherubino's choices about exactly how and where he was building the wall; she then proceeded to encourage, help and take over the building of the wall. The exercise brought to the fore the three characters' relationships, and, compellingly, the singers were not 'acting', they were simply playing the game.

A SINGER'S RESPONSE TO BARRIERS

- *My aria became a duet – we were really listening to each other's words and movements.*

EXERCISE: *Manipulation*
Pairs/Ongoing

- One person tries to get the other to do something against their will; for example, sit down on a chair, undress (within limits), move across the space.
- The exercise is about persuasion, not about applying force.
- The person being manipulated is usually singing. The manipulator can represent any other character or theme.

EXAMPLE: *The Magic Flute*

Monostatos, No. 13 Aria 'All the world is always lusting'/'Alles fühlt der Liebe Freuden'

- This is another example of physicalising the metaphor. When we created the Character Lists, it revealed that Monostatos feels the rest of the world is against him; indeed, they might be. Whilst Monostatos sings about his intention to assault Pamina, a singer representing Sarastro's Brotherhood continually attempted to get Monostatos to sit down: by tapping him on the shoulder, nudging, pulling at him. The music bristles and, by the end of the exercise, every nerve in the singer seemed to be on edge; the music was alive in his body.

EXERCISE: *Questioning*
Pairs/Group/Ongoing

- Whilst you sing, one or more people verbally challenge everything you sing about. They question, argue, rubbish, dismiss, invalidate, undermine, belittle, reject and ridicule every statement you make by speaking under, and over, the music.
- This exercise gives you another barrier to press against; you meet resistance whilst singing and this incites you to sharpen your own words in opposition. You must justify your thoughts through words.
- The questioners might represent the voice of doubt in your character's own mind, or the society that opposes them, or their ancestors' standards and expectations; whatever best suits the story.

EXAMPLE: *The Magic Flute*

- Sarastro, No. 15 Aria 'Before our holy altar'/'In diesen heil'gen Hallen'
  - Sarastro is laying out for Pamina exactly *how* he will treat his enemies. The tempo is *larghetto* and Sarastro restates the same views repeatedly. The singer playing Sarastro found this aria sedate and worried it would be boring. When we did this exercise, the singer realised that Sarastro is having to assert his views and lead the Brotherhood with the constant awareness that there is an alternative viewpoint; embodied in the Queen of the Night. Indeed, the Brotherhood often define themselves through their opposition, disconcertingly, to women. It helped the singer understand his Objective; he needed to face down other opinions in order to survive. A seemingly sedate hymn suddenly had purpose.
- Speaker, Tamino No. 8 Finale 'What rash adventure brings you here'/'Wo willst du kühner Fremdling hin?'
  - This exercise was particularly useful for the Speaker. Similar to Sarastro, the Speaker exudes a knowing calm and yet, when pushed by Tamino, he reveals a brief spark of anger; a forte chord precedes 'I may not break my solemn vow!/Die Zunge bindet Eid und Pflicht!'. We wanted to explore the possible tension underlying this calm and so, during the scene, when the other character was singing, Tamino and the Speaker would constantly challenge each other's views. It created a tension in the scene which seemed to underpin the deliberate, slow pace of the Speaker.

A SINGER'S RESPONSE TO QUESTIONING

- *Arguing and questioning – this tool is so useful to generate a new impulse to each word and sentence I sing.*

EXERCISE: *Spectrum*
Group/Ongoing

- Write down two conflicting ideas, present in your scene, on separate pieces of paper. Place these pieces of paper at either end of an imaginary line. As you sing the scene, explore your character's shifting relationship to these two ideas; how far along the imaginary line, the spectrum, towards one idea or the other do you travel?
- Every character in the scene can explore their own spectrum simultaneously.
- There may be multiple ideas you want to explore; in which case play the scene again with different ideas at either end of the line, or add a third point to travel towards.
- This tool, introduced to Opera Works by Barbara Houseman, allows you to directly engage with and explore a theme or Point of Concentration.

- It prompts you to make decisions; you *must* land somewhere along the spectrum when you sing a line. Whether that decision ultimately feels right or wrong will help inform your eventual journey through the scene.

EXAMPLES: *The Magic Flute/The Marriage of Figaro*

- Pamina, No. 17 Aria 'Now I know'/'Ach ich fühls'
  - In rehearsals we explored Pamina's conflicting thoughts about 'Love' and 'Rejection'. We discovered that, sometimes, it felt right for Pamina to walk in opposition to the words she was singing; for example, the line, 'if you spurn the love I offer' saw the singer driving towards 'Love'. The exercise helped clarify the subtext for the singer; it seemed to be that Pamina, despite singing about her rejection by Tamino, continued to invest in the hope of love throughout the aria.
- Count, No. 17 Recit and Aria 'You've won the case already!'/'Hai gia vinta la causa!'
  - We explored the idea of 'Entitlement' and 'Self-doubt' in response to the Count overhearing Figaro and Susanna's plot against him. Again, it gave the singer the opportunity to physically engage with the subtext; it made the underlying thoughts present in his body. This helped to develop other layers of the Count's character; for example, it seemed his rage might sometimes be being driven by his self-doubt, rather than his sense of entitlement. Understanding this, ultimately, helped us to understand the Count's eventual appeal for forgiveness at the end of Act Four; he became a complex human being, rather than simply an outline of a monster.

SUMMARY

- The tools fall into two categories; those dealing with the structure, sound and language of the text, and those Displacement Strategies that engage you with the underlying subtext of the scene.
- They help engage your whole self with the thought, the image in your mind's eye, and the words and the music.
- They invite your personal response to the feeling of the language and alert you to other possibilities within the language and music.

TO DO

- Make the tools on structure, sound and language part of your process when learning new roles; they will help you to memorise the words and music.
- Explore different Displacement Strategies throughout your process of creating character and rehearsing an opera; work by yourself if necessary but, ideally, find a way to incorporate these tools into your rehearsal process with fellow singers.

- Use the tools to refresh audition arias that you have been performing for a long time.
- Ask yourself; am I engaged with the words, in my body, through the music? If the answer is, '*no*', explore these exercises to see how they might help you.

SINGERS' RESPONSE TO WORDS AND MUSIC IN ACTION TOOLS

- *Working on text reveals the music to you in a new way.*
- *The composer responds to words to create music, so if feels like going on a journey they might have made. Listening to the sound of the words is particularly useful and when I saw how they relate to the melody, I found it magical. I can approach the music much more easily now, I frequently lose myself in notation rather than the text but this frees up the voice as you don't have a chance to worry about techniques or how you sound.*
- *They help me think about phrasing: how to 'colour' through images and dynamics.*
- *They brought about a series of different thoughts about how to interpret character.*
- *They helped me get out of my head and took me away from worrying about technical points.*
- *I made discoveries about singing whilst focusing on something else. My body was very free for the same reason.*
- *The thing that will stick with me from working with these tools is the huge contribution the audience makes with their own imaginations; that you fuel the collective audience imagination by seeing images in your own mind's eye. It actually means you can reduce your gestures and actions.*
- *They help me in being rooted to the ground, being individual, being yourself; and with the confidence that springs from this.*
- *Worrying makes you hold your breath – these tools stop me worrying!*
- *Being a singer or an actor or both isn't enough – you need to be an artist. These tools help bring artistry to our craft. We can communicate more than words or the notes: imagery, colours, thoughts and emotions.*
- *I found it very interesting that the meaning of the words came so easily. Being dyslexic I often find that I can read a passage over and over again but the meaning may still not be processed. I think these exercises are a more effective way of understanding a piece better and quicker.*

Part Two In Practice

7 Preparing for Rehearsals

WHAT CHALLENGES DO YOU FACE WHEN PREPARING FOR REHEARSALS?

- *It's especially difficult when you haven't found out about the production, or the director's vision, to know how much character detail to go into.*

- *The unknowns are challenging. Many's the time you take a piece, read through a synopsis and create the character based upon your specific interpretation, only to find months later that the director sees the piece taking a different shape. Having the ability to remain malleable in that situation but without forsaking all the work that has been put in previously.*

Throughout your career you will work on a multitude of different projects, each varying in scale, repertoire, rehearsal time and the collaborators you will work alongside. The one constant will be *you*.

How do you bring a sense of continuity as you navigate and embrace these projects? How do you actively engage with your journey as an artist? How do you develop from one project to the next? How do you best use your time in preparation?

Your process begins, on each project, before you meet your vocal coach or enter the rehearsal room; your process begins with yourself and the score. Developing an approach to the early stages of your work connects your various projects and lays the foundations for you to embrace each rehearsal process with a sense of confidence and freedom. This section shows how you can build your own process towards creating truthful character by using the tools already laid out.

You are not aiming to go into rehearsals with a fully formed character or an immovable view of the dramatic world within which this character exists. You do, however, want to go into the rehearsal room with an understanding of the possibilities that the score presents, with ideas to offer and ditch, and with a readiness to use rehearsals to explore different options. You want to have cracked the spine of the opera and to have begun to alert yourself to the opportunities that lie within it.

The Challenge

Before rehearsals commence, you will be expected, in almost all circumstances, to have learnt your part and be off copy. This is perfectly understandable; it takes a certain length of time to learn the music for a role and arriving having not learnt your part significantly impacts on the frequently short amount of time in rehearsals. This, however, presents certain significant challenges.

Actors in theatre will, by and large, not be expected to have learnt their lines before the start of rehearsals; it is understood that lines tend to be memorised, unavoidably, in certain hard-to-break patterns. Text is the result of a process of thought and the actor remains more flexible in the delivery of their lines, if the lines are absorbed through a process of examination of the subtext. The process of learning the text, therefore, is underpinned by a deep understanding of the flow of characters' thoughts and motivations.

Music takes much longer to learn than text. However, the composer is giving you more information through the music than words alone and offers the singer a clearer guide as to *how* to memorise and present the score. Yet each production will interpret this information differently and your, very real, challenge is to learn the part whilst remaining open and flexible to integrating and incorporating the ideas that are discovered in rehearsals.

An Approach

So, how do you do this? How do you remain receptive to a wide range of ideas and not lock yourself down to certain fixed assumptions about character before entering the rehearsal room?

Stanislavski talks about the first impressions of a text having a special freshness and that one's first acquaintance with a part can be the best possible stimuli with your artistic enthusiasm and commitment.[1] It's important that you give time and space to this first reading of a score.

However, it is likely that you will already have seen performances of, for example, *The Marriage of Figaro* or *The Magic Flute*. You may already have been influenced by the performance of a Pamina or Susanna; good or bad, you will have responded and formed an opinion and, either way, the performance will have become a point of reference. Yet this performance is simply one interpretation and, significantly, not one that originated from your connection with the role. With these challenges in mind, here are some thoughts on how to approach the early part of your process:

- Avoid watching too many other productions whilst learning the part, either in the theatre or online. I've worked with singers who arrive in rehearsals appropriating somebody else's performance – adopting their mannerisms and physicality – without a real understanding of why they are doing something. Remember you are the artist; the audience want to see *your* interpretation of the character.

- Avoid over-listening to one particular recording. If you find it useful to listen to recordings, mix it up so that you do not get fixated on one particular reading of a role (the wonder of streaming services!).

- Avoid taking too many ideas about a character from others, early on in your process.

---

[1] Stanislavski, K. (1981) *Creating a Role*. Translated by E. R. Hapgood. London: Eyre Methuen, p. 3.

- Beware of your own particular affinities and prejudices. You might be drawn to play Susanna because you want others to perceive you as similar to that character, or you might distance yourself from Monostatos for the opposite reason. These judgements can blur your approach.

- Even if you feel you know a piece well, attempt to let go of your previous acquaintance and read it again, as though for the first time. Allow yourself to meet the work *now*; at this moment in your life. Adopt a variation of the Royal Court Theatre's maxim; you must treat every new opera as a classic, and every classic opera as a new piece.

- Note all your early impressions, thoughts and emotions in a Rehearsal Notebook (in pencil for editing) but avoid seeking to make decisions until these ideas have crystallised. You need to *do*, in order to embody and fully understand character; so be ready to explore these possibilities in rehearsal.

- Develop a systematic approach to the preparation of creating character alongside the process of learning the music. Do not treat this as an 'add-on' but as something integral to your preparation of a role.

- Throughout this approach always ask 'What *if*. . .?' Collect possible 'What *ifs*. . .?' to explore in rehearsal and work with an empathetic imagination; seek to understand *why* your character behaves in certain ways.

- Preparation is, in large part, about helping to take away certain blocks or obstacles as you go to work in rehearsals. Each rehearsal room process will be led by a different director and conductor but the more you know the opera and the possibilities that lie within it, the readier you will be to explore their process and ideas and – ultimately – the freer you will feel to let go and try something new!

- And engage with a fitness routine! Remind yourself of the exercises in Chapter 1: Foundations in order to continue your work on physical and psychological release, expanding your imaginative resources and developing your readiness to play.

Coaching

Your work with your vocal coach will be incredibly important. This might be the first time you have worked with them, if they have been engaged by the opera company you are working for, or you might share a long history together, but either way they will probably be the first person you will share your thoughts about the character with. This will involve a huge amount of trust and it is important to recognise that at this stage you do not need to arrive with, or indeed leave with, a firm idea of your character: impressions, hunches, possibilities, thoughts to explore are enough. Your vocal coach will perhaps offer you their thoughts and impressions in a similar fashion. These thoughts will probably be incredibly useful as you develop your character but you do not need to take them as incontrovertible facts. Gather these observations as part of your research; collect a variety of thoughts and ideas and collate them in your Rehearsal Notebook. They are part of your information toolkit, research that you will need to eventually edit through in order to select what helps you understand and embody the work in rehearsal.

Whilst working with your coach don't be tempted to start to 'perform'; it will be too early to present any kind of result. Be on your feet; play, explore exercises, engage with Actions and Objectives. Use this period to excavate and mine the work. Be a detective and gather a forensic knowledge of everything the music and libretto give you.

Even when doing simple exercises on a technical matter, use it as an opportunity to play. Every exercise must have an imaginative imperative; an underlying story or motivation. For example, go on an extraordinary imaginative journey whilst practising scales; each note or scale might represent a different picture to navigate in your mind's eye. Embracing a spirit of play at this early stage helps to hardwire a flexible approach into your work; you learn in an adaptable way.

Remember, as you begin to prepare to go into rehearsals, that a character is always transforming. You must not think about creating one static character but seek to investigate the possible layers of a character that will enable you to eventually respond and react to each moment. The text and music are the guide for you to map the changes your character will undertake. Every Event marks a change of direction on your character's journey, so it is useful to plot these out and to distil the information from the text and music to fully understand where these changes are.

Where to Start

What follows is a list of eight sets of tasks that you should, ideally, do whilst learning the music prior to rehearsals. This is a recapitulation of some of the tools from previous chapters and suggests a sequence in which to work through these tools.

Ultimately you will select which tools work best for you, in order to devise your own process to create operatic character. Certain factors will guide *how* you prepare each role and your process will adapt to these: your familiarity with the repertoire, your knowledge of a particular director and conductor's process, the length of rehearsal period, the role itself. The less rehearsal time you have, the greater the imperative to prepare. The smaller the role, the greater the need to draw upon your imagination.

All these tools are about gathering fuel to power your rehearsal process. Notebook ready . . .

1. Words in Action

- Before even thinking about the music, start by reading the libretto through: aloud and by yourself, in a quiet place. Speak all the repeats through and in a natural speech rhythm.
- Read though your text again but this time speak the words in the rhythm set by the composer. Try to make these rhythms 'natural', not simply measured in time. Speak recitative in your own rhythm.
- Use the tools on Structure, Sound and Language in Chapter 6: Words and Music in Action. Unless you are good friends with a willing répétiteur, it may be difficult to do the extensions to these tools; in which case, either sing unaccompanied or speak the rhythm of the words the composer sets. You can also explore these tools in coachings.

STRUCTURE

EXERCISE: Walking the Punctuation, p. 213
EXERCISE: Walking the Sentence, p. 214
EXERCISE: Changing Chairs, p. 215
Ideally you need a partner to target with this exercise (ask a friend!) but if that is not possible, it is still worth doing the exercise to explore where the thoughts land.

SOUND

EXERCISE: Release of Emotion, p. 217
EXERCISE: Exploring the Consonants, p. 218
EXERCISE: Exploring the Vowel, p. 220

LANGUAGE

These tools are particularly useful when working in a foreign language.

EXERCISE: Three Times Through, p. 220
EXERCISE: Physicalising Words, p. 221

2. Initial Questions

Ask these two questions at the beginning of your preparation:

- *How similar am I to the character I am playing?*

  As you work through your analysis of the score, create a simple of list of everything you share with your character; your nationality, age, relationship status. As you begin to know the character better, note traits and behaviours you share with them, however uncomfortable these truths might be. You must ultimately reveal these truths in performance; it is about taking yourself to the character rather than bringing the character to you and foisting yourself onto them.

- *How different am I to the character I am playing?*

  In a separate column, list everything that is unfamiliar to you about your character and their life. This will underline those areas of research you need to undertake. It will also suggest where you especially need to engage your empathetic imagination; engaging the idea of 'What *if…?*' to seek to understand behaviour that might feel unfamiliar.

The following nine questions are your reference points before starting work on the opera; refer to them scene by scene, as you work through the opera. You will not answer all these questions before starting rehearsals but they will help guide your early thoughts in preparation. Remember, your character will respond to change and adapt throughout the story, so it is important to continue to ask these questions at the beginning of every scene:

1 *Who am I?*
   (relates to all personal and historical Facts about your character and their Core Beliefs)
2 *Where am I?*
   (relates to cultural and environmental Facts)

3 *When am I?*
   (this, again, relates to environmental and cultural Facts)
4 *What has happened and what is anticipated is going to happen?*
   (this relates to the Immediate Circumstances and the Future Prospects)
5 *What relationships do I have?*
   (refers to Relationship Lists)
6 *What do I want?*
   (refers to your character's hierarchy of Objectives)
7 *What do I want it for? And what is at stake if I don't get it?*
   (relates to the consequences of your Objectives)
8 *What is in my way?*
   (relates to your Obstacles; both internal and external)
9 *What do I need to do to overcome them?*
   (your Actions).

3. Facts and Questions[2]

Remember, as you prepare, you will have many more Questions than Facts. You cannot begin to answer your Questions until you begin rehearsals. Even some Facts will change as you get to know the production design. By thinking about the Questions that arise from the text you will be more focused to discover the answers through your rehearsal process:

- Begin the process of gathering the information from the libretto: all the environmental, cultural, personal and historical details. Create two columns to collate your response; Facts and Questions.

- Divide each of these columns in four: YOUR CHARACTER, THE WORLD, IMMEDIATE CIRCUMSTANCES and FUTURE PROSPECTS.

YOUR CHARACTER
From the Facts you have gathered, think about how you might complete the following Character List:

- Name
- Age
- Weight
- Height
- Relationship status
- Health

---

[2] See Given Circumstances, p. 48.

- Place of birth

- Place of residence

- Occupation

- Income

- Class and social status

- Education

- Cultural identity (a group you might belong to)

- Physical characteristics

- Posture

- Gesture.

CORE BELIEFS[3]
Begin to think of possible Core Beliefs and look for where these might change. You do not need to determine any of them.

THE WORLD
Anthropological Lists:[4] Look at the Facts of the opera through the anthropologist's lens. Remember, this approach is particularly useful when embarking on creating a chorus character or playing a smaller role.

IMMEDIATE CIRCUMSTANCES
List the Facts relating to what has happened immediately before the action of the opera begins and prior to each scene.

You will have many questions to answer in rehearsal relating to this; not only *what* happened but also *how* it has impacted upon the world of the opera and the characters.

FUTURE PROSPECTS
Scene by scene, write down any information relating to what your character imagines they might be doing in the future.

CHARACTER LISTS[5]
Working through the opera, write on separate lists, divided scene by scene, everything:

- your character says about themselves

- your character says about the world

- your character says about other characters

---

[3] See Organising Information: Other Approaches, p. 62.
[4] Ibid.
[5] See Exercise: Character Lists, p. 56.

- other characters say about your character
- the librettist and composer (see below) say about your character
- relating to the imagery your character uses.

Summarise all these lists with observations based on each list.

RESEARCH

At this point in your preparation I would only start light research relating to your character and the general historical context; you do not at this point know enough about where and when the production will be set.

Remember:

- If possible, seek out any research with images: drawings, painting, sculptures, photographic, film.
- Look at the original source material, for example, the Beaumarchais play in the case of *The Marriage of Figaro*.
- Look at the historical context of the opera's conception. For example, details about the rise of freemasonry at the time *The Magic Flute* was written shed light on the symbolism within the opera.
- Look at the librettist's and composer's biographies; there may be important clues about the characters or the world.
- Unless you manage to speak with the director about their ideas for the opera, save research on gesture, clothes, detailed cultural, political research until the beginning of rehearsals.

POINTS OF CONCENTRATION

As you work through the Facts and Questions of the opera, collect possible Points of Concentration that you can use in rehearsal and through to performance.

4. The Music

Make a note of what appear to be the composer's intentions regarding the character's subtext. Remember, the music does not lie! Seek out any musical clues about what the musical terrain might suggest about the character's emotional state and journey, even if, at this point, they are quite general observations. Make a list of notable shifts, changes or tendencies relating to the:

- melodic shape and patterns
- contrasting harmonies
- orchestral accompaniment
- relationship between vocal line and accompaniment
- tempo markings
- rhythm

- modulations of key
- musical accents; breaths, pauses, accented words
- dynamics.

5. Plot

Dividing up the opera makes it easier to grasp its constituent parts.

EVENTS

- Note all the Events or turning points in the opera with an (E).
- Write these Events out as a list, to give yourself a detailed plot outline of the entire opera.
- Note some possible pre-opera or pre-scene Events.
- Note the possible first significant Event.
- Highlight all *your* Events through the opera.
- Alongside this, make a simple note of all the interactions you have with other characters in the opera (include references to those interactions that occur outside of the onstage action of the opera).

TIMELINE

Begin to construct a timeline for your character; accept the many gaps and questions you will have at this stage. Refer to your Facts to gather details of the time, location and Immediate Circumstances before each scene.

6. Objectives, Obstacles, Actions

There is a huge amount to think about in this area. Again, do not commit or attach yourself to anything; have fun listing the possibilities you can take into the rehearsal room to discuss and play.

OBJECTIVES

Responding to the music, plot and Given Circumstances:

- begin to divide your scenes into Units of action
- list possible Scene Objectives, ideal outcomes and possible stakes
- list possible Act Objectives
- list possible Through-Lines of Action.

It is really very early in your process but you might have hunches about:

- Super-Objectives
- Counter-Objectives.

Consider, with reference to the Character Lists, your character's:

- Perception goal relating to each character
- Relationship goal relating to each character.

OBSTACLES
Consider possible Obstacles alongside every Objective; they will be internal Obstacles, other characters or external Obstacles.

ACTIONS
Allow your imagination to roam and consider possible tactics to get your wants. In rehearsal, so many more possibilities will be released when you are playing opposite *real* people! You can keep your early suggestions very simple; you might literally say 'I enter', 'I address you'. These possibilities are important starters; they will provide a spark for other ideas.

As you look at the libretto make sure you do not just look at your own lines. What are your Actions in *other* characters' arias? How are you provoking or inciting them to sing? What Obstacle might you be presenting to their Objective?

7. Physical Characterisation

Again, the text and movement work will absolutely inform each other; consider them separately initially but with an awareness of their inter-relatedness. You will already have gathered many thoughts about physicalising character from your work on the role so far; these tools will help to shape and define them:

LABAN

- Consider your character's dominant Laban Effort and Rhythmic tendency.
- Are there particular gestures or qualities that seem appropriate?
- Explore these early thoughts in your coachings; do any appear to resonate?

LECOQ

- Explore different points of Undulation and consider which Body Parts might lead your character.
- Consider whether your character has a dominant State of Tension, or if a particular Event might trigger a change of State. Make a note of it or try it in a coaching.
- Begin to consider which Animal you might research to layer your characterisation.

ADDITIONAL

- In response to your early musical analysis, consider your character's Inner Tempo Rhythm.

At this point you may have no clear idea whether there will be the time or encouragement to develop physical character in the rehearsal process you are preparing for. However, you will have a list of options to explore for yourself through rehearsals. Having clear intentions means that, if a decision does not feel right or the feedback is not positive, you know what you were intending, you will have a language to express it and other possibilities to shift the intention.

8. Operatic Story-Telling Conventions

You are preparing to tell a story. You will shortly join a creative team who will have been considering *why* and *how* they will tell this story now. To understand some of the factors they might have considered through the design process, reflect upon some of these questions that help frame your characterisation and the story they are part of:

- What is the subject of the opera; how might you sum up the opera in one sentence?
- What are the major themes of the opera? Write them down and consider how these themes conflict. For example, in *Figaro*, Love versus Sex, Control versus Freedom.
- What is your character's relationship to these themes; how do they respond to them?
- As a starting point, this is a world in which it is natural to sing. How else might we define the form of the opera? Is it pertaining to naturalism, expressionism, impressionism, romanticism, classicism? Is it a comedy, farce or tragedy?
- Within this form, are the characters archetypes? Do they serve specific functions? If so, what function does your character have?
- What relationship do the characters have to the audience? Is there a fourth wall and, if not, what qualities are the audience imbued with: judge, best friend, confessor?

The further away the world of the opera moves from realistic depictions, the harder you must search for clues to help you construct this unique world. This, of course, is the main purpose of the rehearsal room: to build a collective world, however extraordinary, in which all the characters can behave coherently and truthfully.

VOCAL COACH: JANE ROBINSON

Jane Robinson is ENO's Head of Training. She studied at the Royal College of Music and the National Opera Studio and specialises in vocal and professional development. Jane has also worked on the music staff at Glyndebourne, Nancy, Lyon, Brussels and Palermo and is an Associate Artist and vocal coach at Birmingham Opera Company. Jane was Music Director of ENO Opera Works and so we worked closely over many years. I wanted to ask Jane about that part of the singer's preparation that, as a director, I do not usually get to see.

How should a singer prepare for rehearsals?

I think it's best when a singer arrives at rehearsal with the music learnt perfectly, vocally ready, and with clear ideas that you're ready to completely abandon depending upon what the director and conductor want to do. You can't arrive like an empty page as an opera singer. You need to engage with your own ideas but you have got to be prepared for somebody to say, 'I don't want that at all'. Then, you need to be ready to make another offer. You need a toolbox of different approaches to be able to help you prepare.

What does a singer focus on in your coachings?

Well, first of all you're focusing on getting the music right. That's the foundation; the rhythms, the tuning, the dynamics. And, alongside that, you've got to consider who the character is. You can hear who the character is in the voice.

For example, I've just been coaching the Governess, from *The Turn of the Screw*, and the singer sounded awfully old when approaching Mrs Gross on the line '*Listen, my dear*'. I had to remind her that the Governess is, perhaps, only 18 and much younger than Mrs Gross. Additionally, she's just arrived at this place: Bly. It is unfamiliar and, perhaps, a little unsettling. These thoughts an audience can *hear* in the voice.

You have to be in character when you're learning the role. From day one, you have to be asking, 'Who am I?' You're an actress from the beginning, as well as a singer. If you're asking these questions, it feeds into the decisions you make about phrasing, sometimes subconsciously. You will sing the text in a different way. You will engage with it differently emotionally.

You must also think about what's happened before the opera started. With the Governess, for example, you might ask: is she in love with the Guardian? What were her family like? This will inform every phrase. Just like in life, where you come from informs how you say something; you can have eight people in a room, saying the exact same line, and they'll all say it differently depending upon who they are. Of course, it's really important to remember that you may have to shift some details in order to align your thoughts about the character with the conductor and director's thoughts.

When you're working with singers, you ask these questions?

Of course! Where have you come from? Why are you here? What has just happened?

If a singer is singing in a way that might not be reflecting the character, do you ever give them a technical note to correct this?

Yes, for example, someone might be singing in a chest voice and it might be inappropriate for the repertoire and for the character; it might age the character. If somebody is singing, for example, Sophie, the younger sister in *Werther*, it's got to *sound* like she has the energy of a fourteen-year-old. Of course, it's about the suspension of disbelief, you're acting, but it's about how you breathe and how you move.

You can have a set of notes – the same notes in the same rhythm – but you breathe differently depending on who you are and what it is you have to say. The intensity of need will inform your breath; you sing something in reaction to something, or you might be reacting to what's going on inside yourself. You need to be thinking about what you're *actually* saying – what underlies the text. You need to be thinking about the Actions and Objectives of this character from the beginning. You're an artist, you're not just a technician; your thoughts are important.

You're breathing to sing, in order to produce whatever high notes there are. You have to put the breathing rhythm into the already allotted of structure of the piece and *sing it in* prior to the first day of rehearsal; because you can't be constantly thinking 'is my jaw released, how's my breathing, how are my ribs, my pelvis'. If you're somehow blocking the air, you are going to be blocking everything else; if you feel uncomfortable, you will be blocking your interpretation. You can't be thinking about your breath in performance, or even in rehearsal. Rehearsals aren't for rehearsing your singing. You need to be free in your mind to engage with what the director wants.

What expectations do you have of a singer?

When a singer comes to a coaching, I'll expect them to know the music already; I'm not there to teach the notes. They need to be bringing repertoire that they can do *now*. There's no point preparing the role you feel you might sing in ten years' time, you might not be doing it in ten years' time! It's about thinking for *now;* knowing yourself and accepting yourself.

I feedback depending on what they want when they come to a coaching: I might be checking the vocal technique, the repertoire, whether that fits who they are. When we are working on a role that they're about to go into rehearsals for, the questions I ask will be targeted; I'll ask about the character and the scene that they're in.

They will generally move around the space; some will stretch, some will be moving in character, some singers will always bring a great intensity of intention to every single line they sing. You need a huge amount of time to prepare really well. It's like being an athlete in the Olympic Games; being at the top of the tree in your profession demands this. It's about how good can you be *today* and, in order to do this, you'll have to bring a consistent focus.

VOCAL COACH: ANGELA LIVINGSTONE

Angela is Head of Opera Vocal Performance at the Royal Welsh College of Music and Drama. She has worked extensively as a pianist and répétiteur, alongside leading conductors including Sir Charles Mackerras, Sir Simon Rattle and Jiri Behloavalek, amongst others. Angela is also a panellist for the live audition round of *BBC Cardiff Singer of the World*. I've worked alongside Angela to train young singers over a number of years and I wanted to discover more about how, as a vocal coach, she helps prepares singers prior to rehearsal.

Can you describe the work you do with singers?

The relationship between the coach and singer is a very personal relationship. It must be a safe place, in order for the singer to make discoveries, take risks and to get things wrong.

I think it's often where singers uncover the piece. Working with a coach is, of course, about getting to know the notes, the rhythms, the pronunciations, the composer's intentions, the nuts and bolts, but out of that always comes some kind of discussion about how these characters are feeling, what's going on with them and how the music supports that or sometimes works against it.

All these points arise out of these sessions with the coach and evolve depending upon where the singer is at with their instruments and their performing personality. Working with somebody who's hugely experienced is, of course, very different from working with somebody who's just starting out. The pitfalls, however, remain the same: namely the fear of not technically achieving certain parts of the role.

What effect does this fear have on the singer?

It can become a distraction and a physiological hindrance that then impedes their flow of *playing*. When you're at play, you're exploring what the music might mean for the character.

Look at a child at play; that's when we learn most. A child can't play, in that free flow state, if they're scared of falling off the wall. When a child climbs on the wall to do imaginary battle – to play – they're not thinking 'I'm going to be very careful about how I put one foot in front of the other'. I suspect none of us thought that as kids; we climbed the wall, and maybe fell off the wall, but we still continued to play.

How do you work to alleviate those fears?

My approach is to locate where the area of discomfiture is, isolate it, and sort it by finding another area of the voice that works really well and taking that physical state into the area of difficulty. When the singers become comfortable, they realise what they weren't doing to get through a corner. It's about positively reinforcing what they are doing well.

What expectations do conductors, directors and companies have of young singers before rehearsals?

The expectation nowadays is that they have to arrive and absolutely hit the ground running. They have to be completely prepared to deal with a room in which a number of people will ask things of them, in the same moment. They've got to be able to multitask; be multi-skilled at listening and processing. The young singer has to combine, or synthesise, all of those demands; they have to be very practical and very pragmatic.

How does the singer prepare themselves to deal with such various demands?

For many singers, you can see that their characters start in their feet; this keeps them grounded and in contact with the floor. If you're going to do something difficult, you're not going to stand with one foot off the floor, or shift your weight upwards, as it becomes weak. Indeed, if singers do this, it is perhaps because of self-consciousness. It's important that singers understand that an audience is looking at the character; that's who they're there to see.

Sub-texting is an important way of preparing for rehearsals in coachings. This is the process of asking what a character is *actually* saying when they sing a line; what is really being communicated. This is especially useful when working in foreign languages. You can translate a libretto literally, or you can *subtext* in everyday parlance; using words that really mean something to you personally. For example, Zerlina sings to Masseto 'non mi toccò la punta delle dita' ('He did not touch even the tips of my fingers') but, if you were playing Zerlina, you might *subtext* this section by talking around the line: 'He didn't lay a finger on me! How could you possibly think that? I mean, he started it, not me'. As a coach you can learn a lot about the singer by playing this game; I can discover routes forward and, also, any misunderstandings that the singer might have about the part. As a singer, it's important that you start to explore what you think is important to the character, in your own words. Then you can go to your first day of rehearsal ready with contributions and ideas.

Before a singer even goes to a coach, it's useful for them to have a map of their character's journey: perhaps they'll have identified where the character's biggest challenges or Obstacles are in the story, the various situations that they find themselves in. I might then follow up by asking a range of questions about the character: how old are they? What do you think they like doing when they're not at work? What's their favourite colour?

When preparing for rehearsals, it's worth remembering that conductors and directors don't always have all the answers, and don't always get it right. And importantly they're not having to do it. Rehearsals have to be a two-way street; it's important to find your voice, to stand up and be counted.

CONDUCTOR: MARTIN FITZPATRICK

Martin Fitzpatrick is a conductor and is ENO's Head of Music. He studied at Oxford University, followed by the Guildhall and the National Opera Studio. Martin has conducted many productions at ENO. We first worked together as assistant director and assistant conductor early in our careers. I wanted to ask Martin about what expectations a company like ENO might have of young singers and how a singer should prepare to meet them.

How do you remain flexible and responsive to the possibilities of character when learning a role?

It's not about *how* you learn the notes but how you *approach* learning the notes. Taking *Figaro* as an example, it's about asking, what's the reason Mozart has put that there? Approaching the score in this way immediately frees up your dramatic thinking. If your focus and energy is on, 'I have to sing on the fourth beat', then you're closed off. It's about looking at the score and seeking to understand, for example, why Figaro responds to the Count at a certain moment, or why he comes in sooner than you might expect him to.

It's about enquiring into, and interpreting, the choices that Mozart has made?

If they are an operatic composer of genius, then there's going to be a reason why they've chosen to set a particular word on a particular note. Why have they made that choice? Why have they set it like that? If you have these questions in mind when you're learning it – from the top of your process – then you're always going to approach things with that enquiring spirit.

That's what a singer like Simon Keenlyside does; he has such a fresh approach. He has no barriers between the music and the drama – indeed, you almost forget he's singing – it becomes communication in a heightened way.

What are the specific challenges for singers when preparing a role?

The problem for young singers now is that they have access to 73 different performances and that means that it's very easy for them to take someone else's performance and replicate it. I don't want to hear Pavarotti again; I want to hear what *you* do with Cavarodossi. I don't want to hear what Mirella Freni did – because she can probably do better than you – but if you have some fresh ideas, or have thought long and hard enough about a role, then you're going to bring your own qualities to it. That is of more interest to me than compiling a generic idea of a role.

You must always ask, do I want to do what the composer has written or is the performance history more interesting? Maybe you've often heard people taking a breath in a certain place but the composer has written a slur over it; I think it's much more interesting to ask, what do I understand by what the composer has written and how does that inform what I want to do?

So, if we ask how we can bring freshness and flexibility to creating a role, it's about having an active dialogue with the score?

Exactly. You must be asking *why did the composer write these notes?* If it's a Verdi or a Mozart, then there is usually a very good reason. As Verdi gets older, you see him less and less interested in what the rules of aria and cabaletta are. By the time he writes *Falstaff* and *Otello* he's saying, 'Well, the words mean I have to put in eight bars here', or 'The text means I have to change key here; rather than, here I've got a traditional structure of a slow bit and a fast bit'. The only reason to perform opera is that the music adds something meaningful to the drama. It's not film music, the reason to write opera is to add a layer. For me, looking at *Porgi Amor*,[6] Mozart has written the essence of the character in the sixteen-bar introduction. You *know* that character before she opens her mouth.

Is there anything else a singer should be thinking about in preparation?

If an opera is based on another medium like *La Traviata*, *Figaro*, *Billy Budd* or *The Turn of The Screw* then knowing the original source is important. Knowledge about where the composer was in his or her life is also important; for example, why did *Peter Grimes* chime with Britten? Reading around the subject as much as you possibly can.

---

[6] *The Marriage of Figaro* Countess, No. 10 Aria 'Hear my prayer'/'Porgi, Amor'.

8 Rehearsals

WHAT QUESTIONS DO YOU FACE WHEN REHEARSING?

- *I find it difficult to commit to a role during the rehearsal period in the same way I would on stage during performances.*
- *How do I stay in character when I'm not singing?*
- *Can I bring my own life experiences and characteristics to the piece?*
- *Am I turning this character into me?*
- *Am I doing strange things with my body without knowing it?*

Rehearsals are the crucible for all ideas, observations and viewpoints about the opera to interact and create something new. They are a laboratory where ideas are tried, tested, discarded and selected to bring definition to a collective interpretation of the opera. Together with your fellow collaborators – the other performers, the director, conductor, choreographer and designers – you will embark on a journey to discover how you reveal the truth within the story.

The real joy of rehearsals is in acquiring the knowledge and understanding of the various layers, shades and textures of the world and, through collective effort, bringing these to life; translating this understanding into specific sound, physicality and emotion, and making the ephemeral, tangible. At the beginning of the process no-one – the director, conductor, designer – knows *exactly* what form this story will take. The alchemy of many different parts will create a unique and heightened realisation of a world. Of course, this process will be guided; the director's and conductor's job is to establish the parameters, the metaphorical ball-park, in which you will play. The result, however, will only emerge through many and various mistakes, mis-steps and collisions, founded upon the collective imagination of the assembled team.

Every rehearsal process will be entirely different. As an actor and assistant director, I experienced a multitude of approaches; from those where blocking was executed from a preconceived written-out plan, through to those where the improvisations extended from rehearsals through to performance. As a performer, traversing these varying landscapes, you will need to be responsive and open to each new way of working whilst, alongside this, developing an approach through the rehearsal period that allows you the time and space to explore and evolve a character and an understanding of the world. This is where your toolkit comes in.

This chapter looks at what might be expected of you and how you can use each stage of the rehearsal process to build your character using the tools that you have acquired through the book.

Expectations

Bring discipline to your approach and you will find the freedom to explore and play. At Opera Works we collectively established some ground rules for creative, respectful work.

These points are those that the singers thought important:

- Be punctual;[1] meaning, do not be exactly on time but arrive at least ten minutes before the scheduled start time.
- Leave mobile phones outside the room.
- Ditch any sense of hierarchy; all singers will ultimately create and communicate the world together.
- Bring commitment and energy.
- Be vocally and physically warmed up and ready to work.
- Always be prepared.
- Be supportive of your collaborators.
- Bring a willingness to participate; a 'Yes and . . .' attitude (see p. 38).
- Bring a willingness to learn from others.
- Leave your little worries and minor difficulties outside the room.
- Have a notebook.
- Consider your clothing; you might need to move around freely or bring specific items of clothing for your character.
- Ask for specific feedback.
- Be ready to receive feedback; the outside eye is the audience's eye.
- Write the feedback down to consider it later.
- Listen, and be open, to new ideas.
- Be at as many rehearsals as possible, including, where appropriate, those rehearsals when your character is not in the scene. The decisions that are being made will affect your characterisation and understanding of the world.

Music Calls

Music calls are, increasingly, a luxury in a cash-strapped operatic landscape but, when funds allow, they provide an invaluable period to explore the music with the conductor and fellow

---

[1] The esteemed director Mike Alfreds worked with us throughout Opera Works. At his first session, one of the singers arrived late. Mike looked at her directly and said 'Don't be late, no-one will like you'. Through the rest of that year, no-one was late again.

cast members. Ideally, the director will also be present to integrate the process from the beginning.

The calls provide an opportunity to work through all numbers with the conductor and to sing through duets and ensembles with the rest of the cast. They help to establish the style of music-making that the conductor will encourage through rehearsals and give you useful pointers on character. You will get a sense of tempi and with it, the speed with which your character and others, think or move. Additionally, certain phrases will receive emphasis, the length of pauses defined or dynamics expanded upon. All these suggestions should be noted to help bring detail and definition to your earlier preparation. Bear in mind that many of these suggestions might change and adapt through the rehearsal process.

Rehearsals

The aim of rehearsals is to translate from the score all Given Circumstances, all characters' underlying thoughts and Objectives and all inner pictures and impulses, into action. This action must be played out in a cohesive, coherent world and be communicated truthfully to an audience.

As already mentioned, the route to bringing the piece to life will be different every time you set foot in a rehearsal room: dependent upon the opera, your role, your fellow singers, the director, conductor, choreographer and extended creative team, the budget, the design, the company and the time available. There is rarely enough time given to the process of rehearsal. A rehearsal period ideally should be six to eight weeks to allow the depth of work necessary. In the UK, however, the standard period is closer to four weeks, with many productions coping with much less than this. Added to this are the traditional non-availability requests – rare in the theatre and dance world – that gnaw at the fabric of collective endeavour.

How best to use the time, to navigate an unfamiliar process, to continue the journey of exploration you began in your preparation, to evolve an understanding of the world and the realisation of your character in action?

Day One

The first day of rehearsal can often be an overwhelming experience for all involved. To begin with, over breakfast or on your journey to the rehearsal room:

- Write down how you feel. The mix of adjectives you use to describe your feelings, both positive and negative, will probably be felt by many of the team, the director and conductor included. These emotions all too frequently render first day of rehearsal entirely forgettable and yet there is a wealth of information to access that can help facilitate the process ahead.

- First up, if it is all a bit overwhelming, take some deep breaths and find a moment to do the backward circle. (See Exercise: Backward Circle, p. 24.)

- A lot of information will be handed over; have your notebook handy but know that you do not need to remember everything.

- Say 'hello' to as many people as you can. Most companies begin the process with a meet and greet, which is a good opportunity to meet collaborators who may not be part of your process until later in the rehearsal period: lighting, set and costume designers, the wardrobe and production team. Make friends but do not worry about remembering names!

- You may do a read-through of the libretto or a sing-through of certain scenes or the entire opera; this may be in front of the wider team. This is not a test; when reading through, take your time. Use it as an opportunity to hear the words spoken or sung by others for the first time.

Design Presentation

The first day of rehearsals usually includes a showing of the model box and costume drawings. This will provide a wealth of information for you:

- suggesting a theatrical style in which the opera will be presented; for example, naturalistic, expressionistic, classical, absurdist, epic

- suggesting a treatment of the plot and themes

- presenting the *subject* of the opera from the viewpoint of the director and designer; how the production will communicate the story of the opera

- suggesting *your* function in the story

- informing you about the period of the production

- providing numerous details to incorporate into your list of Facts: for example, you will now know exactly how many doors, windows, etc.

- defining some of the Questions you still need to answer; what does the character see on the fourth wall, how might the characters use the space (especially if the space is abstracted)?

- setting some clear research tasks

- providing a basis for the beginning of your work on visualisation

- suggesting how the structure of the story will flow from scene to scene

- revealing the challenges you might need to negotiate as a singer.

In these ways the model will help you begin to understand the parameters and edges of your world.

Space affects each of us differently: we will have certain preferences in terms of colour and light, certain structures will resonate. The model showing might be surprising, perhaps challenging, but see it as an invitation and the spark to ignite the pursuit of a very real question: how would I behave in this space?

Costume drawings can be, similarly, a little unsettling; you are presented with decisions that have already been made, about a character that has yet to evolve. However, view the drawings as a useful source of information: a world of further Facts to help define your character and their world. The drawings will likely provide clues about your character's comparative status, their wealth, their job, their perception of themselves and the society they live in.

They will also highlight the work you need to do to make these costume drawings *your clothes*. You might need to research a particular period or society or group of people. You will need to become familiar with the particular cut of the clothes: with the restrictions they might bring, the way they might affect your movement, the gestures they suggest.

Practicalities

STAGE MANAGEMENT

The stage manager, deputy stage manager and assistant stage managers are vital collaborators on your journey to create character:

- They will provide useful information about the practicalities of using the design. Once the model box leaves the room, continue to study photographs of the design that will likely be in the rehearsal room, in order to develop your understanding of the story it tells and the way in which you will use it.

  Seek to understand how the design corresponds to the mark-up in the rehearsal room; are there different levels represented only by a line on the rehearsal room floor? Which way do the doors open? Are video projections used and, if so, what are they of? Get to know your world in detail.

  Opera and theatre director Katie Mitchell often marks up those rooms that lead off from the rooms onstage and invites the cast to continue to improvise the scene that follows on from the written scene.[2] Even if the rehearsal room in which you are working does not replicate this, the principle of Mitchell's use of external space should be embraced in your imaginative journey through rehearsal.

- Ask stage management for props, or substitutes, whenever needed in a scene. The imagination can only do so much and having to mime drinking a cup of tea is pointless if ultimately you will be provided with a cup and saucer.

  Additionally, there may be props you will need to be working with, early on in the process, to explore how they inform your characterisation and to develop a familiarity with. For example, in a production of *The Magic Flute* I directed, the Queen of the Night used a walking stick and smoked using a cigarette holder, Papageno lived out of a shopping trolley, Sarastro wore spectacles and the Speaker, a trilby hat. The singers had to get to know how to use these props; *how* they used them informed who these characters were.

- The DSM will assimilate a meticulous understanding of the production throughout rehearsals; they will ultimately be conducting, empathetically with the conductor, the timing of all movement of set and lighting onstage. Their forensic record of the production in the rehearsal room book, alongside that of an assistant director, is an

---

[2] Mitchell, K. (2009) *The Director's Craft: A Handbook for the Theatre*. London: Routledge, p. 173.

incredibly useful resource to help fill any gaps in your memory about decisions that have been made in the rehearsal room.

- Together with the assistant director and company manager, the DSM will look after the rehearsal room schedule. Sometimes a scheduled rehearsal overruns, delaying the beginning of your rehearsal; whilst it can be frustrating to wait, use the time constructively working through possible Actions, detailing character biographies and creating visualisations.

WARDROBE

Your costume fitting is an opportunity to get to know the clothes you will be wearing, in more detail. Speak to the team about the fabric, the manner in which it might be worn and the historical background; gather as much information as possible. They might also have mood boards and visual sketches that provided the original inspiration for the design; this will provide further fuel for your characterisation. You might feel self-conscious in the costume fitting, wearing clothes that are not your own, but keep an open mind, engage in a discussion with the team and seek to bring elements of the costume (or similar substitutes) into the rehearsal room. The height of a heel, the tightness of a waistcoat, the restriction of a corset, all inform the physical and emotional life of a character.

An Approach

The length and structure of a rehearsal period can vary enormously but throughout any process, the approach and tools you bring to the room can provide a meaningful and effective process.

The 'yes and . . .'[3] attitude must be at the heart of every collaborative exchange; a team of newly assembled artists can only build a world collectively with such a sense of purpose.

It is important to remember that, even with a readiness to play, you cannot achieve everything at once. The skills and understanding you will acquire throughout rehearsals take time and a combination of patience, tenacity and focus are necessary. If you are playing Susanna, for example, you may have to learn to play the guitar, to dance the fandango and to adeptly sew flowers onto a wedding hat, at the same time as constructing an understanding of the history, thoughts, inner images and motivations of the character. Your character will not simply fall into place in a moment of inspiration; you will need to layer, one strand at a time, every element of their personality, and the world in which they live, in order for the character to evolve.

Constructing the thought process for the character takes longer than the music allows. It is useful, where possible, to begin each rehearsal by simply speaking the text. This gives you the freedom to more easily stop, ask questions and consider the thought, rather than being swept along by the music.

Throughout all this, you must embrace the fact that your process will be littered with all manner of attempts and failures, for it is only through repeated trial and error that you will uncover the truth about your character.[4]

---

[3] See The Rules of Play, p. 38.
[4] See 'We suck and we love to fail!', p. 38.

ENSEMBLE BUILDING

It is much easier to embrace this spirit of creative failure when your team of collaborators is doing likewise. A rehearsal process may or may not place an emphasis on building a sense of ensemble; if it does, embrace the opportunity to break down the social conventions that get in the way of creativity and to develop trust through play, with your fellow story-tellers.

Use the rehearsal room before rehearsals begin, if possible, to physically warm up, so that you are physically ready to explore movement; your commitment might inspire others to do likewise and a process of group warm-ups and play can begin to develop.[5] A production may engage the skills of a movement director or choreographer; get to know the warm-ups they lead as they can be invaluable for you to use throughout the process and into performance.

If a process does not give time for this, still attempt to bring an openness to your approach. You may, at times, feel vulnerable but it will inevitably inspire others you are working with to work in the same way; to close off defensively, however comfortable this might make you feel in the moment, will ultimately prevent you from receiving the new information you need to respond to.

EXPLORATION

A process of rehearsal might begin with table work – the company gathered together in a collective intensive analysis of the opera – or, alternatively, simply a quick chat about what the scene might be about. Regardless of the nature of the process, you should initially free yourself to be in the Ideas Room and carry the spirit of 'What *if*. . .?' with you. Be ready to contribute the early ideas from your investigations in preparation, filtered through the lens of what you have learnt from the design presentation; this now defines the boundaries of the world in which all ideas will play out. Be just as ready to let go of your ideas in order to explore other ideas, however surprising or confounding.

The possibilities presented by the score need to be explored and either embraced or discarded; you cannot know the exact nature of travel until you set out in a given direction. So, resist the temptation to 'fix' all the elements too early; an impression of the world and character will emerge through rough sketches. Even in the quickest of processes, where an opera is blocked to within an inch of its life at the beginning of rehearsals, it is possible to find room to play. The discoveries you make during this period have to sustain you, not just through rehearsals, but during the entire run of performances.

Layer your understanding of:

- the words and music; beat by beat, how your thoughts form the foundation of the action
- the character; how do you behave, physically and psychologically?
- relationships; with other characters and, perhaps, the audience
- the world; how do the details of each part of your world evolve through collaboration?

---

[5] See Chapter 1: Foundations, for physical release, warm-up and ensemble building exercises.

The distinction between each of these strands may not be so clearly drawn through a rehearsal process. You can distil the decisions made with the director, conductor and other singers and continue your individual work on the various layers: Facts, Questions, relationships and motivations. This separation of the various layers can bring a sense of order to your process; it allows you to identify where you need to bring focus and enables you to target your questions in rehearsal. Your Rehearsal Notebook becomes a vital companion throughout your process; it will chart your dialogue with the score and be a constant reference point throughout your journey.

RESEARCH

Following the design presentation and early discussions with the director, you will have a much clearer context for your research. Begin research early in your process. You will have already researched the composer's and librettist's biography, with an eye for details that enlighten you about the reasons for their decisions. You can now expand your research to the particular time and place the production is set in, regarding:

- political history
- clothes
- dances
- hobbies
- music
- literature
- art
- gesture.

Contribute this research, when appropriate, to the rehearsal room (remember, research images are always especially potent). Use research to answer your Questions about the world and character.

RELATIONSHIPS

Begin an early dialogue with your fellow singers about the history and nature of your relationships. You will need to negotiate to create shared character biographies, with reference to the work on Character Lists and agreed Facts.

SKILLS

A production of *The Magic Flute* I directed was set in a circus and, so, alongside the work on score analysis and character in the rehearsal room, the singers had regular sessions at NoFit State Circus in Cardiff. Over the six weeks of rehearsal, they became (almost) expert acrobats, aerialists, jugglers and unicyclists. Identify early which new skills you will need to acquire and begin immediately to develop them. This might be dancing, stilt-walking, puppeteering, playing an instrument or more rudimentary but perhaps unfamiliar behaviours such as rolling cigarettes or applying make-up. The more accustomed to these skills and behaviours you become, the more adeptly you can bring expression through them; *how* does your character do these behaviours, at this moment in the opera, and to what intent?

STAGING

The stage space is usually broken down and referred to in the following way:

Upstage Right (USR)	Upstage Centre (USC)	Upstage Left (USL)
Stage Right (SR)	Centre Stage (CS)	Stage Left (SL)
Downstage Right (DSR)	Downstage Centre (DSC)	Downstage Left (DSL)
	The Audience	

The process of staging, blocking or choreographing a scene will be approached differently in every process. Some directors will want to lock down staging immediately, others, to allow the singers to discover their relationships within the space through playing Objectives. Whatever the process, this check list should be considered before getting on your feet:

1 The Facts about the world; especially the time, place and weather.

2 The Immediate Circumstances; what has just happened to your character.

3 Your Scene Objective.

4 The Events in the scene.

5 In response to these Events, your shifting Objectives and ideal outcomes.

6 Your Projected Circumstances.

7 Any relevant Core Beliefs.

8 Your inner images.

9 Your perception of self and Status.

10 Your relationships with others referred to, or in, the scene.

11 A readiness to actively listen.

The logistics of staging an opera mean that you might not always work chronologically in rehearsals. By charting your passage through each scene in the way this list sets out, and with reference to your preparation, you will begin to create an arc for your character's journey that makes it easier to jump in at a certain point.

If the process is one where blocking is dictated, you will need to find inner justifications for every move your character makes. If any move onstage is not motivated by an internal impulse it will be meaningless and empty; you will have disengaged from the very essence of your character. So, ask *why* have I moved to this place at this moment; find a reason rooted to your character's Objective. You can find freedom in *how* you move to a particular place; even within the most restrictive of processes, there is always room to play.

If you actively listen to other characters, and allow yourself to engage and respond to what they are singing, you will be continually motivating your own movement. Every single thought moves you, so, regardless of whether you have been directed to stand downstage left for an entire duet, your character will still be on a journey if you are always reacting.

In certain rehearsal processes, you will be asked to discover your movement through the space through the active pursuit of your *wants*. As a performer, alongside a very real engagement with the world of the opera and your character's inner thoughts, you will need to bring an awareness of the following for clarity of storytelling:

- Every story in opera is played out within the confines of structured time. This will define your thinking, your reactions and your movement. Listen to the orchestration and you will likely discover, exactly, when to start to walk, when to sit down or land an idea, when to kiss another character (with what intensity and for how long). Everything you do must be united with the music.

- Your connection with the conductor is vital. The flow and exchange of thoughts are guided by them; they are the ever-present metronome of your internal rhythm. You do not need to stare intently at them to follow or pick up a beat but, for much of the time, your peripheral vision must allow their presence. Of course, this is not always possible and the relationship and trust you develop through rehearsals will enable occasional breaks of connection. In the theatre, it might be that your connection with the conductor is facilitated through monitors. These are unlikely to be in rehearsals, and occasionally the conductor might move in the room to replicate the position of the monitors in the theatre. Check with stage management where these monitors will be, so that you can carry an awareness of this as you move within the scene.

- The angles you find when singing, and listening, to another character will be crucial in clearly communicating the sound and action to the audience. Essentially you want to be singing downstage to another character, and allowing them to sing downstage to you. This might only require the slightest shift of your weight, from one side to the other. Bringing an awareness of this when you move in the space will mean the director does not have to continually stop to correct this and will, therefore, give you much greater freedom in the decisions you make.

- An alternative to this is engaging what has become known as 'The Ant and Dec Principle'. The two television presenters will always face the camera when talking to the other, whilst the listener (the presenter not talking) will always face the person talking. At the moment the speaker is about to finish talking, they look to the listener and an exchange or handover takes place. It is a convention that allows the audience to receive everything that the speaker is saying, whilst suggesting that the conversation is simply between the two presenters on screen. This principle is invaluable in opera, particularly in large spaces, but both singers must be equally engaged or it will risk looking 'stagey'.

- Be aware of not masking other singers.

- Explore your use of, and relationships with, furniture, props and clothes. You may need to explore and familiarise yourself with these elements prior to playing a scene.

- Bring an awareness of Laban's principle and how expression can be built through your character's relationships with the space (its depth, levels and particular areas), other characters and the audience. Think about direction, time, flow and weight in terms of your movement through the space.[6]

---

[6] See Laban (p. 130).

A PROCESS

Directors and conductors largely determine the process in the rehearsal room. The suggestions, hitherto, are to help you navigate your own individual process through their various approaches.

If there were any possibility of informing or influencing the process in the room – if one day the director were to walk into the rehearsal room and ask 'What would be useful for you to do today?' – then the following process might be a useful approach to take when first exploring a scene on its feet:[7]

- Firstly, use the space to work through the exercises on Structure[8] to explore the movement of thoughts through the scene.

- Next, remind yourself of the list of Initial Questions: from 1 to 9.[9] Spend time, in silence, to reflect upon the pre-determined Immediate and Given Circumstances.

- Remind yourself of your Scene Objectives and Events in the scene.

- Next, walk the space in which the scene occurs (or the space from which your character enters), again in silence, and turn over your Scene Objective: why you want it, the consequences of achieving it or otherwise, the Obstacles in your way. As you walk, explore where in the body these feelings of *need* arise from.

- When you are ready to speak, do so (do not sing yet). Speak the scene through in pursuit of your Objectives. Do not concern yourself with speaking the text correctly; this should be partially improvised. If you miss lines or create new ones, it does not matter; achieving your Objective is your primary concern.

- Once finished, discuss the Events in the scene; did they mark a clear change in your Objectives?

- Repeat the exercise, this time speaking the libretto in the rhythm and dynamics marked by the composer (but not yet singing).

- Then, take a moment to look over the Actions that you have previously proposed in your score. Change any suggested Actions in response to playing Objectives.

- Hand your score to your Actions coach,[10] who will feed you your transitive verb before you say the line. The same happens for each singer in the scene. The scene progresses at its own speed, the singer only speaking their line once they feel they fully understand their Action. Throughout this process, stop to negotiate or discuss the Action, in response to what your partner is playing. Work in this order:

  ○ Speak the lines.

  ○ Speak the lines in rhythm.

  ○ Speak the Action (the verb itself) with the music underscoring each spoken verb. Stretch the length of the word/verb, so that it fills the time that the composer has set.

---

[7] See Chapter 4: Objectives, Actions and Obstacles for further ideas.
[8] See Chapter 6: Words and Music in Action.
[9] See Chapter 7: Preparing for Rehearsals.
[10] Remember: the actions coach remains on the periphery of the action, closest to the singers they are coaching.

- ○ Sing line by line, the répétiteur stopping after each line, to allow time for the coach to feed the next Action.
- ○ Sing the scene.

In any play-ins or interludes make sure you pursue Actions or, alternatively, speak aloud the inner thoughts that this music underscores. Commit to the Actions with your entire imaginative and physical being; it is more fun and the results will be more revealing. It is only through *doing*, aligned with the music, that you will truly begin to understand the character. Music, thought and action woven together.

AT HOME

Your work in the rehearsal room, and ongoing work at home, go hand in hand. The rehearsal room signals the work you need to consider at home; the work at home provides the ideas to explore in the rehearsal room. Develop a routine around rehearsals to give yourself time to review and respond to the previous rehearsal, in order to inspire your next day's work; so that in the next rehearsal you are building upon the work, rather than using it to remind yourself of what happened previously.

Visualisations, for example, are a great way to deepen your understanding of your world. Create images in your mind's eye about the history of events referred to in the opera or the Immediate Circumstances of the scene. If you refer to something in the opera, you need to *see* it; in so doing, so will the audience in their mind's eye. For example, when the Countess sings, 'I remember his love so tender'/'Dove sono i bei momenti',[11] she needs to be running through a collage or film of her most loving moments with the Count; or when Figaro sings to Cherubino, 'Here's an end to your life as a rover'/'Non più andrai', Cherubino needs to replay images of war that he has previously seen in paintings.

Alternatively, keep a diary for your character or create stories from their past; you will begin to see the pictures you write about.

It is in this way that you begin to embody your character; their thoughts and images live within you and their Actions and Objectives find foundation. They are not merely *wants* and *verbs* expressed on a page but deeply held feelings springing to life from within your body.

REPETITION

We rehearse to discover and select the behaviour that will best express each beat of the story. Having done this, we then have to repeat this behaviour in response to the same Events, many times over, whilst still giving the impression that this is happening for the first time without a pre-ordained outcome.

Repetition is vital to give time for your character's traits and behaviours, unfamiliar in your own body, to become habitual. The manner in which a character opens a door, sits on a chair, holds their lover's hand, is unique and requires a different set of tensions carried through your body than you will be used to. The very act of singing creates additional physical demands which often make such behaviours more difficult. Repetition enables you to make these behaviours your own and bind them intimately to the music. Paradoxically, it

---

[11] *The Marriage of Figaro*, Countess, No. 19 Aria, 'I remember his love so tender'/'Dove sono i bei momenti'.

is through repetition that you acquire the security and freedom to adapt and alter your performance in the moment; to be spontaneous. As we have already discussed, this spontaneity is the key to creating truthful life onstage.

To simply repeat a scene without purpose can ultimately deaden the life of the thoughts; never allow it to become routine. You must continue to explore the inner stimuli to action and this is best achieved through exploring different Points of Concentration.[12] Select a theme or a Given Circumstance, or a relationship detail, and take a moment to explore how this idea resonates for your character before repeating a scene. It is in this way that you add layers to your understanding of your character and their world.

RUNS

The nature of each process will determine how early a run of an act, or of the whole opera, will take place. When you begin to do runs, do not be tempted to think of them as a test set by others. Each run will provide important information and useful opportunities:

- This is an opportunity to integrate the different layers of your work.

- Explore your character's Through-Line of Action. Gather a sense of their journey through the story and of how one Objective links to the next. Are there any missed beats? Are you clear what happens in the passage of time between acts and how this affects your character? Do all the Objectives point in same direction? Are the stakes high enough?

- With each run of an act, set a Point of Concentration for yourself. Just as when you repeat a scene, always focus on playing your Objectives.

- Depending upon the nature of the production, as you begin to run the opera more frequently you could introduce a subtle game into the action.[13] This must not undermine the integrity of the world but could help you experience the action from a slightly different angle; for example, play the game that you will avoid standing closer than a metre to anybody.

- Most importantly, listen. There will always be new moments to respond to; the conductor will adjust and adapt their tempo, a fellow singer will bring new emphasis to a word, note or gesture. If you are listening and receiving intently, you will react differently every time you play the opera.

- Always make notes of what you discovered after a run. Be honest with yourself: if there are moments that remain unclear, note them, and interrogate them later. Look for the surprising discoveries, be aware of new feelings.

- Listen to the notes from the director and conductor. Write them down, consider them. If you can, before the next run, work into them.

- In the next run of the opera, do not aim to reproduce something that previously went well. Start afresh, with a renewed focus.

---

[12] See Points of Concentration, p. 110.
[13] See The Clown, p. 190.

Troubleshooting

Collaboration can be a messy and chaotic endeavour; a team of over one hundred people, including the orchestra and chorus, have a matter of weeks to create an entirely new world that responds to a piece written, perhaps, two hundred years ago, with the aim of telling a story that resonates today.

THE DIRECTOR/CONDUCTOR RELATIONSHIP

You may find yourself in a situation where you disagree with the ideas of the director or conductor. Firstly, examine the root of your disagreement; for example, is it that you have an affinity with previously received ideas? Secondly, discuss your views with them; it might open them up to other possibilities and, at least, give them further opportunity to explain their ideas from another perspective. Finally, if there is no movement from them, you must ultimately find a way of embracing their ideas; look at how you can make the idea your own and find your own justification for it.

Conversely, you might find that you are getting insufficient feedback or guidance; this can be a lonely experience. In the first instance, ask questions, not in the hope of seeking general approval but specifically targeted to gain details about the character or music. If this yields little, then engage with the assistant director, assistant conductor or répétiteur. If not, explore the tools laid out in this book; it is important to have a dialogue throughout a process but that can be with the composer, the librettist, other singers or your own thoughts in your rehearsal notebook.

It is almost inevitable that divergent opinions occur in the making of an opera; those that affect you most directly are between the director and conductor. Occasionally it can feel as though one is pointing in one direction and the other in another. How best to deal with this? In the first instance, try to engage both of them in the conversation at the same time, not to highlight any conflict, but to seek an understanding. Listen to what both are saying: maybe the apparent difference of opinion can be answered through an entirely different approach, in which case, offer these possibilities up. Finally, you can speak with the assistants to see if they can help provide a way of progressing that respects both ideas. Ultimately, try not to get frustrated, or favour one side over the other, but continue to seek other ways of exploring the scene.

THE SINGER/SINGER RELATIONSHIP

You might find yourself in the situation where you are working with a fellow singer who, through mistakes, inexperience or lack of commitment, is making it difficult for you to play your scene. What to do? In the first instance, if the situation is due to mistakes or inexperience, offer to work with the singer outside the rehearsal room; share the thoughts from this book and engage in a dialogue. Bring your focus to the specific positive elements of their performance, in order to engage more easily with them.

More difficult to respond to is a lack of commitment. If this is the case, try reframing the singer's behaviour as belonging to the character; what *if* their disinterest is startlingly attractive, what *if* their lack of truthfulness is a mysterious personality trait. It is important that you do not allow their energy to affect you so, whatever they offer, take it and respond to it within the context of the story.

Sitzprobe

German for a 'seated rehearsal', the sitzprobe usually takes place towards the end of studio rehearsals and is the first time you will sing the opera with the orchestra. The focus of the rehearsal is the integration of orchestra and singers; the conductor will be particularly concentrating on entrances, phrasing and changes in tempi. The task of integrating the two forces requires tremendous focus and you be will expected to have your score with you and make notes where necessary.

After weeks of rehearsal with piano accompaniment, it is an opportunity to listen afresh. Details that the piano score cannot capture will present themselves to you. Be alert to how these orchestral colours and textures might bring new emphasis to certain sub-textural thoughts. Indeed, if there has been an opportunity to be in orchestral rehearsals, prior to the sitzprobe, take it.

The musical precision that the conductor will need from you in bringing the entire score to life will also help define the structure of your thoughts; the arrival of an idea will be pinpointed by the downbeat of the baton. They are often exhilarating rehearsals and, whilst the focus in the room is often on the musical detail, use the opportunity to start to integrate your character's thoughts and the music at a deeper, more nuanced level.

Stage and Piano Rehearsals

Moving from the rehearsal studio, in which you have created the production, to the stage, on which you will present it, is a fragile moment. The rehearsal room will have afforded a certain focus, the rehearsal props and furniture grown familiar. You will have adapted your singing and physicality to the size of the rehearsal room and connected certain thoughts to particular points in the room.

The stage will have numerous distractions to contend with: moving scenery from all directions, lighting, video, trap-doors and different levels. The team of collaborators will have grown to include stage crew, lighting, sound and video designers and technicians, fly men and women, set and costume designers, the wardrobe and make-up team and the producers.

Stage and Piano rehearsals are primarily technical rehearsals with only piano accompaniment. They are led by the director from the auditorium and the stage manager from the stage. All elements of the staging are brought together and integrated for the first time. This takes time and, importantly, it is the first opportunity many of the creative team will have to create their art. This is what to bear in mind:

- Firstly, be patient; the rehearsals will stop and start and you will have to wait, sometimes without knowing the reason why. The task of bringing together so many elements in a short amount of time takes time.

- Remain focused, onstage and off.

- When your scene is being rehearsed onstage, commit to everything you worked on in rehearsals. It can be frustrating for the creative team if you are marking your acting performance; it can be difficult to know if this is an intentional choice.

- The theatre can be a dangerous workplace; be alert to flying pieces and moving scenery.

- Familiarise yourself with your backstage routes; certain entrances onto the stage might take more time or energy (and breath) or be more difficult to access than you imagined.
- Find opportunities to conserve your energy when not working.
- Familiarise yourself with props, furniture and set. There will be elements that you have not worked with before; take time to get to know them, so that you are ready for when you work on the scene.
- Familiarise yourself with make-up, wigs and costume. If you have quick changes, know where these will take place.
- Consider the audience sightlines, the position of the conductor in the pit and the whereabouts of the monitors of the conductor.
- Explore the acoustics of the larger space.
- Set new points of focus; for example, exactly where are the 'pinewoods' that the Countess and Susanna refer to?
- Be aware that the order in which scenes are rehearsed might change. The director might also decide to do a 'cue to cue' rehearsal where the focus is entirely on rehearsing the technical elements and you will jump certain parts of the scene.
- Note that staging will change. The director will respond to what the theatre brings and adapt accordingly; for example, it might be that you need to be in a certain place to catch your light. You will need to justify these changes for your character.
- You will receive a great deal of information over the course of these rehearsals; when you get an opportunity, note it down, so that you can reflect upon it afterwards.

EMBRACING THE SPACE

When transitioning from a small rehearsal space to cavernous theatre, bear in mind that you will need to support your physical communication to clearly reveal the story to the audience, in the same way you support your voice in order to be heard:

- Be in a state of balance and readiness; feet firmly planted and on the balls of your feet. Remind yourself of the exercises in Release, p. 14.
- Energise your body; the tapping exercise, p. 20, is particularly useful.
- Energise your thoughts; find a reason to raise the stakes and, therefore, the *need* to get your Objective. This will bring energy to your breath and to your Actions. It is the *precision* of an Action that carries across space; it is not about doing something *bigger*. Be absolutely clear of your target: this will energise your gestures in response to them.
- The beginnings of phrases, the beginning of an action, are where the idea is usually most focused and imbued with the feeling of *need*.
- Do not tail off at the end of a phrase or gesture; sustain the thought.
- Projecting, both vocally and physically, means *sharing* with the audience. It does not mean pushing out to them; it means allowing them into your conversations. Keep the truthful connection with the thought from which the action derives.

- Find good positions in relation to your partner; a millimetre shift to one side or the other onstage can result in the end ten seats on each row of the audience hearing and seeing you.
- Get to see the lighting from the auditorium, if you can. The effect that is being created may not be clear from onstage and seeing it from the front will help provide useful character and world information. It will also help you to see where to stand, and in which direction to angle, to be best caught by the light.
- Bring this awareness to your work onstage and get used to feeling the heat of the light on your face; in cross-light, be careful not to block others or be blocked by them.

EXERCISE: *Embrace*
Solo/2 mins

- Imagine that your kinesphere – your globe of personal space – extends out into the theatre.
- Be on the balls of your feet, close your eyes and imagine holding an enormous beach ball that extends from you, into the auditorium.
- Keep your shoulders relaxed and stand upright.
- Imagine growing taller, your shoulders wider and your outstretched arms longer, as the beach ball slowly expands.
- Feel that you comfortably embrace the ball.
- Then open your eyes and take a breath from the imaginary beach ball, as you slowly lower your arms with a feeling of height, width and space.

Stage and Orchestra Rehearsals

Once all the technical and design elements have been integrated, the orchestra join the rehearsals. These are led by the conductor, who will determine the order in which to work. In these rehearsals it may feel as though the focus is on your voice and audibility in the theatre. A large part of the conductor's job in these rehearsals is to focus on balancing the sound of the singers with the orchestra; this takes time and it is important not to panic. Do not begin to push vocally and remind yourself to embrace the space. Use these rehearsals to think about how the music might inform your journeys through the space; what additional details might become clear that were not present whilst working solely with the piano?

Dress Rehearsal

Depending upon the time available in the schedule there might be a piano dress rehearsal, followed by an orchestral dress rehearsal. Orchestral dress rehearsals are often open to an invited audience: anyone from sponsors of the company, to friends and family. It might therefore feel like a first performance, although it is important to remember, as indeed it is with all performances, that the production remains a work in progress. Look ahead to Chapter 10: Performance for how to approach performances. The dress rehearsal will be an important opportunity to engage, moment by moment, with the audience's response. This does not mean performing to the audience but, rather, having an awareness of how clearly you are communicating the story. Of course, in a comedy you will be able to respond and adjust, with the conductor, to the necessary space that must be allowed for laughter. Use the dress rehearsal to heighten your awareness of your character's Through-Line, why their over-arching Objective matters and what is at risk.

After the dress rehearsal you will undoubtedly receive feedback from a range of different sources: friends, family, colleagues, coaches who might have been in the audience. Treat this feedback carefully; whilst you can listen to the feedback, you are under no obligation to take it and a judicious filter is best applied. Indeed, you have a responsibility to the production you are performing in, and the fellow performers you are performing with; you, therefore, cannot make changes to your performance without consultation. Of course, there might be useful thoughts about minor adjustments relating to diction, clarity and audibility but often these notes will refer to the *result*, without looking at *how* you achieve them. There will be notes from the director and conductor at some point after the dress rehearsal, so any concerns you have should be talked through with them.

9   Rehearsals in Depth

Here we examine how you can approach the different factors you will meet in opera rehearsal rooms: the various musical numbers, repertoires and directors' approaches to creating opera.

Opera is traditionally divided into different kinds of music and poetry: recitative, aria and ensemble. Each of these forms requires a unique dramatic approach. They have each developed throughout operatic history, so we must also consider the varying demands of different repertoire. The focus here is not a study of operatic history, but rather an exploration of how we approach each form in order to create believable stage characters.

Rehearsing Recitative

Recitative is the pitched speech used to capture the rhythm of natural dialogue. It is usually written in blank verse, with only the occasional flourish of rhyme. Evolving from the more heightened *recitar cantando* of early opera,[1] the distinction between recitative and the aria developed around the mid-seventeenth century with later Monteverdi and Cavalli operas.[2] This simpler style of recitative was adopted by most Italian and French composers from this point through to the 1820s, when it was gradually replaced by the more dominant style of a seamless, continuous musical framework. Melodically and harmonically simpler than aria or ensemble, utilising less vibrato and fewer sustained notes, the function of recitative is to carry the plot and action of the drama forward with clarity, leaving the aria and ensembles to reflect upon, and investigate, the major themes or issues of the piece.

Recitative from this period generally falls into two categories:

- *Recitativo accompagnato* (accompanied recit) – is accompanied by the orchestra. It requires a stricter adherence to the score; it must be sung as marked and with reference to the pitch and rhythm. For example, the exchange between Tamino and the Speaker, at the beginning of the Act One finale in *The Magic Flute*.

- *Recitativo secco* (dry recit) – is usually accompanied by punctuating chords from the harpsichord, with occasional help from the cello or bass. Its aim is to replicate the rhythm of speech, so whilst the pitch of the notes must remain as written, the rhythm set down in the score is flexible; it is a guide that can be adapted by the singer to

---

[1] Listen to Monteverdi's *Orfeo* as a good example.
[2] Compare *Orfeo* to Monteverdi's *The Coronation of Poppea* or Cavalli's *Giasone*.

represent, as near as possible, the rhythm of natural speech informed by the character's Objectives.

EXERCISE: *Recitative*
Solo/Pairs/Group/Ongoing

How to approach preparing and rehearsing recitative:

- Using the score, speak the recitative aloud in the rhythm in which it has been written, walking and turning on each grammatical or musical punctuation.[3]
- What do you notice? It is interesting to do this to discern the rhythmic clues that the composer might have written in.
- Next, repeat the exercise, adjusting the rhythm so that it sounds more like that of natural speech.
- Do this again but slow the words down to the tempo of the music; generally, composers will set the words slower than we typically speak.
- Having learned the recitative, next speak the words whilst playing the scene engaged with your Objectives.
- Then, try Actioning the scene, again just speaking the words.
- Bring emphasis to certain words, shift the length of words, play with pauses.
- Repeat this, Actioning line by line, but this time try singing the text on one comfortable note, using your speaking rhythm. The répétiteur will have to sympathetically hold up chords if the Actions coach needs a little time to feed the action.
- Now, sing the notated pitches whilst Actioning.

Rehearsing Arias

Arias tend to employ heightened poetic text with fixed rhyme structures, and more complex melodic and harmonic structures than simpler recitative. Many arias manipulate time to function as a suspended moment for the character to explore conflicting emotions or ideas. Plot tends to move more gradually through arias but the characters are always *in action*: battling, challenging, determining, pursuing. The music expresses this internal action through elaborate melody, extended vocal lines and rich orchestral accompaniment often in contrast to the sparse variance of text in the libretto; the words are often repeated, with the music to which they are set suggesting their shifting meaning.

The da capo aria became the defining feature of *opera seria*; defined through its ABA structure, with the return to the A section an opportunity for highly decorated vocal lines. Handel, the foremost exponent of the form, worked with complex narrative plots to ensure each character had a number of contrasting arias throughout the opera. Operatic

---

[3] See Chapter 6: Words and Music in Action.

conventions adapted over time, and the aria developed greater flexibility through Mozart's operas, yet they remained the primary means of accessing a character's emotional journey and, indeed, of presenting opportunities for virtuosic singing.

Exploration

Stanislavski suggests that in all arias, 'no matter how brief they may be, there is the seed of a larger piece at work. In each there is a plot, conflict, solution, and a Through-Line of action and Given Circumstances all leading to a Super-Objective'.[4] Any exploration of an aria must therefore be within the context of the whole opera. The narrative function of an aria can vary greatly; we only have to look at the range of arias from *Figaro* and *Flute* to see the variety of different reasons a character might *need* to sing in such a heightened way for an extended period. The German opera director Walter Felsenstein supports this, arguing: 'The dramatic happening must take place on a level where music is the only means of expression. The singer must not give the effect of being an instrument or component part of music that already exists but that of being its creative fashioner'.[5]

At the heart of most arias is an argument the character is trying to make through the employment of numerous rhetorical devices. The conventions of classical Greek rhetoric formed the foundations upon which early opera was conceived. A character will repeat words, shift tempi and dynamics, use simile and metaphor to work through and present their thoughts; every line the character sings is part of the logical progression of their argument. The theatre and opera director, Peter Hall, suggests Mozart's arias are public debates.[6]

The initial questions to ask when exploring an aria are:

- What is the aria *about*; what is the character's central argument?
- What is the antithetical argument; the central conflict in the character's thoughts?[7]
- How does a character make their argument?

For example, in the Countess's first aria,[8] she makes an argument, through prayer, for her sorrow to be soothed by having the Count's:

'love be reawakened or. . . .'
'or' is the important pivot point, leading to the conflicting argument. . . .
'forsaken let me die'.

Similarly, in *The Magic Flute*,[9] Pamina makes the argument to Tamino that she has:

'loved, and loved in vain. If. . .'
again the argument pivots around an important small word, 'if'. . .
'you spurn the love I offer only death will bring me peace'.

---

[4] Stanislavski, K. (1998) *Stanislavski on Opera*. Translated by E. R. Hapgood. London: Routledge, p. 22.
[5] Fuchs, P. P. (1991) *The Music Theatre of Walter Felsenstein*. London: Quartet Books.
[6] Hall, P. (2000) *Exposed by the Mask: Form and Language in Drama*. London: Oberon Books, p. 83.
[7] A conflict in an aria often pivots around a relatively small word; a simple *but* or *then* mark the transition from one idea to the next.
[8] *The Marriage of Figaro*, Countess, No. 10 Aria, 'Hear my prayer'/'Porgi, Amor'.
[9] Pamina, No. 17 Aria, 'Now I know'/'Ach ich fühls'.

As an exercise, when speaking the aria through, place one argument on one hand, and the other argument on the opposite hand. This will quickly help you to get a sense of the way in which the characters are balancing and weighing each argument against the other.

Both characters employ various rhetorical devices to expound their arguments to God (the Countess) or to their lover (Pamina): they repeat lines, with the music placing stresses on different words each time, they build and diminish dynamics, they present two possibilities. What unites the two arias is that while each character is appealing to the reason of other characters (God, Tamino), they are also rationalising their thoughts for themselves.

Map the Journey

Once you have discerned what lies at the heart of the aria, the next task is to begin to map your character's journey through the aria and gather an understanding of their Objective. The next questions to ask are:

- What is the character's journey through the aria?
- What does the character discover about themselves?
- How does this relate to the character's journey through the opera?
- How is the character changed in some way by singing these words and music?
- What are *you* (the artist) aiming to reveal?

Begin by looking at where the character starts the aria. What state are they in? What thought and Action precedes the play-in to the aria? What is their initial Objective?

Next, examine the turning points within the aria itself. How does the antithetical argument emerge? Where is the character at the end of the aria and what thought seems most present? Have they reached a resolution?

If we look at the conventionally structured Handel da capo aria, the B section will usually present a new argument or, at least, a shift in the perspective of the character. At the end of the B section, a new Objective must have taken shape to justify re-engaging with the repeated A section; there must be a *need* to return to the A section, based upon a discovery in the B section. You will often need to assume the role of a dramaturg to write a clear journey through many of Handel's arias; on first inspection a conflict or transition of thought may not reveal itself. Indeed, it is the music that, more often, suggests the shift in thoughts in the context of the Given Circumstances and Through-Line of Action. As Stanislavski suggests above, the aria must be seen in the context of the over-arching Objective for the character; by examining this, the journey of the character through the aria, as a constituent part of their Through-Line, will become clear.

A shift from recitative to aria often suggests that the subject the character is singing about really matters to them. The music suggests the emotional state of the character but this state, mood or feeling must not be 'played'; the result, as discussed, will be sentimental and indulgent. The character has something too important to resolve to spend time reducing their own story to emotional parody. They are working something out; they *need* to sing, in order to achieve something.

In deciding what Objective to play through an aria, you first need to consider three factors:

- the context of the past
- the present action
- the future intention.

EXAMPLE: *The Magic Flute*

Pamina, No. 17 Aria 'Now I know'/'Ach ich fühls'

- The Context Of The Past

Pamina arrives in the opera having been separated from her mother, confined by Sarastro and sexually assaulted by Monostatos. She has then met and fallen in love with Tamino, who is here to rescue her. She has subsequently been separated from Tamino, encouraged to murder by her mother and been threatened with rape by Monostatos.

- The Present Action

Pamina is reunited with Tamino. He resolutely refuses to talk to her.

- The Future Intention

She had hoped to escape with Tamino.
Pamina's Objective might be:

> '*I want to* attempt to make sense of this situation' or
> '*I want to* reach an understanding of the profound impact Tamino's rejection will have'.

Having identified this Objective, look again at mapping the journey through the aria:

- The Beginning

Identify the trigger that sparks the character's need to sing at the beginning of the aria. For Pamina, it is Tamino's determined refusal to reply to her repeated questions; his silence triggers her aria. In this case it is interesting that the play-in is a mere half a bar; she is immediately wounded by the silence and she unpacks and examines her feelings through the aria. The play-in seems to suggest that Pamina analyses her feelings at the very moment she sings, rather than contemplating them before or after.

- Mid-Point

Does the music suggest a raising of the stakes at some point? Is there a turning point at a moment in the aria where the character makes a discovery or realisation?
Pamina hits a top B flat almost immediately after singing that only 'death' will bring her peace. The dramatic shift in pitch suggests, perhaps, that this realisation takes place in the moment of singing; that she has not considered this possibility before.

- The End

What is the culmination of the aria? What does the play-out reveal to the character and, through them, the audience? How does the aria inform the dialogue that follows? In what way is the character changed?

Pamina's aria culminates in an extended, defeated descent and a three-bar play-out. There is a sense of having gathered a deep understanding of the consequences of Tamino's rejection. The play-out might be about Pamina sitting with this realisation or, alternatively, it might be about handing over this understanding to Tamino. Through an analysis of Pamina's Through-Line and Given Circumstances, an Objective and a journey through her aria emerges.

TARGET

At every moment, on every line, your character is communicating with someone or something: themselves, another character onstage or off, gods, the audience, an object or idea. Before singing a line, always determine:

- Who or what is my target?
- Who else can hear what I sing?
- Where are they?
- What is my shifting relationship and attitude to them?

As we examined in Actions, p. 89, when we communicate our energy and focus can be classified as being in one of three circles in relation to our target:

- 1st Circle: when connecting to an inner thought or an idea in your mind's eye.
- 2nd Circle: when communicating directly to someone in the same room.
- 3rd Circle: often used when addressing a large group of people. Also, when focusing on the horizon.

Target: You

If you spend *too* long in 1st Circle, whilst singing to yourself, your thoughts risk being unclear. If your character is repeatedly singing the same line in an aria, without shifting from 1st Circle, the audience will wonder why you are repeating something to yourself that you already know. You can communicate with yourself but shift between all three Circles. In 1st Circle, you might target an idea in your mind's eye. In 2nd Circle, you might make that idea *present*, as though you could actually hold it. In 3rd Circle, the idea might be projected onto an imaginary cinema screen in front of you.

If you are *doing* something to yourself, take it into 2nd Circle by externalising the physical Action. For example, imagine your character talking to themselves in a bathroom mirror: *driving, urging, berating, comforting.*

Do not assume that because a character is targeting themselves they are necessarily being truthful with themselves. Of course, removal from the public sphere allows layers of a character's persona to be peeled back but their idealised vision of themselves might still not allow for absolute revelation; there is often tension within this 'internal' exchange.

Target: Visualisations

We can see images in our mind's eye in 1st Circle, or we can see them projected onto an imaginary landscape in middle distance in 3rd Circle. The more time you spend building and detailing these images, the more you have to engage with.

If I asked you where you ate lunch yesterday, after a brief pause, your eyes might roll up and to the left, you would recall the memory, and communicate based on the pictures you see. If I asked you to describe your ideal job, you might look into the middle distance and see yourself onstage, next to certain famous performers, in a theatre of your choice.

To be able to do this, honestly, you must invest time creating these images as though you have lived your character's past and dreamed their future. Audiences are good at spotting lies!

You might see these images as a film, connecting with a quality in the music. They might travel towards you like a river, or track in front of you as a moving landscape. What is your attitude to them? What do you want to do to them? Do you face them head on or, instead, distance or side-line them?

Target: Others

When singing an aria, it is always better to have an external target. Of course, you may have many shifting targets throughout your aria but it is easier to communicate ideas to other characters, or objects, in the room.

EXAMPLE: *The Magic Flute*

Sarastro, No. 15 Aria 'Before our holy altar'/'In diesen heil'gen Hallen'

The decision could be made to sing Sarastro's second aria, in *The Magic Flute*, as a general statement of a philosophy; indeed, the music is stately and considered:

We worship at the altar
of man's humanity to man.
So if a friend should falter
we'll help him if we can.
He will go forth from our embrace,
to make the world a better place.

If, however, the aria is addressed to Pamina, as an introductory lesson, or to his followers, as a demonstration of his magnanimity, or to the recently departed Monostatos or Queen, as a coded threat or, even, to himself, as a way of calming himself after uncovering

---

a threat to his life, we have a much more dynamic piece of action. The majestic music, then, has possible undercurrents of violence sustaining it and the subtext is revealed as Sarastro's desire to destroy the threat of women meets the Obstacle of maintaining his regal public persona.

These are the choices you make as an artist; you must decide what the aria is actually about and *how* you choose to reveal it.

Target: The Audience

There is a central paradox when singing an aria to the audience; often you are expressing something incredibly intimate that you would not share with another character, and yet you are engaging a mass of people you have never met before and, in all likelihood, cannot see very well.

Firstly, you need to imbue the audience with a character and have an attitude to them. They could be your best friend, a judge or other self. How do you regard them? How do you think they regard you? Does this change throughout the aria?

Secondly, your communication with an audience will be more detailed and direct when singing to them in 2nd Circle. If you sing to them in 3rd Circle it will resemble a political rally and not an environment in which your character will want to share personal revelations. Embrace the audience as though in a dialogue of mutual exchange.

EXAMPLE: *The Marriage of Figaro*

Figaro No. 26 Aria 'You foolish slaves of Cupid'/'Aprite un po' quegl'occhi'

Figaro's explosive tirade against women, and the men who love them, can be played either to the women and men in Figaro's past, hypothetical figures, or directly to the audience. The latter is the most exciting approach; it gives the singer a direct relationship with *real* people, to *reproach*, *mock*, *belittle*, *accuse*. The audience are grabbed and pulled firmly into the action in a way that can only be done in live theatre. It is visceral, bold and challenges an audience's attitude to questions in their own life. Again, if this interaction is in 2nd Circle, Figaro can ask a question and expect to get a response: the interaction becomes specific and urgent.

The key to any aria is to consider it a dialogue; a duet, where the target happens not to sing. Imagine that, at potentially any moment, you might be interrupted and, immediately, the words seem to matter more.[10] Remember that your relationships with your targets are always shifting; it is always important to physicalise these shifting relationships. Remind yourself of Exercise: Concretising Thought and Exercise: Spectrum[11] as a way of exploring these relationships. Additionally, ask yourself and your target the following questions before singing your aria:

- what do you think I think of you?
- What do you think I think you think of me?

---

[10] See Exercise: Covert Relations, p. 230 in Chapter 6: Words and Music in Action.
[11] Chapter 6: Words and Music in Action, p. 226 and p. 235.

OBSTACLE

The aria will be powered by the Obstacle your character faces; without one, there is no need to continue singing. Your character might face a number of different Obstacles in one aria. Indeed, the movement from the A section to the B section, in Handel arias, usually occurs as a new conflict emerges. With reference to the arias mentioned above:

- Pamina's Obstacles are her own lack of understanding of the situation and Tamino's silence.

- The Countess's Obstacles are that no-one appears to be listening (her prayer is unanswered), her powerlessness to change the situation and, in turn and opposing her Objectives, her desire to end it all. For a character experiencing internal conflict, their Obstacle and Objective will be interchangeable.

- Sarastro faces the internal Obstacles of what he would actually like to do to traitors, set against his Objective of wanting to appear magnanimous and in control.

- Figaro's Obstacles might be the disregard of the audience to his words of advice or, alternatively, his very real love for Susanna.

Sometimes, you will need to search hard for an Obstacle: engage your skills as a dramaturg. For example, in Papageno's No. 2 Aria 'I'm sure that there could never be. . .'/'Der Vogelfänger bin ich ja' it is difficult to observe an Obstacle; he simply seems to want to befriend the audience. However, locate a simple Obstacle; the audience do not know who he is and Papageno will, therefore, have to work harder to win their friendship.

SUBTEXT

The subtext in an aria often lies in the conflict between the Obstacle and the Objective, or between the conflicting wants of the character. Look again at Exercise: Physical Essence, p. 206. Embodying one of your character's wants – the Objective they are trying to hide or dismiss – and then covering it and only allowing it to be revealed through one simple movement, can elucidate the character's inner conflict for the audience.

For example, in Sarastro's aria, he might present himself as calm, considered, and controlled but his right hand might be imagining crushing a tiny, imaginary Queen of the Night. You could reduce the physical volume of this crushing action but it will still reveal the conflict within the character. The subtext of an aria is best located through an exploration of the tools detailed in Chapter 6: Words and Music in Action.

ACTION

Every line in an aria requires an Action driven to a target, underlined by understanding of what the ideal outcome would be. Each repeated line must have a fresh impetus, and be connected to the previous line and the one that follows through a logical progression. The music will guide the choice of Actions, from line to line, and these Actions must be physically engaged through the whole body.

Figaro, No. 3 Cavatina 'So, little master, you're dressed to go dancing'/'Se vuol ballare'

This aria is Figaro's first opportunity to address the Count directly, following the news of the Count's desire for Susanna and after Susanna's exit. Except, of course, the Count is not actually there. The target remains the Count despite this.

Figure 9.1 Figaro aria.

In this section the same lines are repeated five times; 'You'll see'.[12] They are very simply set to music but Mozart brilliantly distinguishes one line from the next; 'you'll' is sung on a C each time, the 'see' is sung one note higher with each repeat. This perhaps suggests that Figaro is attempting to keep the lid on his desire to hit The Count, whilst perhaps raising the threat to The Count with each repeat. The fact that the interlude shortens between the final two repeats gives further indication of an intensification of threat. Figaro's Action, on each repetition of the line, might remain the same. It might be 'I jab you' (the 'you' being The Count). The music, however, guides us toward *how* the Action should be played each time; the physical jab perhaps getting a little bit harder each time.

ORNAMENTATION

Every note your character sings has to be motivated; every ornament or cadenza needs a purpose. The challenge is that ornaments are often determined before rehearsals have even begun; before you know who the character is and what they want. Hold off determining ornaments for as long as possible, until you understand your character, and their circumstances, more fully.

In certain repertoire the words become lost; increased volume or higher pitch preferences the vowel over the consonant. However, if the breath is triggered by an internal psychological impulse and the sound consequently motivated, allied with the physical embodiment of the Objective, the intention will be communicated to the audience. The story will continue.

Rehearsing Ensembles

One of the most extraordinary aspects of opera is the ability to hear two or more characters' thoughts at the same time; the music and text suggest the moments their thoughts and feelings converge and separate. This is rarely possible with text alone and, in duets, trios and larger ensembles, the effect can be dramatically and musically exhilarating; the simultaneous juxtaposition of contrasting attitudes to the one event is the inspiration for the highest drama and most dazzling comedy.

Mozart's ensembles in *The Marriage of Figaro* are the perfect illustration of this point. The Act Two finale begins with the pain and violence of the duet between the Count and Countess and tumbles into ever increasing comic befuddlement, with the addition of more and more characters, as the act reaches its climax. In the Act Four finale, Mozart uses the ensemble to swiftly unfold the plot and bring focus to the isolation of the two characters at the centre of the storm.

Challenges

There are a number of challenges for the singer when trying to clearly communicate the character's journey through ensembles:

- Too often the stage action becomes static and the dynamics of the drama, all too present in the music, are not reflected on stage.

---

[12] In Italian 'saprò' actually means 'I'll know', but the sentiment remains the same; Figaro is singing to the Count 'you'll see, I'll know'.

- It is very easy for the action to become confused. Take Susanna and the Count's duet:[13] one moment the two are singing to each other, the next to themselves (or the audience).

- When all characters are singing exactly the same text, it is easy for an individual character's journey to become indistinct.

The most important task, in order to clearly convey the individual strands of story through ensembles, is to first actively listen to the music. The music will highlight exactly when the changes must happen; the constant shifts – usually melodic, rhythmic or dynamic – highlight a string of narrative Events through the ensemble. Whatever occurs onstage in an ensemble must occur in absolute synchronicity with the music; if the structure of the story – of each of the character's shifting beats and Events – becomes detached from the musical structure, the audience will be adrift. Here is a list of those factors to consider when conveying character through ensembles:

- Identify your character's journey through the ensemble, in the same way as you would with an aria. More time will often be spent preparing an aria; you are the only one singing and, as a result, it can feel as though the focus is entirely on you (actually, the focus is often on what you are doing to your targets). However, because so many different journeys happen simultaneously in an ensemble, it is vital that your journey is drawn boldly and distinctly.

- You must psychologically and physically connect with your target. When the audience are receiving a lot of information at the same time, they need clear indications of exactly who you are referring to. As the music shifts and motifs are repeated, it is important that your targets also shift. As the logic of the story and the changes in the music dictate, you must shift your focus from one character, to another, to yourself or to the audience. Ensure you physicalise your shifting attitude to your targets. The audience will see this and read the story visually, even if they cannot hear exactly what you are singing.

- Have a clear understanding, at every moment in an ensemble, of those characters that can hear you and those that you can hear. Then, find a way of making this clear to an audience. Much of this will be about staging; it is easier for an audience to understand that certain characters have formed an agreement about a certain point if they are in close proximity. The general note, however, is that an economy of movement, with clear shifts of direction, energy and weight when needed, will help to highlight the important information to the audience.

- When another character has a lengthy aside to a third character or the audience, your task is to believably sustain or extend your thought, in order to allow the aside to take place without your knowledge of it. Your sustained idea might need to be played at a quieter physical volume than the character singing. If you cannot sustain your idea, find a new idea. Any vacuum of thought, or lack of commitment to a thought, will draw the audience's eye like a magnet. A good way of sustaining a thought is to engage in a detailed interior monologue; script this monologue for yourself to help maintain focus.

---

[13] Count and Susanna, No. 16 Duet, 'How could you be so cruel'/'Crudel! Perchè finora'.

- Understand how time shifts; the story can move from a naturalistic exchange in the present tense, to a suspended moment inside the characters' heads, in a single beat. The naturalistic conventions of theatre rarely apply in ensembles; seek to find a clear shift of target, or movement from one Circle to another, to clearly convey this movement of time to the audience.

- At certain moments in a large ensemble you will need to make your vocal line more present; you will be guided in this by the composer or conductor. Your physical storytelling at these moments is vital. You will need to match your presence in the vocal line by becoming *more present* onstage. You can do this in a number of ways; the most obvious way is for the director to find a reason for you to step downstage, closer to centre stage, or into a different lighting state. However, you can also connect your core[14] and heighten, if only slightly, your physical gestures.[15]

Rehearsing Chorus

Who am I? Who are these people? Why am I singing the same words as them?

These questions can lead us towards an understanding of the function of the chorus in the story and define the dramatic conventions at play.

EXAMPLE: *The Magic Flute*

Act One Chorus

- The first chorus is an off-stage response by male voices to Tamino's questions about Pamina. The chorus are Sarastro's brethren and are collectively guiding Tamino towards his entrance into the Temple.

- The male chorus are next seen and heard as 'slaves', alongside Monostatos, attempting to recapture Pamina; they are singing the words that they magically hear in their heads, inspired by the music of Papageno's bells.

- We first see and hear the full male and female chorus within the Temple. They are Sarastro's followers, singing a hymn in praise of Sarastro; this is collective worship demonstrating the passion of Sarastro's disciples.

    Within this scene, *how* the chorus communicate changes; they have a collective spontaneous response to Tamino and Pamina's embrace and thereby demonstrate the fundamental deep-seated opposition of the brethren to overt displays of emotion.

- The final two choruses in Act One are both presented in the form of collective worship. The first, a reprise in praise of Sarastro; the second, in praise of their plan to 'Sanctify the state of man'. How might these be communicated? The chorus might sing from hymn sheets; scripted within the reality of the world. They might alternatively be collective outbursts of fervent belief; they just happen to be singing the same words and are united in their desire to *praise, celebrate, uplift* and *worship*.

---

[14] See Exercise: Core, p. 21.
[15] See Exercise: Embracing the Space, p. 269.

Characterisation

Who the chorus are – the way in which they communicate and their function within the scene – can change throughout the opera. In response to this, the way in which directors stage and define the chorus also varies greatly; from embracing a naturalist approach to executing highly stylised choreography.

An understanding of the function of the chorus and the approach of the particular production is vital; this will frame your behaviour and establish the guidelines that determine your own individual response to the piece. Within these constraints of convention, however, it is important to bring the character imaginatively to life for yourself, in order to create an engaged characterisation:

- Consider the Given Circumstances and construct a character biography based upon these, the conventions established in the rehearsal room, and your own imaginative response.
- Create relationships; collaborate with fellow chorus members and singers to build shared histories.
- Understand your Objectives, your Ideal Future, Obstacles and Actions. The same work must take place on these factors as it would if you were singing a solo role. The only difference is that your Objectives, Targets and Actions might well be shared with the rest of the chorus/community. The style of the production will define how much freedom you have to choose *how* to pursue your Objectives.

  If you are given a general collective note that relates to an emotion, for example, 'you are all scared', resist *playing* this emotion. Unpack the instruction and ask 'Why am I scared and what does my character want to *do* in response to this?'
- Related to this last point is the importance of your Target. When a chorus is singing the audience are receiving a lot of information at once and, often, a shared target is important for the clarity of storytelling.
- Your physical engagement with the world should be detailed and specific. Who are you? How do you respond to certain factors? Too often, for example, I see a chorus in opera acting 'cold' by generically patting their upper arms. People feel the cold in different ways: some more in their toes, others the end of their nose. If it is the production's intention for the audience to *believe* in your behaviour, then your behaviour must be, to some extent, personal and individual.

  Consider also *how* you physically contact others; give physical contact the value it deserves in the context of the story.
- Also, remember that this contact must continue to be specific when a character is singing to you. Who is this character to *you*? Who this character is to you may, indeed, be very similar to who they are to the person standing alongside you. However, you must act in response to your own impulses within a group; you cannot act *exactly* the same as the group.

ANTHROPOLOGY

The work you do to create a believable character as part of a chorus will involve a great deal of dialogue and negotiation with the director and fellow singers to characterise the whole world. This world is the very fabric of the opera that the plot unfolds within. If the world is incoherent, so too will be all the characters' actions within it. Work on creating the world can be negotiated through reference to the anthropological questions we looked at earlier.[16]

Rehearsing Text

Many operas incorporate spoken dialogue. The use of dialogue derives from the particular genre in which the operas were written, or from the composer's desire to explore the full range of vocal expression. *The Magic Flute* and, for example, the operettas of Offenbach and Sullivan follow the traditions of their form; singspiel and comic opera have their roots firmly in the traditions of popular theatre. At the turn of the twentieth century, composers such as Schoenberg and Berg (following on from the experimentation of Bizet and Humperdinck) developed *sprechstimme* (speech-voice): text spoken at the pitch written by the composer.

Consider why, to what purpose, the composer employs spoken text; it might be simply to communicate more information in a shorter period of time, or it might be to bring particular attention to a specific moment in the opera.

Spoken text must be supported by the breath and articulated in a similar way to the sung word. There are some very important books on developing the actor's speaking voice listed at the back of the book. Healthy singing demands that you support your speaking voice in everyday life to reduce the likelihood of fatigue. Take another look at the vocal warm-up at the beginning of Chapter 6. The exercises in this section present terrifically useful tools for initial and ongoing exploration of the sound, rhythm and subtext of the language.

EXERCISE: *The Telephone*
Solo/Ongoing

Explore the possibilities for the expression of meaning in spoken text, by bringing your attention to those same elements that composers consider when bringing expression through music.

- Imagine you are having an imaginary conversation on the telephone using only the word 'yes'.
- First, explore how expression can be brought by varying only the rhythm with which you speak. Then, the pitch. Then, the dynamics.
- Of course, you will inevitably overlap and change all three elements at certain points.
- Now, write down a list of Actions: *I tempt* you, *I urge* you, *I distance* you, *I welcome* you, *I invite* you. Try the exercise, using only 'yes', with these Actions.
- Repeat the entire exercise with the sentence: 'Can I help you?'

---

[16] See Organising Information: Other Approaches, p. 62.

Transition from Speech to Song

Moving from speech into song, and back again, can be precarious. The listener's ear is attuned to one mode of expression and, when another is introduced, it can strike a false note. This can alert the audience to the artifice of the form and, as a result, distance them from the action. The following needs to be kept in mind:

- The impetus to begin the song must be present in the last line of text. There must be a need to begin to sing: to explore an idea, to reach for a clearer understanding, to communicate a thought or feeling more urgently. Intensify your Objective as a way of heightening this need.

- This Objective must be translated into the line before you sing, in order to energise the line. As an exercise, try singing the final line of spoken text and imagine that the impulse to sing materialises earlier. Do the same with the first line of spoken text after singing; build a bridge between the two means of expression.

- Be alert to the tempo-rhythm of the song and marry this to the thought and text before, and after, the transition. Do not suddenly create a different energy for the song out of nowhere and then drop it as soon as you finish singing.

The same rules apply when performing spoken text as when singing on stage.[17] It is important not to shout in order to be heard. The text carries through an energised sound, produced through an energised body and clear intentions. Your focus should be on what you are saying, rather than how you are saying it. The consonants, as with singing, carry the meaning of the word – Exercise: Exploring the Consonants, p. 218, is good to look at. Finally, have the intention of *sharing* your text with the audience rather than projecting to the back of the theatre.

Rehearsing Translations

You need to consider *how* to sing in English. When you are approaching performing an opera in Italian or German the focus will often be on how to sing in that language; attention will be brought to the vowel sounds and where the consonants lie. When singing in the vernacular this work is just as essential in order for an audience to understand what is being sung.

A good translation is no easy task: it will encapsulate the meaning of the line, fit the rhythm of the music, place stresses in the correct place so that the verbal text and musical text (both of which were informed by the original language) meet, incorporate open vowels on high notes and, perhaps, rhyme. If a translation is difficult to sing, then it is worth asking for a change. However, the integrity of the entire world is bound up in the translator's choices; they are as integral a collaborator as the composer and original librettist. Be mindful, therefore, that the more a translation is changed, the greater the risk that the fabric of the world begins to unravel.

---

[17] Look at Chapter 8: Rehearsals.

TRANSLATOR: JEREMY SAMS

Jeremy is a director, writer, composer, orchestrator, musical director and lyricist. His work has been performed on stages across the world. I wanted to speak to him in his role as a translator of opera. Jeremy has translated more than twenty operas from their original language to English and his work offers the most eloquent argument for opera to be performed in the language of the audience. Throughout the book we are referring to Jeremy's translations of *The Marriage of Figaro* and *The Magic Flute*. I asked Jeremy about how he approached the process of translation and why he felt it was important to perform opera in English to an English-speaking audience.

How do you approach the process of translating operas into English?

What I'm after is something that absolutely captures the flavour and the feel of the original; something that's immediate and, most specifically, something that doesn't necessarily go word for word with the Italian. This is true of all the Mozart titles that I've translated. For example, *'Dove Sono'* isn't called *'Where Are'*, *'Dies Bildnis'* isn't called *'This Picture'*, and *'Come Scoglio'* isn't *'Like a Pedestal'*. I really want to imagine a text which arrives on Mozart's doorstep in English. He sets it to music and the result is what we hear.

Take, for example, *'Ach Ich Fühl's':* what is this aria about? It's about Pamina saying *'Ah, I get it. Love does not last forever, the things you thought would be endless are not. Ah!'* So, that's why it's *'Now I Know'* and not *'Ah! I Feel It'*. I know what the exact translation is in German, but what I'm after is something where the words and the music, if possible, cohere together like cling film. Many translations don't aim for this because they're so concerned with replicating the vowel sounds and the consonants. I try to go back beyond the original words because all words and all music are symptoms of what a character feels in the story.

Mozart starts with people in stories with problems. Fiordiligi has a problem with these blokes in disguise who are trying to woo her and she asks, *'What do I do about it? Well, I have to respect my boyfriend'*. She's got a problem and the solution is the aria; she is trying to work out what to do about it and examining her feelings.

What else do you consider?

I'm very observant of rhyme, although in some operas more than others. The most rhymed opera of all time, for example, is *The Magic Flute* which is understandable as it's all about ringing and singing and pairs; it's about music!

The other thing I try to do is to keep the vowel sounds the same as the Italian, particularly if there's coloratura or melisma. Da Ponte is very careful. He ends most of his big arias with *'Ah'* sounds, except for Pamina's arias which end on *'E'* sounds, presumably because the first singer to play Pamina loved to sing on this vowel.

Most translations have been for new productions; Bryn Terfel first sang my *Figaro* translation. Many ideas that I've included in translations have come from the director, or possibly some of the singers, of these productions. As a translator one does have the chance to editorialise as well. For example, in *The Magic Flute* I had a conversation with the director, Nicholas Hytner, about downplaying the racism and the misogyny inherent in the original libretto.

What do you think singers should consider?

There will always be, in a singer's mind, a ghost version of the translation, which is the Italian version of the opera. I've even heard singers wanting to breathe according to the Italian words; but that's no good whatsoever. Only imagine this: that you've received a new text of an English opera by Mozart hitherto undiscovered. Otherwise, as a singer, you will be in a perpetual state of grief about not singing in Italian. In fact, what you are doing is singing in a language that your audience will immediately understand, just as Mozart's audience did.

Many people are very anti-opera translations, but composers aren't. They generally want things to be in a language in which they can be understood. Wagner, when he first comes to France, insists *Tannhauser* and *Lohengrin* are in French.

I recommend every singer tries to translate at least a page of the score from the original. Have it make sense, get the rhymes right, try not to go backwards and always move things forward; just like the music and the story.

Rehearsing the Original Language

The imperative, when singing text that is not your first language, is that you understand what the text means. This means understanding each and every word that you are singing and, also, the sentence structure. Without a clear sense of the structure of the sentence the process of thought will not be correct. The words and music result from the thought and, if we cannot understand this result, we will never understand the thought that created the impulse for it.

Understanding a word does not mean simply knowing its literal translation. It means connecting with it, as we do our own language, on a visceral level; we must *need* the words that the characters sing in order to express their thoughts. When you sing 'I love you' it will resonate in a deep and profound way that 'Ti amo' or 'Ich liebe dich' will probably not. The words you sing in your own language carry with them a lifetime's associations; they will give you more immediate access to your inner life and pictures. The same is true for an audience; if the story is told in their own language the words will be received more directly, and with greater urgency, than if they are listening to a language that holds fewer associations.

You must therefore build your association with these words. Of course, the best way to do this is to live in the country whose language you are singing in and build associations through the experience of living the language. Alternatively, the Tools laid out in Chapter 6: Words and Music in Action help connect you, physically and psychologically, to the words you are singing; I particularly recommend Exercise: Physicalising Words (p. 221) as an immediate way to create a direct route from the word to your imagination.

Cover Rehearsals

The Challenge

The challenge when covering a role is to discover how to be true to the production and the decisions that somebody else has made about the character whilst, at the same time, creating a truthful character that you can bring to the performance. It is about finding the balance between following predetermined decisions and bringing yourself to the production. Disregarding the production risks confusing the rest of the company, especially if you have to go into the production at a late stage. Replicating what has already been created by somebody else will simply render your character lifeless.

An Approach

- You will have the established parameters within which to interrogate the role. This is similar to the experience of seeing the model box on the first day of rehearsal; a set of decisions has already been made but they invite you to create within the specific definition of the world.

- When covering a role these parameters are more clearly drawn; the world has been realised and the decisions the character makes in response to this world have been determined. See as many rehearsals as possible to layer your understanding of this world.

- Work within these boundaries; the Objectives, Obstacles and Actions are laid out for you to investigate and justify in the same way you would the score. *How* you play them, however, must come from you.

- The more you get to know and understand the score, together with the world of the production, the greater freedom you will have to discover the character for yourself. Be detailed in your study of these two elements and approach the task with flexibility.

- Martin Fitzpatrick, Head of Music at ENO, works with many cover casts[18] and explains that, 'The process must begin with going back to the score and asking "Why is it written on the page like that?"' You need to bring your own spirit to it which comes from your interrogation of the role. It remains *your* process. If you don't first understand why a certain character you are covering moves over to a chair, ask the question 'Why might they do that?' or, alternatively, 'That doesn't make sense to me, what can I do that won't put other people off but is true to what I think about the scene?' Maybe you still move to the chair but you don't sit in it, or you go to the table next to it. You mustn't be a vacuum ready to be filled by somebody else's ideas. You must have thoughts about how you want to do this role. However, you need the flexibility to be able to modify how you were thinking about this character because of the production you're in; to know what is non-negotiable and to ensure that everything that is negotiable is where you explore the possibilities.

Revivals

The same approach should be taken when re-staging an opera first staged some time ago as it would when covering a role. The advantage with a revival is that you will, most likely, not be the only one to be exploring the production for the first time.

You cannot replicate *exactly* everything that happened in the original production but you must acknowledge and honour the original decisions. Working within these boundaries, your approach to creating character should remain the same as it would were you part of a team creating a new production.

---

[18] Interview, May 2018. Martin and I first worked together conducting and directing the cover cast for the production of Poul Ruder's opera *The Handmaid's Tale* at ENO in 2003.

10 Performance

The performance is another step on your journey of creating character. Throughout rehearsals you will have been layering information about the character's physical and psychological behaviour, their relationships with others and the world defining these behaviours. Through stage and piano, and stage and orchestra, rehearsals you will have layered knowledge about the technical demands of the space, set, costumes, wigs and props that will help you to communicate with clarity. The added element in the performance is the audience; your engagement with them, and the story you are telling them, is founded upon the layers of information you have built about your world and character.

Nerves

Every singer's response to a performance is different. Some will experience feelings of excitement and anticipation; others physiological or psychological fright. This fight-or-flight response is a perfectly normal reaction; the body releases waves of adrenaline, cortisol and norepinephrine in response to a perceived threat. The heightening of the senses that such a rush of hormones brings can be useful in performance; it can bring a sense of energy and focus. It can also create unnecessary tension, constricting the airwaves or restricting physical movement, so it needs to be controlled and managed.

It is important to remember that every performance is another small part of the journey. Your process up to this point will support you, you will learn through the performance, and have the opportunity to build on what you have learnt in your next performance.

Preparation

Your preparation before a performance should be specific and tailored to you and what you need; you may need to focus on releasing energy or, conversely, on energising the body. Think about your preparation in advance. Create a plan or routine and begin to use this through stage and dress rehearsals.

Arrive early for a performance and in advance of the half-hour call.[1] Give yourself time to check props, wigs, costume and make-up and time for your vocal, physical and

---

[1] The half-hour call is the typically contracted call time for performers: thirty-five minutes before the performance begins.

psychological warm-up. Draw upon the work of your process so far, as it will provide everything you need for your preparation. Remember that there is the support of a team of people working to tell this story collectively; it is not just down to you!

Physical Warm-Up

- Remind yourself of the release exercises in Chapter 1: Foundations and the energising exercises in Chapter 8: Rehearsals. You will have used these through rehearsals and will know which work best for you.
- Do not forget to warm up your back; it is too often neglected and engages your whole body in the expression of your story. A quick massage from a colleague, or pressing a ball against a wall either side of your spine, does the trick. In addition, do a few spine rolls and a 'Composite Sha'.[2]
- Connect the mind and body by:
  - reconnecting to your character as the Animal
  - exploring your character in different States of Tension whilst imagining them in different scenarios in their everyday life
  - walking an imaginary line that tracks through your character's biography and, as you do so, physicalising your character at different ages
  - re-engaging your character's Psychological Gesture.

EXERCISE: *Response to Words*
Solo/Group/5 mins

Write a list of themes from the opera onto separate pieces of paper, shuffle them and lay them on top of each other like a stack of cards. Stand in neutral, physically centred. Uncover the first word and physicalise your character's response to the word. This does not mean miming a representation of the word but, rather, capturing your character's attitude in a freeze frame in the body. Breathe into this and let the thoughts and physicality extend.

Psychological Warm-Up

- Again, remind yourself of the focus exercises in Chapter 1: Foundations.
- Spend a good ten minutes with your character and their inner thoughts and pictures. Consider the list of nine questions in Chapter 7, p. 243. The reduced list is: who, when, where, what and why?
- Consider your Character Relationships.

---

[2] Chapter 1: Foundations, p. 17.

- Focus on one particular object that resonates for your character; hold it whilst you replay the stories it connects to in your mind's eye.[3]

- Imagine the night before this day: the day the story of the opera begins. Picture your character's bedroom; imagine lying on your bed and closing your eyes; focus on what you hope to happen the next day. Imagine waking. What thoughts and pictures fill your mind? What do you want to achieve today? What is your over-arching Objective?

- For every performance think about a particular Point of Concentration.[4] Turn over all your thoughts associated with this theme or idea as part of your warm-up. Come back to your Point of Concentration just before you enter the stage.

EXERCISE: *Dropping the Anchor*
Solo/10 secs–10 mins

At ENO Opera Works we worked with performance psychologist Jacqueline Branson Thom. This exercise is invaluable for helping to ground you and is something you can do before walking onstage or going into an audition. The more you practise it, the deeper it builds the associations, the quicker you will be able to access the state in future. The visualisation at the end of the exercise will help to slide you into your character.

- Feet on the floor. Eyes closed.
- Begin with a breath out, with a soft tummy, and allow the breath in.
- If *calm* were a colour, what colour would calm be for you?
- If *calm* were a sound, what sound would calm be for you?
- If *calm* were a feeling, how does calm feel for you?
- Imagine a light above your head and pour the calm colour, sound and feeling into the light. On a breath out imagine a wave of the calm colour, sound and feeling flowing down over you and carrying any tension away, down into the ground. With each breath out a wave of the calm colour, sound and feeling showers you; washing away any excess tension.
- Then imagine, from the soles of your feet, golden roots of light. Imagine these roots going down through the floor, down through the building, down into the earth, down through all the strata of the earth and down to the very centre of the earth: the electro-magnetic core.
- Draw that gravitational energy up through the roots of light and through your feet, legs and the base of your spine to below your navel; you will feel stronger and grounded like a tree. Because these are roots of light they move with you and connect you with the centre of the earth wherever you move.
- Focus on that point below your navel and imagine a light there; the light is a source of vibration and energy.

---

[3] The Mind: Awareness Focus, p. 25.
[4] Points of Concentration, p. 110.

- Every time you breathe in, that light gets brighter and stronger. The rays of light fill the whole of your body: out to your fingertips and out to fill the whole of your mind.
- When you're completely filled with the light, imagine allowing it to shine out of every pore. Allow it out around you as a sphere of light. At the centre of this sphere of light, you belong.
- Then, imagine a silver cord at the base of your skull held aloft: supporting you from above.
- Next, think of a person, or an animal, who you feel completely comfortable with. Notice the comfortable feeling: where it begins in your body and where it moves to.
- Give that feeling a colour and allow a wave of that colour over the whole room.
- Then, remember a time you felt good: the way you'd like to always feel. Imagine you are there in that moment: seeing what you saw, hearing what you heard, feeling what you felt. Take that feeling onto the stage with you.
- Then step into the world of your character. Where are they? What are they seeing, hearing, feeling, smelling and tasting around them? What do their clothes feel like? What are the pictures, sounds, feelings, hopes and dreams that are playing on the surface of their mind?

The more you repeat this exercise, the quicker you will be able to access the state of readiness the exercise brings.

The Wings

Just before entering the stage:

- If you need to release tension there are two quick ways. Firstly, push against a wall (as though trying to push the wall over, both palms placed on the wall around shoulder height) and breathe deeply. Secondly, clasp your hands behind you, fingers interlocked, and push your hands away from your back before releasing your hands.
- Revisit the Point of Concentration you loaded earlier. This will help you *see* and *hear* afresh onstage.
- Run through, in your mind's eye, the *Immediate Circumstances*: the events that have just happened for your character prior to entering the scene.
- Focus on your Scene Objective. Locate in the body the place your *want* is centred.
- Remember – the scene begins when you are in the wings and only finishes after you have left the wings.

Onstage

Entering the Space

The aim in performance is to act moment to moment, as if everything were happening for the first time; the action immediately and instinctively triggers a reaction, followed by a conscious decision to respond.

In the first instance, place your trust in the layers of the world and details of character you have created and come to understand through rehearsals: these will work on a subconscious level. You can only consciously do one thing at a time and so your focus must be on pursuing your Objective. An engaged pursuit of your Objective will lead to active and dynamic listening; you need to see and hear your partner's response to understand how successful the pursuit of your Objective is. Listen with your *whole* self: not just your ears but your entire body connected to your partner's actions and reactions. As an extension of this, Stanislavski makes a useful note (that I've slightly adapted); that you must sing, not to the ear, but to the eye of your partner onstage.[5] This transaction of actively listening engages the inner and outer character.

This demands an openness and a vulnerability, together with an understanding that events onstage cannot be exactly repeated; things will change. Allow yourself the flexibility to adapt to others; by first contemplating a Point of Concentration, you will hear different emphases in the story. Respond to these and allow your new response to be translated into your Actions. The Action itself will not change but *how* you react to your partner must; you will still *kiss*, *push*, *entice* but how you do it will alter, if only minutely, night after night.

For example, if in a particular performance of *The Magic Flute* the singer playing Tamino decides that the Point of Concentration is his age, he might hear the Speaker's accusation 'High sound words for such a youth!' delivered with greater intensity.[6] It might resonate to the extent that his action to defy the Speaker, on his next line 'Yes, hatred of iniquity', might then be more forceful. This, in turn, the Speaker will receive and perhaps respond to with intensified mockery: 'You will not wound us with your slander' and so on. The singers, beat by beat, will adapt to the new information in the body and sounds of their partner.

Play

The process of playing, improvising, listening and responding in the moment must continue onstage. You will have built strong foundations and a deep understanding of the character and the world and this will give you the freedom to let go and react spontaneously.

Of course, you will take with you a dual consciousness; you will connect intimately to the world of the character and opera, whilst at the same time carry an awareness of the performance itself. You will be connecting with the conductor, finding your light, finding the angle to sing at and listening to another character. This process of assessing the action onstage should begin in the wings, alongside the process of inhabiting the world of the character; weighing the tempo, the energy of the scene and the responsiveness of the audience in readiness to join the action.

Craft

Throughout rehearsals, and especially stage rehearsals, you will have carried an awareness of how to use the space to best convey the story to the audience. Remind yourself of the factors we looked at in Chapter 8: Rehearsals:

---

[5] Stanislavski, K. (1999) *Building a Charcter*. Translated by E. R. Hapgood. London: Eyre Methuen, p. 152.
[6] *The Magic Flute*, Act One, Finale.

- Embrace the space, rather than pushing.
- Find ideas from out front, the auditorium of the theatre becoming, at once, a literal fourth wall and a playground for your imagination.
- Raise your eye level to allow the audience to access your ideas.
- Attune yourself to the audience: allow this connection. If you are in a comedy, it is absolutely critical that you, the other performers and the conductor are playing the scene *with* the audience. This does not mean playing up to them but allowing space for their response and adjusting the tempo and rhythm of the scene accordingly.

Troubleshooting

Tension, and its physical and psychological manifestations, can return onstage. This is what to bear in mind:

- That first moment onstage can sometimes be disorienting: there is a lot of information to take in. As you enter, just focus on one specific object or idea to root you in the space.
- If you begin to feel self-conscious, return to this object or idea; it is the *camera out* exercise in Exercise: The Camera, p. 26. The answers to most matters, in performance, lie outside you: throw your focus on your partner, an object in the space, the images projected by your mind's eye.
- You can 'Drop the anchor', in a beat, onstage. You need to have worked it up over time. It can instantly ground you and bring a sense of belonging to the space.
- Things will go wrong; it is live performance. React to these changes in character. Do not block or ignore them but find a way of incorporating them into the action. If a chair breaks, your character should respond to it. The response might be to blame the chair, or the person that gave them the chair, or to attempt to hide the broken chair from another character.

After the Perfomance

Each performance is an opportunity to continue to develop your character; you will always know your character, and their world, better at the end of a run of performances than at the beginning.

Continue your work on building character by:

- analysing your performance for yourself. The next day, find time to track through the whole opera and honestly assess what happened through the previous performance. If something felt unsatisfying then consider why; how can you engage with your process to resolve it? Discuss this with your fellow performers, the conductor and director.
- remembering that you cannot simply repeat a performance if it felt right. You can analyse what you were engaged with at the time, technically and imaginatively, but

you must take this and continue to be open to new possibilities in the next performance. Otherwise, the Objective will shift to recapturing something from the past, rather than responding to your character in the present.

- being open to the notes of the conductor and director; they will be responding to the information the audience has given them and aiming to help to clarify the storytelling. The work does not finish after the first performance.

- approaching feedback from those outside the production with caution. If necessary talk to the director or conductor about any feedback that negatively affects you or your thoughts about the work. Reviews are best avoided; whether good or bad they can have an effect on your performance which is not usually helpful. Sometimes they are unavoidable. As with any advice from outside the production, treat the comments with caution. The printed word can carry unwarranted importance; it is just one person's view, motivated by a range of possible factors. If any reviews highlight areas of concern, continue a dialogue with the conductor, director or their assistants.

EMOTION IN PERFORMANCE: SUZANNE MURPHY[7]

Suzanne Murphy is a soprano who has worked closely with Welsh National Opera, singing roles ranging from Adina in *L'Elisir d'amore*, to Madame Lidoine in *Dialogues of the Carmelites* and the title roles in *Tosca*, *Norma*, *Lucia di Lammermoor*, *Fanciulla del West* and *Fidelio*. She has also sung major roles with English National Opera, Opera North and Scottish Opera and around the world.

When I was singing Violetta in La Traviata I kept breaking down when I was rehearsing. I couldn't get to the end of the scene because I was crying so much. I had to do the final scene over and over; by rehearsing it a number of times it allowed the emotion – my response to what was happening – to sit a little deeper. I felt it in my stomach rather than on my voice.

By the time you get to performance you are a channel, from the music to the audience. The performance is for the audience's emotions – you don't have to do too much emoting and mustn't seek to do so!

A little while ago I had to sing in front of my teacher; a recital in celebration of her ninetieth birthday. When I was thinking about it and rehearsing it, I couldn't help but get emotional! So I asked myself, how do I control this emotion to allow myself to sing? I reframed the event in order not to break down. I created a story about why I was here, and what the event was, that help me to see it in a slightly different way. I wrote a different story.

---

[7] Interview, Cardiff, 2017.

11 Auditions

WHAT ARE YOUR CONCERNS ABOUT AUDITIONS?

- *How do I hold onto the character and not just worry about my singing, the panel and how I look?*
- *In performances that are non-stage based, auditions especially, my movements become quite stiff – how can I develop the flexibility I have onstage when in an audition?*
- *How do I physicalise my ideas in an audition and recital?*

An audition is an opportunity for the opera company to hear and see your suitability for a role, and an opportunity for you to introduce yourself and demonstrate your abilities and your potential, both for the role and as a collaborator. Auditions will generally fall into one of two categories: the general audition or the role audition. The general audition will be, perhaps, a first introduction to the company and a chance for them to consider you for a range of different repertoire for some time in the near to mid-future. They will be considering where you are vocally, your technique, the aptness of the voice for their theatre, how you engage with and present character, how you move, how you might work alongside other singers, and how you might collaborate with a creative team.

The role audition is where the panel will be assessing your suitability for a specific role. Alongside all other considerations they will be considering how your voice balances with other cast members, how you look (for the part and alongside the other singers) and how adaptable you are.

It is not a perfect process. The amount of time that both sides have to convey and receive information is limited. Any judgement the panel make will be based upon a myriad of different factors and influenced by anything from the time in which you go into an audition, to the conversations between the panel.

It can be uncomfortable being so closely scrutinised and can often feel as though you have no control over the situation. However, you can develop your audition technique and take some ownership of the process through preparation.

Preparation

A call to audition can come at any moment and it will help to be ready for that moment. It is easy to feel unprepared, especially if you have not recently been in rehearsals creating a role. When rehearsing a role, you are fully engaged with your voice and the process of creating character. In the time between roles, it is also important to remain engaged with all parts of your craft. You may continue to work with your vocal coach. Opera Works singers set up various Facebook pages with conversations about how they were exploring their new tools, or debates about performances they had seen at the Coliseum. Others would arrange trips, not only to the opera, but to dance, theatre and exhibitions. A dialogue with others provides fuel for your creative journey and a sense of readiness when an audition arrives.

Choice of Repertoire

You should have a portfolio of about six to eight arias ready at any one time. Usually a company will ask for two or three in contrasting styles and languages, so you do not need to bring your whole portfolio; for example, a contemporary piece may not be relevant to a particular company, or for the role you are auditioning for. Have a range of arias ready that are solidly in your voice, repertoire and mind. Therefore, if you are asked to audition at very short notice, you will be ready.

If you are in a general audition you will, more than likely, be able to choose which aria you begin with. If you are singing for a specific role then you will probably be asked to begin with an aria that character sings or, at least, from the same repertoire. In choosing your arias select those that fit you; those that are within your capabilities vocally and dramatically. Additionally, consider who you are, and where you are at, as an artist; and, therefore, what *type* of role a company might see you for. This requires a good degree of honesty. There is no point auditioning with Wagner, however much you see yourself as Brünhilde, if your voice is still relatively light. Similarly, you may have sung Marcellina in a college production of *The Marriage of Figaro* but it is unlikely that a professional company will consider you for such a role if you are still in your early twenties. Listening to feedback from coaches, conductors and directors is vital when making these decisions. Think about the length of the aria; time in auditions is often limited and it might be better to give the panel the opportunity to hear and see you sing two shorter contrasting arias than one very long one. Avoid long play-ins or interludes, or make clear workable cuts to them. It is, however, useful to be able to offer arias that have recitative preceding them; a panel will be able to judge much about your psychological engagement with a character through the way you approach recit. Most importantly, be well prepared and avoid, where possible, auditioning with a piece you have only just learnt.

Investigating the Aria

The first question you should ask yourself, having chosen an aria to audition with, is 'What is it that I wish to convey about the character with this aria?' This places a creative pursuit at the centre of the audition process and stops it from becoming about all about you and the panel.

When preparing the arias, remind yourself of the process of preparing and rehearsing arias detailed in Chapters 8 and 9. Alongside this, consider the following:

- Know the whole opera! This is the most obvious way to get to know an aria. The music and libretto give you a wealth of information for free, and yet I have lost count of the number of times in an audition a singer has told me that they like the aria but have no idea what the opera is about.

- Use the Given Circumstances to direct your interpretation of the aria.[1] Create an incredibly detailed idea of what has just happened, what you can see, what the weather is like, what time of day it is, what the light is like, what the other characters look like, what is behind you, what surface you are standing on, what is above you, etc.

  The more detail, the more you can invest in the moment of the audition, the less likely you are to be drawn into hopeless considerations about what the panel are thinking. Your imagination needs to play harder without the inspiration of other people.

- Then place your Objective at the centre of this scene. Connect this to your Through-Line and Super-Objective.

- Plot through the journey of the aria. How do you imagine the other characters respond to your actions? How do you react in return? Do you imagine the other characters move at any point? Ideally, in preparation, play the scene with somebody else.

- When creating this scene in your mind's eye, make decisions that result in your character *not* having to move around the space; this can be distracting in an audition.

- In an audition you need to be able to access the world of your character incredibly quickly. Once you have decided upon your Given Circumstances and constructed a reality in your mind's eye, as an exercise, close your eyes and locate yourself in the world. On a breath in, open your eyes and imagine transporting yourself to within the bubble of this reality. Locate exactly where everything is around you, including the character you are singing to.

- If this imaginative bubble was a colour, what colour would it be? If it had a texture, what texture? What smell? What temperature?

  Load these sensory stimuli into your imaginative bubble before an audition; you might then find it swifter to access the world of the character in an audition.

- Alternatively, what if, through your aria, you were singing in response to abstract ideas or images travelling on a stream towards you? Or, a storyboard of images tracking across an imaginary projected cinema screen on the horizon line? Or, shifting memories that are projected in 3rd Circle and then absorbed in 1st Circle?[2]

- Be clear with where your points of focus, or targets, are and your changing attitude to them. Try the Exercise: Concretising Thought[3] to help develop relationships with your targets.

Movement

Wherever your audition is held, a small rehearsal room or the main stage of the theatre, it is generally considered best not to move around the space too much in an audition. Certainly,

---

[1] Pamina, No. 17 Aria, 'Now I know'/'Ach ich fühls'.
[2] The Three Circles, p. 95.
[3] Chapter 6: Words and Music in Action, p. 226.

do not enact the 'blocking' or 'staging' from a previous production. It is best to think about preparing to *respond* to your imagined world within the confines of your kinesphere: a step forward or back is fine.

Reduce the scale of your physicalised character; look at the Physical Essence exercise, p. 206. There is a tendency in auditions (and onstage) to over-use hand gestures; you do not need to explain your Objectives. Pursuing Objectives, in connection with your Targets, will release you from demonstrating. Actioning an aria can help to keep the ideas alive and active within the body.

If you are auditioning in a larger space you will need to consider how you energise your movement whilst still remaining, more or less, within your kinesphere. The images in your mind's eye will fill the auditorium. See the tools in Chapter 8.

Create a Psychological Gesture[4] for each aria; it is a quick way to physically re-engage with the character before entering the audition.

Professional Engagement

If you are preparing for a general audition, get to know a little about the company: the repertoire they stage, any recent productions and the teams they work with. If you are auditioning for a specific role: research the character, the opera and the composer. If you can find out who will be at the audition, do a little research into them. This will help give you a sense of ownership over the process.

CV

The company will probably already have a copy of your CV that you will have emailed previously but have a couple of extra copies with you to distribute at the beginning of the audition should the panel need any additional copies.

The CV should be there to give the panel quick, easily accessible information about you in a way that does not detract from what you are doing in the audition. They will not have time to read all the CV; keep it clear, clean and concise. Avoid clutter, diverse fonts and confusing information.

Points to remember and include when creating your CV:

- keep it to one page
- your name, voice type and contact information (including website) should be located at the top
- where you have trained and who you are studying with (if appropriate)
- what roles you have done and where. Alongside this, possibly the conductor and director of each project. Present this positively; the eye wants to be drawn to the more important roles you have performed
- any prizes and additional skills in separate sections

---

[4] Exercise: Psychological Gesture, p. 85.

- avoid any information that is conflicting (if you stopped singing mezzo roles five years ago, these credits are going to be confusing)

- a simple photo (a headshot, no soft focus or big frocks!) within the body of the CV. Do not attach a separate photo.

What to Wear

This is, frankly, a minefield! Everybody I have worked with on audition panels seems to have a slightly different idea as to what is 'appropriate'. As a director wanting to explore character, however briefly in an audition, my priority is that the singer wears something they feel comfortable to move in. However, other panellists seem to have strong views as to the exact length of a skirt and cut of a suit, to the nearest centimetre; hopefully, this kind of prescription is becoming less common.

When considering what to wear, it would be fine to ask the company about the formality of the audition at the time they offer you the audition. Different companies, in different territories, will have different views. Do a little research, if you can, to judge if certain places will frown if you do not make an appearance in a full ball gown or suit. My advice is to err on the side of simplicity: wear something that you feel comfortable to move in but that is also a little smart. Avoid ripped jeans and very high heels and anything else that falls into these categories.

It is useful to think about the role you might be auditioning for. For example, if you are auditioning for Cherubino or another 'trouser role', wear trousers. If it is a general audition, wear something that expresses who you are and the kind of role you might be cast in.

Preparing 'You'

At Opera Works we worked with actor, director and charisma-coach Alex Maclaren.[5] Alex works all over the world training everyone from CEOs of international companies to politicians and singers, helping them to embody charismatic behaviour. The work is about presenting the best side of yourself. Alex suggests thinking about this as creating a character remarkably similar to yourself to take into the audition room; this version of yourself is just more confident, composed and ready to communicate. Here are some pointers:

- Slow down. Charismatic people aren't in a rush. Take time to consider your replies and move smoothly and deliberately.

- Either be still, or move with purpose. Arrive where you want to be and stop. Avoid shifting from foot to foot.

- Make clear, decisive gestures rather than making small repetitive movements. Keep your hands in view and avoid touching your face.

- Smile freely. Be warm and empathetic. Avoid being defensive.

- Enjoy eye contact without it becoming a prolonged, intimidating stare.

---

[5] Alex Maclaren leads the London-based theatre company The Spontaneity Shop.

- Take up the space around you, without invading others' space.

- Hold your head stiller than normal.

- Mount an agreement, not an argument. If you can't agree with the person you're talking to, validate their point of view.

Practise these charismatic behaviours in different environments, so that they become habitual: at home, in the pub, at work. Remember, you are still *you*; these behaviours simply highlight the best of you.

Nerves can be debilitating if not kept under control. Look at the strategies in Chapter 10: Performance, especially Exercise: Dropping the Anchor, p. 293.

The duality of a performer – simultaneously in character whilst assessing the performance – is necessary when performing a role. However, in auditions the Inner Critic can often be turned to full volume. Counter this by focusing your attention out into the room (remind yourself of the idea of having your camera out[6]) and carry in your thoughts the imaginative realities of operas you are about to enter.

The Composition of an Audition

Arrival

Arrive at least ten to fifteen minutes before your allotted audition time. Employ the charismatic behaviours before entering the building. There might not be a room to warm up in, in which case, utilise the toilets. This should include a physical warm-up; look at Chapter 8 for the exercises which best suit you. Use this time as an opportunity to:

- Drop the Anchor

- revisit the bubble of Given Circumstances

- re-engage in your Scene Objective

- enact your Psychological Gesture.

You could do this for the each of the arias you will be offering to the panel in the audition room.

The Introduction

The audition begins before you even enter the room to meet the panel. The person who will meet you and convey you to the room is an important member of the team and will often be asked their opinion of auditionees by the panel. Be friendly and engaged whilst remaining focused on your preparation.

- Walk into the room with your camera out; notice details about the panel. Embody charismatic behaviours; smile, be assured, ready and positive.

---

[6] Exercise: The Camera, p. 26.

- If you have a CV, place it down on the panel's table and take a couple of steps back.

- Do not shake hands unless they move to do so. Stop walking before speaking. Introduce yourself, warmly, whilst maintaining steady eye contact.

- If it is a general audition just state the aria that you would like to begin with:

  'I'd like to begin with Pamina's aria from *The Magic Flute,* "Ach ich fühls"'.

- You can then tell the panel of the other arias you have brought after you have sung this first aria. It is a good idea, even if you are singing the aria in English, to give the original title of the aria. It is also worth naming the composer, before the title of the opera, for less well-known repertoire.

- If you have been asked to prepare for a particular role, suggest beginning with this aria but also mention the other arias you have with you: 'I've brought Pamina's aria from *The Magic Flute,* "Ach ich fühls". I also have, etc'.

- The panel might suggest you include a cut. If you have brought a Handel da capo aria, it is wise to mention this when you introduce the aria and to ask the panel if they would like you to cut it and, if so, where. If they don't have a suggestion, be ready to make your own.

- By having in mind what you would like to do, or by being ready to accept their suggestion without hesitation, you reassure a panel that you know what you are doing. If you know your own mind then there is no need to rush.

The Panel

It is important to remember that the panel will also be feeling a certain amount of pressure during auditions. They will want to make the right casting decisions; ultimately, you are potentially the one who will be delivering their interpretation to the audience. Even if it does not necessarily feel like it, most panels are on your side and will want you to do well. They might be tired, or involved in an internal debate about the direction casting should take, but they will genuinely be hoping that you will be right for the part they are seeking to cast. If they make judgements about the pieces you are presenting, do not apologise for what you are offering. I worked with a casting director who would sigh heavily whenever a Menotti aria was offered; and another who delighted in informing the singer that they were the fifth person to offer 'Quando me'n vo'. Do not worry about it; you cannot anticipate their response.

During Opera Works we would improvise an audition scenario with Alex Maclaren. The singers gleefully took up the various roles of the panel and performed detailed impersonations of a hybrid of various producers, casting directors, conductors and directors. Alex would usually give the singer auditioning a private instruction: imagine that you are a lion but instead of eating the panel, you are going to take care of them. It seemed to work.

If ever you get the opportunity to be part of a panel, take it. It is fascinating to see how auditionees sometimes present themselves and I have no doubt you would find it immensely instructive.

The Répétiteur

- Once you have spoken with the panel, head over to the répétiteur: your collaborator for the next ten minutes. Do not walk away from the panel too quickly; I have noticed that this journey can often carry the sense of 'Thank goodness, I've escaped!'
- Be clear, precise and friendly with the pianist. If the panel have suggested making a cut in your aria, point out where this is on the score. You might mention your desired tempo.
- You need to make this the briefest of talks, so ensure your score is clearly marked up. Avoid bringing scores covered in scribbles or marked with breaths and ornaments that you do not do. Do not bring huge heavy scores or loose sheets. Your music should be cleanly stuck together and easy to manage.

Before You Sing

- Take a position a step or two away from the piano.
- The time it takes to walk to this position is yours. Take your time and gather the information from your Given Circumstances bubble that you have created in preparation.
- When you arrive at the spot, root your feet. Breathe deeply and, as you do so, allow all the images in your mind's eye to fill the room; enter the character's world. This might be the moment you recall the sensory information of your bubble. As you release your breath, engage with your Objective.
- Turn to the répétiteur and give them a simple head nod as a signal you are ready. Stay in character.

The Aria

- Find your points of focus in the space. See the Targets and engage with them.
- You will rarely be invited to sing to the panel. When preparing for your audition, place the Targets in your aria, generally, just above the head level at which the panel will be sitting. This means you will not risk staring directly at them but will still be clearly seen.
- Keep engaged with your imaginative reality. If your imaginary partner is the point of focus, keep them in sight. Do they move? You will have considered this in preparation.
- Most importantly: pursue your Objectives.
- Do not be distracted by the panel if they talk or look through your CV. The more you engage with the images in your mind's eye, the less you will think about the panel.

The Second Aria

You will not always be asked for a second aria; this is nothing to worry about and could be for a multitude of reasons.

- After you have finished your first aria, hold the thought for a moment after the end of the music. Then take half a step back and leave your character's world.
- The panel will usually guide you by suggesting what they would like to hear. If they do not, simply ask: 'Would you like to hear a second aria?'
- They will probably make a choice from the repertoire you have offered. If they offer you the choice, it is a good idea to present something musically and dramatically contrasting from the first aria.
- If you need to return to the répétiteur, do so briefly and concisely. If not, take a moment to look down and enter the new bubble of this second character. See the world of the character as you breathe in and look up. As you breathe out, engage the Objective.
- Signal, again, to the répétiteur when you are ready to begin, whilst remaining in character.

NOTE:

- As with all live performances things do, occasionally, go wrong: memory lapses happen, or the tempo set by the répétiteur is inaccurate, etc. Do not worry about it; *how* you deal with it will say more to the panel than what actually happened. Do not blame anyone: simply stop, apologise and ask for a moment, speak to the répétiteur or take a moment to compose yourself, thank the panel, and continue your aria (do not go all the way back to the beginning of your aria if you are half-way through but, instead, find a good place to pick it up from).
- The panel might stop you at any point during the audition. Do not act surprised and do not take it personally. This can happen for a wide range of reasons.

The End

- At the end of your second aria, again, hold the thought for a couple of beats.
- Look to the panel, thank them, thank the répétiteur whilst collecting your music and exit confidently, without apology.
- Do not anticipate that the panel will want to talk to you afterwards. If they do, inhabit the charismatic behaviours.

Outside the Audition Room

- You are still auditioning! Do not talk too loudly or begin a post-audition analysis of your performance.
- Politely thank the person who has met you, gather your stuff and leave.

Analysis and Follow-Up

- The outcome of any audition is out of your hands. The panel will have an inordinate number of factors to balance and consider. The final decision can often be quite arbitrary and relate to who seems to best fit with another performer.

- It is worth asking for feedback, especially if you know or trust the opinion of someone on the panel. However, it is rare that companies have the resources to offer feedback.

Take a moment, a couple of hours after the heat of the audition, to go through and note down how you felt you presented yourself and your arias. In addition, note any comments you received in the room.

Keeping it Alive

You face similar challenges keeping your audition repertoire alive and fresh as you face when performing in a long run of an opera.

- Use different Points of Concentration when warming up outside the audition room.
- Try some of the exercises in Chapter 6: Words and Music in Action to re-enliven your arias.
- Play your aria opposite someone; each time you do, you will learn something new.

Websites

Websites and social media are a tremendous professional tool. Just remember that they are a *professional* tool and aim to present the side of yourself you would like prospective employers and colleagues to see.

Your website should:

- be easy to navigate.
- not contain too much information; keep text concise and to the point. Similar to your CV, ensure you do not include contradictory or irrelevant information.
- be regularly updated: especially the biography section. If you have a news or diary tab, this can be also useful for casting directors looking to solve a last-minute emergency but, again, it must be kept up to date.
- feature professional media. Photos: avoid big frocks, soft focus or personal and family shots. Video and audio: companies will most likely want to hear how you sound now but, if you do feature it, ensure it is simply and clearly presented. Shaky recordings, or those from a long time ago, are not so useful.
- get feedback from trusted colleagues before launching your website.

CASTING DIRECTOR: SARAH PLAYFAIR

Sarah is a casting director and consultant and has worked with most of the major UK opera companies over a forty-year career. She was Director of Artistic Administration for over ten years at Glyndebourne Festival Opera. She regularly casts for Garsington Opera, Birmingham Opera Company and Tête à Tête. I wanted to draw on Sarah's extraordinary knowledge and experience of auditioning and casting young singers throughout the UK.

As a casting director, what do you want from an audition?

I think the worst thing in the world is auditioning and the second worst thing is listening to auditions. It is a nightmare! What am I looking for? I'm looking for a package. Initially, of course, we're looking for musicality but I think what I want to see is the *real* person. I am looking at that person to see if they are going to fit into whatever piece or company I'm looking for; this may be a more generic consideration or it may be quite specific. It may be that I've already cast someone in one of the roles; for example, I have cast a really good soprano who is rather short and I therefore can't be looking at a six-foot five tenor if that does not meet the needs of the production. Alternatively, I might be looking to balance vocal weight within an ensemble. There are an awful lot of things to consider and every time it's different.

Every audition we're approaching from a different angle, with different parameters, but as someone auditioning you can't know any of that. How can you? Unless you've been specifically briefed, how can you know what we're looking for? You can't try to second guess the audition panel; if you don't get the role, it may be for a reason that you can do nothing about.

When you audition singers for one project, are you also considering possible future projects?

Absolutely. It may be that a singer is not what we're looking for now: they just don't fit within the ensemble that we've already got together or the director, or conductor, might be thinking of this role in a certain way. However, it might well be that you keep this person in mind for something coming up, for another opera in the season.

As a singer, is it appropriate to ask if there's anything particular the company are looking for?

I think you can, depending upon where you are in the business. If you're a young singer, starting out, it might be more appropriate for an agent to ask on your behalf. If you're a young singer without an agent you can always ask the question but probably the answer will be that this is a general audition. If you've been specifically asked to come and audition for Zerlina, for example, it may well be that in the course of the audition you find out how the production will present the character. With most of the companies I work with – for a very specific role audition – the conductor or director will want to explore the character within the audition. We warn the singers in advance that this might be a mini working session. For example, they might ask you to sing the aria three times in different ways. What we want to see is what you can bring to the table; we usually don't start off with a rigid idea, there's always an element of flexibility.

And singers should bring this same flexibility to the audition process?

Absolutely. Be prepared to be flexible. Don't be thrown in an audition. I think the one thing you should come prepared for is *anything*! Bring more arias than are requested, in as wide a range as you can, so that if the panel say 'Have you got anything else?' you are ready to make an offer. I think always be overprepared for an audition.

Expect to be stopped in the middle of an aria and know how to behave if you are. An absolute must, if you're doing a da capo aria, is to introduce your aria by saying that it's a da capo aria and to immediately ask if they'd like you to cut and, if so, how. Have in your mind what you'd like to do if they say, 'you choose'.

You must be balanced and show yourself. Don't try to be something you're not because then you hide your own charisma or stage presence.

Auditions are not perfect. There are some people who are brilliant at auditions and not very good in performance, but many more who struggle in auditions and are really good in performance. It's a very unsatisfactory way of choosing but it's all we have. We can't get to see everyone in every performance. And when we see someone onstage it may not relate to what we want them to be doing.

What is your advice for preparing for an audition?

As a freelance singer you always have to be ready. You may get a call from a company who have just lost a singer and need you to come in at 11 am the next morning. If you're not quite ready, you've lost it.

Use the time well when you're looking for work; this is a good time to be preparing your audition arias. Don't get into a rut with your aria; if, for example, you have been singing Figaro's arias since you were an undergraduate and are still singing them the same way out in the profession, think how you can develop them. Again, it's about remaining flexible and musically and dramatically engaged. Every singer should be constantly developing the arias they have been working on.

Alongside this, singers need to be expanding their minds in other ways: going to the theatre, a gallery, reading, going to opera. It will, no doubt, inform how you then approach your aria in auditions; listen to other singers, conductors, orchestras, watch actors, do workshops in acting and improvisation.[7]

VOCAL COACH: JANE ROBINSON

Jane is Head of Training at ENO and has spent much time on audition panels as co-Director of ENO Opera Works and leading the ENO Harewood Artist's Programme.

What should singers consider when preparing for an audition?

I think singers need to choose arias that are really absolutely right for them: vocally and dramatically. And then they need to be really prepared with a performance; they've got to be ready to stand there and create the essence of a full performance around them. The best auditions that I've seen are those where you believe there's a production all around them. The performance might be physically reduced but they've got the same level of engagement of thought as they would if they were standing on stage. They've snapped into another world, they're seeing all those images, and they're really relating to the other characters: even though there's no one there.

You, the singer, have to give the panel confidence that you can give a performance. You have to have done the work before you get the job; so be as completely prepared as you can. This will help you feel confident. This preparation is huge because it's such a difficult environment in an audition room. You have to create your *own* process in order to do this. So, you need a toolbox and, of course, this extends into the rehearsal room. You might arrive on day one and be working with the director who says 'over to you'. When I worked with the director Peter Hall, at Glyndebourne, he used to say 'Well, show me something. Do something.'

---

[7] Many theatre companies run workshops for actors, alongside the work they are making. Be sure to check their websites. In the UK, The Actor's Centre offers a full range of workshops year-round. It is an incredibly important resource to help you to continue to build your skills; see www.actorscentre.co.uk.

Part Three Interviews

Opera is the result of an incredible variety of collaborations. As a singer, at the heart of the creative process, you will work most closely with the conductor, director and other singers. In this section we return to our exploration of rehearsals, and performance, with a series of conversations with those primary collaborators. We talk to conductors about how to create character with reference to a range of different operatic repertoire; to directors on their various approaches to working with singers in the rehearsal room; and finally, to singers, at various stages of their careers, about the way in which they approach creating and performing roles. Throughout the conversations we take numerous diversions to explore the reasons for each artist's passion for opera, in the hope that their reflections prompt you to further explore your relationship with the form.

12 Repertoire

- EARLY MUSIC: CHRISTIAN CURNYN
- MOZART: JANE GLOVER
- BEL CANTO: DAVID PARRY
- VERDI: CARLO RIZZI
- TWENTIETH CENTURY: WYN DAVIES
- NEW OPERA: JONATHAN DOVE

Different repertoire brings with it a unique set of challenges when creating character and a diverse range of approaches from those practitioners who work, most often, with the operas of particular composers.

Over the next chapter we explore the work of different conductors, specialising in different repertoire, in the rehearsal room and in the pit. The chapter ends with a conversation with composer Jonathan Dove about the process of composition and his collaboration with singers.

EARLY MUSIC: CHRISTIAN CURNYN

Christian Curnyn founded the Early Opera Company in 1994. Since then the company has produced operas throughout the UK and formed a close association with the Royal Opera House, creating work in smaller theatres. Christian has a strong association with ENO, having conducted a range of Handel, Purcell and Rameau operas for the company. He worked closely with ENO Opera Works and brought great insight to how to approach the challenges of baroque repertoire; I asked him to elaborate on that work here.

I'd like to start by asking: what initially drew you to opera?

When I was about sixteen I started to go to the Edinburgh Festival and it was at the time the Wooster Group and Pina Bausch were doing lots there. Theatrically this work really intrigued me and, at that time, I'd seen very little opera that engaged me in the same way. When I moved to London I saw David Alden's production of *Ariodante* at ENO which just blew me away; I'd finally seen the sort of theatre, of an abstract nature but in an operatic form, that really excited me. That's when I decided what I wanted to do and I set up the Early Opera Company.

And what was it about early opera that particularly excited you?

Firstly, I just liked the sound of the music and loved the formality of it. I find what can happen within those constraints really appealing. Many of Handel's operas detail a specific location – for example, Rodelinda is Queen of Lombardy – but they're not about the places that they're set, they are about the emotions and the interactions between the characters. So they are an open book for a director and conductor as there are so many different ways of doing these operas; they're not constrained by a later aesthetic.

What are the particular challenges of baroque opera for singers?

Nearly all the characters have to sing incredibly difficult music. Singers are like athletes but, rather than a shot-putt Puccini soprano, Handel requires a more agile type of performer: a gymnast. You have to have a fragility combined with incredibly strong technique; there's something so precise, so filigree about the ornamentation. The risk is it's easy to get lost, which is why I think Actioning works very well in this music; it helps to focus you.

With an opera written before Handel by, for example, Monteverdi, or from after, such as *La Bohème*, characters tend to sing something directly to another character; they generally don't repeat words. With Handel the same words are repeated over and over and over again, so you have to find a reason why you sing it all those times and why you sing it differently each time. You can Action *La Bohème* very easily because it's very plain text and through composed, whereas Handel's operas need to be given a context, which I think is the job of both the director and the singer.

What preparation should a singer do before productions rehearsals?

First of all, learn the notes and know it from memory – that's very important – but with the flexibility of knowing that things may change and with room for growth throughout rehearsals.

When getting to know the music, try not to listen to it from other recordings, even if that means employing a pianist and recording them playing it on the piano for you. The music needs to become yours, rather than learning it through hearing somebody else, or even singing along to somebody else, which can be a disaster. The more coaching, from the right coaches, the better.

I would suggest finding out beforehand what the conductor and director would like regarding ornaments. If a conductor is happy to leave them to you, then arrive, again, with the flexibility to change something that might not work.

Spending time getting to know the character and investigating what's going on in the opera, as you prepare a role, helps you remain flexible; you'll become aware of the possibilities that lie within a role.

What's the best way for a young singer to approach the music call?

I'm not a great fan of music calls. If I do them I tend to focus on recitative, in order to help them become fluid, but I don't like to impose a reading. If I were to say 'now, I think you should take more time over that word' it would be like giving a line reading to an actor; it would simply be telling the singer what to do. There's a full rehearsal process to explore the opera, however, it's important that the director realises that the conductor needs to feed into this process.

How should a singer approach production rehearsals?

I would say there needs to be a dialogue in the rehearsal room. It's important for everyone to sit around a table and discuss what's happening. If the singers can have explored possible Actions before rehearsals begin, rather than analysing everything for the first time in rehearsals, it can help make the process quicker. The important thing is to come into rehearsal room without expectations – good or bad – and to let yourself commit to what's happening. It's important you don't censor yourself.

Singing is such an unreal thing – it's *other worldly* – and so you'll have to get used to singing the role. It's important not to mark all the time in rehearsals. Of course, it is possible to over-sing but it's important to learn how to pace yourself through rehearsals. The risk is that you get to the end of rehearsals and realise you've not sung through large sections of the opera. Singing is all-consuming and it can easily eat up all the other work you've been doing; you have to somehow make space for that other work in your head.

You've spoken about how important it is to Action an aria; what else should a singer do when looking at Handel arias in rehearsals?

I always ask less experienced singers to write out the whole text of their aria. Written out on a sheet of paper it looks like a poem; suddenly, it's not as abstract as when you were singing it with all the notes.

Then, look at the rhetoric; you can cut a Handel aria into segments. You have the opening introduction (the first A section), the middle argument (the B section), and then the conclusion (the second A section); within each of these you can break the aria into smaller sections.

It's interesting to look at which part of the sentence, or which certain word, is repeated in an A section; this offers you different choices. The music can underline certain words in a repeated phrase; look, for example, at how Handel turns a phrase around when he sets it to music.

The B section tends to be just one very clear thought: the lynchpin. It's important to ask how the B section informs the character's thoughts when returning to the A section; note that the B section often begins with 'but' and therefore presents an alternative argument.

It requires a lot of preparation but, once you've done this, you can use the thoughts as a kind of collage in rehearsals, cutting them out and trying them in different orders throughout the aria. This approach can help construct an inner monologue through the aria; it requires an imaginative engagement but reveals a wealth of possibilities.

The next step is to see how the ornaments affect the da capo. They are not just there to show off; a big cadenza needs to reflect some emotional change. Many singers tend to over ornament, so I'll often ask them to simplify them, but they are very personal to a singer.

Are ornaments infused with a sense of the character within the context of the production?

They absolutely should be. For example, take appoggiaturas. I'm not a great fan of them a lot of the time but of course they have a function: the softening of the line. However, you don't want the line softened by somebody who's a tyrant, unless you want to see them in a different light. For example, at the end of *Rodelinda*, when Grimoaldo realises he's defeated, it may be that using ornaments to soften him – very different ornaments from those he might use at the beginning of the opera – will reveal a different side to him. The character, at every moment, is on a journey and they should have somehow changed through the aria. I think all ornaments need to help highlight what's happening emotionally in the scene.

There are few duets and ensembles in Handel operas, but do they pose any particular challenges?

It's important to pull ensembles apart by Actioning them to each other. What are you trying to say to the other characters? Why are you repeating lines? Duets particularly benefit from Actioning; it's very easy to simply enjoy singing in thirds and to forget to connect with the other singer. As an exercise, if it's possible, it's useful to sing the other character's line. It gives you the other side of the argument and helps show you who you are in the other character's eyes.

Can you talk about how you work with singers on recitative?

Generally, there are two types of recitative: *accompanied*, which you find in Monteverdi and Cavalli, and *secco*, the dry recitatives you find in Handel.

The dry recit in Handel is very much just speech and whenever I do them I always ask the singers to speak the text first. I follow that by asking the singers to speak the text with the chords underneath; you have to pace it and the chords add certain boundaries. Then I might ask them to sing all the recit on one note and encourage them to find natural inflections; the pitch remains the same but the rhythms change and the muscles required for voice production are engaged.

Looking at Monteverdi recits, in a recent production of *The Return of Ulysses (Il ritorno d'Ulisse in patria)*, as an exercise, I asked the singers first to speak the text and then to declaim the text. The singer has to negotiate the way the recit goes into little arias – arioso – and then into full aria. In the arioso I asked the singers to continue speaking but to *think* about singing and then in the aria to actually sing. It helped separate the different sections; whenever the characters needed more space for their thoughts, they broke into singing.

How do you approach the Sitzprobe?

I find it odd when people dress up for the Sitz and everyone applauds at the end of each aria. I tend to treat a Sitz, not as the moment where everything comes together and you don't have to worry about the staging, but rather as two more orchestral rehearsals. There's nothing hallowed about it and I find simply treating it as an additional orchestra rehearsal stops the singers from feeling like they have to give a 'performance' too early on; there is a risk of undoing so much good work. It can't all be about the voice. I've had singers who have sung very well in rehearsals – their work is imbued with a sense of character and clear thoughts – and then in the Sitz it becomes a totally different opera; they are singing twice as loud and twice as fast! It's useful to consider the situation of the character in the Sitz so that it remains a rehearsal.

It is fantastic to open the dialogue between the singers and the orchestra. In baroque music the orchestra is the motor, a rhythm section supporting the action; you get a sense of the energy and of the rhythmic pulse. It's important for the singers to remember that the orchestra will be in the pit during performance; so they shouldn't try to match the volume of the orchestra in the Sitz.

Any other thoughts for the young singer?

Yes! Firstly, in Monteverdi operas certain lines are improvised in the orchestra; they aren't scored. I've never yet had a singer ask 'Do you think maybe I could have a lute copying me here?' or 'I'd prefer the harpsichord in this section. I think it's the right kind of sound for this moment' or 'I think the continuo needs to be more aggressive at this point'; the orchestration is all very flexible and that dialogue would be exciting.

Secondly, I think it's really important that young singers go to see opera. When I taught in conservatoires I was always absolutely staggered: I would say, 'I went to see this amazing performance at ENO', and no one had ever seen it. Almost as important as seeing opera is to go to see other art forms: get cheap tickets at the National Theatre, see dance at Sadler's Wells, wander around the National Gallery.

MOZART: JANE GLOVER

Jane Glover has conducted in major opera houses around the world. She was Director of Opera at the Royal Academy of Music from 2009 to 2016 and is currently Music Director of Chicago's Music of the Baroque. Jane has a long association with Mozart's operas: she was the Music Director of the London Mozart Players from 1984 to 1991 and her book *Mozart's Women* (2005) was nominated for both the Samuel Johnson Prize and the Whitbread Prize for Non-Fiction. I wanted to focus specifically on her experience of conducting Mozart's operas.

What excites you about opera?

I'm just as excited about opera now as I was when I started. As a child I was passionate about the theatre and music and it was logical that I would therefore move into opera where everything comes together. When all the stars are lined up, it is an art form where the total exceeds the sum of the parts. It doesn't always happen by any means. In the eternal triangle of drama, plus music, plus visual presentation at various stages in music history one of the three has been overemphasised at the expense of the others. When they do come into total parity of focus, the results are miraculous.

The three Mozart/Da Ponte operas are perfect examples of that. You get a great librettist and a great composer who, whether they liked each other or not and I'm not sure they did, just hit it off artistically. The results are phenomenal.

We get that same total sympathy with Strauss and von Hofmannsthal and, if it's not completely sacrilegious to say it, with Gilbert and Sullivan. They work perfectly together. This is essential; on the one hand, it's to do with the setting of the words and, on the other, much more than this. Take Handel who, although he lived here for fifty years, never completely mastered the English language and yet if he made mistakes in it, which he often did, he absolutely never failed to communicate what the piece was about. He may have misunderstood the odd stress but he understood the importance of the text. There's an endless fascination in the relationship between words and music.

What is important for singers to look out for when creating character in Mozart's operas?

There are so many clues to draw the singer's attention to; they are on every page. They're almost always text driven, they start with Da Ponte, but they also come from what Mozart has done with the text. For instance, look at 'Dove sono i bei momenti' ('Where are those good times'), the great Countess Aria in Act Three, where she sings 'Ah! Se almen la mia costanza.... mi portasse una speranza, di cangiar l'ingrato cor!' (Ah! If only, at least, my faithfulness . . . could bring me the hope of changing that ungrateful heart!). This aria could have been set in the same vein as 'Porgi Amor' but Mozart chooses, instead, to use these words as a way of turning the character around, ending the scene – this 'To be, or not to be' moment for her – in a very different mood from the one in which she started the scene. He gave insight into the character that da Ponte had not. There are a lot of similar examples of Mozart taking a major decision on a character but that I think is one of the best.

There's also Susanna's last aria, 'Deh vieni, non tardar' ('Oh come, don't delay'), where she starts by play-acting – pretending to be waiting for the Count to annoy Figaro – and then half-way through the aria you realise she's telling the truth about what she feels for Figaro. Whether he realises that or not is another point. Something that starts out as play-acting turns into something unbelievably real, which makes it even more touching. One hooks onto these moments and allows oneself to be led by these two great geniuses of the theatre.

How do you start your work creating characters with singers?

In music calls in the first instance. Of course, one first has to make sure that the music is in the voice and is well memorised but when working on a production I love to have the director at the music calls, largely because there are so many decisions to make and particularly when discussing Mozart recitative. So much happens in these recits that I always want somebody else's input and it's wonderful to have the input of the director. In an ideal world the roles of the director and conductor are interchangeable, with no territory being guarded, and everybody walking the same path. Music decisions are based on dramatic criteria and vice versa.

What do you particularly focus on in Mozart recitatives?

The thing I always encourage students, and indeed fully grown professionals, to do is just to ignore note values. I do not want to hear rests and semiquavers and obedience to time signatures and notation. In recitative, notation is ultimately inadequate; it's merely mathematics and should be ignored. What we have to do is reverse the composer's process, and go back to the text and inflect that as naturally as possible. With recitative I get singers to speak it as much as possible, then they know how to sing it; you must release the text from the shackles of notation.

I also encourage singers to be different every time; not always to react in exactly the same way just because that's how it's written. It's important to actually take your time on a response; to be in the moment. When I left the Royal Academy of Music, my final exhortation to my students was 'remember, in recitative I don't want to hear you reciting, I want to hear you thinking'.

That goes for every performance of every opera?

Absolutely! And it's the same with ornamentation; that should be completely spontaneous and responsive to what's happening in that performance at that time.

You wouldn't necessarily set ornamentation?

No, not at all. It is very unusual, actually, to find someone who's prepared to do it differently night after night but one always aims for that. I know some very distinguished conductors who distribute cadenzas and ornamentation to singers before they've even met them, let alone heard them sing. That seems to me completely bonkers. I mean both Handel and Mozart, my two great gurus, would never write anything for anybody until they'd heard the voice. Mozart's great phrase is 'I like an aria to fit a singer like a well-cut suit of clothes.'[1] He saw himself as a tailor; he knew all about colour and texture and fabric and shape and what fitted that particular body. That's what he did with the voice and an aria.

Does this same approach to recit apply when exploring aria?

Yes, textual nuance has to be completely faithful to the character's intentions. Of course, you don't have nearly the same flexibility as you do with recitative, by definition the music is measured and accompanied. There are other things to take into consideration, like orchestration, the shape, the structure and so on. I am, however, looking for the central truth in the aria. Look at, for example, the arias of Konstanze in Mozart's *Die Entführung aus dem Serail*. They were written for a phenomenal singer, Caterina Cavalieri, but through all the vocal fireworks you have to find an emotional truth. It is there. So, one looks and identifies it and, through rehearsals, discovers how to show it. This will arise from an understanding of the situation of a character; a specific moment of truth might rest upon what's happened to a character in the last five minutes or over the last five years.

Would you have any advice for the singer when translating work from the studio onto the stage?

Hang onto everything! Don't lose that work. I would encourage them to listen: to the other singers, to the orchestra. Another of my exhortations is, 'always learn your orchestrations'; from the word go, know exactly what the orchestra is doing at all times. When the great Christine Goerke did her first Elektra, a role that she now sings all over the world, she went to every single orchestral rehearsal and sat quietly in the corner. There's a wealth of information in the orchestration.

BEL CANTO: DAVID PARRY

David has a long association with ENO and is an important advocate of opera in English; he conducted the Chandos recording of *The Marriage of Figaro* in Jeremy Sams's translation. He has also recorded a great number of Opera Rara's rare operas, mostly from the bel canto repertoire. As David was in the middle of rehearsals for *The Barber of Seville* when we spoke, it was this area of his work that I wanted to speak to him about. He began, however, by talking about his love of Verdi.

---

[1] Taken from a letter Mozart wrote to his father, 28 February 1778.

What initially excited you about opera?

The first performances I remember seeing are of *The Mikado*, when I was ten years old, in Liverpool. I remember crying when it stopped because I wanted it to go on forever. However, at school I saw opera as a rather vulgar idea; it was the most exquisite music but I'm not sure I connected it with a dramatic idea at that point. When I was at university I heard *Aida* live for the first time and that was viscerally exciting. Extreme emotions shown through music; I was hooked.

I think the world view of a composer is important. With Verdi, there are so many shades of grey that nothing is absolute and the level at which he explores human behaviour is extraordinary. His Shakespearean viewpoint really makes him, for me, the greatest composer that ever lived. Alongside this is his incredible melodic gift. That was what got me into opera; amazing melodies that tell you something, not necessarily in terms of a simple plot, but in terms of the characters' emotional journeys.

How does a singer seek to communicate a character's emotional journey?

The singer in performance has to play in the moment at all times – that's the essence of acting, really – and the notes on the page are only a guide; they are a formula. The piece is not what's on a piece of paper, it's what occurs in real time; that's the wonderful thing because it's always slightly different.

For example, at the moment I'm doing *The Barber of Seville*. I've conducted it more than a hundred times, in a variety of productions, and therefore, because I know it so well, I don't have to think about the technical demands of conducting it. This is fantastically liberating and means I can think about how to find a way, with these particular singers, of making it real for them. I can focus on helping them to realise the text in a way that is dramatically present; and by 'the text' I mean the *total* text. I don't separate the words from the music.

You need to think of recitative from operas written before the mid-nineteenth century as more like spoken theatre; it just happens to be on pitch. I ask singers to speak it through and to ignore whatever note values the composer has given the words if they go against how you would speak that line. You have to sing the right notes but if, for example, there's a rest in the middle of a clause, you can ignore it as it's just there to fill in the 4/4 bar.

How do you tend to steer the singers towards an understanding of what the music and words are telling us about who this character is?

It starts in music rehearsals but is a continuous process throughout rehearsals. What I'm doing is getting singers to feel how the total text works together and how it can be properly articulated. For example, in *Barber* that's about the choice of which words you will stress.

Early in rehearsals I see what the singer has to offer because I don't want to start with a preconceived idea of how they're going to sing it. I'm keen to establish an idea of the stylistic parameters of a performance, and that includes everything to do with musical and verbal phrasing, but all singers are individuals and will have different ideas of how to approach certain repertoire; I'm trying to pull it together so that it makes sense as one piece.

These pieces are written to have strong personal journeys, they are all strong characters. So, I'm also listening to what the singers offer in terms of how they see the character.

What is Rossini revealing about certain characters through the music?

He characterises through his music; when you hear Rosina's cavatina you know she is a clever, determined, good person through the melodies he gives her. The Count is romantic and idealistic and, again, this is revealed through his melodies.

I feel Rossini, alongside Mozart, is one of the early proto-feminists in opera; the women always come out on top in his comedies. There is also the recurring idea of people accepting who they are in love with, regardless of who they are. Of course, this is one of the central themes in Beaumarchais's plays; *Barber* and *Figaro*. I think Rossini is more interested in *Barber* because it concerns the idea that people are ultimately defined by their inner beauty. Those people who think Rossini is trivial are very wide of the mark.

Is the perception of Rossini's works being trivial due to idea that bel canto repertoire subjugates character in favour of a celebration of beautiful singing?

The point about bel canto is that it should be about extreme expression through the vocal line. The extreme technical demands that Rossini makes of singers are absolutely connected with the extreme emotion his characters are experiencing. Too often people forget about *why* it's written the way it is. Rossini pushes the ideas in the opera so far that his characters are on the edge. For example, in the finales of his operas it's practically impossible to sing at the speed with which it is meant to go but this brings an incredible intensity to the situation.

Rossini often messes with time in order to reveal the mechanics of the characters' thoughts. You have very naturalistic conversations in the recitative and then the *stretta* of the Act One finale in *Barber* goes into a weird world of craziness.

So, as a singer, you need an understanding of the how the conventions of the world might shift?

Everything initially has to come out of the reality of the character's situation. Rossini then translates these situations to very extreme theatrical and musical expressions. For example, in the Act One finale all the characters arrive at a place where everything's out of control but this has to be connected to their experiences in the piece up to that point.

The big danger when developing an understanding of the characters in this repertoire is that you simply repeat what's already been done; you've a memory of how it has been performed previously and so you don't go back and examine the score. It's very useful to do new, or non-repertoire, pieces to develop the tools for creating a character from scratch; you can then apply this approach to, for example, *The Barber of Seville*. Creating a role without previous knowledge is incredibly liberating because there's no performance tradition; too often people are imprisoned by tradition and performance practice. A singer must learn how begin with the text and work through to a result, rather than remembering a result and aiming for that.

What do you feel are the challenges of singing in Italian?

Young singers in training should, first of all, learn to sing in their own language. It's a question of learning how to connect verbal and musical thoughts, and it's far better to do that in your mother tongue because your thought processes are in that language. A thought isn't something you just add onto the musical phrase but what tends to happen with many productions sung in a foreign language is that the singer doesn't develop this connection between verbal thought and musical thought; between the conscious and the unconscious. You have to be able to ally these two things in order to fully express what is going on.

When a singer is singing anything melodically based I'll often say 'Will you stop singing that as a famous aria; don't just sing the tune'. You have to create it anew; the rhythm and the pitch arrive from the thought. The approach has to be from the words to the tune, not the tune to the word. Therefore, if you learn to sing opera in a foreign language you tend to sing the tune to the words, because the word isn't natural to you.

When you do sing a role in language that isn't your own, you have to understand the meaning of every word that you're singing in that language. Your understanding of the language of the text has to be exhaustive; you must know what the *function* of every word is. You need to understand how the sentence is constructed, and what every element of that sentence does, or your thought process can't be right.

What should a singer think about when approaching performance?

There must be an awareness of spatiality on the stage because that tells a story and helps you to be heard. There's no point doing anything onstage unless you can be heard.

The main trap in performance is to simply think about yourself, perhaps because you're nervous. This makes performance much less interesting. It's important to keep a connection with the other singers; this protects you. Finally, I think the really important thing is not to play, for example, 'funny' in a comedy or 'sad' in a tragedy. You must play the moment and trust that the verbal and musical text will reveal your internal thoughts and feelings. This will have an effect; you don't have to *make* the effect with your voice.

VERDI: CARLO RIZZI

Carlo conducts in major opera houses throughout the world and has a long-standing relationship with Welsh National Opera, where he was Music Director for over twelve years. I worked with Carlo on a production of Verdi's *Falstaff* with young singers training at the Royal Welsh College of Music and Drama. I was particularly struck by the way he worked with the singers to help them create detailed, nuanced characterisations and wanted to ask him about his approach to Verdi.

What is it about Verdi that excites you?

The answer is very simple: it's the theatre. Obviously, his music excites me but for me the key with Verdi is the way that he uses the words; the fact that there is never repetition or beating about the bush just to get to a nice melody. Verdi is very essential; he brings words and grammar together with the music so precisely. He often had problems with his librettists, not because he doesn't like rhyme, but because the dramatic shape of the piece didn't satisfy him. That's what first attracted me to Verdi; he's an incredible composer but it's never all about the music. That for me is the key to opera.

And what do you think the particular challenges are for the young singer when working on Verdi, particularly the non-Italian speaking singer?

The non-Italian speaker needs to learn how to pronounce the words correctly. And then, and this is for Italian and non-Italian singers, it's about the shape and journey of the phrase. You can take the same line, the same aria, the same opera and one singer will know where they're going – the ups and downs in the phrase – whilst another singer can sing the exact same notes but, like a stone, the phrase doesn't go anywhere.

Take *Falstaff*, for example, when in Act Three Falstaff says to Alice: '*Sei la mia damma!*'. Now, technically, '*mia dama*' is '*my lady*' but with a double 'm' – '*la damma*' – it is a female deer. One can learn this but the important thing is that the way you say '*dama*', and the way that you say '*damma*', has to be completely different: '*dama*' is something high class, '*damma*' is an animal. It's not just about adding an additional 'm', it's about the singer having an awareness that the line expresses Falstaff's attention, interest and excitement for Alice. This is not only about pronouncing the line correctly, it is about understanding that, in so doing, you can bring completely different sensations; the line becomes violent, almost like he is forcing himself on her. It is, therefore, not only about the pronunciation but the way in which the singer understands the phrase; understand what is *behind* the words and the drama comes alive.

How do you bring this to a singer's attention?

My music rehearsals are never only about 'Let's do this a little faster' or 'Let's do a ritardando here or a diminuendo there'. If I ever say 'Let's go a little faster' there must be a reason and the reason is very often in the words. I need to work with the singer to discover the meaning of the words. Very often I will ask singers 'What are you saying?' and dutifully they will bring out their copy of the score and show me a literal translation of the words. And I say, 'Thank you very much, I know exactly what this means, I'm Italian but still, what are you *saying*?' It's about asking a singer to *act* rather than *sing*; very often I start by asking the singer to just speak the words.

And by just speaking the words initially you get closer to an understanding of why Verdi set a line in a particular way?

Exactly, and especially in recitative. In the recitative you have the drama. You see the character and their feelings. Recitative is always written in 4/4 but this is just the accepted way of writing it; the recitative should follow the rhythm of the words when spoken. At the same time, Verdi might write a certain chord for the horns on a certain word, and on another word he might write a long *piano legato* with the strings; this means that he wants a certain emphasis and two different expressions. So, one has to see the words and the way they have been set in the score.

Studying character begins with reading the story and knowing the background; with *Falstaff*, for example, you might also read the Shakespeare. Take Verdi's *Otello*; it starts in Cyprus, he doesn't include the first act from Shakespeare's *Othello*, but it is important for singers to know the history of what happened before in order to understand how important Desdemona is to Otello. If the singer doesn't know this history they cannot understand the depth of what is happening and the desperation at the end of the opera. It is important to know these things, even if they are not translated into the opera, otherwise you see *forte* in the score and so, like a typewriter, you sing *forte*.

It's important to start with the words. The music is another level of expression, the music helps, but you must begin by asking: 'Which word is the important word?', 'What am I aiming to translate to my partner?', 'What is the journey of this phrase?'

How does a singer continue to keep the story of the character alive in Verdi's ensembles?

Well, that is a very difficult question to answer because very often in ensembles the music takes over the words. It's difficult to understand the web of four different lines and four different characters singing at once; it is a sort of musical cathedral, with different layers and heights. So, what I generally do, is try to find some moments in the ensemble for one voice to be prominent. This work really has to come from the conductor; they should know all the parts and how the musical cathedral is constructed.

What do you expect from the singer the first time they work with you?

It's very simple, from the first rehearsal I expect a singer to know their part from memory. And then, we talk. A singer might say 'I really would feel more comfortable if this was slightly slower' or 'Could this be a little more legato here?' The conductor needs to understand if this request is in order to show how beautiful the voice is or, importantly, if it's something that can actually help the performance. The job of the conductor is to help get the best out of the performer.

How should the singer approach the Sitzprobe?

The singer should seek to understand the different sound world that's created by the orchestra; the colours of the orchestra. This sound world is an integral part of their character; not just in Verdi but with every composer. For example, in *The Marriage of Figaro,* to hear Susanna's aria in Act Four, first on the piano and then with a clarinet and bassoon, is to receive a completely different message. This is where the young singer can put themselves, and their ideas, in front of the reality of the score.

Also, the orchestra and the piano very often play different tempi. This is not because the pianist, conductor or orchestra are bad. Just think about one person dancing, and then sixty people dancing; there is a different weight, a different noise.

So, I would say there are two things to learn: firstly, that the orchestra will move a little slower and secondly, how to use the sound of the orchestra to help shape the character you're creating.

How should a singer use stage rehearsals?

A singer in stage and orchestras always has the hardest part: they're on stage, jumping around, changing costume, putting hats on the right way and working out how everything is done. It's very complicated and not easy! For this reason, the stage and pianos should be used by singers to clear up everything technical that may go wrong. For every successful stage and orchestra, you need to have had a successful stage and piano.

Do you have any other advice?

If a singer feels there is a discrepancy between what they *feel* and what they are asked to *do*, it is important that they talk about it because otherwise it will hamper their performance. They should ask *why* they have been asked to do something because, at the end of the day, it is their performance. The more a singer is involved and clear about what they're doing and why they're doing it, about why they're singing a certain way, the more their performance will be enhanced. If they just create a role passively it will be like tonic water without the fizz.

TWENTIETH CENTURY: WYN DAVIES

Wyn is Director of Music at New Zealand Opera. He has previously worked on the music staff at Welsh National Opera and the Metropolitan Opera. Wyn's knowledge of operatic repertoire is extensive and wide-ranging. We worked together on Kurt Weill's *Street Scene* and so, alongside more general questions about creating character in opera, I focused on the specific challenges of twentieth-century repertoire.

To begin with, could you tell me why opera excites you?

The reasons have changed. I started off being excited by the proximity to people's voices; I was amazed at the variety of expression people could achieve with their voices. Over the years, I have become a bit less interested in the sheer noise that the voice makes and more interested in the presentation of drama through music, and through singing in particular. Nowadays, when I go to an opera, particularly if I'm in the audience, it is the effectiveness of the drama that interests me more than the sound of the voice.

And was there a reason for that change?

I think there was a time when I realised that those famous voices that you hear in recordings, those really top voices, can't number as many as fifty in the whole world at any given time. What you're much more likely to come across is somebody who's very good at presenting an idea or character through using their voice; you don't need to have one of the world's fifty best voices in order to do that. In fact, it's a different kind of talent. I very often find that the sort of voices that win competitions are not owned by the sort of people who are good at creating decent drama because those people have been concentrating on the pure sound that they make and not necessarily on the communication of the piece of text through singing. I've become much more interested in that over the years because that is what satisfies and entertains me.

What are the particular challenges that you've noticed young singers face when they begin the process of creating character?

I think the particular challenge for the young singer is how to get over the frustration that they are unable to realise what's in their imagination. They will have an idea about what they want to do, they'll have an imagination and a sense of how to express an idea, but they will need help in coaxing their voice to do it. They will need to break the music down and make it more fragmentary and not so pure. If you listen to the greatest singers, they are always fragmenting the music – breaking it up into tiny sections – in order to express what the words say. However, they do it in such a skilled way that you hardly notice it.

To begin with you have to know exactly what every syllable means, and then translate it into the way that you would naturally express it. Of course, that's a bit more complicated when you're singing in a language that isn't your own language, but it is your job, as a singer, to do that. Unless you realise that a certain phrase is a colloquial phrase in a certain language, you cannot express it properly. You need to do a lot of work on understanding the detail of the text before you can start to sing it properly.

As to bringing it all back together again, I think that simply comes by rehearsing the scene. It's a question of repetition.

How does this approach apply when working with twentieth-century repertoire?

Actually, I think it's probably easier in a great deal of twentieth-century music. I mean nobody could set words more naturally than Benjamin Britten, for example, and that's a great help to singers when imagining the way in which to put it across. If you're singing an opera with a deliberately instrumental musical setting but written for voice, as you'll find with some composers, then I think there's no doubt you'll have to master a way to sing it, possibly without the text at all to begin with. It's a different kind of technique. If you're learning to sing, for example, *Pierrot Lunaire* by Schoenberg, you have to learn how to find the notes in your voice before you put the text on it.

How do you work with a team of singers on ensemble?

One can work on an ensemble and make them sound musically acceptable quite quickly but, if you're really going to get the dramatic sense across, you want to give the audience a chance to understand that everybody's singing something different; that is the glory of Mozart finales, for example. If everybody sounds uniform, an audience simply won't understand. Of course, if a group of singers are singing the same phrase, in the same rhythm, I think it's natural to want to find a good blend. However, this sometimes leads to the sound being evened out and, if they're singing different words, you really want to hear the difference that comes from two different kinds of phrases being sung. So, you have to try to go against the grain; for example, the stresses don't need to be made in the same way, especially not if the singers have got different text.

Much twentieth-century repertoire explores a full range vocal expression; how should singers best navigate this?

One of the most difficult things is to move from spoken dialogue, into a sort of sung dialogue, and then into aria. You have to work out vocally how to do this; it's a complicated technical process. I think the use of microphones has made that more difficult because what tends to happen is that you assume your spoken voice is going to be heard because it's amplified and so you don't look after the detail as much. Operettas were written at a time when there weren't microphones so you'd have to work out a way to lift your spoken voice in order that it projects in a way that works with your singing voice.

What is your focus in a music call?

The process is different with every single singer. It depends on whether they're an experienced singer who has already sung the particular role that you're working on, or somebody to whom you're basically teaching the role.

I find it interesting working with people who know roles very well because, very often, they just tend to repeat it in the way that they've got used to singing it. I remember doing a production of Purcell's *King Arthur* and, at one point, the director said to the actor doing the narration, 'I want to do that section again – you didn't do it like that last time' and the actor replied 'Oh, I see you want me to repeat it, I thought we were rehearsing'. What he meant by rehearsing was an exploration of different ways of doing things – of expressing things – but what a lot of opera singers do, instinctively, once they've learnt how to sing a role, is to simply repeat it and to slightly refine the way they produce the notes. So, it is a fascinating process of trying to make people realise that what they're doing is simply *repeating*, rather than *reprocessing* something every time they do it, so that the phrase comes alive even if it's the six thousandth time that they've sung it. You want to be actually in that moment communicating there and then. This involves bravery.

At the other end of the scale is the learning process with people who haven't sung a role before. It's about making them aware of what's going on in the opera; bringing an awareness of what the character is thinking about. Also, singers may not be aware of how the solo voice fits into the general sound of the orchestra at a particular moment. Something you thought was hard to sing might turn out to be much easier when you've got the cushion of an orchestra. It's important that singers don't over-commit, or over-sing, simply because it looks like they need to when singing it with piano. A casualty of the way we work in opera is that we don't get to hear the live orchestra until often a matter of days before we're performing it. The piano can't differentiate one instrumental sound from another and so you lose the colours that you get from the orchestra; these are often one of the biggest clues about how the composer is thinking about the emotional heat of a phrase.

You said bravery is required for performers to rediscover a role that they may have done many times before; what else does a singer need to perform with spontaneity?

You need to be *processing*; that is, thinking through, phrase by phrase, what you're saying, or what it is you mean to say, in the moment that you're doing it. The risk is that you end up *repeating*; merely locating the place in the voice that you know that note has to go, on the vowel that it has to be on; which is a purely a technical thing. That is, of course, highly complicated because the actual process of having to make that sound is a big deal. The singers who I think are most successful at being spontaneous are those who have got the ability to concentrate precisely on what they *mean* to say, and at the *moment* they mean to say it.

It also important not to assume that another character is going to sing, just because they did it in rehearsals last week.

The composer has already timed the phrase, and decided which notes are higher and which notes are lower and, in so doing, determined the emotional intensity of a phrase. The singer can highlight these choices; they can make them more obvious and clearer. However, it's important not to be satisfied with merely singing the right notes in the right place in the way that the composer wrote it because that, in itself, doesn't communicate. It's about working backwards in order to translate all this information that you receive from the composer into *thought*; you have to put yourself in the composer's position and ask yourself, 'Why didn't they write it in another way?'

NEW OPERA: JONATHAN DOVE

Jonathan has written more than twenty operas, in addition to a range of choral, orchestral and instrumental work. I wanted to draw on his vast experience of working with, and composing music for, singers to gain an understanding of what a composer imagines when creating characters and the world they inhabit. Our conversation focuses on his breakthrough opera, *Flight,* commissioned in 1998 by Glyndebourne as a '*Figaro*' for the 1990s'.

How did you begin composing operas?

I was a répétiteur for ten years. I ran out of money very quickly after leaving college and ended up playing for a Handel opera. I'd not really thought about opera before; I'd seen maybe three operas by the time I went to university and I hadn't seen many more by the time I left. Then, suddenly, a whole world opened up. I spent my twenties playing for rehearsals for, mostly, directors Graham Vick and Richard Jones, which was quite an education.

I suppose therefore, I was thinking about the process within a rehearsal room and that conditioned certain choices for me; the singer is the most interesting thing in opera and everything moves around that.

If there's a choice of notation – if I'm thinking one way would be hard for the orchestra to follow, and another would be hard for the singer – I'll choose the one that's going to work most easily for the singer because the orchestra have the notes in front of them and the singers have got to memorise two hours of music. And you really don't want people just staring at the conductor; I've seen that in the kind of opera where the time signature changes in every bar.

Of course, I have written music where the time signature changes a lot, as it does in *Flight,* but I hope that for a singer it's a kind of groove that you can get into and that once you've got the hang of it, you can feel it physically as a kind of dance.

This empathy for singers was borne out working in the rehearsal room?

Yes, and an understanding that the musicianship of singers varies greatly. There are singers who also play instruments but I want to be able to work with anyone who can really sing. I don't think I'm ever writing down for singers but I'm just being aware that they're bringing a lot that an instrumentalist just doesn't have; their voice is unique for a start, whereas one Steinway is much like another. If I'm writing for a particular singer then I really want to show off what they can do and play to their strengths.

Which composers inspired you?

I think if your setting is English then Britten is unavoidable. He's a towering figure and must certainly have shaped my sense of how you sing in English. My work is also coloured a little bit by musical theatre: the possibility of singing something casually or conversationally where not everything is elevated and extended. Obviously, you're always having to choose how you set text. If I set something at speaking speed and pitch I know that it will be much easier to understand; it's just not melodically very exciting for a length of time. If I want a phrase to soar because of the emotion at that moment but I also want to be absolutely certain that everybody has got the words because there's a crucial plot point, there may be an option of singing it once at nearer speaking speed and pitch, and then repeating it and letting it soar. I've not done this so much in *Flight* but I have often used quite a lot of repetition; it's partly because it's fun to inhabit an idea or feeling and explore it for a while.

When you do use repetition in Flight *the music is different and distinct each time; are you thinking about what the characters might be doing on each particular line?*

I'm certainly always trying to feel the energy in the room. I'm asking: what's happening between these people? What's the temperature? How fast is it? How slow is it? How happy is it?

I suppose I'm also trying to find out what the music feels like in a slightly broader way: what key are we in? What's the harmonic context? What's the instrumental colour? What are the various sound worlds and where do they change?

Then, alongside these questions, I'll ask: where are moments where things really articulate? Where is somebody suddenly surprised? Where does something contradict? There needs to be a sense of the beats of a scene.

All of this is probably in place before I work in detail. When this sort of musical material hits the text is when I find out what the melodies really want to be.

Will you tend to start composing with this overview of the sound world?

It's not always like this because sometimes you read a line of text and you go, 'Well, that goes like this' and you can sing it straight away. Or you might see five or six different ways of singing it and you think, 'I wonder which one it is?' In which case, I'll try different variations during the course of a scene.

The idea with the Controller in *Flight* was that she would be singing very high; she's high in a control tower, her voice will float over everyone else's. I worked out the mode in which she would be singing later but when it did reveal itself, for some reason, her particular mode had been associated with travel in pieces I had written before *Flight*, although this was never something conscious. The old woman brings in quite a lot of sadness, although in the music I think you'll feel more a quality of longing. Bill and Tina enter on the white notes with very bright energetic music: quite playful and fun. The Minsks also enter on the white notes but it has a different feeling and that's mainly because of the rhythmic drive. That has to do, partly, with where they are in the story but it is also about their own inner story.

This is all before the characters have sung a note. I'm looking at when the character comes in, what's the feeling that comes in with them, balancing the different harmonic contexts and, fairly instinctively, getting a sense of pace and contrasts. It is very 'big picture'; it's a long shot of the piece.

I can't remember how I arrived at the mode for the Refugee; that may well have had a life outside of my own music. It's certainly *other* and it's different from everyone else's music in the piece. His mode, when it arrived, gave me the kind of colour that I wanted for the

Refugee and the more I lived with it, the more I was able to get out of it; I was able to explore what he was able to do.

When in the process did you decide what voice type the characters were going to be?

I think very early on. Partly because we were casting at least two years ahead of the performance, so I needed to know what I was writing for, but also because certain ideas were very immediate. I thought quite early on that the Controller would be right at the top, down to the Immigration Officer – as a threatening presence – right at the bottom (the bass), with the Refugee right in the middle. I liked the idea of the countertenor for the Refugee because of *otherness* but, as it happened, it also placed him right in the centre of the vocal texture.

The hardest thing was working out whether Bill was a tenor or baritone. I think I started with Bill as a baritone and the Steward as a tenor, but it seemed to me that actually Bill has the more intense experience and so, for that reason, the tenor will reveal that extremity better. I think of a baritone as being more ordinary, more of an everyman, whereas the tenor is able to capture something exceptional.

How did you and April de Angelis (the librettist of Flight*) collaborate?*

The words arrived quite a long way into the process. The way April and I worked was unusually collaborative. There is always a long conversation at the beginning of a process: before a word is written you've got to know that this is a story we both want to tell, these are the scenes we're interested in, this is going to be exciting. But with *Flight* the plot, or treatment, is actually derived from the finished piece. April found out in the writing of it what was going to happen. There were various false starts and wrong turns; for example, scenes would arrive that would appear to be from a completely different story. So, we kind of felt our way together towards what the story was. I would respond vividly to the text; to the text as well as to the drama. The text is just the tip of the iceberg really, it's what's underneath the text that one's plumbing into. I remember that the line '*Look up there*', at the beginning of the opera, made me think of a kind of rushing sound; I heard the line on that scale just imagining that moment.

I don't think I dared to think of writing *Flight* much away from the words, yet there were occasions when it was clear certain kinds of music had to happen for which there weren't yet any words. For example, at the end of the first act, it seemed to me that everyone being grounded would only feel as devastating as it should, if it were preceded by the idea that everyone was about to get on the plane and have this wonderful experience. April hadn't written this scene at this point and I was imagining a kind of carousel baggage conveyor belt, with suitcases flying around. I played a kind of carousel music to April and she went, 'Oh, you mean, like oceans and donkeys and shells and elastic' and the words came pouring out and she just wrote more and more of it.

Did you and April talk about the subtext?

I think I discovered it from the words. The old woman is a good example of that. When she reads what's on the postcard she's received from the young barman in Mallorca, there's almost nothing there but you know that she feels a great deal for him: about that experience with him and what it was like to walk along the beach. So, that's all going to be in the music even though you're looking at almost nothing on the page.

April and I met quite often, talked a lot, and would write to each other; as scenes started to arrive through the fax machine, I would send back ideas and suggestions. It's unusual to be that involved in the process of the evolution of a narrative and I think it's because the narrative didn't previously exist.

When you're setting the words to music, what sort of questions are you asking yourself?

It's actually more like I'm trying to play the scene. I'm kind of imagining being in the situation of the characters and saying those words. Or singing those words; I don't make such a distinction between saying and singing. If there are times when if I can't quite work out the music, I do sometimes speak the lines aloud. I do remember reading the whole of *Flight* aloud with a friend to get a feeling of how it was working and, weirdly, there was something missing; it was the music.

Do the sounds and textures of words lead you towards the music?

Certain words have a distinctive texture like '*lucky donkey*' or '*drinking on an empty tummy*'; there's a rhythm there and it's difficult to say it any other way. When you sing these lines, the fun of it is the feeling that it is just how it sounds when we speak.

On the other hand, the moment where the Minsk man comes back and says '*I've got the feeling, have a longing, and it was love*' is very short on the page. That was something I connected with my own emotional experience; somebody has to have several goes at a declaration like that before it will actually form. So, to write that section I was putting myself in the scene as the character.

Do you see the space through the characters' eyes?

Yes, and I think I probably move fairly freely between imagining being in the audience watching it on a stage and actually being in the thoughts of a character; it's different levels of reality.

I think I was imagining a kind of giant for the Immigration Officer and, when you listen to the music, it kind of sounds like a giant with a limp; it's a very uneven tread but there was something about that kind of quality that felt right. I'm not expecting, however, for the singer to be walking in time with the music. I'm also not really expecting that the stage should look anything like what I've got going on in my mind. That's just part of my process; I need to see something in order to imagine the scene and therefore to write the music for it.

Much of the underlying subtext is expressed through the music; for example, the Minsk man's inability to say 'love' . . .

Yes, and I suppose I feel it's clear but I realise that it isn't always entirely obvious. I'm used to singers bringing an awful lot to the picture. I certainly think if you just sing the notes themselves it's never going to be enough; I've only put so much in the music. I've gone some way, I've revealed some part of the journey to the audience, but it's unfinished. It can make all the difference whether this singer is really seeing something in their mind's eye or not; it makes for a complete musical and dramatic experience. The melody alone is not enough – it's some of it – but it's not everything.

Singers need to imaginatively engage in the character's world, in the same way you do, in order to fulfil and complete it?

I think some singers do this instinctively but not if they're particularly preoccupied with making a beautiful sound. There is often a tension between, for example, making a beautiful line and really articulating: getting enough energy into the particularly unusual words or unexpected language. The audience won't understand unless the singer has really invested in it. You really ought to feel that people are singing to each other and expecting the other person to understand, to respond and to react.

I give the singer quite a lot of freedom. I very rarely write any dynamics into the vocal lines; I write all of them for the orchestra but I'm not expecting the singer to do exactly the same as the orchestra. I tend to use accents only to indicate an exceptional stress; I don't mark the natural stresses of English, including the special stresses we make on words that we are emphasising, because I expect all that to be part of the acting equipment of the singer. In a performance of one of my operas, if I find that something is missing it is usually because it's not being completely imagined by the singer.

13 Approaches to Rehearsal

- ALETTA COLLINS
- LEAH HAUSMAN
- RICHARD JONES
- PHYLLIDA LLOYD
- ROBIN NORTON HALE
- DAVID POUNTNEY

Over the course of your career you will work with many different directors, each with their own unique approach to creating and telling stories in opera. Their work will be informed by their beliefs about what opera should be and how it should communicate with an audience. These conversations with directors and movement directors will, I hope, offer an insight into a range of different rehearsal processes.

ALETTA COLLINS

Aletta began her career as a dancer and choreographer. She is a former Associate Artist of the Royal Opera House and has, in addition, directed and choreographed opera for Opera North, Glyndebourne and the Salzburg Festival. I wanted to focus on Aletta's experiences of creating productions of new opera, particularly Thomas Ades's *The Tempest* and Mark-Anthony Turnage's *Anna Nicole* and *Coraline* and, alongside this, how her work with dancers has translated to her work helping singers create physical character.

Why are you drawn to opera?

It's not that removed from my dance background; the two forms are very close in many ways and in many ways it is an easier thing for me to access than a play. The fact it's lyric, that it's set to music like dance is, immediately makes more sense to me.

I'm also excited by the way you can tell a multitude of stories at the same time; the music takes you in one emotional direction; a visual world which could place you in a different one, whether that's in synergy with or in opposition to the other story; and then the human story. You're able to tell a multi-layered reading of something because the music is there holding everything together. I think that's the same for dance. The difference is that in opera there tends to be more money to work with a larger creative team.

How does your work with dancers translate to your work with singers?

I think I'm only just beginning to trust myself to do that. For ages I was too nervous of a singer being a different sort of artist; I thought that you had to tell them what to do but, because I've had a bit more experience, I realise that I can work with singers more like I'd work with dancers.

I directed *Cenerentola* last year and when working on the Act Two sextet, 'Questo è un nodo avviluppato' ('This is a tangled knot'), I said to the cast, 'If we're exploring where this knot began, we have to go back to the beginning'. So, I gave them the instruction to work alone for ten minutes to come up with physical moving snapshots of the six pivotal moments in their story that got each of them to this point. Once they'd done this, my next instruction was that they had to run them backwards. Once we'd put them together, we basically ran the whole opera backwards to the moment where Cenerentola and the Prince first saw each other in Act One. We then did it all again going fast forwards. This is how you make dance: there's an idea and a task. It was a proper movement response to the situation, rather than me simply teaching them how to dance.

I think that you need super-confidence to introduce the messiness of creating work in this way in opera which, for all its brilliance, doesn't really like messiness. It doesn't really like the question, 'I'm not quite sure what we want to do here ...?' It likes experts and everyone knowing what they're doing but this doesn't leave much room for an atmosphere of play and it's within such an atmosphere that you make discoveries.

In preparation for a role, what can a singer do physically and imaginatively to remain flexible for rehearsals?

The biggest part of the preparation is going to be learning the music and so it's important to enjoy learning it as openly as possible without narrowing your interpretation of the piece as you do so. It will help to read the whole opera and to read about the piece, extracting interesting material whilst doing so. I've been working with a football coach for the last two weeks and he said, 'My role as teacher is to disrupt the players'. Everything is about improvisation, being quick, changing direction; if one player is dribbling a ball *down* a room, everyone else is dribbling balls *across* the room, in order to make it more difficult. How you as an artist embrace that idea of disruption in your practice, so nothing is ever completely set, is worth considering.

Something in all of us wants to know that we're in control, that we're safe. Learning a new role can be quite overwhelming but I think you need to be dribbling that ball whilst learning it, so that you're starting to fuse that learning with the idea of disruption and improvisation.

There's an interesting experiment that's been done with dancers: a group are rehearsing and get to the end of a scene and, instead of repeating, they stop, sit down and simply imagine their way through the scene. They just visualise it. The result was that the dancers knew the scene better by taking half an hour out to visualise it than they would have done spending two more hours in a room doing it.

For singers, it's about finding different ways of learning and embracing the disruptions to your set path. Even a concert is never going to be how you learned it on your own, because you're part of a big living, breathing machine. Of course, it is very hard understanding how to prepare with a new score because you might not have the luxury of having the whole thing. However, you can always ask the creative team if there is something you can be thinking about whilst learning the opera. Maybe try to find out from the director what they are reading and which films they are thinking about.

What qualities do singers need in the rehearsal room?

It's important to lose the idea that speed of achievement equals success. Arrive with a readiness to explore different directions and a flexibility to discover your own understanding of your character within the parameters that the director has set up. Together with this, have a delight in play.

How do you work with a singer to create physical character?

I think it's useful to give an artist who is not used to being that physical a little physical routine that their character might do. I would then encourage them to use it in different places; you begin to see a physical engagement with the character take root. When we did *Coraline* earlier this year, we had no idea when we started rehearsals that her dad really likes dancing. It developed from a moment between the father and daughter early on in the opera; a section of music sounded like a little dance they might share. This grew throughout the production to the point where the dad would be dancing whenever he could; he wanted to be a dancer. So, it's connecting the physicality of the character to the character's Objectives. When we did *Anna Nicole*, Richard Jones, the director, gave the singer playing Anna Nicole the idea that the character has really sticky fingers, like a child. It was a physical trait that ran through the production.

How do you create a physical language for the world of the opera with a company?

It often depends on how you design it. With *Cenerentola* I decided that the family lived above a ballroom school and that Don Magnifico was a ballroom dancing teacher. The overture featured a group of school children dancing alongside the two sisters. It's the story of Cinderella but there's no ball in the opera! So, because I made that decision with Giles Cadle (the set designer), it immediately gave us a world for people to access and to bring ideas to; the environment spurs the ideas.

Do you find that the characters' environment always informs the physical language of the world?

To a degree I think it does. The piece I'm about to do, however, is incredibly abstract; this is a piece where people have mirrors for hands and the men wear giant round cages on their upper body. So that defines what you are and that's a different way into it. With a world that is so abstract, the spatial storytelling will be the strongest narrative card we have to play: moving in circles, moving in straight lines, playing with distance, etc.

I think a lot of the work we do in this country is based around place and time; these are very key ways in. Our European colleagues are not as strict as that and that work can be very exciting.

In this kind of production, I think it's about having a clear dialogue with the company about what the ambition is. It's easy to be pulled in different directions because somebody's understanding of it is slightly different; it's not as clear as saying we're going to do this like Jeeves and Wooster.

Are there any specific challenges in making a new opera?

It's massive that you don't know what the orchestration is going to be and so it's really useful for the music department to be explaining the orchestral score whilst the piano plays in rehearsals. It's very important to really *listen* to the music. I remember working with Sir Simon Rattle and explaining that I can't read music; he said 'That's ok, I'm not a very good dancer'. It was very clear to him that I could *hear* what was going on but that I didn't have the vocabulary for it; I would label sections of music 'shimmery fish' or 'chocolate box'. Every corner in the operas I work on has a name – all the colours and textures of the music inform these names – and it means you're meeting each musical corner as a friend, they all have different personalities. The more you can do that, the more you can move as quickly as the score does.

Our immediate response to music is with pictures, colours and textures. I feel very fortunate that I don't have a musical background; maybe if you do you're connecting with it more intellectually. It's really important to be listening to the orchestration around your voice. The things that are floating past or bubbling under can give you a sense of where you are; literally or emotionally.

Is there anything else you'd say to a singer about creating character?

I think I've pinched this off Richard Jones: in *Coraline*, for example, when we were working with the ghost children, I would ask them to give me five words that define what a ghost child is for them; 'They are lonely', 'They are hungry', etc. Then, after five minutes, I would ask them to tell me five things that ghost children are not. Giving yourself definite attitudes to help define the corners of your character is very helpful; '*I am . . .*', '*These three things are . . .*'. For example, with this piece I'm about to direct the mantra of the chorus will be '*We all believe in Diana and will therefore only walk in circles and not in straight lines*'. If you are a member of the chorus it gives you something to hold on to. This piece is so abstract I'm trying to come up with three core beliefs for each character that translates into behaviour.

It's about giving yourself an arsenal of emotional and practical truths about your character. If your practical truth is 'Whenever I lie I pick my fingers', then when your character lies you've got something practical to do. It's making these character thoughts and traits visible. And it always has to be connected to the music: what does that chord mean? How is it supporting what I'm doing? There's no such thing as a solo moment in opera, there's always the music and where you place yourself in relation to it emotionally and practically.

LEAH HAUSMAN

Leah trained in dance and drama in New York City, and at the École Jacques Lecoq in Paris. She has worked as a choreographer, movement director and director of opera on both sides of the Atlantic. She worked closely with the ENO Opera Works singers and, over subsequent years, invited a number of the groups to help explore and develop ideas for new productions at ENO. I was keen to ask her about her work developing a singer's physical awareness.

What is it about opera that excites you?

When I was starting out I was really interested in theatre and dance – seeing work by Pina Bausch, Robert Wilson and Robert Lepage – and, by comparison, opera seemed pretty dull; those directors hadn't infiltrated opera at that point.

When I came to work in opera, however, I fell in love with it from day one. Coming from a dance and movement background, music is so crucial. Directing opera is like swimming in an ocean; you have the buoyancy of the music, which makes life so much easier. I fell in love with the process and I loved how efficient the rehearsal room was. I also loved that the singers had a kind of openness; mostly they are hard-working human beings who are looking for help in whatever way they could. A singer's training is very similar to a dancer's training in many ways; to have a strong technique is essential, it's your base, and so the dramatic end of things tends to get put off until later, unless you have an unusual teacher who is really good at integrating those things.

What are the specific challenges a singer faces when creating physical character and what can a singer be doing to prepare before going into rehearsals?

A singer's process demands that they arrive with the music already prepared; and that musical preparation is a kind of physical preparation. How you learn the music will really affect how you're going to be able to work on the physicality for a character because the physical attitude is so massively reflected in the voice and vice-versa. When learning a role, it's important to try to keep your interpretation of a character malleable. You don't know what the director might have in mind so you have to explore how to shift in different directions when learning a role. Often singers will have sung a role a number of times, which gives them the opportunity to be relaxed with it and to experiment; on the other hand, the danger is you get fixed.

The danger of fixing things too firmly is that a performance needs to have the space to breathe?

Yes, the singer needs to have the space to be able to react and respond in the moment. This is a challenge for the singer because so many forces are potentially confining; you've got to stay with a conductor, with the musicians, whilst all the time struggling to hear the orchestra when onstage. That is why singers have to be particularly attuned to each other; they have to know what's going on from somebody else's in-breath, not from what they hear but from the other singer's body. It's about *physical listening*. I often lead workshops with singers and the company organising will want me to do individual sessions with the singers but it's not about that. It's about them understanding how to work within a group and how to read each other physically. You can't do that work in an individual session; you have to work with other people.

What qualities do you think a singer needs to work in the rehearsal room?

The saying 'yes' principle must underline every approach. Because performers can be nervous, because there's often something to prove, and because they've done so much preparation, the risk is that when you try to move out of your comfort zone there's a block that stops you.

The 'yes' principle is a foundation for your rehearsal period; before you even think about character, you need to develop the ability to be in a rehearsal room and be ready to accept what's thrown at you. My emphasis for the first weeks of rehearsal is often to get everyone to a place where they're able to communicate with each other. A singer is a stage performer and one of the major requirements is to be able to work with a group of people in the room: including the costume designer, stage technician, other singers, assistants, coaches, etc. How you juggle all of that, is who you are as a performer. It's all about openness and generosity.

How do you help singers to develop character?

I encourage singers to listen with their body and to respond with their whole body, as opposed to only from the neck up. Many singers are awkward with their arms; they can feel their arms and legs are disconnected from their body. The more a singer understands where they're moving from – the core – the better.

Childlike exercises are useful to connect you to being a moving human being, as opposed to an adult singer who stands still at the piano and practises: skipping, jumping, running, hopping, running backwards all help establish a more open state.

Exercises that release tension in the neck and spine are very important: twisting warm-ups that free your arms help here.

The more physically malleable you are, and the more you're aware of your spine, then the more you can elongate your movements, which enables you to really connect to the opera. I don't mean that you must go into slow motion; I mean that you must learn to draw out a movement, take a moment and suspend it. Everything is suspended in opera; each note suspends the intention. In an aria you've got to be able to elongate sung lines and knowing how to do that physically to a movement is really important for a singer. It is essentially psychological; opera often suspends or slows your thought process and it's important to understand how to justify that physically without going into slow motion.

Other tools that I find useful when working with singers are:

- States of Tension: they challenge singers to go to places that they didn't think they could go to whilst still singing. You can reduce that movement to something really small and yet it still gives a totally different quality. I call it *reducing the sauce*; it's like cooking, when you reduce something, it gets richer and more intense. When you reduce the movement it's because you're putting restrictions on it and, therefore, it's hotter and more intense.

- Mask work: is useful to bring a performer's awareness to the physical energy they give off and to highlight what it is that the audience are seeing. It's a way for the singer to understand more about themselves and the more they know about themselves, the more possibility there is of transforming.[1]

Where should a singer begin if they're not getting the kind of work you lead in the rehearsal room in order to create physical character?

There are all sorts of fun things you can do. For example, give yourself a physical Point of Concentration as you're playing the scene to engage your body: 'I'm going to play the scene

---

[1] Both these tools are explored in Lecoq, p. 154.

as though I need to pee' or, 'I'm going to play this as though there are lead weights attached to my ankles'. Give yourself a slightly different intention from what you were playing previously but one that still connects with the character's journey in the scene.

I think it's important to occasionally surprise the other singers by doing something that's going to wake them up; you know, drop your trousers! Too often performers aren't relating to each other, they're not actually in the same space with the other performer.

How do you work with singers to create a world and environment in which everyone is in some way connected?

When I was co-directing Berlioz's *Benvenuto Cellini* at ENO the set and costumes were quite extreme; the characters needed to feel as though they popped out from the set, like in a cartoon. I would break moments in the opera down into individual movements. For example, if the incident was (*I'm walking down the street, see a penny and pick it up*), then you can either run that as one moment, or you can break it down frame by frame. In doing this we were then able to elongate the moment between each frame, so that we the audience received bold, clear pictures of every little thing that was happening; somebody received an idea, the idea lands and they respond.

You can *literally* physicalise the internal dialogue. I remember working on Rachmaninoff's *The Miserly Knight*; it's all about paranoia and greed. We worked with an amazing circus performer who acted as the Knight's alter-ego. He was always following the Knight around, which meant that the singer playing the Knight constantly had someone to respond to. When we felt we weren't *seeing* the singer's thoughts, we would ask the circus performer to touch him and the singer would immediately physicalise what he was thinking and singing about. He had to respond to the touch at that moment. It's a very useful exercise. When we later removed the circus performer, the singer had a muscle memory that seemed to continue to help him make the psychological visible.

Another good exercise in this vein is for the singer, at the end of each line that they sing, to bounce a ball to the other character. It connects the singer with the idea that you must always be trying to *do* something to the other person.

It's important for the cast to watch each other, for example, in other scenes. Given that you are a cog in the whole machine, you need to look at what the whole machine is doing. The more you can understand the world, the more you'll have to work with. This also relates to when you move into stage rehearsals. When you watch everything, you realise what's on everyone else's plate and you become part of a whole thing – part of the production and the story – you are the performer *and* the character.

RICHARD JONES

Richard began his career working with Scottish Opera and the Citizens Theatre. He has since gone on to direct theatre and opera around the world. Richard's productions are consistently revelatory, transforming audiences' perceptions of operatic repertoire. His work incorporates extraordinary psychological examinations of character within highly arresting heightened visual landscapes; I wanted to ask Richard how he worked with singers to inhabit these worlds.

What was it that first excited you about opera?

The lack of realism. People don't go around making that weird noise and, by and large, they're not in those very primitive situations but, at the same time, I knew it was very truthful and fundamental and very real. The first opera I saw was *Boris Godunov* at the Royal Opera House.

Had you seen theatre before that?

Yes, I'd seen theatre at the Old Vic.

And the experience was . . .

. . . different. *Boris Godunov's* got lots of doom bells in it; it's got death, hatred and ritual. It was different from the plays I saw. My early experience of theatre were the Palladium pantomimes; I saw performers like Charlie Drake and Old King Cole. The colours, the light, the kind of artificial event went into my hard wiring immediately. Any parent can tell you about that moment when you're in a theatre with your child and they suddenly go down a rabbit hole. I've yet to surface, unfortunately, because it's a horrible addiction.

What's your starting point when you're asked to direct a piece?

I go to saturation point before I talk to anybody else. Listening to it, looking at it, looking at the words, reading around the author, digesting what was around the author at the time. So, you reach saturation point before you go to your collaborators. And then you have so much to say, you're an unstoppable stream of consciousness, that the designer has got to sort it out with you. That's the appropriate moment to make a shape or a production because the designer will, with you, discern what's essential to what you're saying.

What are the main challenges that singers face when creating a character?

If you're working with a cast of young singers you would hope to be very articulate and hopefully excite them about the stage you've got to with it, and you would make it very clear that the responsibility to continue it, or carry it on, was theirs. That's what you have to do when singers come in on the first day of rehearsals.

The challenges for the singer are, I suppose, to like, digest and be excited by the world the director is suggesting but then to take their own soul, or their own personality, into it. It's frequently not the same casting process as theatre. In theatre you can intuit that the person who you've cast will inhabit and augment your concept, so ideally you would have the same casting process, the same opportunity, to have intuitions about singing artists and if you were in that position I would say you're going to get somewhere.

For example, the next opera I'm directing at Glyndebourne is with singers Alan Clayton and Christopher Purves, both of whom I've worked with. So, I'm making the production with them in mind; they're extremely experienced people who had a theatrical talent in the first place.

What should singers do to arrive ready to work on day one?

Know the narrative of the opera and certainly know the situation of the other characters in the opera; know what everybody else's journey is. This will contribute to the atmosphere in the rehearsal room. And openness; openness is the main thing I'd ask of a singer.

How do you begin creating character with singers?

I have worked with a number of movement directors: Sarah Fahie, Aletta Collins, Lucy Burgess, Linda Dobell. Linda and I used to do backstories for every character and then we'd type them out. The backstories were made up of those things in the text that you couldn't dispute, like gender or class, and the speculative things. I would always give the backstory to a singer and say, 'These are unnegotiable about the character, they are just common-sense things', and 'These, I would put it to you, that you *could* play, but these things are speculative'. It's fine if they just go with the speculative things but it also feels a bit more creative if they take it in a direction which is speculative *and* true. I tend to do backstories during the first three days of rehearsals. I make it a collective process and I then make another singer read aloud the backstory of a character who is not them. This would be a foundation and any changes in the backstory would be announced collectively, so that the whole event is congruent.

So, everything comes out of the backstory?

I think everything does. Who you are comes out of what's happened to you. It's all about what's happened to you prior to the moment you arrive on stage in the story. I don't think you can dispute that, I mean call me old-fashioned.

I think it's really, really important to have that strong meditation about your imaginative connection with somebody who is not you. You've got to have that on a daily basis, otherwise it feels fake.

The performance becomes simply a demonstration of the technical feat of singing?

I mean, there are certain operas, those which are less overblown or less emotional, where I think the singer is actually cornered into playing something naturally. With *The Marriage of Figaro*, for example, apart from 'Dove Sono' or 'Porgi Amor' which can get operatic, the singers have to be in the present playing the situation; they can't generalise. Which is why a poor performance of *The Marriage of Figaro* is often really poor, and a good performance is really great.

I was directing *The Queen of Spades* at WNO, and remember saying to a singer, 'The music doesn't exist. It's not for you to tell the audience to appreciate the music'. When an opera house resurrects a production in two minutes, you see that generally the singers perform a kind of guide to how the audience should experience the music. A singer's body might generate something about the music, and have to on a technical level, but on the whole it's very important to provoke a tension in the theatrical event by not *playing* the music. Katie Mitchell's productions are very good on that. She only works from the Actions, the Objectives, the Obstacles, the situation and I always enjoy her productions for that reason.

But the music informs how you play a particular Objective or Action?

Well, that's what's good about opera, isn't it? If you listen to *Otello* by Verdi, the music is telling you what Iago is actually doing but the text is about the action on stage, or about him concealing those things. There are millions of examples of that in opera. It's really thrilling.

The death of Mimi (*La Bohème*) is a brilliant scene. I mean, Brecht would've despised the death of Mimi for an audience to be manipulated like that. I'd say that it just has to be played as realistically as possible, where people really have to do what they do around a deathbed, which is to pretend it's not going on. The music tells you quite clearly, she's died and the people in the room are unable to negotiate that. In a play you couldn't do a death as invisible as that. The music tells you, the audience, absolutely unequivocally that she's dead. I think one of them realises she's dead, and the others don't, and they are of an age where they don't have the emotional capability to be there with that person's death.

How do you create a world, an environment, with the singers that is cohesive?

You just carry on day to day, incrementally. Incrementally you answer all the singers' questions; the more their questions are answered with a kind of uniformity and love and deliberateness, the more everybody will get onto the same page. And also asking questions, whereby you know that, hopefully, the answers that they arrive at will get them closer together. That's why it's good to do *The Marriage of Figaro*, because *The Marriage of Figaro* has to be played by a team.

I've sat through rehearsals of plays where actors come in and assiduously watch rehearsals of scenes that they're not in. I think it's important that people are coming in all the time. I would encourage singers to watch what's going on, and then if they wanted to go off to a practice room, I think that would be ideal.

What would you do on the first day of rehearsals?

Well, I try not to show a model until the third day of rehearsals. Nobody listens on the first day. I get them to read the story, read the text spoken, then do the backstory; it depends. I'll say, can you research something around the period or why the composer did it, or they might bring something back the next day which is an artefact, or a kind of piece of household equipment which might be in the opera, so we can talk about it. That's always really useful; subliminally it's much better because somebody is listening to somebody else talk and they go 'Oh they're nice, they're human', or 'They're quite funny', or 'Oh, I think I might fancy them, oh dear, that's a worry'. I think this is really useful before you perform. I think there are ways in which a group can combine which relates to the text and are a bit under the radar. And by under the radar I mean people start going 'I had quite a hostile feeling about them when I first met them, but now I quite like them now I hear them talk'. Anyone talking alone is making themselves vulnerable, aren't they? It's very useful where you're put in a position of empathy with another performer. Opera is not addressing those things whatsoever.

And allowing yourself to be vulnerable is particularly difficult when ...

... you're doing something as technical as singing. Especially when you are being judged to see if you can do your high C, and if you can't, you slip on the ice and you're out. It's shit. And I'm not a Pollyanna person, I'm not a person of great heart, but I do know that those things make for much more effective theatre.

What can the singer do about this?

Put the composer and librettist before themselves. And I think, in rehearsal, the singer must relate to the event; all the time they must ask, what's the event? What's going on? The more you point them towards that, they will play it and sing it better, as opposed to self-reviewing. It's always best to be in the situation and it always sounds better.

PHYLLIDA LLOYD

Phyllida has directed opera for ENO, ROH, Opera North and Paris Opera whilst working extensively in theatre and film. Phyllida's productions are always politically vital and defined by incredibly engaged and detailed performances. I wanted to ask her about how she engages singers with improvisation in rehearsals and what she sees as an artists' responsibility to their chosen form.

Why opera?

Well, because of the structure of star-driven, what I call, international opera, where people arrive very late and have often done the role many times before, it's not really possible for me to do the kind of work I want to do, and so therefore I no longer do it.

The question of why opera at all is that I do think that when all the elements are in cohesion – the music, the performance, the visual ingredients, the story, the ideas – that opera has the potential to reach parts of an audience that other art forms just sometimes struggle to reach; it can bypass intellect and connect with some of our deepest channels.

However, there are many impediments to getting to that point. Opera is an extremely unwieldy medium – it's very expensive to have everybody together for enough time and there always seems to be a frantic struggle to get the show on the stage. Fundamentally because singers don't get paid to rehearse, a rehearsal is not what I understand to be a rehearsal. For me a rehearsal is everybody coming together for a minimum period of six weeks and beginning an intensive process of building an ensemble, that is going to somehow create the illusion that they're composing this music as they go along.

What are the challenges for the singer creating work in opera?

With actors and a play, actors have to take a big intellectual ownership of the evening, because there's nobody telling them when the silence should end or begin; there's nobody literally dictating to them rhythm and tempo. If actors don't get intellectually invested in the whole thing, they die. By contrast, one of the greatest sopranos in the world arrives on the day to sing in a production of mine, gets a few 'Don't fall down the hole in the ground' and 'Turn left, turn right' and 'Here's your crown', and on she goes, and blows the pants off the whole crowd.

Now the question for me is, this is fine for a certain kind of audience but what about that next generation? That generation that is now very versed in movie, in TV and great theatre? An audience very attuned to great acting, subtle acting; are they going to watch opera?

Is it dangerous enough? The score of this operatic event binds everybody together like a kind of Evo-Stik. So that actually, if one person stops singing in the middle, the others will fill in their bits and most of the audience won't really notice; the band plays on and everybody's fine. You can often feel that nobody on stage has really got a relationship. And one of the greatest sopranos in the world knows she can not only survive, but thrive with very little preparation.

And maybe she does do a huge amount of character work and is then able to drop into any production; but why? What's motivating her to bother to be more than she is already? What's motivating you, as a young singer?

I remember once going to teach a class at the National Opera Studio and to work on *Don Giovanni*. I asked the group to think about anything in their own lives that had anything to do with the action of *Don Giovanni*. And one guy put up his hand and said, 'Sorry, can I ask what has this actually got to do with my life?' And I just said 'Everything, because it's your life, and your experience brought to this medium, that is going to keep this medium alive'.

And so, we have this problem; the orchestra is Evo-Stik-ing the whole thing together, the conductor's telling you when to sing, so that you don't even have to think about why you come in, and you certainly don't have to listen to anybody else on stage. But what if you did? What if you *really* did? What if you came to rehearsal knowing what everybody else not only sung, but what their text was? What if you were really cognisant of the whole and came to rehearsals with a great kind of energy of excitement, and will, and anticipation of how this is all going to play out?

How have you worked with an ensemble to create this kind of energy in opera?

I remember doing an exercise at the Coliseum when rehearsing *The Rhinegold* and saying 'You all know your text, let's stand in a circle and you're going to pass the football on the last word of your piece of text to the person to whom you have an Action or an Objective'. The first person starts and they're all completely stunned; they're not even sure who's playing which part, because it's day one of rehearsals; but by the end of it, the ball was flying around the room and everybody knew who they were singing to and what they wanted to do to them.

What is your approach to creating work with singers?

I work in both a very forensic way and a very free way. The forensic way is to go through the text; every time there's a full stop, I ask the singers to give Actions and Objectives to the next piece of text. That means putting a transitive verb on that piece of text; supposing the piece of text is, 'We need some help here to move these pots', your Action could be to *inspire*, or it could be to *shame*. Obviously, the music, in some way, is going to give you a clue as to what the Action or Objective is but even within that, there is still a massive range of how that text can be used with the music. And you can change your Actions in response to what other people are singing to you and how they are singing to you; they incite your response. You really must change what you're doing in response to others, otherwise you risk simply *demonstrating* your Action.

It's about gaining ownership of that text and doing something to somebody else on stage that triggers the music that follows; so that, between you, you are composing the piece.

Once we've done this work in the morning, the afternoon will be spent improvising the scenes. There is no répétiteur so nobody's going to bring you in and nobody's going to tell you where to stand. You are going to have to just listen to each other; your body is going to have to start to listen. I did this with *Peter Grimes* and it was no different for *The Rhinegold*.

In setting up an improvisation, it is important to establish boundaries; what is ok to explore, what your Objectives might be. On the Shakespeares at the Donmar[2] we did break some limbs but we were creating riots. Improvisation gives you ownership of the space itself,

---

[2] Phyllida Lloyd directed an all-female Shakespeare trilogy at the Donmar Warehouse: *Julius Caesar* (2012), *Henry IV* (2014) and *The Tempest* (2016). All three plays were presented as a trilogy in 2016.

the relationships with other characters, and, crucially, your own thoughts. You, the singer, explore the length of the pauses, the thoughts you have before a line, and the journey the thoughts go on.

Then when you return to the music, you will begin to make the connections between those thoughts and the music. You will find that you have much more space; that you're not thinking about when you have to come in, but rather exploring this space before a musical entrance and defining what it means for you. So, you'll own it: the space, the thoughts, the pauses, the music.

Collectively you will be composing the music and, in this way, you will be 'not a servant of the music but its master'. And listening is key. You really don't need to keep looking at the conductor in the pit; you can listen to the music, to each other, to everything.

You've focused on directing operas by Benjamin Britten; why is this?

It's because he writes in English. He's a genius but the huge advantage is that working on his operas 'closes the gap' between the singer and text, and then the audience and text. And it means working directly with a composer who is setting the musical stresses to the text you will be working on.

I remember speaking to Josephine Barstow about how, during the early part of her career, she would take opera around the country, to very different spaces, always sung in English. She said it created very immediate productions.

It's really an absurdity working in another language. There's a letter Wagner wrote emphasising how important it was for his operas to be performed in the language of the audience.

Wagner was responding to an Australian director, Emil Sander, who had previously written to the composer in 1877 after seeing one of the first performances of *Lohengrin* in Australia:

> *My very dear Sir,*
>
> *I was delighted to receive your news, and cannot refrain from thanking you for it. I hope you will see to it that my works are performed in 'English:' only in this way can they be intimately understood by an English-speaking audience. We are hoping that they will be so performed in London. We (that is, I and my family) were extremely interested to see the views of Melbourne which you sent me: since you were kind enough to offer to send us more, I can assure you that I should be only too delighted to receive them.*
>
> *Please give my kind regards to Herr Lyster, and, however remote your part of the world may be, continue to be so well-disposed towards.*
>
> *Your most grateful servant,*
> *Richard Wagner*

Do you have any advice for the young singer?

In terms of preparation, go to see the films, read the books, look online, go to galleries and immerse yourself in ideas that relate to your character and their world; these are the supplies and fuel to sustain you on your journey.

The gender politics of opera are a worry. Over the last six years, since 2012, I've become obsessively preoccupied by gender imbalance on stage. It was as a result of a report saying that for every job that was going to a woman in British theatre, there were two jobs going to men. So, at that time I made a call that the Royal Shakespeare Company should consider hiring 50 per cent men, 50 per cent women and then work out how to do their repertoire. I began to think about opera; I'd been asked to do *Billy Budd* and I thought 'yes but are you doing *Dialogue of the Carmelites* in the same season?' Opera is still stuck where it was, not just six years ago, but sixty years ago in this regard. That's going to take some investigation.

Fundamentally, as a young singer and artist of the next generation, you need to ask: why am I doing this? As an artist and as a member of society, why am I telling this story, today? Who is this character *now*? Why am I socially invested in this opera? It is political.

ROBIN NORTON HALE

Robin is Artistic Director of OperaUpClose. The company was established in 2009 and two years later won an Olivier award for Robin's production of *La Bohème*. I particularly wanted to focus on Robin's work creating opera in English for performance in smaller theatres.

What is it about opera that excites you?

For me it is the most complete form of theatre. One of the things that opera does on big stages that I find really exciting is impressionistic-based storytelling, unlike the theatre tradition in this country which is rooted in realism; opera is much more connected to the European tradition of design-integrated theatre. I think the singing leads you to this heightened expression and that can be incredibly liberating for directors.

What do you think the challenges are for singers creating operatic characters in English?

If you're performing in English then people expect to hear every word you sing. That is perhaps an unrealistic expectation because, of course, many operas are not necessarily written for every word to be heard. But I'm not saying that because it is an unrealistic thing, we should not be making every effort to make it possible. The really exciting thing about working in English is the immediacy of storytelling; of understanding what is happening in that precise moment of music, and that precise moment of stage drama. I'm very much against the use of surtitles when singing in English, because the audience's eyes are always drawn to them and you risk losing this immediacy. The challenge for singers is to remain aware that they will be judged more harshly if they're not heard; the audience won't necessarily notice, when you're singing in Italian, German or Russian, how good your diction is.

What do you feel are the advantages of working in smaller spaces?

I think there are massive bonuses to working in a smaller space. It gives you a much broader range of acting options than are available in a large space; really basic things, like being able to sing facing upstage. Music colleges often only train singers to perform on huge stages, and so singers can be terrified by the thought of turning upstage, but in smaller spaces this can be very effective; you can still hear the singers and I always feel that seeing the back of a character, turned to the audience, can be very eloquent. It also means you can play around with delivery, so that, for example, certain lines can be really *sotto voce*.

OperaUpClose began life in a thirty-five-seat theatre above a pub, then moved to the hundred-seat Kings Head Theatre, and now tours to mid-scale theatres around the country (the smallest venues we visit are two hundred seats, and the largest are a thousand). One of the big differences for us in this transition is that now, instead of just a piano, we have an orchestra of about four on stage. In common with a lot of smaller companies there is no conductor, which can be challenging. However, the bonus is that the singers and orchestra are having to work as an ensemble, are intently listening to each other, and are living and breathing the piece together. Importantly, you don't then get the horrible moment where you can see the singer clocking the conductor, something which always breaks the drama.

And the challenges for the singers when working up close?

The acting has to be even better and, of course, not having a conductor is really challenging. Acting on a very big stage demands a different style of acting but it has to start from the same building blocks, the same truthfulness, that you can then turn up the volume on. But the proximity to the audience in smaller spaces means that the audience can literally see your eyes; they can see if you're looking at another character, or if you're responding to another character, or if you're hearing words as if for the first time in the moment.

What preparation do you expect the singer to do before the first day of rehearsal?

One of the really interesting things about opera, and especially core repertoire, is that a singer with a certain type of voice will end up only ever playing a small handful of roles. That means they will get to know the music and those characters incredibly well. The important thing is not to have set ideas about this character. On the other hand, to have thoughts about the character's journey through the opera is important: their life before the opera, what has happened to them, how old they are, where were they born, what their relationship with their parents is like.

What does a singer need to bring to the rehearsal room?

An openness to new ideas and a generosity towards their colleagues. Each person will contribute, in some way, to the creation of each of the characters and the world. The singer needs to have a strong idea of who that character is, but also be open to developing it with the other cast members. That can mean letting go of some things that they absolutely thought were true of that character.

The readiness to approach these pieces as if they're new writing is vital; we need to imagine we've never met Violetta before and seek to understand why she makes the decisions she makes.

How do you work with a singer to create character and how does the music inform the decisions you make?

I start by creating lists of Facts and Questions: gathering all the information we can glean from the libretto. It's a useful way of shedding assumptions. We also work out timelines and sometimes we create maps of places. We might have a week of massive pieces of paper moving around the room: working out when the characters met each other, family trees and so on.

I intersperse that with a lot of physical work. I like to use exercises that clearly connect to the task of creating the character; for example, we'll start off with everyone walking around the room, leading with different parts of the body. We might then spend time thinking what characters are like when they're sitting alone in a room: what's the pace of their thoughts? Do they sit still? Is there tension in the body? We do this every day, in order to build up a sense of what the character's like under normal circumstances, away from the stresses that can take place in the stories of opera; it's useful to do this before we take the characters into the high drama situations of the opera.

In this way the singers are developing habitual physical behaviours?

Exactly! We'll do an exercise later in the process which is to do a repeated task that the character would do each day: brushing their hair, or cleaning their gun if they're a soldier. We'll do this for ten minutes each day to get a sense of who this person is because, of course, singers have to be incredibly physically comfortable within themselves, in character, in order to make that incredible sound. Almost every production I've done, the singers have requested that we do this ten-minute physical character task warm-up, before the show.

How does the music help when creating character?

The question of what is the internal metronome of this character is really interesting. Sometimes the music does not seem to represent the character's internal thought process or metronome. There might be ten people on stage and it might be somebody else's music. In opera generally, unlike a play, you know how long a thought is, because it's written in the music, and you know where the crisis point in that thought is, even if the singer is not singing, because that's in the music too. So, when the music comes in, it's not dictating to us, it's additional information; what a particular melodic phrase is suggesting is subjective, so this is why it's useful to have initially thought about the Facts and Questions from the libretto, so that we don't simply rely on a stock interpretation or a narrow response to the music.

DAVID POUNTNEY

David Pountney was Director of Productions at Scottish Opera from 1975 to 1980, at ENO from 1980 to 1993, and Intendant of the Bregenz Festival from 2003 to 2014. He has been Artistic Director of WNO since 2011. I wanted to ask David about his process of rehearsing opera and, especially, the way he engage singers to create characters in abstracted, stylised and highly theatrical worlds.

Why opera?

I came to it from the point of view of a musician: I was a boy chorister and then I played the trumpet and the piano. My family were very much involved as good amateur musicians in all kinds of things, so music was a regular language for me.

We were also always going to the theatre as a family. In the days of weekly rep we'd go on a Wednesday evening, this was in Oxford, and they were fantastic touring productions;

most of the West End shows, pre-super high tech, would tour to Oxford on their way to London.

I remember seeing the original production of *West Side Story,* for example, and some opera too: English Chamber Opera's production of *The Turn of the Screw*, Sadler's Wells Opera and so on. I suppose the way in which music tells a story remains the thing that interests me most.

Could you take us through your process, or processes, of rehearsal?

The first thing I do is to set the context in which singer has to develop their role. A lot of the decisions that are going to dictate the environment in which the singer is working will have been taken way in advance. This context will significantly affect the behaviour of the characters. If we take something like my recent production of *The Force of Destiny*, for example, we came up with a pretty abstract set of images for the telling of that story. That clearly influences the way in which the characters behave, because we're not asking them to be naturalistic aristocratic Spanish figures in a kind of opulent drawing room setting, we're treating them much more emblematically than that.

My first job, therefore, as quickly as possible in rehearsal, is to make clear what the environment is, what I'm expecting of the singers, and what kind of performances I'm expecting them to find. Once we've established those basic rules of the game, the singers will of course offer stuff. It's a very important discipline for me to be very, very open and alert to things that might nudge the whole production a bit to the left, or a bit to the right; in this direction, or that direction. Everybody is working with a fresh mind in those first couple of weeks and so, if the director is too obsessed with his or her plan and is forcing this plan upon everybody else, that element of reaction and spontaneous development is being smothered.

After that period, it is actually about getting the whole thing to work, which is rather more pedestrian but opera is a big, cumbersome thing and it needs to be repeated often.

I think an artistic discipline, in the first period, is to keep yourself open, to be able to react quickly to solve scenes, and to go with the flow. You have your plan, those things that you've decided already which are fixed – the nature of the costumes, the kind of style of the set, the style of the production – but within that there is a lot of room for everybody to develop in different ways.

Then comes the period when it's no longer about inspiration, it's about administration; you must make everybody comfortable and make sure it all fits with the timing of the music.

Do you expect the singers to approach rehearsals with the same open mind?

If people have done these roles before, there's no point pretending that they're not going to bring some of that baggage with them. Hopefully they are receptive to other ideas, and you may, as a director, have to deliberately destabilise them to see if there could be different ways of doing this. Nobody is an island, everybody is arriving with all kinds of bits and pieces of understanding, but it's important to try to find a common language somewhere.

There is a skill and technique, as a singer, to getting the best out of your director. If you arrive defensively, clinging on to some preconception you have, you are almost automatically creating a barrier between yourself and the director. As a singer, you should approach the director as a resource, as something to be exploited; what can this person tell me about how I can develop my part?

Is introducing the design on the first day of rehearsals important in establishing a common language?

It's very important, yes, because everyone needs to have a clear understanding of what environment they are operating in. If you're doing, for example, *The Marriage of Figaro* in a period context, then there is a certain discipline to the behaviour which the singers need to be comfortable with. The understanding of the environment the singer is working in will have a big influence on the way they develop their character and on the way they portray their character.

I don't very often work in that kind of environment. I'm more often working in an abstract or slightly more contemporary environment, which is very different. Actually, in some respects, a more abstract approach by the director, I think, will tend to liberate the singers, because they're not being constrained by an environment that seems to entail genteel behaviour in a period context, whilst also singing in a way that you would not speak in that context. I think it's always likely that an operatic performance will deviate from what one would consider a *naturalistic performance*, simply because it's being sung.

But you'd still work with the singers to understand the characters' wants or needs?

Yes, I think the psychology becomes even more important in this respect. The psychology remains true, and even amplified, in the circumstances in which naturalistic behaviour is no longer relevant. The psychological drive of the characters is their primary motivation.

For example, in *The Force of Destiny* I created a scenic device which was that the spot where the father fell, when he was shot accidentally in the opening scene, continued to ooze blood for the rest of the evening. Those characters who felt obsessively responsible for this death were left dealing with this suppurating wound throughout the evening; it gave expression to the psychological obsession and was a psychological motivator for these characters throughout the opera.

And how does this relate to the music?

I still follow one of director Walter Felsenstein's rules, which is that the action or the behaviour of the character should inspire the music to happen, not the other way round. Some directors look at the music as initiating the action but to my mind the character should initiate the music.

If the music has a sudden kind of energy, that energy should come from the character having that energy and the music is describing the energy of the character, not the character acting out the energy of the music. The singer needs to ask, why is that music describing what I'm doing? They have to supply the motivation for that music to exist.

What do you see as the main challenges of working with music and text?

The primary acting instrument of the singer is the voice; a successful opera performer will act with a voice more than with any other part. The way you sing should be an absolutely integral part of the character which you're performing and you should sing like the character. One of the main ways in which a singer can grasp that interpretive possibility is by the use of the words; the words massively give contour to the representation of the character through the voice. There is a lot of misunderstanding about this, because there is a lot of expectation that the main thing is to sing beautifully, whereas on the whole, in opera, singing beautifully has very little to do with it. It's much more about singing *appropriately*. The way in which the words are invested with energy, and with the relish of the pronunciation of the words, obviously interferes with that kind of beautiful singing that you might employ if you were singing lieder.

How might you access the libretto to come to a clearer understanding of who the character is?

In the case of Verdi, for example, it involves an understanding of the political and social backgrounds of where these stories came from and why he chose them. In representing complex human beings, in a complex artistic framework, having a wide-ranging mind and looking widely around you at the implications of these pieces is very helpful. An artist, in this context, has to be a rounded person with a broad worldview to get hold of the humanity that is expressed by someone like Verdi or Janacek. I think to be invited to do a role in *The Marriage of Figaro*, for example, is also an invitation to understand the social and political context of that piece and the society we're talking about, and that may require a bit of research.

You talked about the necessity of repetition in the rehearsal process. Alongside this how do you encourage the singer to bring spontaneity to a performance, in order to suggest to an audience that this story is happening for the first time?

I think there are three distinct phases:

- The creative phase, where you lay down the basis of what you are aspiring to.
- The administrative phase, where you almost deliberately exclude spontaneity, because what you're creating is a secure platform where basically everybody knows how the performance functions and the singers know exactly what they have to do: when, where and how.
- The final stage, when, standing upon that solid platform in the performance, they are liberated to be spontaneous again because they have total confidence in the action around them: the interaction with their colleagues, with the conductor, all the technical stuff, getting the voice where they need it, their breathing and their body, wearing their costumes and sweating under their wigs all rests on this secure base.

You need the rehearsal process to kill off spontaneity for a while, in order to be sure that when they go out to perform they are safe enough, so that they can risk being spontaneous. That's, of course, what you want in a performance but you need a launchpad: I think a singer is actually playing a game of football and reciting poetry simultaneously. They're doing something intensely physically demanding, whilst dealing with words, and acting the portrayal of a character; and so they need to stand solid and then the excitement takes off.

How do you encourage the singer in their work in that third stage?

I do try to not be a picky director. I try to increasingly let them feel, without necessarily saying so, that they are responsible at this stage, that I'm not going to be there. My job is to make myself redundant, so that by the first night nobody needs me any more.

When rehearsals move to the stage, how do you help the singer to continue to develop their character?

Stage rehearsals are very often very technical and when you get to the final run-through in the studio before you get on stage, you should feel that you're very close to performance level, because in the first three quarters of the stage rehearsals you're going to go backwards. Because suddenly you're dealing with a whole other load of technical stuff, it tends to go downhill. Hopefully, by the last stage and piano rehearsal you've built that back up again. And then at the first stage and orchestra, of course, it goes completely downhill again, because you're suddenly hearing seventy musicians instead of one pianist, and the conductor is suddenly three times further away. It's a series of rebuffs and rebuilds.

Do you have any other advice to the young singer?

Not to be afraid to ask. I said at the beginning that the director's job is to set the parameters for the context in which this production is going to be developed. In some cases it might be something quite wacky; for example, somebody just did *La Bohème* set on a spaceship and as a young singer you've got to feel comfortable in that context. You shouldn't be afraid to ask, 'Why are we here? Why are we on the moon?' You don't want to be hostile, because that's just going to create a barrier between you and the director, but you are entitled to understand what you're doing. You need to understand in order to engage with that idea, that's part of getting the best out of your director; there are no stupid questions.

When it comes down to it, when the curtain goes up, you're the one in the spaceship; not the director, they're in the bar. So you need to understand why you're there and you need to find your way to fall in love with that idea.

14 Singers' Case Studies

- KATHRYN HARRIES
- ELIZABETH LLEWELLYN
- WILLIAM MORGAN
- CLARE PRESLAND
- ANDREW SHORE
- PABLO STRONG

The following conversations explore the singer's process from preparation through to performance. The featured singers are at different stages of their careers: a number are graduates of ENO Opera Works and all have a close association with ENO.

KATHRYN HARRIES

Kathryn (soprano) sang leading roles for all the major international opera houses. She was Director of the National Opera Studio from 2008 to 2017.

How do you prepare to create a character before a rehearsal process?

It's a process that begins the minute I start learning the music and text. Text is of paramount importance because the music has generally been composed in response to the words. In order to honour the composer's wishes, I always wanted to discover how and why he set the text the way he or she did.

The physical singing-in of each phrase is done concentrating on vocal technique and, in particular, breath control and placement. I developed a personal system of practising the words separately, alongside my singing, and when I reached the stage of putting the two elements together, I used very specific techniques of my own to articulate the text as clearly as possible. I developed this approach over time. When I started out in opera, my diction wasn't as clear as it subsequently became, not because I didn't respect the value of the words, rather because no one ever told me how to go about physically articulating vowels and consonants.

As I became familiar with the words and music, the personality of the character I was playing would gradually emerge. The more deeply I went into the character and the character's situation within the opera, the more the ideas presented themselves. I'm very fortunate in having good mental and physical co-ordination; maybe all that sport helped!

Taking time to study the character in real depth is essential if the singer is going to give his or her own unique and honest account of the character he or she is playing. I always aimed to arrive fully prepared on the first day of rehearsal and then I welcomed the ideas given to me by both conductor and director. Provided I was true to the words and the music, the character then developed greater and greater depth, independent of my conscious thought.

How did you approach a first day of rehearsal?

The first day of rehearsal was always rather terrifying because I felt I had to prove myself worthy of having been cast. Being a good colleague was always of paramount importance and I had no time for singers and musicians who tried to undermine each other. Opera was always a team effort, as far as I was concerned, and it behoved us all to be kind, helpful and professional towards everyone we encountered, regardless of his or her place in the jigsaw.

What did you find challenging when creating character in rehearsal and what have you found helps the process?

The only challenge I remember facing in rehearsal was when the director didn't have a clear vision of who my character was within the opera: where she'd come from and what had led her to this point in time. Bad directors rob you of your own ideas and replace them with nothing concrete or honest. Fortunately, I can say this only happened on three occasions in my career and I was obliged to draw on my own skills and imagination to make up for the director's lack of ability.

How does the music help you create character?

The music always told me a huge amount about the character. It's important for singers to listen to the harmonic landscape and to let their imagination run free in response to the music. It's not enough to think only of one's own vocal line.

I never had an acting lesson in my life, which meant that I was free to respond in an entirely genuine and natural way to the music and drama. I was able to physicalise the character just by thinking about what my character was thinking. If I was singing in a language that was not my own, I practised the text in English until it became ingrained in my subconscious to the point where I felt I was singing in my native tongue.

How do you think about physical characterisation?

I was always happy to take direction on how much physical characterisation was appropriate. My tendency was to take things too far, so knowing where to draw the line was important. I believe it's vital that all the members of the cast have the same acting style and seriousness of approach if the production is going to be honest and touch the audience.

I was never a fan of playing games to unlock my imagination; it seemed artificial and, for me, it had nothing to do with getting to the heart of the words and music.

Are there any rehearsal processes that have fed into the way you work in the long term?

The very best process for me was to work with the conductor and director around the piano, exploring each phrase in infinite detail. Staging then followed very naturally and relatively quickly. I also enjoyed 'Verbing' or Actioning: using transitive verbs to express each phrase, meant that the observer could always tell my character's state of mind. It's a useful tool when one's imagination lets one down and it helped with dynamics, phrasing and physicalisation. I was incredibly fortunate to work with some of the greatest directors of my day and for that I shall forever be profoundly grateful.

How did you use stage rehearsals?

I always gave the rehearsals my total concentration, so that I could achieve greater and greater understanding of the person I was playing. I never 'marked' my acting.

How did you prepare for a performance?

A balance of rest and activity on the day. I would go through the music and text at least three times to bring everything I wanted to do to the front of my mind. I was always very nervous, so it was relief to get on stage and get on with the show!

What did you do in the wings before you went on?

I didn't have a particular routine – it depended on the character I was playing. Sometimes I was happy to have a word with my colleagues and other times I needed to be entirely alone. I was fortunate in being able to switch in and out of character very easily and this probably helped me keep relatively sane when I was playing really challenging roles like the Kostelnika, Didon and Kundry.

ELIZABETH LLEWELLYN

Elizabeth (soprano) trained in the inaugural year of ENO Opera Works. She has since performed leading roles at ENO, Royal Danish Opera, Glyndebourne and Seattle Opera, and is about to make her debut for the Metropolitan Opera.

What do you find difficult about auditions?

Oddly enough, I don't find auditions difficult any more! The only thing I find hard is when the panel ask me to sing sections of arias rather than the whole aria, because of time or because they want to hear something specific (e.g. coloratura, top notes, etc.). I find it hard to 'click in' to that section and sing it just as well as if I was singing it in context.

What has helped you to do auditions?

Some time ago, I decided to make each audition my personal ten-minute gala concert to which the panel happens to be invited. It helps me to relax, and to own the space and time I have, rather than feeling judged or that I need to please or impress the panel.

How do you prepare to create character before a rehearsal process?

As basic preparation, I translate the entire score if it is in a language which is not English. This would include descriptions of scenes or other characters in the score, as well as what everyone else says, even if my character never meets them. It is essential for me to understand what is going on and being said in the world in which my character finds herself.

Recently, I had to learn *Madama Butterfly* in six weeks entirely on my own, so most of my time was spent learning the music and memorising text at break-neck speed and then 'singing in' the role before rehearsals began. To help to understand the culture, country and unique world which was completely alien to me, I spent any spare time I had watching documentaries about why and how girls became geishas; what it meant to them, what sacrifices are made, and what benefits are gained. I even researched if there are, or were, any black people living in Japan, and what it is, or was, like for them. The whole exercise was utterly fascinating and very moving but, most importantly for me, it gave me a real-life context in which to build my own Cio-Cio San.

If I have the time, I like to do a comprehensive character analysis, which can take some weeks. This is largely based around a career-defining weekend I spent on the ENO Opera Works course with Mike Alfreds, who coached us using his book *Different Every Night*. We were encouraged to forensically analyse the character and their environments, using the information given to us in the vocal score; I find it useful to build a list of Given Circumstances for my character – their social status, the time of year, day, the era, the place, etc. – in order to build a detailed picture of what would be informing my decisions and the way in which I behave within the space. The process is basically:

- What is my character's Super-Objective (what do I ultimately want)? This is quite a profound question and one I tend to answer at the end of the analysis.

- What is my Objective for this act or scene? What are the Obstacles to me getting what I want?

- What does each of the other characters say about me?

- What do I say about the other characters?

- What do I say about myself?

- With everything I say, what is my specific and concrete Action, not emotion (what do I want the other person to do or feel)?

I find it a great help being specific onstage, and not getting sucked into generic, operatic vagueness of 'emotion'. For example, *how* I play each Action, or *how* I respond to my Given Circumstances can be different every night, but my performance is always rooted in something tangible. I think this has now become a hallmark of my work in opera.

How does your work with a vocal coach support this?

It is really important to have another pair of ears whom you trust, not only to help iron out any technical issues and to make sure that you are at your singing best in terms of tone, diction and phrasing, but to help you to strike the right tone and balance in terms of your character, and in terms of what houses expect to hear from someone who sings your roles.

I remember being surprised when my teacher told me to 'give less' in terms of volume for my first Donna Elvira: she said, 'You have more than enough voice for this; you can afford to give less'. As a result, it freed me to pay more attention to the delivery of text, especially in recitatives, and not push so much vocal weight around for her arias and ensembles which have a great deal of coloratura.

How do you approach a first day of rehearsal?

With confidence and with openness! I mostly sing either title roles or leading ladies, so the confidence comes from being certain that I have prepared thoroughly and that I am equal to the challenge. The openness is about being open to the ideas of the director, conductor and other singers, even though I will always arrive at a first rehearsal with an informed opinion about my character. I think it is helpful to a director or conductor if I have a thoughtful shape to my character, as it tends to give rise to interesting and helpful discussions. In the end, my ideas may have to yield to the production, but they provide a starting point. It is good not to be too fixed in my ideas about a role at the beginning, and be prepared to explore other avenues as they present themselves over the rehearsal period – often, I can come to a new conclusion about my character which I had not considered before.

What do you find challenging when creating character in rehearsal?

Going with an idea from a director which I do not agree with, understand fully or find comfortable.

What have you found helps the process of creating character in rehearsal?

Challenging myself to remain open for the duration of the rehearsal period. Sometimes it is hard to see what is being created until a section is finished. For example, I remember being in the chorus for Richard Jones's new production of *Falstaff*. The entire cast and chorus were called to rehearsals every day, even if we were not singing in that scene: there were lots of 'extras' as shop-keepers, passers-by, etc. It was difficult to understand why it was important for us to be there until we eventually ran the scene; the result was one of exceptional beauty, interest, commitment and humour.

Around the halfway point in the rehearsal process, I tend to sketch a kind of flow-chart for myself, to check my understanding of what my character does and why, as well the practical issues of entrances, exits and costume changes. It helps me to see where the holes or inconsistencies are.

How does the music help you create character?

The music is very much the *how* characters speak, and on many occasions the orchestra 'says' what cannot be said or articulated onstage. For me, the music also forms the emotional world in which my characters live. I pay close attention to how my role is written, especially at moments of acute distress; how the composer uses the various registers and 'sweet spots' in a soprano's voice to create a particular impression.

For example, much of Cio-Cio San's music is very lyrical and steps up and down quite logically, even in the 'big' moments. However, the mere thought of returning to the life of a geisha produces her only angular music in the whole opera with cries of 'Morta!' and 'Ah! M'ha scordata?!'. I came to the conclusion that Butterfly has been rigorously trained to be genteel (sometimes imperious, heightened by her perceived status in Act Two) and always controlled, until something or someone touches on something raw.

How do you think about physical characterisation?

I think physicality is possibly the most important thing I can think about. The audience – or even just people in everyday life – read my body language long before they register what has come out of my mouth. I found it hard to embody Butterfly, whose movements seem smaller, stylised and controlled. Also, I think how I move – and therefore breathe – informs the vocal colour I want to create. So, as soon as I have memorised the role, I try to work on what might be asked of me physically in the rehearsal room, and embody some of those ideas.

Are there any processes you have found challenging and why?

The role I am currently singing in Seattle, Bess from Gershwin's *Porgy and Bess,* I am convinced is physically strong, but emotionally very complicated. She has an addiction to cocaine and she is also addicted to her boyfriend, Crown. Her scene and duet with him in Act Two are very intense and extremely physical; she tries a number of times to run, he catches and overpowers her. The music is a big sing with lots of brass in the orchestra, and pretty bluesy in vocal style; these elements together make for quite a cardio-vascular workout. I insisted that we run the scene every few days until it was physically easy for me to manage; the opera director Calixto Bieto once said that 'The rehearsal room is the gymnasium for the voice', and now I understand what he means!

How do you use stage rehearsals?

It can be difficult because this is the point at which I am most acutely aware that my bosses, and my colleagues backstage, can sit in on rehearsals at any time or hear the rehearsals via the tannoy all over the building. There is a strong temptation to play to that, and to try to give a performance in order to impress.

I try to get as detailed an overview as possible from the director and conductor as to how they will be using the stage-time and make sure that I too have a plan based around what they need during that time.

Tech week can be exhausting and frustrating, so I try to be clear about what I want to achieve in each rehearsal. If I do not want to sing out, and concentrate instead on navigating the set, or checking sight-lines, or working with the addition of wigs and costumes, I will make sure that the conductor knows this.

Or it may be that I want or need to build stamina vocally, or understand how the theatre works acoustically, and so sometimes I sing a lot in stage rehearsals to help me in that area.

Each role and production brings different challenges, so I try to remind myself that the stage rehearsals are still *my* rehearsals, and my priority is to make sure that I feel confident, safe and secure – even final dress rehearsals, which opera houses now generally open to an audience, I use as an opportunity to make adjustments.

How do you prepare for a performance?

I try to get a proper night's sleep the night before, and definitely stay away from alcohol, food which I have an intolerance for and noisy environments.

I stay away from people as much as possible! Lots of friends, journalists, agents have asked for meetings on performance days which I routinely refuse. For me, people sap energy and focus, and tire me vocally, and the show is my priority.

I try to eat proper meals at regular intervals, with the last meal being the largest, around four hours before curtain-up. I find it difficult to eat and digest food shortly before a performance, so I need fuel to keep me going for the evening (that said, I will always pack an emergency banana just in case!).

I almost always do some form of exercise to wake up my body or to put me in touch with how my body is feeling that day. Exercise helps me to clear my mind, and 'reset' for the working day ahead. It also helps me to notice new things – sights, sounds, smells – and generally heighten my awareness.

It is important for me to spend at least an hour with the score that day, going through my performance mentally and reminding myself of what I want to achieve. Having my notes to hand from my character analysis is really useful here. I want my performance to feel as fresh and spontaneous as possible, rather than going through the motions, so it is really important to renew focus and to have fresh ideas about the role.

I get in to the theatre at least three hours before curtain-up, so that I can warm up slowly and in relative solitude. Sometimes, my voice isn't working the way I would like it to, and so needs a little more coaxing. It is important I understand what is happening in my body that day (e.g. tiredness, tensions, coming down with a cold, etc.). Usually, I have a hair and make-up call straight after this warm-up, so I can relax a bit and do a final warm-up and go through my 'hit-list' once my costume is on. My 'hit-list' is a list of between ten and twenty musical or vocal things which I know can be a little tricky and which need a bit of special attention.

What do you do in the wings before you go on?

I try to greet all of my colleagues backstage; we are a team and my success is very dependent on theirs. Apart from that, I try not to get into conversations; it is a time for me to be still and focused. Sometimes, my singing colleagues can be nervous and/or hyperactive, and they have a tendency to try to draw everyone around them into their drama; I block them out and mentally visualise a bubble forming around me, where I can see and hear them, but where I am protected from their 'energy'. I simply concentrate on *why* my character is about to enter the space, *how* they will enter that space and *what* they want to achieve when they get there.

WILLIAM MORGAN

William Morgan (tenor) trained with ENO Opera Works and is currently an ENO Harewood Artist. He has worked with, amongst others, Scottish Opera, ROH, Glyndebourne and OperaUpClose.

What do you find difficult about auditions?

Everything! Who likes auditions? They are necessary but extremely hard to enjoy, and enjoyment is very necessary for good performance; it breeds curiosity and opens the mind to options. In auditions there are all sorts of barriers: having a strange sort of audience who are looking to employ and assess, rather than to enjoy themselves like a regular audience; having to perform without rehearsing with the pianist; building an atmosphere in a potentially very dead space; the question of 'doing enough' versus 'doing too much'.

What has helped you when auditioning?

A number of things: having performed the piece in production before auditioning with it and therefore having a physical memory of the role, knowing the space or the room beforehand, knowing the pianist, having a lot of Points of Concentration to play with in order to keep my mind from wandering, various techniques for keeping the mind in the present, listening and being attentive at each moment. In the best cases an audition is more like a working session; there is a dialogue with feedback and ideas.

How do you prepare for creating character before a rehearsal process?

I love words and I have no time for opera performances in which I cannot hear the words landing. So, I will always start with text and become familiar with the whole piece: writing down ideas, the Given Circumstances in each scene, etc. I like to think about the structure of the opera and the character's journey, through Objectives and Events. I love the 'three times through' exercise and like to get maximum freedom with the words before introducing any music. I find that starting from this point of intimate knowledge of the words gives the most options when the rehearsal process starts; good exercises don't predetermine any outcome, they are just a process that gives us food to work with later.

Actions are great; I always try to write down a few, but not worry too much if they're not immediately obvious. I try not to nail anything down. At this point it's just about having options.

How does your work with a vocal coach support this?

Vocal coaches that I like to work with ensure that I am delivering every word with clarity, freedom and intention. They can hear if I drop the ball or am skimming over something a bit. I am currently working with coaches to prepare Tom Rakewell in *The Rake's Progress*; a fairly long role. My main priority is to work with someone who has a deep knowledge of the architecture of the piece and who can tell me things about their experience of preparing it in the past; this can feed my dramatic ideas for Tom.

How do you approach a first day of rehearsal?

This is a great day! It's about listening to everyone else, finding out how the piece will fit together and hearing it for the first time as a group. When it's a new work, and none of it has ever been heard before, that's particularly thrilling.

What do you find challenging when creating character in rehearsal?

The challenge is that a lot of people are always trying to help, which can be very enjoyable, but also tricky to manage. And often, time is short so we can become fixated on quick results rather than trusting a process.

The big challenge is allowing it to go wrong! I always think it's best to push ideas as far as possible, and then you can rein them back if necessary. I also suspect it's easier for directors and colleagues if you offer something in this way and allow them to respond and filter.

What have you found helps the process of creating character in rehearsal?

It is always interesting to see how you fit in with other characters in the piece and to allow your responses to them to develop. I love the physical act of *trying* things in rehearsal. I like trying to find a different thing to focus on each time: refreshing an Objective or trying a new Action and seeing how that influences the scene. In *The Turn of the Screw*, Peter Quint's two related Objectives 'To save Miles' and 'To get rid of the Governess' became the main things I played with. The Objectives became my mantra: '*She has to go . . . He must be free . . . She has to go . . .*'. The clearest Objectives to play are often the most simple.

How does the music help you create character?

Music always contains a lot of information we can use to play with but most often I think it just helps us to delineate where the beats are. Often the music change inspires a new Action; it doesn't tell me exactly what the Action should be, but it tells me there has to be one! I might be working with music where I have quite a lot of freedom (for example, Donizetti's recit provides only a loose framework), or, contrastingly, very little rhythmic choice at all (Stravinsky), but the music always guides us towards where to place beats.

How do you think about physical characterisation?

I like to think in terms of rhythmic constructs, effort qualities, leading with body parts. Character archetypes can be fun! Physical actions can inspire thoughts, as much as the other way around. We had a tricky exercise in *The Turn of the Screw* because under our theatrical rules, the ghosts and children were not allowed to look at each other directly, so the way we interacted physically was very important. Miles took on some of Quint's physicality and vice versa.

Are there any processes you have found challenging and why?

There are lots of good challenges! Playing against my natural movement qualities has been challenging for me. I often tend to play quite urgent, enthusiastic character types but in *Paul Bunyan* I had to play someone (Hot Biscuit Slim) who is charismatic but also very laid back. I kept having to think about sitting back into the ground and feeling the weight in the pelvis and hips. He lets people come to him, rather than going to them.

The processes I remember being the most challenging are those in which I've had a small role, or covered a role. There has been a huge amount of waiting around followed by suddenly having to be really alert for a very short period of action time.

Are there any rehearsal processes that have fed into the way you work in the long term?

I have loved working with actors and choreographers, as well as musicians and directors. Seeing the way actors bring text to life by playing the Through-Line has been inspirational. Some of this drive is given to us as singers through the pacing of the music, but we can't take it for granted; we need to make it our own.

I had an amazing rehearsal process on *Between Worlds,* a new commission and my first solo role for ENO. It didn't have the big, theatrical, larger-than-life moments that opera often has; it was really necessary to employ very clear Actions at each moment and play them, honestly, as myself. I sort of realised that character for me was less about putting on a mask of someone else or doing a vast amount of 'pretending' to 'be' a certain person and was more about thinking very specifically about Circumstances, Objectives and Actions. And I developed an understanding that you can only fully play one thing at once; you might need to leave some aspects for the next scene.

How do you use stage rehearsals?

Stage rehearsals are often pretty scarce in opera! They are a fraught time; I try to pace it so that once the technical work is done, and scenes can be run in their entirety, I can really step up and view them a bit more like a performance.

How do you prepare for a performance?

I think that if the rehearsals have been good, the performances are the easy bit! I try to just centre myself, be aware, be rested and allow myself to be excited! I love putting things before an audience; it can really transform a show for the better.

I think it's really important to perform just as we have rehearsed: with open-mindedness, an awareness of colleagues and a sense of company spirit. It seems incredibly obvious, but some singers I know seem to change their mindset in performance and become very blinkered and closed off, especially if management are present, etc.

What do you do in the wings before you go on?

It varies. I always aim to bring focus to the present, whether that's through the breath or some other physical sensation. I refresh the Given Circumstances of that scene, especially if I've had a long gap since the last scene. In *The Turn of the Screw* there is quite a large gap between some of Quint's appearances; I remember finding a lot of enjoyment in reminding myself of the present danger in each scene. If I know the show extremely well, after many performances, the Given Circumstances can become automatic, so I will try to find a new interesting Point of Concentration. I did many performances of a small-scale production of *Die Fledermaus*; playing Alfred, to keep it alive and fun for myself, I would play games like focusing on Rosalinde's necklace and finding it the most desirable object ever; the next time, it might be her shoes; the next time, I would try to make her dance. It's all about having options, as long as they are all consistent with the show, the overall Objective and are generous towards colleagues.

CLARE PRESLAND

Clare (mezzo soprano) trained with ENO Opera Works. Clare now works internationally with companies such as ENO, Théâtre des Champs Elysées, ROH and Opéra de Lyon.

What do you find difficult about auditions?

It has taken me some time, with a lot of reflection, thought and analysis, to figure out how I 'work' in auditions! What's difficult is that you have a small time frame to 'deliver' and you don't always know if there will be warm-up facilities, or a rehearsal with a pianist, beforehand, so the circumstances can bring their own challenges. There's this idea of 'proving yourself'; wanting work opportunities from the audition but not appearing too 'needy'.

I have to say that role-specific auditions are much easier than generals. With role-specific auditions, everyone knows what they're casting for and there is a clear requirement of repertoire and, of course, decisions follow fairly soon after; so you know where you stand, a little more, in the whole process. General auditions are a great opportunity to sing but it doesn't always mean things will come from it. And the other thing about general auditions is that the casting board have to really understand how to cast you from what they hear from the audition pieces you performed.

What has helped you to do auditions?

- Having space before to get into the best 'mental space' I can.
- Finding the right repertoire for me, as opposed to 'fitting into some kind of box'!
- Having an aria that I always start with and that I know I can deliver even if I'm feeling under par; something I am truly committed to and in.
- Staging the arias! I find it so much easier to audition with roles I have performed and if I haven't sung the role, well, I stage them myself: seeing your set, cast, etc. really helps bring different vocal and theatrical colours.
- Realising that if I focus on proving myself I will give off the wrong energy, an energy that is too 'in your face' perhaps, now I sing for my love of singing and I enjoy having the opportunity of doing so.

How do you prepare to create character before a rehearsal process?

I really think that the creation of a character starts from the minute I highlight my score and write my translation in (if I'm working in another language). When I read the libretto, I tend to underline text that moves me or informs me of who the character is. The music then gives us so much information about character – harmony, melodic line, etc. Once I have the music learning underway I tend to write Actions underneath phrases. This gives me clear direction and also allows the breath and emotion to colour the voice.

How does your work with a vocal coach support this?

Having a coach who has good ears and who you trust is essential. It's so important to be singing in the right groove from the start and, as the music informs so much, this in turn all adds to character development.

What do you find challenging when creating character in rehearsal?

I approach the first day of rehearsal with an open mind but I think the only challenge is if a director or conductor views the piece, or character, in a very different way from how you do and what your instincts say. But, this can always be discussed and sometimes you find different routes that work better! Hence why I try to be open-minded.

What have you found helps the process of creating character in rehearsal?

Having a rehearsal period! This time dedicated to delving deep is just precious. I recently worked with a director who gave me the most incredible subplot to basically every line I sang; it had meaning and an edge that I had never considered before.

How do you think about physical characterisation?

I start from the breath; this can really inform how you characterise naturally by truly engaging and feeling and breathing as the character would. And then I try to think of one physical characteristic and use this as the 'physical anchor'; a gesture, a movement, etc. added as another layer.

Are there any processes you have found challenging and why?

It can be challenging if a director keeps making changes, big changes, right up until the last moment, as then there is no time to physicalise what is required deep into your muscles. But then again, this can be positive because it keeps you on your toes to find new things continuously.

I really believe that every process informs and builds me as an artist, I always walk away having learnt something, or many things.

How do you use stage rehearsals?

To play, discover, delve deeper and really get the music, and the role and staging, into my muscles. And to laugh with my colleagues ... there's always laughter and banter as the cast bonds!

How do you prepare for a performance?

This all depends on what time the performance starts. For evening performances, I find those days quite tricky as I'm never sure how much to do during the day. I'm still finding my way with this but, generally, I try to have a little more sleep as you need the concentration and stamina later in the day. My schedule tends to run like this:

- I have a big meal in the afternoon.
- Do some light vocalising.
- Arrive at the theatre for hair and make-up, during which time I revise my score.
- Then I stretch.
- Warm up vocally.
- Get into costume.
- And then, once in the wings, I touch my toes and roll up 'vertebra by vertebra'.
- I follow a tapping ritual where you tap the different pressure points in your body – hand, heart, head, stomach, etc. as I speak through positive thoughts and learnings to myself. I assure myself that no matter what I 'accept myself, am prepared, can do this if I enter the role, the piece, the music, etc.'
- Have a sip of water.
- Take three short breaths in, and three out to get the breath going!

ANDREW SHORE

Andrew (baritone) has worked in all the major opera houses of world. He has performed more than thirty-five roles at ENO.

How do you prepare for a role?

The difference between opera performers and straight actors is that an actor doesn't have to do any preparation at all before he meets the rest of the cast; they want the character to grow from the interaction with the other actors and the director.

That's impossible in opera because you simply can't spend time in rehearsal learning the music; you've got to learn the music beforehand. It's a case of learning it precisely and learning it in whatever language it's in; it's months of preparation.

What I tend to do is to keep singing through the role before rehearsals, over and over again, and thinking about the character as I'm doing it; thinking of all the possibilities. I find when I start working on a character it actually occupies my mind virtually twenty-four hours a day; I might be having a shave in the morning and something will just occur to me, my brain will have been percolating and I'll have a sudden shaft of thought, 'That's why he's saying that' or 'That's what he must be thinking when he's saying that'. It's like something gets in the brain and is working away there all the time.

How does your preparation vary when approaching different repertoire?

If it's a modern piece – a piece like *Woyzeck*, or *Jakob Lenz* by Wolfgang Rihm – I'll really want to dig away at the psychology of the character. *Jakob Lenz* was based on the real person and there are diaries written by the chap who tried to help him in the eighteenth century: someone who would now be called a psychiatrist. When you get historical material like that to work from it becomes really fascinating; it gives you a real insight into his thought process.

If I'm working on a piece that's entirely fictional, I often find contemporary inspirations. For the comic roles that I do, like Bartolo or Dulcamara, a lot of my inspiration comes from modern-day television comedies.

There was a sort of convention in operatic comedy; the performers played as if saying, 'This is where the laugh *should* be', and the audience understood, and so there was a polite acknowledgement that this was a funny moment in the music. As a young singer, I thought, there must be a way of making it *genuinely* funny. That's when I started thinking about my enjoyment of those comedians – the likes of Morecambe and Wise, Arthur Lowe, Tommy Cooper, Frankie Howerd – with their particular physical mannerisms and verbal tics, who actually make the audience laugh involuntarily, spontaneously. It is possible to find the moments in *The Barber of Seville* and *Don Pasquale*, for example, that can provoke a spontaneous outburst.

It's about encouraging performers to find those moments. When you're performing opera it's so easy to be cushioned by the music, to feel that as long as you sing the music in the right place, it'll all fall into place. I think young performers have more freedom and more courage to do this now than they did perhaps forty or fifty years ago.

How do you approach the rehearsal process?

It's such a blank canvas that you can create anything, everything is open to be explored. Through rehearsals I'm very keen on the idea of not getting stuck on one interpretation straight away; I will deliberately change moves or thoughts. I think it's important to keep shaking things up. It's important to keep rattling the bag, to see where the pieces land and, eventually, you'll find the ideal combination. If you get stuck too rigidly into one way of doing it too soon, then you'll never know what other possibilities there were.

How does the music help you create character?

The great advantage of opera is the time; it is pre-determined. Now some would say this is a restriction but actually it can be a tremendous freedom, because if you know precisely that a certain amount of business has only a defined amount of time to happen in, then within that you can carefully judge and balance the moves to arrive just where the music needs them to be. In that sense you're getting inside the music and feeling the freedom within the confines of the time given.

Recitative is different because you can have much more freedom within that, although even within recitative one has to be responsive to the movement of the harmony and the expectation of certain harmonic shifts.

Peter Sellars, the American director, experimented some years ago with long silences between certain lines on his production of *Cosi Fan Tutte* at Glyndebourne. In a play, if there's no reason for the next person to speak immediately, you'd have a pause, a silence, and the dramatic tension would be there within the silence. What I found when he did it with recitatives, however, was that there was a feeling that something had gone wrong; suddenly the music stopped. I could see what he was trying to do, to inject absolute realism into the dialogue, but it's the music and the harmonic progressions that suggest the way the conversation is going. I think it's a mistake to ignore that; I don't think you can treat recitative entirely like dialogue.

I think you've got to allow yourself to be open to actually feel the music. You've got to feel as though the music is coming through you; it can inform the smallest gesture or evolution of a thought.

How do you think about physical characterisation?

Michael Chekhov's concept of the Psychological Gesture is a very interesting tool to help an actor find what he calls the central spine of the character. You begin by asking yourself what the character's overwhelming desire at a particular moment is, finding a simple gesture to express that desire and letting it grow into a full physical gesture. Constantly enacting this gesture has the psychological effect of helping the feeling from which it began to grow. I think there's a lot in it. For an opera singer, the music has got to be the source for that Psychological Gesture; the feeling or desire has to be informed by what the music is suggesting.

What do you do in the wings before you go on?

I ask myself, what is the character's basic driving desire in this particular moment?; I let that become the focus and it will then suggest all sorts of other things. It informs how I arrive on the stage: I ask myself as the character, Where am I? What am I doing? Where am I in the story? How far am I in my ambitions at this point in the story? And that gets the energy going and then, as you walk out on stage, you're bringing that on with you. You're already there in that moment before you arrive on stage.

How does the work in rehearsals translate to the stage?

You need to let it be seen that you've already thought of the thought that you're going to sing in a few bars' time, unless it's spontaneous and you're reacting at that very moment. When I watch opera, I want to see in your eyes that you've already formulated, or you are formulating, the thought that you're about to express. The audience will be with you then, even before you sing that line, because they can see that you're absorbed in something which will then come out. It comes down to the strength of the inner thoughts and feeling how the music is linked to them.

You also develop the ability as a singer, over the years, to think in two parts; you're going on the journey of imagination through the character but there's a small part of you keeping an eye out for the beat, the practicalities of the stage and, very importantly, a sense of the link between you and the audience.

For example, when Falstaff comes back from the ducking in the river and is sitting by himself outside the inn, if you sense that the audience understands the character, you can play the subtlest things. He is essentially saying 'Who'd have thought that a man of my distinction would have ended up being thrown in a river?' and you can play with the idea that he is very arrogant or, alternatively, that he is genuinely shocked; in so doing, you can draw different reactions from the audience.

What are your experiences of singing opera in English?

I can only really do such things as I've just described when I'm playing in English to an English-speaking audience. Sticking with *Falstaff*, when I was in America we were singing it in Italian, so the audience were having to read the surtitles. We had this issue of timing; I got completely frustrated that I was constantly singing lines against a lot of laughter because the laugh lines, and he's got quite a few of them, were coming up at the very moment I began singing. As I was singing these glorious phrases, all I could hear was laughter from the audience having read the line before I'd sung it.

The question of audibility and clarity when singing in English is answered by the singer having the desire to communicate their thoughts and words to the audience. If that desire isn't there, you'll get sloppy wording and a lack of clarity.

This is a dual desire: the desire of the character to communicate their thoughts, and of the singer to communicate the story. This goes back to this idea that there's a cushion of the music; we know that if the singer just keeps singing then the performance will start, it will go through and it will come to an end. Unlike an actor who has got to keep the performance going through the sheer will of communication.

In opera, if there's an energy of thought, it will be communicated through the words. This is the answer to so many of the problems regarding the lack of diction.

PABLO STRONG

Pablo (tenor) trained with ENO Opera Works. He is a member of the ENO chorus and has sung and covered numerous roles for ENO.

As a member of the ENO chorus, how do you approach a first day of rehearsal?

The first day of production rehearsal is often an exciting one. We are shown the concept for the production and sometimes given some context about our characters. When rehearsing *The Girl of the Golden West* at ENO, Richard Jones took great care in helping each individual chorus member build a backstory for their character and I feel this brought a lot of depth and individuality to the chorus's work through rehearsals and once we were on stage. Different directors have different approaches to this stage of the rehearsal, and indeed towards a chorus in general. A good director will work with the chorus to help us each establish a character and to properly understand our place within the story. However, some directors will overlook this important step and immediately start blocking the chorus as a group, without much explanation. I always feel this is a missed opportunity to develop greater depth in the individual performances of a chorus; it runs the risk of leaving a chorus feeling alienated and seeming like an afterthought in the final production.

What different approaches, from directors or choreographers, have you experienced to help you create character in the chorus of an opera?

Developing the individual backstory is very useful. Many directors show us visual examples of what they have in mind: set, costume ideas. Sometimes directors will want to hear us sing some of the music and then give us an idea of how they imagined it, so that straightaway we are working on building the character of the chorus through the music. It's helpful when choreographers give us an idea of the physicality behind our characters and the reasons for this physicality; it means we can then build and develop our physical character.

How does the music help you create character in chorus?

Knowing the music extremely well is one of the best things to aid the process of building a character, as once the singing of the music is automatic, it frees you up to focus on the character and the story. Much of the time in opera, the drama is already there in the music, so to a certain extent, by learning the music properly you have already made a big step in establishing how to act the role.

How have you approached physical characterisation?

A movement director will sometimes suggest physicality for us to adopt, either individually or as a group. In the case of developing a sense of the group's character, the exercise where you mirror other people's physicality is often very useful. It varies; as a chorus we are sometimes required to be very specific with our movements, and sometimes we are required to blend in and perform as a unit. We are also often required to use very abstract movements; I feel that the key to establishing these movements is to keep building on them, experiencing this new physicality in your day-to-day life.

How do you use stage rehearsals?

I use stage rehearsals, initially, to help anchor the memory of the music to physical movements and my location on the stage. Then I trust that through repetition the physical movements and singing will become more and more relaxed and natural. I try not to become too specific with my actions; I want there to be a certain amount of spontaneity in my performance (of course within the framework of the production). I think it is very important, especially in a chorus, for individuals to retain a certain degree of freedom and spontaneity in their performance. This stops the group reacting in a blob and disengaging from the performance; it helps keep the scene alive and naturalistic.

In this way, the journey of a chorus member doesn't feel any different from that of a soloist. Once the reality of singing the same words and music with other people is accepted as the norm, then I just react naturally to what is happening in the music and on stage.

How do you prepare for a performance?

I don't have any specific rituals to prepare for performance. In fact, if I ever feel like I am developing a ritual I will drop it, because I fear this is a slippery slope towards neuroses! By the time we get to the performance, all the music and the movements are so deeply ingrained that I just trust that when the scene takes place I'll know what to do. It is very important that, as a performer, you have this degree of preparation through rehearsals; otherwise you are forced to think about the technicalities of your movements and music, which will disengage you from the action happening on stage and this will be seen by the audience.

List of Exercises

Part One: The Tools

1 Foundations: Where to Start

THE BODY: RELEASING TENSION

Understanding Outer Tension Solo/5 mins
Understanding Inner Tension Solo/2 mins
Extreme Tension Solo/2 mins
The Baby Solo/5 mins
Observing Tension Pairs/10 mins
Feet Solo/8 mins/ + tennis ball
Align Solo/5 mins
Roll and Align Solo/5 mins/ + a wall
Align: Semi-Supine Solo/10 mins
Massage 1 Solo/5 mins/ + tennis ball + wall
Massage 2 Pairs/10 mins
Energise Solo/Group/10 mins
The Dagger Group/5 mins
Core Solo/1 Min
Three Angels Pairs/5 mins
Backward Circle Solo/5 mins
Net Throw Solo/5 mins

THE MIND: AWARENESS AND FOCUS

The Camera Solo/Group/2 mins
Active Senses Solo/Ongoing
Receive Pair/3 mins
Follow Pairs/2 mins each
The Circle Group/Ongoing
Ball Throw Group/Ongoing/+ two different coloured tennis balls + a bottle

IMAGINATION

Imaginary Impetus Solo/Ongoing
Visualisation Solo/Pair/Ongoing
Diary Solo/Ongoing

PLAY AND SPONTANEITY
Yes and . . . Pairs/5 mins
Find the Game Group/Ongoing

4 Text and Music

GIVEN CIRCUMSTANCES
Character Lists Solo
Map Visualisations Solo/Group
Circles of Concentration Solo
Timeline and Diary Solo/Group
Improvising Pre-Opera or Pre-Scene Events Group
What If . . . Solo/Group
Hotseat Pairs/5 mins

ORGANISING INFORMATION: OTHER APPROACHES
Core Beliefs Solo/Group
Anthropology Group
Musical Response Solo/Group

ORGANISING INFORMATION: THE MUSIC
Musical Response Solo/Group
Words in Music Solo

OBJECTIVES
The Pen Group/5 mins
Motivation Challenge Solo/Pair/5 mins
Sung Motivation Challenge Solo/Pair/5 mins
Psychological Gesture Solo/15 mins

ACTIONS
The Shoe Pairs/Group/2 mins
Actions Gym Pairs/15 mins
The Play-in Solo/10 mins
The Interior Film Solo/Ongoing
Connecting Targets Solo/3 mins
Comparing Actions Solo/Ongoing
Clap and Response Group/5 mins

OBSTACLES
Your Obstacles Solo/5 mins

POINTS OF CONCENTRATION
Point Of Concentration Improvisation Rehearsal/Performance
Concentration of Attention Solo/Group/Ongoing

EVENTS

Montage Rehearsal/5 mins
Events Improvisation Group/15 mins
Scene Improvisation Rehearsal

FURTHER TEXT TOOLS

Basic Meisner Repetition Pairs (with an Observer)/Ongoing
Line Repetition Scene/Ongoing

5 The Body and Movement

MUSIC

Follow the Leader Pairs/15 mins

LABAN

Exploring the Structural Model Pairs/Group/10 mins
Rhythmic Constructs Solo/Ongoing
Exploring Rhythmic Constructs Solo/10 mins
Efforts Exploration Group/45 mins
Exploring Gestures and Rhythm Solo/15 mins
Spatial Relations Pairs/10 mins
Efforts/Rhythmic Constructs Actions Gym Pairs/15 mins
Isolation Pairs/5 mins

LECOQ

Balance, Control, Focus Solo/20 mins
Push and Pull Pairs/Group
Balancing the Space Group/20 mins
Undulation Solo
Reverse Undulation Solo
Body Parts Solo/Group
A States of Tension Journey Solo/Group/10 mins
Becoming Your Animal Solo/Group/20 mins
Translating Your Animal into Character Solo/Group/20 mins
Wearing the Neutral Mask Group/A Neutral Mask/5 mins
Waking Up Group/3 mins
The Sea Group/5 mins

CHARACTER TYPES AND *COMMEDIA DELL'ARTE*

Moulding Pairs/5 mins
Commedia *and Rhythm* Pairs/One Person to Lead Clapping/Ongoing
Commedia *and The Inner Monologue* Pairs/*Commedia* Mask
Commedia *and Lazzi* Pairs, Threes and More/*Commedia* Mask

THE CLOWN

The Clapping Game Group/10 mins
The Sock Game Group/Ongoing
Restrictions Solo/Group/10 mins
Status Group/A Pack of Playing Cards (removing King, Queen, Jack and Joker)/20 mins

DEVISING

123 Pairs/3 mins
Text Improvisation Pairs/3 mins
The Journey Pairs/Group/5 mins
Life Story Solo/10 mins
A Story String Group/5 mins
The Flock Group/Music/Various Objects/20 mins
Élan Pairs/Three/Four/20 mins
Physical Essence Solo/Ongoing

6 Words and Music in Action

Spoken Text Vocal Warm-Up Solo/10 mins
Walking The Punctuation Solo/Ongoing
Walking The Sentence Solo/Ongoing
Changing Chairs Pairs/Ongoing
Release Of Emotion Solo/Group/Ongoing
Exploring the Consonants Solo/Ongoing
Resistance Group/Ongoing
Exploring The Vowel Solo/Ongoing
Three Times Through Solo/Ongoing
Physicalising Words Solo/Ongoing
Task Solo/Ongoing
A Circle Group/Ongoing
Spaces of the Mind Solo/Ongoing
Inner and Outer Landscape Solo/Ongoing
Drawing a Picture Solo/Ongoing
Concretising Thought Solo/Pairs/Group/Ongoing
Marking Thoughts Solo/Pair/Group/Ongoing
Building Structures Solo/Pair/Group/Ongoing
Covert Relations Group/Ongoing
Making Contact Group/Ongoing
Shifting Alliances Group/Ongoing
Barriers Pairs/Group/Ongoing
Manipulation Pairs/Ongoing
Questioning Pairs/Group/Ongoing
Spectrum Group/Ongoing

Part Two: In Practice

8 Rehearsals

Embrace Solo/2 mins

9 Rehearsals in Depth

Recitative Solo/Pairs/Group/Ongoing
Target You Pairs/Ongoing
The Telephone Solo/Ongoing

10 Performance

Response to Words Solo/Group/5 mins
Dropping the Anchor Solo/10 secs–10 mins

Further Reading

Text and Music

Adler, S. (2000) *The Art of Acting*. New York: Applause.
Alfreds, M. (2007) *Different Every Night*. London: Nick Hern Books.
Alfreds, M. (2013) *The What Happens*. London: Nick Hern Books.
Benedetti, J. (1998) *Stanislavski and the Actor*. London: Routledge.
Chekhov, M. (1985) *To the Actor*. New York: Harper and Row.
Donnellan, D. (2005) *The Actor and the Target*. London: Nick Hern Books.
Hagen, U. (1973) *Respect for Acting*. New York: Wiley.
Meiner, S. and Longwell, D. (1987) *Sanford Meisner on Acting*. New York: Vintage.
Merlin, B. (2007) *The Complete Stanislavsky Toolkit*. London: Nick Hern Books.
Mitchell, K. (2009) *The Director's Craft: A Handbook for the Theatre*. London: Routledge.
Stanislavski, K. (1980) *An Actor Prepares*. Translated by E. R. Hapgood. London: Eyre Methuen.
Stanislavski, K. (1980) *My Life in Art*. Translated by J. Benedetti. London: Routledge and New York: Theatre Arts Books, R. M. MacGregor.
Stanislavski, K. (1981) *Creating a Role*. Translated by E. R. Hapgood. London: Eyre Methuen.
Stanislavski, K (1998) *Stanislavski on Opera*. Translated by E. R. Hapgood. London: Routledge.
Stanislavski, K. (1999) *Building a Character*. Translated by E. R. Hapgood. London: Eyre Methuen.

The Body and Movement

Boal, A. (1992) *Games for Actors and Non-Actors*. Abingdon: Routledge.
Callery, D. (2001) *Through the Body*. London: Nick Hern.
Grantham, B. (2000) *Playing Commedia: A Training Guide to Commedia Techniques*. London: Nick Hern Books.
Graham, S. and Hoggett, S. (2009) *The Frantic Assembly Book of Devising*. Abingdon: Routledge.
Kemp, R. (2012). *Embodied Acting: What Neuroscience Tells Us about Acting*. Abingdon: Routledge.
Lecoq, J. (2000). *The Moving Body*. London: Methuen Drama.
Newlove, J. (1993). *Laban for Actors and Dancers: Putting Laban's Movement Theory into Practice: A Step-by-Step Guide*. London: Nick Hern Books.
Newlove, J. and Dalby, J. (2004). *Laban for All*. 1st edn. London: Nick Hern Books.
Preston Dunlop, V. (1998) *Looking at Dances: A Choreological Perspective on Choreography*. London: Verve Books.
Rudlin, R. (1994) *Commedia dell'Arte: An Actor's Handbook*. Abingdon: Routledge.
Spolin, V. (1999) *Improvisation for the Theater*. Evanston: Northwestern University Press.
Wright, J. (2006) *Why is That so Funny: A Practical Exploration of Physical Comedy*. London: Nick Hern Books.

Words and Music in Action

Berry, C. (1993) *The Actor and The Text*. London: Virgin Books.
Berry, C. (2001) *Text in Action: A Definitive Guide to Exploring Text in Rehearsal for Actors and Directors*. London: Virgin Books.
Berry, C. (2008) *From Word to Play: A Handbook for Directors*. London: Oberon Books.
Houseman, B. (2008) *Tackling Text and Subtext: A Step-by-Step Guide for Actors*. London: Nick Hern Books.
Rodenburg, P. (2007) *Presence*. London: Penguin/Michael Joseph.

Opera and Theatre

Abbate, C. and Parker, R. (2012) *A History of Opera: The Last 400 Years*. London: Penguin Random House.
Brook, P. (1990) *The Empty Space*. London: Penguin Books.
Ewans, M. (2016) *Performing Opera: A Practical Guide for Singers and Directors*. London: Bloomsbury Methuen Drama.
Fuchs, P. P. (1991) *The Music Theatre of Walter Felsenstein*. London: Quartet Books.
Glover, J. (2005) *Mozart's Women*. London: Macmillan.
Hall, P. (2000) *Exposed by the Mask: Form and Language in Drama*. London: Oberon Books.
Kerman, J. (1989) *Opera as Drama*. London: Faber and Faber.
Sutcliffe, T. (1996) *Believing in Opera*. London: Faber and Faber.
Taylor, G. and Wilson, P. (2015) *Dramatic Adventures in Rhetoric: A Guide for Actors, Directors and Playwrights*. London: Oberon Books.
Till, N. (ed.) (2012) *The Cambridge Guide to Opera Studies*. Cambridge: Cambridge University Press.

Broader Interest

Berne, E. (1992) *Games People Play: The Psychology of Human Relationships*. London: Penguin.
Carter, R. (2008) *Multiplicity: The New Science of Personality*. London: Little, Brown.
Damasio, A. (1994) *Descartes' Error: Emotion, Reason and the Human Brain*. London: Penguin.
Damasio, A. (1999) *The Feeling of What Happens: Body, Emotion and the Making of Consciousness*. London: Penguin.
Feldman Barrett, L. (2017) *How Emotions are Made: The Secret Life of the Brain*. London: Macmillan.
Nachmanovitch, S. (1990) *Free Play: Improvisation in Life and Art*. New York: Tarcher Penguin.
Nettle, D. (2009) *Personality: What Makes You the Way You Are*. Oxford: Oxford University Press.

Index